Symbol	How it is read	What it means
$\mathrm{SE}(\bar{x}_1 - \bar{x}_2)$	standard error of difference between two means	Pooled sample variance of two sample means
t	t value	t value from Student's t distribution
t_α	t sub alpha	t value corresponding to a specified tail area α
$\overline{X}$	X-bar	Sample mean; mean of x values
$\overline{Y}$	Y-bar	Mean of y values
Z	Z score	Standard normal score

II. Symbols taken from letters of the Greek alphabet

α	alpha	Significance level
α error	alpha error	Type I error in hypothesis testing
β error	beta error	Type II error in hypothesis testing
α	alpha	y intercept of population regression line
β	beta	Slope of population regression line
χ^2	chi-square (pronounced "ki-square")	Test statistic for contingency table
δ	delta	Mean difference of population observations
Δ	delta (capital delta)	Δx means change in x
μ	mu	Population mean
μ_0	mu sub zero	Baseline value of μ
$\mu_{\bar{x}}$	mu sub x-bar	Mean of sampling distribution
σ	sigma	Population standard deviation
σ^2	sigma squared	Population variance
$\sigma_{\bar{x}}$	sigma sub x-bar	Standard error of the mean
Σ	the sum of (capital sigma)	Sum the values that follow
ρ	rho	Population correlation coefficient

III. Mathematical symbols

$|x|$	absolute value of x	Take the numerical value of x, ignoring the sign
$n!$	n factorial	$n(n-1)(n-2)\cdots 3 \cdot 2 \cdot 1$
$>$	greater than	Number on left is larger than number on right
$\geq$	greater than or equal to	Number on left is larger than or equal to number on right
$<$	less than	Number on left is smaller than number on right
$\leq$	less than or equal to	Number on left is smaller than or equal to number on right
$\neq$	not equal to	The two values on either side of the symbol are not the same value

Basic Statistics for the Health Sciences

Fifth Edition

Jan W. Kuzma
Loma Linda University

Stephen E. Bohnenblust
Minnesota State University, Mankato

Boston   Burr Ridge, IL   Dubuque, IA   Madison, WI   New York   San Francisco   St. Louis
Bangkok   Bogotá   Caracas   Kuala Lumpur   Lisbon   London   Madrid   Mexico City
Milan   Montreal   New Delhi   Santiago   Seoul   Singapore   Sydney   Taipei   Toronto

Higher Education

BASIC STATISTICS FOR THE HEALTH SCIENCES, FIFTH EDITION

Published by McGraw-Hill, a business unit of The McGraw-Hill Companies, Inc., 1221 Avenue of the Americas, New York, NY 10020. Copyright © 2005 by The McGraw-Hill Companies, Inc. All rights reserved. No part of this publication may be reproduced or distributed in any form or by any means, or stored in a database or retrieval system, without the prior written consent of The McGraw-Hill Companies, Inc., including, but not limited to, any network or other electronic storage or transmission, or broadcast for distance learning.

Some ancillaries, including electronic and print components, may not be available to customers outside the United States.

ISBN   978-0-07-284403-0
MHID 0-07-284403-5

5 6 7 8 9 0 FGR/FGR 0 9

Editor-in-chief: *Emily Barrosse*
Publisher: *William R. Glass*
Executive editor: *Nick Barrett*
Director of development: *Kathleen Engelberg*
Development editor: *Lynda Huenefeld*
Executive marketing manager: *Pamela S. Cooper*
Production services manager: *Jennifer Mills*
Production service: *Melanie Field*

Manuscript editor: *Thomas Briggs*
Design manager: *Preston Thomas*
Cover designer: *Lisa Buckley*
Interior designer: *Linda Robertson*
Art manager: *Robin Mouat*
Illustrator: *The Asterisk Group*
Production supervisor: *Tandra Jorgensen*

The text was set in 10/12 Palatino by Thompson Type and printed on acid-free, 45# New Era Matte by Quebecor World Fairfield.

Library of Congress Cataloging-in-Publication Data

Kuzma, Jan W.
    Basic statistics for the health sciences / Jan W. Kuzma, Stephen E. Bohnenblust.—5th ed.
        p. cm.
    Includes bibliographical references and index.
    ISBN 0-07-284403-5
    1. Medical statistics.   2. Statistics.   I. Bohnenblust, Stephen E.   II. Title.

RA409.K88 2004
519.5′02461—dc22

2004053885

www.mhhe.com

To my mother, Elizabeth, my wife, Kay, and my children, Kim, Kari, and Kevin, who have given me faith, love, and joy. —J.W.K.

To my loving family—wife and friend, Sandy, and three wonderful children, Steve Jr., Mandy, and Sam. —S.E.B.

Contents

8 One-Sample Significance Testing, Point Estimates, and Confidence Intervals   123

9 Two-Sample Significance Testing, Point Estimates, and Confidence Intervals   154

10 ANOVA   174

11   Inferences Regarding Proportions   194

12   The Chi-Square Test   207

16 Life Tables   297

Preface

Statistics is a peculiar subject. Unaccountably, many students who handle their toughest studies with aplomb view statistics as a nearly insurmountable barrier. Perhaps this derives from the inherent difficulty of viewing the world in probabilistic terms, or from the underlying mathematics, or from the often abstruse mode of presentation. Our hope is that *Basic Statistics for the Health Sciences* is a step toward overcoming these problems.

The purpose of this book is to present some of the concepts, principles, and methods of statistics in as clear and understandable a manner as possible. The level is appropriate to students with a limited mathematical background but for whom a working knowledge of statistics is indispensable. We have found this approach to be particularly effective with students of medicine, nursing, public health, and the allied health sciences.

Because statistics allows us to use data to gain insight into a problem, we emphasize understanding rather than mastering a statistical technique. Therefore, the underlying objective of this book is to introduce concepts intuitively rather than via rigorous mathematics.

Certain features of this book's organization have proven to be especially effective. These include—in each chapter—an outline, learning objectives (which may easily be used as review questions), highlighting of important terms, a concluding statement, and a list of newly introduced vocabulary. We and many of our colleagues have found these to be simple but effective aids for any student striving for mastery of the material. Many of the examples and exercises are adapted from actual data in health research, so students are quite likely to appreciate the relevance of the material to their chosen field. Our teaching, research, and life philosophy are reflected in the recurring theme of these pages— the effect our lifestyle choices have on our health.

This text goes somewhat beyond the coverage of most elementary statistics books by including a number of special topics for students of different disciplines and interests. Some key principles of epidemiology are introduced; the topics of age adjustment and relative risk are covered. A chapter on probability, often reserved for more sophisticated treatments, is included. By understanding probability, students gain a better insight into several of the subsequent topics. There are chapters devoted to correlation, regression, and analysis of variance, as well as to distribution-free methods. Chapters on vital statistics and life tables are included to meet the special needs of medical and public health students. Two important subjects—how to perform a health survey and how to evaluate a research report—should be of real benefit to those who will carry out or use the results of research projects.

This text can be used for a course of three quarter units or three semester units, depending on the topics the instructor chooses to emphasize. It contains the material we have found to be uncommonly effective in motivating students' interest in statistics, so they begin to see it as a very satisfying form of detective work. The book should be especially useful for students who enter the course with some lingering doubts about their ability to master statistics or for those who initially question the relevance of studying the subject.

Changes in the Fifth Edition

We have been delighted with the positive reception of this text by individuals from diverse institutions across the country—students, instructors, and reviewers. Clearly, the strong public health and health sciences emphasis of this text has become an outstanding feature of this book. This fifth edition builds on the philosophy and pedagogic approaches of the previous four editions. It includes improvements that we hope will make this new edition even more useful in meeting the teaching objectives of instructors and will make it even easier for students to comprehend.

Although the basic content and outline of previous editions remain, there have been some significant changes to the fifth edition. This edition continues to emphasize a "hands-on" approach to statistics, but there is more emphasis on the use of computer programs and—more importantly—the interpretation of computer outputs.

New material to this edition includes:

- New health science material to exemplify and illustrate concepts
- Extensive new information on selecting appropriate samples
- New information on measuring and interpreting skewness
- New information on degress of freedom and population estimates
- SPSS software information throughout appropriate chapters

Acknowledgments

It is my pleasure to be able to continue the work started by Jan Kuzma. Dr. Kuzma did an admirable job of taking a very difficult subject and making it understandable to those students who might initially view a statistics class as an unwanted requirement. I only hope that I have been able to build on that tradition.

We would like to thank the many students, instructors, and special reviewers for their thoughtful and helpful suggestions on improving this edition:

Priya Banerjee, SUNY–Brockport

Toni Cade, University of Louisiana at Lafayette

Simon Geletta, Des Moines University

Marcy Parry, Ferris State University

We wish also to acknowledge the cooperation of the various publishers who generously granted permission to reproduce tables from their books.

We wish to thank Dr. Thomas Glover and Dr. Kevin Mitchell, both of Hobart and William Smith Colleges for their input regarding Chapter 3: Organizing and Displaying Data.

Writing a textbook is a labor of love—characterized by both pleasure and frustration. Dr. Kuzma and I wish to thank the many people who have helped and inspired us over the years. We first need to acknowledge the many students we have encountered in our teaching careers. Nothing is more enjoyable than working with young, inquisitive minds. The transition from terrified student to a student with a developing sense of confidence and understanding is something all of us find exciting and rewarding.

I also must thank the many friends and colleagues who have helped shape my professional career. The staff at McGraw-Hill is outstanding. My colleagues at Minnesota State University–Mankato have been incredibly supportive. I especially wish to thank my colleagues within the Department of Health Science, including Judy Luebke, Dawn Larsen, and Linda Winans. Their friendship has been invaluable. My family has also been a tremendous source of support. As any professor knows, there are times when scholarly effort is a long and lonely process. Without the help of my wife, Sandy, and my daughter, Sam, the process would be much longer and much lonelier. Thank you.

—S.E.B.

1

Statistics and How They Are Used

CHAPTER OUTLINE

✔ LEARNING OBJECTIVES

After studying this chapter, you should be able to

1. Define *statistics*
2. List several reasons for studying statistics
3. Distinguish clearly between
   a. descriptive and inferential statistics
   b. surveys and experiments
   c. retrospective and prospective studies
   d. descriptive and analytical surveys
4. Define *bias*
5. Describe the purpose and components of a clinical trial

1.1   THE MEANING OF STATISTICS

One way to understand statistics is to consider two basic questions: (1) What does the term *statistics* mean? and (2) What do statisticians do? Once we have the answers to these questions, we can delve into how statistics are used.

What Does *Statistics* Mean?

The word **statistics** has several meanings. It is frequently used to refer to recorded data such as the number of traffic accidents, the size of enrollment, or the number of patients visiting a clinic. Statistics is also used to denote characteristics calculated for a set of data—for example, mean, standard deviation, or correlation coefficient. In another context, statistics refers to statistical methodology and theory.

In short, statistics is a body of techniques and procedures dealing with the collection, organization, analysis, interpretation, and presentation of information that can be stated numerically.

What Do Statisticians Do?

A statistician is usually a member of a group that works on challenging scientific tasks. Frequently engaged in projects that explore the frontiers of human knowledge, the statistician is primarily concerned with developing and applying methods that can be used in collecting and analyzing data. He or she may select a well-established technique or develop a new one that provides a unique approach to a particular study, thus leading to valid conclusions. Specifically, the statistician's tasks are as follows:

1. *To guide the design of an experiment or survey.* A statistician should be consulted in the early planning stages so that an investigation can be carried

out efficiently, with a minimum of bias. Once data are collected, it is too late to plan ahead. By then, it is impossible to impose an appropriate statistical design or compensate for the lack of a randomly selected sample.

2. *To analyze data.* Data analysis may take many forms, such as examining the relationships among several variables, describing and analyzing the variation of certain characteristics (e.g., blood pressure, temperature, height, weight), or determining whether a difference in some response is significant.

3. *To present and interpret results.* Results are best evaluated in terms of probability statements that will facilitate the decision-making process. Mainland (1963:3) defines statistics as the "science and art of dealing with variation in such a way as to obtain reliable results." The art of statistics is especially pertinent to this task and involves skills usually acquired through experience.

The interpretation of statistics is both an art and a science. When results are said to be **significant,** the statistician is making a probability statement. He or she is saying that the differences are *most likely* real differences rather than chance or random differences. Because probability is often linked with sample size, large samples can yield seemingly impressive results. However, when the statistician scrutinizes the sample more closely, she or he may realize that, even though the results appear impressive, they have little or no practical value. An excellent example of the effects of a large sample is presented in Chapter 13 and involves the Pearson correlation technique.

Statisticians can also help with another key aspect of interpretation: Are the results applicable to other groups? Subject selection, especially the nonrandom selection of patients with specific study eligibility requirements, poses a particular problem. The statistician can help determine if the results from a published study are applicable to a somewhat different group of patients. For example, a clinical study on drug efficacy might find certain effects in the study group, but would those same effects be found in an elderly population? Are studies on cardiovascular disease, which have historically focused on men, applicable to women? Are bone density studies, in which women have been studied most extensively, applicable to men? Although statisticians may not be able to give definitive answers, they should be able to give objective advice to consider prior to making a judgment.

1.2   THE USES OF STATISTICS

It is helpful to distinguish between the two major categories of statistics. **Descriptive statistics** deals with the enumeration, organization, and graphical representation of data. **Inferential statistics** is concerned with reaching conclusions from incomplete information—that is, generalizing from the specific.

Inferential statistics uses information obtained from a sample to say something about an entire population.

An example of *descriptive* statistics is the decennial **census** of the United States, in which all residents are requested to provide information such as age, sex, race, and marital status. The data obtained in such a census can then be compiled and arranged into tables and graphs that describe the characteristics of the population at a given time. An example of *inferential* statistics is an opinion poll such as the Gallup Poll, which attempts to draw inferences as to the outcome of an election. In such a poll, a sample of individuals (frequently fewer than 2000) is selected, their preferences are tabulated, and inferences are made as to how more than 80 million persons would vote if an election were held that day.

Statistical methods provide a logical basis for making decisions in a variety of areas when incomplete information is available. Here are some examples of scientific questions to which the application of statistical methodology has been useful:

1. How can researchers test the effectiveness of a new vaccine against the common cold?
2. How effective is a trial that seeks to reduce the risk of coronary heart disease?
3. How effective have several family planning programs been?
4. How much, if at all, does use of oral contraceptives increase a woman's chances of developing a thromboembolism?

The four specific studies described next further amplify the application of statistics.

Example: Smoking During Pregnancy

A pioneering study of the effects on the newborn infant of smoking during pregnancy was reported by Simpson (1957). She examined data on 7499 patients in three hospitals in and near Loma Linda (California) University and found from the records that prematurity rates increased with the number of cigarettes smoked per day. A more recent review of the various studies on this topic is given by the Surgeon General's Report on Smoking and Health (U.S. Department of Health, Education, and Welfare, 1979). The principal conclusion of that report is: "Maternal smoking during pregnancy has a significant adverse effect upon the well-being of the fetus and the health of the newborn baby."

Example: The Multiple Risk Factor Intervention Trial (MRFIT)

Paul (1976) reported on a national study of the primary prevention of coronary heart disease. The study's approach was to determine whether the risk of coronary disease in middle-aged men can be significantly reduced through intervention. This intervention entailed simultaneously reducing their serum cholesterol levels, treating any high blood pressure, and encouraging the men to stop smoking. The 7-year trial involved 20 clinical centers and 12,866 subjects, all initially healthy but at high risk for coronary disease. At random, half the men were assigned to be followed through the intervention program, and the other half through their usual medical care, which included annual physicals and lab tests. The report of the results was prepared by the MRFIT research group and appeared in the *Journal of the American Medical Association* (1982; 248:1465–1477). Investigators observed that the risk factor levels declined in both groups. Furthermore, during the 7-year follow-up period, the mortality rates for coronary heart disease (CHD) were 17.9 deaths per 1000 for the intervention group and 19.3 deaths per 1000 for the untreated group. This was a nonsignificant difference, and the lack of a positive result has generated considerable discussion. There may be more plausible reasons for this outcome: (1) It is difficult to show a significant drop due to an intervention when the entire country is experiencing a multidecade decline in CHD rates; (2) the intervention strategy may not have been drastic enough to show a significant difference; and (3) because a report of the assessed risk factors was sent to the physicians of those in the untreated group, members of that group may have benefited from whatever "treatment" their physicians had prescribed for them.

Because skills, facilities, and funds are never unlimited, the problem arises as to how to extract the maximum amount of information in the most efficient manner. With the aid of statistics, it is usually possible to achieve greater precision at minimum cost by effectively using the resources available.

Example: The Framingham Study

Perhaps the most famous longitudinal study ever conducted was the Framingham Study. In 1948, the small city of Framingham, Massachusetts, was chosen for an ambitious project in health research. At that time, little was known about the general causes of heart disease and stroke, but the death rates from cardiovascular disease (CVD) had been increasing steadily and had reached epidemic proportions. The primary objective of the study was to identify the factors or characteristics that contribute to CVD. To this end, 5209 men and women, ages 30–62, who had not yet developed overt symptoms of CVD or suffered a heart attack or stroke underwent the first of many extensive physical examinations and lifestyle interviews.

The results of this study and subsequent analysis have directly contributed to our knowledge about the major risk factors for CVD—high blood pressure, high blood cholesterol levels, smoking, obesity, diabetes, and physical inactivity—as well as providing a great deal of valuable information on the effects of related factors such as blood triglyceride and HDL cholesterol levels, age, gender, and psychosocial issues. This knowledge of CVD risk factors has influenced clinical practice and treatment, and prevention programs aimed at reducing the incidence of CVD. This study is continuing with second- and third-generation groups, or **cohorts.** As of the summer of 2003, 879 scientific articles had been published using data obtained from the Framingham Study and listed at the following Web site: www.nhlbi.gov/aboutframingham/.

Example: The STAR Trial

The STAR (study of tamoxifen and raloxifene) Trial is an example of a **longitudinal study** that is just getting started. According to their Web site the STAR Trial is "one of the largest breast cancer prevention studies ever" (www.nci.nih.gov/clinicaltrials/digestpage/STAR). The trial will involve 22,000 postmenopausal women at increased risk of breast cancer, from 500 centers in the United States, Puerto Rico, and Canada. The primary purpose of the study is to determine whether the osteoporosis prevention drug raloxifene (Evista®) is as effective in reducing the chances of developing breast cancer as tamoxifen (Nolvadex®). Statisticians will play a key role by analyzing the data and determining which drug has an effect, how great the effect is, and whether widespread use of one or more of these drugs is warranted.

1.3   WHY STUDY STATISTICS?

Many students ask, "Why should I study statistics?" or "How useful will statistics be in my future career?" or, especially if this is a required class, "Why do I have to take this class?" The answers to these questions depend on their career objectives.

A knowledge of statistics is essential for both understanding and conducting research in any of the health professions. Those of you using this text are probably taking your first statistics class, and for many of you, it may be your only statistics class. Whatever health profession you ultimately enter, there is likely to be a strong emphasis on science and the scientific method for advancing the profession. Whenever a new method, drug, device, or intervention is developed, a key question is, "Does it work?" Statistics are used to analyze the data and help you decide if the new idea is worthy of being incorporated into your professional lives.

For example, consider these research questions: "Is the drug raloxifene (Evista®) as effective in reducing the chances of developing breast cancer as tamoxifen (Nolvadex®)?" "Does the Atkins Diet lead to weight loss?" and "Can touch therapists detect a human energy field?" Such questions require researchers to gather data, statistically analyze the data, and then interpret the results within the context of their profession. To keep abreast of these and other current developments in their field, they need to review and understand the writings in scientific journals. And full understanding of these writings often requires a working knowledge of statistical terminology and methodology. For persons active in research, a basic understanding of statistics is useful not only in the conduct of their investigations but also in the effective presentation of their findings in papers and reports for publication, and at professional meetings. Some proficiency in statistics is also helpful for individuals who are preparing or may be called upon to evaluate research proposals. Furthermore, people with an understanding of statistics are better able to decide whether their professional colleagues use statistics to objectively view the issue or merely to support their personal biases; that is, it helps them decide whether the claims are valid.

A knowledge of statistics can help anyone discriminate between fact and fiction in everyday life. This is especially true in relation to the multitude of health claims in newspapers and magazines, on television and radio, on the Internet, and even in ads for pharmacies and grocery stores. A working knowledge of statistics is one more tool to use in making these daily comparisons and evaluations.

Finally, a course in statistics should help you know when, and for what purpose, a statistician should be consulted.

1.4 SOURCES OF DATA

In observing various phenomena, we are usually interested in obtaining information on specific characteristics—for instance, age, weight, height, marital status, or smoking habits. These characteristics are referred to as **variables;** the values of the observations recorded for them are referred to as **data.** Data are the raw materials of statistics. They are derived from incredibly diverse sources. Knowing our sources provides clues to our data—their reliability, their validity, and the inferences we might draw.

Surveys and Experiments

Data may come from anywhere: observational surveys, planned surveys, or experiments. The two fundamental kinds of investigations are **surveys** and **experiments.** Data from a survey may represent observations of events or phenomena over which few, if any, controls are imposed. The study of the effects of the explosion of the atomic bomb on the inhabitants of Hiroshima and Nagasaki is an example of a survey. In this case, the radiation to which the survivors were exposed (referred to as "treatment" in statistics) was in no way controlled or assigned. By contrast, in an experiment, we design a research plan purposely to impose controls over the amount of exposure (treatment) to a phenomenon such as radiation. The distinction between them is that an experiment imposes controls on the methods, treatment, or conditions under which it is performed, whereas in a survey, such controls are seldom possible.

A classic example of an experiment is the Veterans Administration Cooperative Study. It began in 1963 and involved 523 hypertensive men who were patients in 16 Veterans Administration hospitals (Veterans Administration, 1970,

1972). The study demonstrated that oral hypertensive medications, judiciously administered, could significantly reduce blood pressure levels, whereas **placebos** (substances or treatments that have no therapeutic value) had no effect on blood pressure.

Although experimental investigations are preferable to surveys, in some cases there are reasons for not conducting them—for instance, ethical reasons, as when a beneficial treatment may be withheld from one of the groups; or administrative reasons, as when an experiment may seriously disrupt the established routine of patients' care.

Health researchers conduct surveys on human populations all the time. These surveys may be categorized as retrospective or prospective.

Retrospective Studies

Retrospective studies (commonly referred to as **case-control studies**) gather past data from selected cases and controls to determine differences, if any, in the exposure to a suspected factor. In retrospective studies, the researcher identifies individuals with a specific disease or condition (cases) and also identifies a comparable sample without that disease or condition (controls). The purpose of the comparison is to determine if the two groups differ as to their exposure to some specific factor. An example is a study that compares the smoking habits of women who bore premature babies with those of women who carried their pregnancies to term. Given the comparative data, the researcher then seeks to determine whether there is a statistical relation between the possible **stimulus variable,** or causative factor (smoking), and the **outcome variable** (prematurity).

A disadvantage of retrospective studies is that the data were usually collected for other purposes and may be incomplete. Surveys frequently fail to include relevant variables that may be essential to determining whether the two groups studied are comparable. This absence of demonstrated comparability between cases and controls may envelop the results in a cloud of doubt. In addition, because of the historical nature of such records or the necessity of relying on memory, serious difficulties may attend the selection of appropriate controls. Unknown biases frequently hinder such studies.

The major advantages of retrospective studies are that they are economical and are particularly applicable to the study of rare diseases. Such studies also make it possible to obtain answers relatively quickly because the cases are usually easily identified.

In retrospective studies, sample selection begins with the outcome variable (disease). The researcher looks back in time to identify the stimulus variable (factor). In prospective studies (discussed next), the stimulus variable is known in advance, and the study population is followed over time, while occurrences of the outcome are noted. A generalized **2 × 2 table** may be used to illustrate the study design; Table 1.1 shows an example. This table is applicable to both retrospective and prospective studies, and is called a fourfold table because it consists of four elements—*a, b, c,* and *d:*

Table 1.1 Generalized 2 × 2 Table

Stimulus Variable	Outcome Variable		
	With Disease	Without Disease	Total
Present	a	b	$a + b$
Absent	c	d	$c + d$
Total	$a + c$	$b + d$	

1. Element a represents persons with the stimulus variable who developed the disease.
2. Element b represents persons with the stimulus variable who did not develop the disease.
3. Element c represents persons without the stimulus variable who developed the disease.
4. Element d represents persons without the stimulus variable who did not develop the disease.

Prospective Studies

Prospective studies are usually **cohort studies,** in which the researchers enroll a group of healthy persons (a cohort) and follow them over a certain period to determine the frequency with which a disease develops. An example that was briefly described in section 1.2 is the Framingham Study. Framingham subjects were analyzed statistically based on the presence or absence of one or more variables (e.g., smoking, diabetes, high blood pressure, obesity) that at the beginning of the study were only suspected of being related to CVD or stroke. In a prospective study, we must first look at the key variables of interest simply because the disease or diseases being studied have not yet occurred. In the Framingham Study, as subjects either developed CVD or had a stroke, the key variables were compared for the individuals who acquired the disease and those who did not. Based on the data analysis, the researchers could then begin to determine the degree of importance of each variable in relation to CVD or stroke.

The primary advantage of prospective studies is that they permit the accurate estimation of disease incidence in a population. They make it possible to include potentially relevant variables (e.g., age, gender, ethnicity, occupation) that may be related to the outcome variable. Furthermore, data are collected under uniform conditions and for specified reasons, and there are better opportunities to draw appropriate conclusions or make appropriate comparisons while limiting or controlling the amount of **bias,** which may be considered systematic error. For example, in the Framingham Study, researchers were able to collect data *before* subjects developed CVD or stroke. The net result is that our current understanding of CVD and stroke is better than if they had waited for subjects to develop the disease and then tried to understand why. The primary disadvantage of prospective studies is that they take considerable time (Framingham started in 1948) and are expensive, especially if the disease studied has a low incidence rate.

Although prospective studies provide useful data, they typically are not used to establish or "prove" a causal relationship, because the variables cannot be randomly assigned or manipulated. We simply cannot randomly assign subjects to either a smoking group or a nonsmoking group and then see if the CVD or stroke rates differ over time. Typically, subjects are identified as either smokers or nonsmokers and studied over time. Then a statistical analysis is performed to determine if and how much the CVD and stroke rates differ from those of nonsmokers. Although this may yield strong evidence for a relationship between smoking, CVD, and stroke, we would still have to make sure that smoking was the real cause. Some risk factors from the Framingham Study are also emerging. The data suggest that these factors are related to CVD and stroke, but as of yet, a causal relationship has not been established. Three factors identified are homocysteine, Lp(a) (a lipoprotein that may prevent the breakup of clots), and various infectious agents (www.framingham.com/heart/4stor_02.htm). With these emerging risk factors, there may be "a point in the accumulation of evidence when it is more prudent to act on the basis that the association is causal rather than to await further evidence" (McMahon and Pugh, 1970:22).

Comparison of Ratios

For each type of study, it is instructive to note the different ratios that can be constructed and the questions that can be answered. For *retrospective* studies, the ratios to be compared (using the notation of Table 1.1) are

$$\frac{a}{a + c} \quad \text{and} \quad \frac{b}{b + d}$$

By comparing them, we can answer the question, "Were mothers of premature infants more likely to have been smokers than mothers of full-term infants?"

For *prospective* studies, the ratios to be compared are

$$\frac{a}{a + b} \quad \text{and} \quad \frac{c}{c + d}$$

This comparison answers the question, "Which group has the higher frequency of premature infants—mothers who smoke or mothers who do not smoke?"

Descriptive and Analytical Surveys

Retrospective surveys are usually **descriptive surveys** that provide estimates of a population's characteristics, such as the proportion of individuals who had a physical examination during the past 12 months. Prospective surveys may be descriptive or analytical. **Analytical surveys** seek to determine the degree of association between a variable and a factor in the population. An example is the relationship between having (or not having) regular physical examinations and some measure of health status.

1.5 CLINICAL TRIALS

A **clinical trial** is a carefully designed experiment that is generally considered to be the best method for evaluating the effectiveness of a new drug or treatment method. Clinical trials are used extensively to test the efficacy of new drugs and treatments. The federal Food and Drug Administration (FDA) requires clinical trials before drugs and other medical products under their purview receive approval.

Prior to starting a clinical trial, it is essential for the investigator(s) to write "a prospectively written **protocol** that describes in detail the design of the proposed research" (Schechtman, 2000:117). Included in the protocol are clearly defined hypotheses, detailed delineation of inclusion and exclusion criteria for study subjects, descriptions of the proposed interventions and the randomization process, a detailed explanation of how bias may be minimized, a description of the procedures to minimize errors in the collection and analysis of data, a justification of the sample size, and an a priori explanation of the statistical techniques used for data analysis (Schechtman, 2000). What this means is that all facets of a clinical trial must be carefully considered *before* the trial is begun and *before* data are collected. The protocol should also be considered a contract between the investigator(s) and whoever is sponsoring the research (Chew, 2000).

Two key features of a clinical trial are randomization and blinding, each of which helps minimize bias. **Blinding** means that the study subjects and/or the investigators do not know who is in the control group and who is in the experimental group. As Schechtman (2000:118) aptly puts it, "The purpose of blinding is to reduce the likelihood that study assessments will be biased because subject or investigator behavior has been influenced by knowledge of treatment group assignment." In a **single-blind study,** the subject does not know if she or he is in the treatment or the control group. An even better approach is to design a trial known as a **double-blind study.** In this case, neither the subject nor the investigator knows to which group the subject is assigned. A neutral party keeps track of who is in which group and typically discloses it only at the conclusion of the trial.

The second key feature in a clinical trial is **randomization.** True randomization, while not guaranteeing equivalent groups, is the method most likely to consistently reduce bias by producing equivalent treatment and control groups.

(The **treatment group,** which receives a potentially therapeutic agent, is compared with a **control group,** which receives a placebo or the standard therapeutic agent.) In the most basic randomization procedure, each subject in the trial is randomly assigned to either the experimental or the control group; this assignment is fully independent of all preceding assignments. Because the use of controls doubles the size of the sample, some investigators have tried alternatives such as historical controls—subjects selected from a set of records after a study has been completed. Historical controls present problems, however, because of changes in the population over time and because there is no way to eliminate selection bias. Volunteer groups have also been used as controls. Because such a group is self-selected, it is usually atypical of the rest of the population, thus limiting the inferences that may be drawn. Some investigators have chosen controls from patients in certain hospital wards. But this method presents problems of selection for a particular kind of disease or condition and may overrepresent patients hospitalized for a long time or those recently admitted. It is important to remember this: "The consistent message is that trials that use nonrandom assignments tend to produce biased overestimates of true therapeutic efficacy" (Schechtman, 2000:117).

As mentioned previously, an a priori explanation of the statistical procedures is an important component of a protocol. Before collecting data in any type of study, it is important to know how you will analyze the data. Consulting a statistician will help you not only with the analysis but also with the procedures and data collection. We have seen situations in which the data had already been collected when the statistician was consulted. Sometimes we look at what has been done and realize that, if relatively minor adjustments in the data collection process had been made at the beginning, the data might have been much easier to analyze, and the results would have been more meaningful. Regardless of whether we are discussing a clinical trial or any other type of study, we cannot overemphasize the importance of a well-written protocol *prior* to beginning the study.

Example: The Salk Vaccine Clinical Trial

The 1954 clinical trial of the Salk poliomyelitis vaccine is a good example of how a clinical trial can be used to solve an important public health problem. At that time, outbreaks of polio were unpredictable. Because the disease caused paralysis and frequently death, such outbreaks were of great concern to both parents and children. Enter Dr. Jonas Salk. Salk developed a vaccine that proved safe and effective in a laboratory setting in producing antibodies against polio. The question to be answered, then, was whether this promising vaccine could prevent polio in exposed individuals.

To find the answer, a clinical trial was set up. Statisticians recommended that at least 400,000 children be included in the study: 200,000 children in the treatment group and 200,000 children in the control group. The large numbers were needed to provide an adequate number of cases in order to get valid results. An adequate number could be obtained only with these large sample sizes because the incidence rate of polio cases was estimated to be 35 per 100,000 children. The 400,000 children in the study were randomly assigned either to a treatment group (the group receiving the active Salk vaccine) or to a control group (the group receiving a placebo, which consisted of an injection of salt dissolved in water). Because of this precaution—the addition of the double-blind feature—neither the children nor the administrators of the treatment knew which children received the vaccine and which received the placebo. Furthermore, those who examined the children to determine whether they had contracted polio were also unaware of their patients' group status.

It was important that the study group be randomly allocated so that the two groups would be comparable. If this procedure had not been followed, it is likely that the treatment group would have been biased because children from higher socioeconomic levels, whose parents were aware that they were at greater risk, would have been more likely to participate. Such children were at greater risk because their environment was more hygienic than that of children from lower socioeconomic strata, and they were less likely to have developed an immunity to the disease.

The tabulation of the collected data indicated that the incidence rate of cases in the treatment group was 28 per 100,000 versus 71 per 100,000 in the control group. Statistical analysis of these rates showed that the Salk polio vaccine was indeed effective and that the clinical trial (one of the largest ever) and its cost ($5 million) were justified.

Some students may be concerned about the ethical problem of withholding treatment from half of the study group. However, before the clinical trial, there was no definite proof of the effectiveness of the Salk polio vaccine, and without a control group, there was no available scientific, rigorous procedure by which to provide definitive answers. A clinical trial had to be carried out. Once it was— and the evidence was convincing—the public health authorities had the ammunition necessary to mount a national campaign to virtually eradicate polio. Their efforts were successful; polio is no longer considered a public health threat.

1.6   PLANNING OF SURVEYS

The previous sections discussed several types of medical surveys that may give rise to data. Before starting a survey, it is essential to formulate a clear plan of action. An outline of such a plan, including the major steps that should be followed in pursuing the investigation, is given in Chapter 17.

1.7   HOW TO SUCCEED IN STATISTICS

Studying statistics is somewhat analogous to studying a foreign language because a considerable number of new terms and concepts need to be learned. We have found that students who do this successfully scan the chapter outline, read the conclusion and the vocabulary list, and review the learning objectives before coming to class. Also, as soon as possible after the class, they study and learn the relevant terms, concepts, principles, and formulas in the textbook. After doing the assigned exercises, they try to reformulate the objectives as questions and then answer them. We suggest that you do the same. The questions you form from the objectives also serve as excellent review questions you can use to help prepare for tests and exams. If you are not sure of some of these objectives, you may need to go back and reread the chapter or do additional exercises. Doing as many exercises as possible is one of the best ways to learn statistics. If anything is still not clear, make up questions you can ask at the tutorial session or in class.

In addition, read essays dealing with the application of statistics to a variety of fields. Also, because many of the exercises involve a large number of measurements, you may find a calculator helpful. Finally, keep in mind that students who are successful in mastering statistics do not allow themselves to get behind.

◆ CONCLUSION

A statistician designs efficient and unbiased investigations that provide data that he or she then analyzes, interprets, and presents to others so that decisions can be made. To do this work, the statistician uses techniques that are collectively called "statistics." Students of statistics learn these techniques and how they may relate to their work and to everyday life. In particular, they learn how to make correct inferences about a target population of interest based on sample data. Students need to know not only how to understand the scientific literature of their field but also how to select from various kinds of investigations the one that best fits their research purpose.

◆ VOCABULARY LIST

analytical survey	descriptive statistics	randomization
bias	descriptive survey	retrospective study
blinding	double-blind study	significant
case-control study	experiment	single-blind study
census	inferential statistics	statistics
clinical trial	longitudinal study	stimulus variable
cohort	outcome variable	survey
cohort study	placebo	treatment group
control group	prospective study	2 × 2 table
data	protocol	variable

◆ EXERCISES

1.1   Suggest and describe briefly a survey and its objectives.
    a. Is it a descriptive or an analytical survey?
    b. What are some potential sources of bias?

1.2   Suggest and describe an experiment.
    a. What research question are you testing?
    b. What is the "treatment" in this experiment?
    c. What are some potential sources of bias?

1.3   Suggest a clinical trial for some phenomenon of interest to you, such as drug use or exercise.
    a. How would you select and allocate cases?
    b. What would be the treatment?
    c. What would be the outcome variable for determining the effectiveness of the treatment?
    d. What double-blind feature would you include, if any?

1.4   Find a newspaper or magazine article that uses data or statistics.
    a. Were the data obtained from a survey or an experiment?
    b. Is the study descriptive or inferential?
    c. What research question was the author trying to answer?
    d. How did she or he select the cases? What population do the cases represent?
    e. Was there a control group? How were the control subjects selected?
    f. Are possible sources of bias mentioned?
    g. If conclusions are stated, are they warranted?
    h. Make a copy of the article to turn in with your answers to these questions.

1.5   Define: *bias, clinical trial, experiment, survey,* and *statistics.*

1.6   Explain what is meant by
    a. descriptive statistics
    b. inferential statistics

1.7   Answer the following questions regarding the Salk vaccine trial:
    a. Why was such a large trial necessary?
    b. Why was a control group needed?
    c. Why was it important to include a double-blind feature?
    d. If volunteers had been used in this trial rather than a random sample of individuals, of what value would the results have been?

1.8   U.S. census statistics show that college graduates make more than $254,000 more in their lifetime than non-college graduates. If you were to question the validity of this observation, what would be your basis for doing so?

2 Populations and Samples

CHAPTER OUTLINE

✔ LEARNING OBJECTIVES

LEARNING OBJECTIVES

After studying this chapter, you should be able to

1. Distinguish between
   a. populations and samples
   b. parameters and statistics
   c. various methods of sampling
2. Explain why the method of sampling is important

(Continued)

3. State why samples are used
4. Define *random sample*
5. Explain why it is important to use random sampling
6. Select a random sample using a computer statistical program
7. Suggest methods for dealing with missing data

2.1 SELECTING APPROPRIATE SAMPLES

A **population** is a set of persons (or objects) having a common observable characteristic. A **sample** is a subset of a population.

The real challenge of statistics is how to come up with a reliable statement about a population on the basis of sample information. For example, if we want to know how many persons in a community have quit smoking, or have health insurance, or plan to vote for a certain candidate, we usually obtain information on an appropriate sample of the community and generalize from it to the entire population. How a subgroup is selected is of critical importance. Take the classic example of the *Literary Digest* Poll. This poll attained considerable prestige by successfully predicting the outcomes of four presidential elections before 1936. Using the same methods, the *Literary Digest* in 1936 mailed out some 10 million ballots asking persons to indicate their preference in the upcoming presidential election. About 2.3 million ballots were returned, and based on these, the *Literary Digest* confidently predicted that Alfred M. Landon would win by a landslide. In fact, Franklin D. Roosevelt won with a 62% majority. Soon after this fiasco, the *Literary Digest* ceased publication. A postmortem examination of its methods revealed that the sample of 10 million was selected primarily from telephone directories and motor vehicle registration lists, which meant that persons with higher incomes were overrepresented. In 1936, there was a strong relation between income and party preference; thus, the poll's failure was virtually inevitable.

The moral of this incident is clear: The *way* the sample is selected, not its *size*, determines whether we may draw appropriate inferences about the population. Modern sampling techniques can quite reliably predict the winner of a presidential election from a nationwide sample of less than 2000 persons. This is remarkable considering that the nation's population today is more than twice what it was in 1936.

The key to selecting an appropriate sample is that the sample be representative of the population. This means that, whatever variable you are studying, a relatively small sample should very closely approximate the population. The previous two paragraphs present an example in which an extraordinarily large sample did *not* represent the population. The next time a major election approaches, notice the various polls that attempt to predict the probable winner. Many of these polls will come very close to the actual vote count—and do so with a much smaller sample than was used in 1936.

As another example to illustrate populations and samples, we might identify the health issues of college students and then develop programs or provide health care resources depending upon their needs. Let us consider all the students at your school. Is this a sample or a population? It depends. If you are looking at college students in general, your school would be a subset (i.e., sample) of the population. If only students at your school were sampled, could the information gathered be used to make inferences about all college students in the United States? Probably not. The simple reason is that there is likely to be something unique about your school that makes it nonrepresentative of college students in general.

But let's suppose we are only interested in the health issues for students at your school. Under these circumstances, you would view these students as a population. If you want to know what chronic conditions are present, how much students drink or smoke or use marijuana, what prescription and over-the-counter (OTC) drugs are taken, or what serum cholesterol levels are, how do you go about gathering these data? One way would be to survey or examine every student. Realistically, however, this is simply not possible. So what alternatives do you have? What if you were to take a small sample of the population and then, based on this sample, make accurate inferences about the population. Note that the population may consist of persons, objects, or the observations of a characteristic. The set of observations may be summarized by a descriptive statistic called a **parameter.** When the same characteristic pertains to a sample, it is called a **statistic.**

Suppose your school is large enough to have a pharmacy. What drugs should the pharmacy carry? You would need to determine which prescription drugs are most commonly used by students at your school. To do this, you would select a sample. Remember that you want this sample to represent the population. The preferred, and the most likely, method of obtaining a representative sample is to select a **random sample.** The basic principle behind random sampling is that every subject (in this case, students at your school) has an equal chance of being selected. Although this does not guarantee a representative sample, it is the technique most likely to yield a representative sample.

Random sampling might seem to be the best route, but there are often considerable obstacles. Let us assume that you we have a health questionnaire that includes questions about prescription drugs. Your goal is to select a random sample of students to complete this questionnaire. Selecting a random sample is fairly easy. Using a statistical program, you can assign each student a number and then generate a random sample. You next send the questionnaire to the selected students. Here is the problem: What will your **response rate** be? How many students will return the questionnaire? Without resorting to various techniques for improving the response rate, you may be doing well to get a 50% return. Remember that the primary purpose of random sampling is to obtain a representative sample and then, based on the sample statistics, to make inferences about the population.

Is a 50% response rate good enough to ensure a representative sample? Often, you simply do not know. Think about the situation at your school, and ask yourself whether students who complete and return a survey are different from those who do not. Researchers often assume that the responses are representative, but that assumption may not be valid. This leads to possible **sampling bias.** Bias occurs because some segment of the population might be either over or underrepresented. For example, females, or freshman, or health science majors may be more likely to respond than males, seniors, or English majors. Thus, the statistics gathered from such a survey may have some **bias,** which means the sample may not be representative of the population. Without getting into specific techniques for increasing the response rate, whatever technique improves the rate is likely to ensure that the sample is representative of the population.

Often, however, a random sample is not feasible. It may be too costly to randomly select a group and then mail out a survey. In the case of a clinical study of a specific treatment for a particular disease, it may be of no value to have three patients from California, one from Idaho, two from Tennessee, and so on. You need to identify an adequate number of subjects quickly and efficiently. At a college or university, you might include all members of one or more classes until you have the sample size you want. This is often referred to as a **convenience sample.** Let us assume that the stats class you are currently in is selected. Most, if not all of you, will probably give your **informed consent** to participate. If the researcher is trying to find out something about your health status, you might complete a questionnaire, or perhaps some type of measurement will be taken, such as height, weight, or blood pressure. Although the researcher is able to gather large amounts of data quickly and efficiently, the key question remains: Is this sample representative of the population? If your class is used, think about how your class differs from and is similar to your school's population. Presumably, you have a higher percentage of students pursuing some type of health major. Are health majors different from other students? You probably also have a disproportionate number of students at a certain grade level. Perhaps there are gender, ethnic, or religious differences that may impact the results. Although a convenience sample may be quick and efficient, and yield large numbers, it still may have limited utility because it is not representative of the population.

Clinical trials frequently employ a nonrandom sample. If a new drug, medical device, or medical procedure is being tested, there may be only one or two test sites. The sample would be those patients who met the criteria for testing the new drug, device, or procedure. The frequent assumption is that, whatever results are found at the test site, similar results will be obtained at other sites and with different subjects. This assumption is tested when the new product is approved for general use and researchers find that either the product is indeed useful or it does not meet the original expectations. A large nonrandom study is the STAR Trial, which was briefly discussed in Chapter 1. In this study, 22,000 postmenopausal women who are at an increased risk of breast cancer are being recruited from more than 500 centers. By the time you read this, there may be some reported results. Because the sample is so large and the scope is so broad (more than 500 centers), there will probably be little or no discussion about the sample. The assumption will be that the results are generalizable to the population of postmenopausal women who are at an increased risk of breast cancer.

2.2   WHY SAMPLE?

You may be wondering, "Why not study the entire population?" There are many reasons. It is *impossible* to obtain the weight of every tuna in the Pacific Ocean. It is too costly to inspect every manifold housing that comes off an assembly line. The Internal Revenue Service does not have the workforce to review every income tax return. Some testing is inherently destructive: tensile strength of structural steel, flight of a solid propellant rocket, measurement of white blood cells. We certainly cannot launch all the rockets to learn the number of defective ones; we cannot drain all the blood from a person and count every white blood cell. Often we cannot justify enumerating the entire population—that is, conducting a census—because for most purposes we can obtain suitable accuracy quickly and inexpensively on the basis of the information gained from a sample alone. One of the tasks of a statistician is to design efficient studies utilizing adequate sample sizes that are not unnecessarily large. How to determine a sample size that is likely to give meaningful results is discussed in Chapter 9.

2.3   HOW SAMPLES ARE SELECTED

At this point, you should begin to recognize the importance of selecting a sample and then using that sample to draw inferences about the population. But how reliable are our inferences regarding a population? The answer depends largely on how precisely the population is specified and on how the sample is selected. Having a poorly specified or enumerated population or an inappropriately selected sample will almost certainly introduce bias. Although you cannot guarantee that bias will be eliminated, you can take steps to control it. The best way to limit bias is to use random sampling, a technique that is simple to apply (it is sometimes called "simple random sampling"). The basic principle behind random sampling is quite straightforward: Each subject in the population has an equal chance of being selected. Cappelleri and Trochim (2000:149) succinctly describe three important reasons for random sampling: "(1) It avoids known and unknown biases on average; (2) it helps convince others that the trial was conducted properly; and (3) it is the basis for statistical theory that underlies hypothesis tests and confidence intervals." As you progress through this chapter, reasons 1 and 2 should become increasingly clear.

As for reason 3, the key point to remember is that a random sample allows us to draw the most representative sample and then, based on the sample statistics, to make inferences about the population. You will study many of these statistical methods as you progress through your statistics class.

Samples can be selected in several other ways. In convenience sampling, as previously noted, a group is selected at will or in a particular program or clinic. These cases are often self-selected. Because the data obtained are seldom representative of the underlying population, problems arise in analysis and in drawing inferences.

Convenience samples are often used when it is virtually impossible to select a random sample. For instance, if a researcher wants to study alcohol use among college students, each member of the population—that is, each college student—ideally would have an equal chance of being sampled. A random sample of 100, 1000, or 10,000 college students is simply not realistic. How will the researcher collect data about alcohol use among college students? Often he or she will survey college students enrolled in a general education course, such as English 101. The underlying assumption on the part of the researcher is that a general education class, which most or all students must take, is a representative sample of college students and therefore accurately represents alcohol use at that college or university. The logical next step is to assume that the colleges or universities surveyed are representative in terms of college and university students' alcohol use. You can see how the use of a convenience sample may eventually lead researchers to inferences about alcohol use among college students that are inaccurate or misleading.

Systematic sampling is frequently used when a **sampling frame**—a complete, nonoverlapping list of the persons or objects constituting the population—is available. We randomly select a first case and then proceed by selecting every nth (say $n = 30$) case, where n depends on the desired sample size. The symbol N is used to denote the size of the entire population.

Stratified sampling is used when we wish the sample to represent the various **strata** (subgroups) of the population proportionately or to increase the precision of the estimate. A simple random sample is taken from each stratum.

In **cluster sampling,** we select a simple random sample of groups, such as a certain number of city blocks, and then interview a person in each household of the selected blocks. This technique is more economical than the random selection of persons throughout the city.

For a complete discussion of the various kinds of sampling methods, you should consult a textbook on the subject.

2.4 HOW TO SELECT A RANDOM SAMPLE

Selecting a random sample is one of the easiest procedures you will learn. The process can be as basic as putting all the names of a population on slips of paper, putting the slips in a container, mixing them up, and selecting however many names you want. Many calculators will generate random numbers. Also, a random numbers table is included in Appendix E. However, the most widely used technique, and therefore the focus of this section, is the use of a computer program to select random numbers. Without attempting to explain how, we will simply state that computer statistical packages such as SPSS are programmed to allow for the quick selection of random numbers.

In Chapter 3, Table 3.1 lists characteristics of 100 of the 7683 participants in the Honolulu Heart Study, which investigated heart disease among men ages 45–67. This data set is also included in a spreadsheet that is available on this book's Web site at www.mhhe.com/Kuzma5e. Suppose we want to randomly select 25 cases from the 100 cases contained in Table 3.1. If you are using SPSS (we used version 11.5), here is how to select a random sample of 25 from the 100 cases listed in Table 3.1. First, go to the menu and find the Data box, which is the fourth box after File, View, and Edit. From the Data Box, go down to the next-to-last choice, Select cases. Once you have found Select cases, choose Random Sample of Cases. In the Select Cases box, next choose Random Sample of Cases. Then hit the button just below Random Sample of Cases, labeled Sample. Another box, Select Cases: Random Sample, will appear. Under Sample size, you will have two choices: (1) Approximately X% of all cases, or (2) Exactly X cases from the first XX cases. If you choose option 1, all you need to do is pick a number between 1 and 99, and that percentage of cases will be selected. If you choose option 2, you can select the exact number you want where you see the X (blank space in the Dialog box). Where you see XX (another blank in the Dialog box), you will typically enter the total number of the subjects in the data set. Using the data from Table 3.1, we would enter the number 100.

Let us use option 2 and choose 25 from the 100 cases in the Honolulu Heart Study. Enter 25 in the first space and 100 in the second. Click OK. Next, look at your screen with 100 subjects. If you scroll down, you will notice that some of them have a slash across the number. There are 25 numbers selected that do not have a slash. This is your random sample of 25. The 75 numbers that have slashes represent the 75 cases the computer did not randomly select. You may wish to repeat this process. Note that each time you repeat the process a different set of 25 is selected. In the next section, we will use this process to illustrate how a random sample can provide you with a sample average that comes very close to the average of the 100 subjects in this data set. At least, this will happen most, but not all, of the time.

2.5 EFFECTIVENESS OF A RANDOM SAMPLE

Students who encounter random sampling for the first time are somewhat skeptical about its effectiveness. The reliability of sampling is usually demonstrated by defining a fairly small population and then selecting from it all conceivable samples of a particular size, say, three observations. Then, for each sample, the mean (average) is computed and the variation from the population mean is observed. A comparison of these sample means (statistics) with the population mean (parameter) neatly demonstrates the credibility of the sampling scheme.

In this chapter, we try to establish credibility by a different approach. Let us return to Table 3.1, which lists characteristics of a representative sample of 100 individuals from the 7683 participants in the Honolulu Heart Study, which investigated heart disease among men ages 45–67. Five separate samples of 100 observations each were selected from this population, and the mean ages were compared with the population mean. The results of this comparison are shown in Table 2.1. We can see that the population parameter is 54.36 and that the five statistics representing this mean are all very close to it. The difference between the sample estimate and the population mean never exceeds 0.5 year, even though each sample represents only 1.3% of the entire population. This comparison underscores how much similarity you can expect among sample means.

Let us take another random sample, using SPSS, from the 100 subjects listed in Table 3.1. First, display the data from Table 3.1 on your computer screen. Next, have the computer display the mean (average) age for the 100 subjects. To find the mean, choose Analyze from the menu, and scroll down to the second item, which is Descriptive Statistics. Within the Descriptive Statistics category, you have five choices. Choose the second one, Descriptives. Select variable number 4, which is Age, and then click OK. You will see a display indicating, among other things, that the number (N) of total subjects is 100 and that the mean (average) is 53.67.

Based on the 100 subjects, next select five random samples of 20, 30, and 40 subjects, using the method described in the previous section. If you write down the sample means (averages), notice how most, if not all, of them should be reasonably close to the average age of 53.67. Again, this illustrates how a randomly selected sample can closely approximate the numerical values of the population. Table 2.2 shows the values we obtained from the five samples of 20, 30, and 40.

2.6 MISSING AND INCOMPLETE DATA

In the opening section of this chapter, we discussed the problem of obtaining a random sample from a well-defined population, such as all students at your school. Regardless of whether you are conducting a survey or using some other data collection technique, if you are only able to collect data from some subjects in your sample, the sample may not be representative of the population. If your sample is biased, there is the very real risk that the sample statistics may differ significantly from the population statistics or parameters. For example, what is the average (mean) number of alcoholic drinks consumed by college students, over a specific time period? Suppose you select a random sample from all students at your school and mail each student a questionnaire. Whatever

Table 2.1 Hypertension Study Cases by Diastolic Blood Pressure, Sex, and Dietary Status

ID	Diastolic Blood Pressure (mmHg)	Sex	Vegetarian Status	ID	Diastolic Blood Pressure (mmHg)	Sex	Vegetarian Status
01	88	M	V	42	70	M	NV
02	98	M	V	43	102	M	NV
03	64	M	V	44	84	M	NV
04	80	M	V	45	74	M	NV
05	60	M	V	46	76	M	NV
06	68	M	V	47	84	M	NV
07	58	M	V	48	84	M	NV
08	82	M	V	49	82	M	NV
09	74	M	V	50	82	M	NV
10	64	M	V	51	74	M	NV
11	78	M	V	52	70	M	NV
12	68	M	V	53	92	M	NV
13	60	M	V	54	68	M	NV
14	96	M	V	55	70	M	NV
15	64	M	V	56	70	M	NV
16	78	M	V	57	70	M	NV
17	68	M	V	58	40	M	NV
18	72	M	V	59	83	M	NV
19	76	F	V	60	74	M	NV
20	68	F	V	61	56	F	NV
21	70	F	V	62	89	F	NV
22	62	F	V	63	84	F	NV
23	82	F	V	64	58	F	NV
24	58	F	V	65	58	F	NV
25	72	F	V	66	82	F	NV
26	56	F	V	67	78	F	NV
27	84	F	V	68	82	F	NV
28	80	F	V	69	71	F	NV
29	56	F	V	70	56	F	NV
30	58	F	V	71	68	F	NV
31	82	F	V	72	58	F	NV
32	88	F	V	73	72	F	NV
33	100	F	V	74	80	F	NV
34	88	F	V	75	88	F	NV
35	74	F	V	76	72	F	NV
36	60	F	V	77	68	F	NV
37	74	F	V	78	66	F	NV
38	70	F	V	79	78	F	NV
39	70	F	V	80	74	F	NV
40	66	F	V	81	60	F	NV
41	76	M	NV	82	66	F	NV
				83	72	F	NV

NOTE: ID = identification; mmHg = millimeters of mercury; V = vegetarian; NV = nonvegetarian.

Table 2.2 Effectiveness of a Random Sample ($N = 100$)

Sample Size (1)	Average (Mean) Age				
	1	2	3	4	5
20	52.95	53.50	54.35	53.45	51.80
30	52.80	53.60	53.70	53.57	52.97
40	53.15	53.70	54.10	53.60	53.15

technique you use to distribute, the questionnaire will almost certainly leave you with a significant percentage of nonrespondents. If you use a true random sample, is it possible that the alcohol consumption levels of the respondents may differ from those of nonrespondents? If, instead of a random sample, you use a convenience sample, such as composition or general education classes, is it possible that those students attending class and completing the questionnaire might differ from those absent in terms of alcohol consumption? It is possible.

It is important to recognize that bias may be introduced because of possible differences between respondents and nonrespondents. This may limit the ability to accurately draw inferences about the population. The next question is, What can be done to determine if bias exists? Frequently, the answer is nothing. The researcher simply states that the response rate is adequate or the convenience sample is representative and then proceeds with the analysis. Or the researcher may acknowledge a possible weakness or bias and make some type of qualifying statement about the results. Yet another possibility is to try to identify some objective method of determining if the nonrespondents differ from the respondents.

If this problem were posed to you, at your school, how might you objectively determine if nonrespondents differ from respondents? One possibility would be to determine whether any population data exists for students. For example, most schools could give you the number of males and females, their years in school, and their grade point averages (GPA). If your questionnaire also asked for the respondent's gender, GPA, and year in school, you could easily compute the sample percentage of males and females; the sample percentage of freshman, sophomores, and so on; and the sample GPA. Then you could compare that to the population parameters already identified. What if you find that your sample has a higher GPA than your population. Remember that you are trying to determine how much alcohol is consumed overall, based on a sample. If the GPA is indeed higher for the sample, would you question the validity of taking the sample alcohol consumption data and generalizing to the population? Maybe so. It is quite plausible, and some might argue probable, that students with lower GPAs might consume more alcohol than their peers.

Therefore, a sample with a higher GPA might potentially underestimate the amount of alcohol consumed by students at your school.

The previous discussion focused on the problem of nonrespondents when data are collected only once. What about a situation in which there are multiple observations from the same subject? These are referred to as **longitudinal studies.** This is the case in most clinical trials. Subjects enter the study with some specific criteria such as a disease or condition at a well-defined stage or grade. An example might be patients with moderately elevated serum cholesterol levels entering a study to test the efficacy of a new cholesterol-lowering drug. The study protocol will require serum cholesterol levels to be measured at various times.

Whenever you have a study that requires two or more data collection points, you run the risk that subjects, for a variety of reasons, will drop out, and you now have a problem with missing data. How do statisticians handle the problem of missing data? One potential method, again, is simply to ignore it. Therefore, your analysis includes only those subjects who complete the study. But there are obvious problems with this approach. These center around the reason(s) subjects leave the study. If you are doing a clinical test of a new drug, such as a cholesterol-lowering drug, what are plausible reasons for dropping out? Some reasons might be relatively benign, such as subjects moving away from the study site or simply failing to keep appointments. However, other reasons might directly relate to your ability to determine the efficacy of the new drug. Perhaps a subject's condition worsened rather than improved; perhaps some subjects were experiencing unpleasant or even dangerous side effects; or perhaps one or more subjects died during the study period. All of these reasons would lead you to question the efficacy of the new drug. However, if all subjects with missing data are dropped from the study, what is left is an analysis of only those subjects who either had a beneficial reaction to the new drug or at least avoided some of the more serious adverse events. Obviously, conclusions drawn solely from those who completed the study would be legitimately questioned. Many peer-reviewed journals would reject articles that ignored dropouts and only analyzed data from subjects who completed the study.

This analytical challenge is known as the missing data problem. Fortunately, there are ways of dealing with the problem. One commonly used technique is a type of **carry-forward analysis** called **last observation carry-forward** (LOCF). Ting (2000) describes an example in which subjects in a 4-week clinical study were evaluated at week zero (frequently referred to as the baseline) and at weeks 1, 2, 3, and 4. Drug efficacy measurements were taken at five points during this 4-week study. With LOCF, subjects may drop out anytime after the baseline data is collected. If you are using the LOCF technique for missing data, you "take the last observed value prior to dropout from each of these subjects and treat them as final data (i.e., carry forward the last observation from each subject who dropped out before the week-four evaluation)" (Ting, 2000:104). A hypothetical example of a 4-week trial to lower serum cholesterol is shown in Table 2.3.

Table 2.3 Cholesterol Levels with Missing Data (Simulated)

Subject	Baseline	Week 1	Week 2	Week 3	Week 4	LOCF
1	281	280	272	256	242	NA
2	291	294	298	—	—	298
3	287	275	266	266	—	266
4	266	252	279	249	240	NA
5	295	294	271	268	232	NA
6	273	273	260	288	—	288
7	254	231	240	226	222	NA

Because dropouts are frequently treatment failures, using this technique may give a more accurate picture of the true efficacy of the drug being evaluated. A more complete discussion of carry-forward analysis may be found in an article by Ting (2000).

◆ CONCLUSION

Assessing all individuals in a population may be impossible, impractical, expensive, or inaccurate, so it is usually to our advantage to instead study a sample from the original population. To do this, we must clearly identify the population, be able to list it in a sampling frame, and utilize an appropriate sampling technique. Although several methods of selecting samples are possible, random sampling is usually the most desirable technique. It is easy to apply, limits bias, provides estimates of error, and meets the assumptions necessary for many statistical tests. Missing or incomplete data can also introduce bias. Carry-forward analysis is one technique for accounting for missing or incomplete data. The effectiveness of random sampling can easily be demonstrated by comparing sample statistics with population parameters. The statistics obtained from a sample are used as estimates of the unknown parameters of the population.

◆ VOCABULARY LIST

bias
carry-forward analysis
cluster sample
convenience sample
informed consent
last observation carry-
    forward

longitudinal study
parameter
population
random sample
response rate
sample
sampling bias

sampling frame
statistic
stratified sample
stratum (*pl* strata)
systematic sample

◆ EXERCISES

2.1 Describe the differences between
  a. a parameter and a statistic
  b. a sample and a census
  c. a simple random sample and a convenience sample

2.2 Describe the steps you would take if you were asked to determine the
  a. proportion of joggers in your community
  b. number of workers without health insurance at companies with fewer than 100 workers in your community
  c. number of pregnant women not obtaining prenatal care in your community
  d. number of homeless people in your community

2.3 Why is the way a sample is selected more important than the size of the sample?

2.4 List and briefly explain the importance of the three reasons for random sampling.

2.5 a. Explain why a convenience sample, such as the selection of students in one or more general education classes at your college or university, might not be representative of all students at your institution.
  b. Explain why students at your college or university might be representative of college students in general.

2.6 a. In what ways are a random sample, convenience sample, and systematic sample different? In what ways are they similar?
  b. Describe a situation in which it would be appropriate and more efficient and cost-effective to use a random sample, convenience sample, systematic sample, or cluster sample.

2.7 Using the data from Table 2.1 and a computer statistical package such as SPSS, choose the variable Diastolic Blood Pressure and find the mean (average) for the 83 subjects. Choose samples of 15, 25, and 35, and find the mean of each of these samples. Note how close the various sample means are to the overall mean of the 83 subjects.

2.8 Suppose in the previous exercise you had selected the sample by taking two simple random samples of 10 from each of the two dietary groups. What label would you apply to such a sample?

2.9 Using the data from Table 3.1 and a computer statistical package such as SPSS, choose the variable Serum Cholesterol Level and find the mean (average) for the 100 subjects. Choose samples of 20, 30, 40, 50, and 60, and find the mean of each of these samples. Note how close the various sample means are to the overall mean of the 100 subjects.

2.10 Describe the population and sample for
  a. Exercise 2.7
  b. the data in Table 3.1

2.11 Explain why missing or incomplete data may affect the validity and bias the results of a study.

3 Organizing and Displaying Data

CHAPTER OUTLINE

3.1 **Classifying and Organizing Data**
Explains and illustrates numerical scales, and distinguishes among qualitative data, discrete quantitative data, and continuous quantitative data

3.2 **Figures, Tables, and Graphs**
Gives a brief overview of each

3.3 **Creating Tables**
Gives instructions on how to organize data in the form of a frequency table

3.4 **Graphing Data**
Discusses and illustrates various methods of graphing, with an emphasis on those that apply specifically to frequency distributions

✔ LEARNING OBJECTIVES

After studying this chapter, you should be able to

1. Distinguish between
   a. qualitative and quantitative variables
   b. discrete and continuous variables
   c. symmetrical, bimodal, and skewed distributions
   d. positively and negatively skewed distributions

2. Construct and interpret a frequency table that includes class intervals, class frequency, valid percent, and cumulative percent

3. Indicate the appropriate types of graphs for displaying quantitative and qualitative data

4. Distinguish which forms of data presentation are appropriate for different situations

(Continued)

5. Construct a histogram, frequency polygon, ogive, bar chart, and box-and-whisker plot

6. Distinguish among and interpret various graphs

7. Determine and interpret percentiles from an ogive

3.1   CLASSIFYING AND ORGANIZING DATA

To successfully explain your data, one of your first tasks is to classify and organize the data. There are three general ways of organizing and presenting data: tables, graphs, and numerical techniques. Each of these methods will be illustrated by reference to a sample of 100 individuals, selected by systematic random sampling from the Honolulu Heart Study population of 7683 (Phillips, 1972). The data for this sample are presented in Table 3.1 and are also on this book's Web site at www.mhhe.com/Kuzma5e.

Nominal, Ordinal, Interval, and Ratio Scales

Before proceeding, we should discuss the meanings attached to various numbers. One approach is to identify data by measurement scale. There are four commonly used scales: nominal, ordinal, interval, and ratio. The scale used to classify the data to a large extent determines what can be done with the data. This statement is best explained by using specific examples, starting with the **nominal scale.** Nominal scales are used primarily for grouping or categorizing data. Variables that yield nominal-level data are frequently referred to as **qualitative variables** (e.g., zip code, hair color, gender, name of college or university, social security number). In Table 3.1, ID (number) and smoking status (smoker versus nonsmoker) are qualitative variables. Note what these variables have in common. All can be used to group or categorize data; you can organize subjects based on any of these characteristics. Also note that these variables do not typically have a numerical value associated with them. However, to use these variables in some type of statistical analysis, it is necessary to assign them a numerical value. For instance, as in Table 3.1, smoking status might be given the numerical values of 0 and 1 for smoker and nonsmoker, respectively. Hair color might be anything from 1 to however many categories you choose to create. Subject identification number (ID) is typically some unique number for each subject. It can be something as simple as the order in which their individual data are entered into the spreadsheet.

Note that these numbers are used simply to group or categorize data and that mathematical manipulations will yield meaningless information. For example, if your class were organized by gender or hair color, of what value would be the average gender or average hair color? Or, using the data from Table 3.1,

Table 3.1 Data for a Sample of 100 Individuals from the Honolulu Heart Study Population of 7683 Persons, 1969

ID	Educational Level	Weight (kg)	Height (cm)	Age	Smoking Status	Physical Activity at Home	Blood Glucose	Serum Cholesterol	Systolic Blood Pressure	Body Mass Index (BMI)
1	2	70	165	61	1	1	107	199	102	25.7
2	1	60	162	52	0	2	145	267	138	22.9
3	1	62	150	52	1	1	237	272	190	27.6
4	2	66	165	51	1	1	91	166	122	24.2
5	2	70	162	51	0	1	185	239	128	26.7
6	4	59	165	53	0	2	106	189	112	21.7
7	1	47	160	61	0	1	177	238	128	18.4
8	3	66	170	48	1	1	120	223	116	22.8
9	5	56	155	54	0	2	116	279	134	23.3
10	2	62	167	48	0	1	105	190	104	22.2
11	4	68	165	49	1	2	109	240	116	25.0
12	1	65	166	48	0	1	186	209	152	23.6
13	1	56	157	55	0	2	257	210	134	22.7
14	2	80	161	49	0	1	218	171	132	30.9
15	3	66	160	50	0	2	164	255	130	25.8
16	4	91	170	52	0	2	158	232	118	31.5
17	3	71	170	48	1	1	117	147	136	24.6
18	5	66	152	59	0	2	130	268	108	28.6
19	1	73	159	59	0	2	132	231	108	28.9
20	4	59	161	52	0	1	138	199	128	22.8
21	1	64	162	52	1	1	131	255	118	24.4
22	3	55	161	52	1	1	88	199	134	21.2
23	2	78	175	50	1	1	161	228	178	25.5
24	2	59	160	54	0	1	145	240	134	22.8
25	3	51	167	48	1	2	128	184	162	18.3
26	3	83	171	55	0	1	231	192	162	28.4
27	2	66	157	49	1	2	78	211	120	26.8
28	4	61	165	51	0	1	113	201	98	22.4
29	2	65	160	53	0	1	134	203	144	25.4
30	3	75	172	49	0	1	104	243	118	25.4
31	4	61	164	49	0	2	122	181	118	22.7
32	1	73	157	53	1	2	442	382	138	29.6
33	2	66	157	52	0	1	237	186	134	26.8
34	1	73	155	48	0	2	148	198	108	27.8
35	2	61	160	53	0	1	231	165	96	23.8
36	3	68	162	50	0	2	161	219	142	25.9
37	2	52	157	50	0	2	119	196	122	21.1
38	5	73	162	50	0	1	185	239	146	27.8
39	1	52	165	61	1	2	118	259	126	19.1
40	1	56	162	53	1	1	98	162	176	21.3
41	3	67	170	48	1	2	218	178	104	23.2
42	1	61	160	47	0	1	147	246	112	23.8
43	3	52	166	62	1	2	176	176	140	18.9
44	2	61	172	56	1	2	106	157	102	20.6
45	3	62	164	55	1	2	109	179	142	23.1
46	2	56	155	57	1	2	138	231	146	23.3
47	1	55	157	50	0	2	84	183	92	22.3

(*Continued*)

Table 3.1 (*Continued*)

ID	Educa-tional Level	Weight (kg)	Height (cm)	Age	Smoking Status	Physical Activity at Home	Blood Glucose	Serum Choles-terol	Systolic Blood Pressure	Body Mass Index (BMI)
48	3	66	165	48	1	2	137	213	112	24.2
49	1	59	159	51	0	2	139	230	152	23.3
50	3	53	152	53	1	2	97	134	116	22.9
51	5	71	173	52	0	2	169	181	118	23.7
52	2	57	152	49	0	1	160	234	128	24.7
53	2	73	165	50	1	1	123	161	116	26.8
54	3	75	170	49	0	2	130	289	134	26.0
55	3	80	171	50	1	2	198	186	108	27.4
56	4	49	157	53	0	1	215	298	134	19.9
57	4	65	162	52	0	1	177	211	124	24.8
58	2	82	170	56	0	2	100	189	124	28.4
59	3	55	155	52	0	2	91	164	114	22.9
60	3	61	165	58	0	1	141	219	154	22.4
61	2	50	155	54	1	2	139	287	114	20.8
62	5	58	160	56	0	1	176	179	114	22.7
63	1	55	166	50	1	2	218	216	98	20.0
64	5	59	161	47	0	2	146	224	128	22.8
65	2	68	165	53	1	1	128	212	130	25.0
66	2	60	170	53	1	2	127	230	122	20.8
67	1	77	160	47	1	1	76	231	112	30.1
68	5	60	155	52	0	1	126	185	106	25.0
69	3	70	164	54	0	1	184	180	128	26.0
70	2	70	165	46	0	1	58	205	128	25.7
71	3	77	160	58	1	1	95	219	116	30.1
72	5	86	160	53	0	2	144	286	154	33.6
73	2	67	152	49	1	2	124	261	126	29.0
74	3	77	165	53	1	1	167	221	140	28.3
75	3	75	169	57	0	2	150	194	122	26.3
76	2	70	165	52	0	2	156	248	154	25.7
77	2	70	165	49	1	1	193	216	140	25.7
78	1	71	157	53	0	1	194	195	120	28.8
79	1	55	162	49	0	2	73	217	140	21.0
80	2	59	165	53	1	2	98	186	114	21.7
81	3	64	159	50	0	2	127	218	122	25.3
82	1	66	160	54	0	1	153	173	94	25.8
83	4	59	165	60	0	2	161	221	122	21.7
84	3	68	165	57	0	1	194	206	172	25.0
85	5	58	160	52	0	1	87	215	100	22.7
86	1	57	154	65	1	1	188	176	150	24.0
87	2	60	160	65	0	2	149	240	154	23.4
88	2	53	162	62	0	1	215	234	170	20.2
89	2	61	159	62	1	2	163	190	140	24.1
90	1	66	154	62	0	1	111	204	144	27.8
91	1	61	152	67	0	2	198	256	156	26.4
92	2	52	152	66	0	2	265	296	132	22.5
93	1	59	155	62	0	2	143	223	140	24.6
94	1	63	155	62	1	1	136	225	150	26.2
95	2	61	165	63	0	2	298	217	130	22.4

(*Continued*)

Table 3.1 (*Continued*)

ID	Educational Level	Weight (kg)	Height (cm)	Age	Smoking Status	Physical Activity at Home	Blood Glucose	Serum Cholesterol	Systolic Blood Pressure	Body Mass Index (BMI)
96	2	68	155	67	0	2	173	251	118	28.3
97	1	58	170	62	0	1	148	187	162	20.1
98	3	68	160	55	0	1	110	290	128	26.6
99	5	60	159	50	0	2	188	238	130	23.7
100	2	61	160	54	1	1	208	218	208	23.8

Code for variables:
Education: 1 = none, 2 = primary, 3 = intermediate, 4 = senior high, 5 = technical school, 6 = university
Weight: in kilograms
Height: in centimeters
Smoking: 0 = no, 1 = yes
Physical activity: 1 = mostly sitting, 2 = moderate, 3 = heavy
Blood glucose: in milligrams percent
Serum cholesterol: in milligrams percent
Systolic blood pressure: in millimeters of mercury
Body mass index = weight (kg) ÷ height (m)^2

of what value would be the average smoking status or average physical activity level. When you use a computer statistical package such as SPSS, nominal or qualitative variables are often used as **grouping variables.** Whereas the average smoking status or average gender is of no value, the difference in systolic blood pressure between those who smoke and those who do not may be quite important. It might also be important to find the difference in serum cholesterol levels between smokers and nonsmokers. Using smoking status as the grouping variable allows you to do this particular analysis. In fact, this is the type of analysis that you may do in the comprehensive exercises in the chapter on two-sample significance testing.

Numbers may also be organized on an **ordinal scale.** Ordinals represent an ordered series of relationships. (e.g., first, second, third, and so on). They may be applied to such diverse situations as the rank order of causes of death or the standings in the Eastern Division of the American League. The five leading causes of death are, in order, heart disease, cancer, cerebrovascular disease, chronic respiratory disease, and unintentional injury. The standings in the American League East typically are New York Yankees, Boston Red Sox, Toronto Blue Jays, Baltimore Orioles, and Tampa Bay Devil Rays. In both examples, what you know is which are first, second, third, fourth, and fifth. In other words, you know the *order.* What you don't know is the *difference.* For example, what is the difference in the numbers of deaths due to heart disease versus cancer? Or how far is New York ahead of Boston? You know which is first and which is second, but you can't quantify the difference with the information provided. Ordinal-level data provide useful information, but without being able to quantify the differences, the information is limited.

The final two measurement scales are **interval** and **ratio,** also considered **quantitative variables.** These variables are measured numerically. Examples from Table 3.1 include weight, height, age, and serum cholesterol. The main distinction between interval and ratio data is whether the number 0 is a true or absolute zero, which means the data are ratio, or an artificial 0, which means the data are interval. True or absolute zero refers to the total *absence* of the characteristic being measured. An example that college students might identify with is $0. If you have $0 in your wallet, you have a total absence of money. The most widely used example of interval data is temperature. Temperature is usually measured using either the Fahrenheit or the centigrade scale. In both scales, the 0 is artificial because it does not represent the total absence of heat.

A key feature of both interval and ratio data is that any differences are measurable and meaningful. For example, if person A has $10 and person B has $20, you know that the difference is exactly $10 and that person B has twice as much money as person A. You also know that 60°F is 30° warmer than 30°F. However, because the Fahrenheit scale is an interval scale, you cannot say that 60°F is twice as warm as 30°F. You can meaningfully compute ratios for ratio data, but not for interval data. This is the only situation in which the distinction between interval and ratio data has any statistical importance. Throughout this text, the various statistical procedures that use interval data are just as effective with ratio data, and vice versa.

Quantitative variables can be further classified as **discrete** (discontinuous) or **continuous.** The number of children per household, the number of times you visit a doctor, and the number of missing teeth are discrete variables; they must always be integers—that is, whole numbers (e.g., 0, 1, 2). Variables such as age, height, and weight may take on fractional values (e.g., 37.8, 138.2, 112.9). They are referred to as continuous variables.

Statisticians often treat discrete variables as continuous variables. An example that you probably have noticed is the number of children per household. You may see a number such as 2.4 children per household. Obviously, you cannot have 0.4 child, yet this is a widely used statistic. The reason for treating discrete variables as continuous variables is that it significantly improves the accuracy or predictability of the data. If a community group such as a school is trying to estimate the number of children who will need services, how should that estimate be made? Suppose a community anticipated that it would have 100 new households in the next 5 years. If the number of children per household is treated strictly as a discrete variable, then the average number of children per household would be 2, and the estimate for 100 new households would be an increase of 200 children. Treating the discrete variable as a continuous variable (2.4 children per household) would yield an estimate of 240 children. In all likelihood, 240 would be the more accurate estimate.

Different types of variables are analyzed differently. Know what type of data you have. This will help you to select the appropriate method of analyis.

Hints for Entering Data into a Spreadsheet

Should you have to enter data into a spreadsheet, here are some hints that may help. If you have to manually enter data, as professors do with grades, remember to verify the accuracy of your data input. Any statistical program will correctly analyze the data provided. If incorrect numbers are entered, the analysis will be mathematically correct, but there will be the infamous "computer error." For example, if you get the wrong grade in the class and the professor claims a computer error, what he or she is really saying is, "I entered the wrong numbers." The computer will correctly compute your grade based on the numbers entered. Throughout this course, you will be either working exercises from this text or using examples from your professor. The most likely reason for incorrect numerical answers will be that you entered one or more wrong numbers. We cannot overemphasize the importance of checking the accuracy of your data. Remember: *Verify, verify, verify.*

Typically, the default setting on a spreadsheet, such as in SPSS, is two decimal places. If you are entering nominal or ordinal data, you may wish to change the setting to zero decimal places. In the spreadsheet that was created from the data in Table 3.1, educational level, physical activity, and smoking status were all changed to zero decimal places. Those three variables are most likely used as grouping variables, not for computations such as average (mean).

Finally, you need to think about subject identification (ID) numbers. If you are doing a study in which the subjects have their own ID numbers, you will need to enter them into a column, probably the first one. You will also want to reset this column to zero decimals. If the subject ID number is simply the order in which the data are entered, you do not actually have to enter ID numbers. The spreadsheet will assign each subject a number that appears to the left of the first column. This is what we did with the Table 3.1 spreadsheet: The numbers 1–100 represent the order in which subjects were entered.

3.2 FIGURES, TABLES, AND GRAPHS

You have undoubtedly seen many examples of figures, tables, and graphs. In this section, we will briefly explain what they are and how they are used. To define and distinguish each of these terms, we draw on the *Publication Manual of the American Psychological Association* (APA), Fifth Edition.

Figures are simply "any type of illustration other than a table" (APA, 2001: 176). Types of figures include charts, graphs, photographs, and drawings. In this chapter, we give examples only of graphs. Because a **graph** is one particular type of figure, the correct APA format is to label a graph as a figure. Typically, a **table** is used to display quantitative data. For example, Table 3.1 displays raw data—that is, data that have not been transformed or analyzed. Again, notice that qualitative data such as smoking status have been assigned numerical values (0 = nonsmoker, 1 = smoker).

The primary purpose of graphs and tables is to visually display information in a manner that makes it easy for readers to comprehend. If the information is quantitative, and so presented as a table, does that table adequately display the data in a way that is easily understood? Table 3.1 is an example of a table that is easy to follow. The title clearly indicates the content of the table, the column heads are short but descriptive, and explanatory notes are given at the bottom. The same basic principles also apply to graphs. A well-done graph or table will enhance the accompanying explanation.

3.3   FREQUENCY TABLES

In this section we will discuss how to create tables using the SPSS statistical program. Any statistical program allows for ease of table construction, but not all computer-generated tables adequately display data. Remember that the primary purpose of a table is to provide a visual representation that makes the data clear and understandable. Perhaps the most convenient way of summarizing or displaying data is by means of a **frequency table.** Table 3.2 is an example of a simple frequency table constructed using the systolic blood pressure readings from the Honolulu Heart Study sample. This table was constructed using SPSS 11.5.

Creating Table 3.2 was a very simple procedure. In the menu bar, we chose Analyze. The second item in the Analyze scroll bar is Descriptive Statistics. From Descriptive Statistics, we selected Frequencies and then chose the column labeled SysBP (for systolic blood pressure). The table was then automatically created. The only further change was to retitle the table and save it.

Table 3.2 may contain some terms that are not familiar. In the first portion, you will see N. Valid, and Missing. The "N" is the number of subjects used in the analysis. In this example, we used all 100 from Table 3.1. "Valid" means we had 100 cases with data entered. Because there were no missing cases, 0 was entered after "Missing." Looking at the main table, you can see the systolic blood pressures listed in ascending order. Should you choose to list the data in descending order, you could change the settings. **Frequency** refers to the number of cases with a particular value. For example, there is one case with a systolic blood pressure of 92 and eight cases with a reading of 128. **Valid percent** is the percentage out of 100, using only those subjects with data. Because all subjects have a systolic blood pressure score listed, in this table, the valid percent is the same as the percentage. **Cumulative percent** is the percentage of all previous cases plus the current interval. To illustrate, look at the cumulative percentage for a reading of 108. It is 15.0. That means there are 15% of the cases beginning with 92 and ending with 108. There are also 4% of the cases at 112. The 4% of these cases, plus the previous 15%, yield the 19.0% you see under Cumulative Percent.

Table 3.2 Systolic Blood Pressure Frequency Distribution (SPSS)

Statistics		
SysBP		
N	Valid	100
	Missing	0

SysBP

		Frequency	Percent	Valid Percent	Cumulative Percent
Valid	92.00	1	1.0	1.0	1.0
	94.00	1	1.0	1.0	2.0
	96.00	1	1.0	1.0	3.0
	98.00	2	2.0	2.0	5.0
	100.00	1	1.0	1.0	6.0
	102.00	2	2.0	2.0	8.0
	104.00	2	2.0	2.0	10.0
	106.00	1	1.0	1.0	11.0
	108.00	4	4.0	4.0	15.0
	112.00	4	4.0	4.0	19.0
	114.00	4	4.0	4.0	23.0
	116.00	5	5.0	5.0	28.0
	118.00	6	6.0	6.0	34.0
	120.00	2	2.0	2.0	36.0
	122.00	6	6.0	6.0	42.0
	124.00	2	2.0	2.0	44.0
	126.00	2	2.0	2.0	46.0
	128.00	8	8.0	8.0	54.0
	130.00	4	4.0	4.0	58.0
	132.00	2	2.0	2.0	60.0
	134.00	7	7.0	7.0	67.0
	136.00	1	1.0	1.0	68.0
	138.00	2	2.0	2.0	70.0
	140.00	6	6.0	6.0	76.0
	142.00	2	2.0	2.0	78.0
	144.00	2	2.0	2.0	80.0
	146.00	2	2.0	2.0	82.0
	150.00	2	2.0	2.0	84.0
	152.00	2	2.0	2.0	86.0
	154.00	4	4.0	4.0	90.0
	156.00	1	1.0	1.0	91.0
	162.00	3	3.0	3.0	94.0
	170.00	1	1.0	1.0	95.0
	172.00	1	1.0	1.0	96.0
	176.00	1	1.0	1.0	97.0
	178.00	1	1.0	1.0	98.0
	190.00	1	1.0	1.0	99.0
	208.00	1	1.0	1.0	100.0
	Total	100	100.0	100.0	

Table 3.3 Systolic Blood Pressure Frequency Distribution with Missing Data (SPSS)

Statistics		
SysBP		

N	Valid	95
	Missing	5

SysBP

		Frequency	Percent	Valid Percent	Cumulative Percent
Valid	92.00	1	1.0	1.1	1.1
	94.00	1	1.0	1.0	2.1
	96.00	1	1.0	1.1	3.2
	98.00	2	2.0	2.1	5.3
	102.00	2	2.0	2.1	7.4
	104.00	2	2.0	2.1	9.5
	106.00	1	1.0	1.1	10.5
	108.00	4	4.0	4.2	14.7
	112.00	4	4.0	4.2	18.9
	114.00	4	4.0	4.2	23.2
	116.00	5	5.0	5.3	28.4
	118.00	6	6.0	6.3	34.7
	120.00	2	2.0	2.1	36.8
	122.00	6	6.0	6.3	43.2
	124.00	2	2.0	2.1	45.3
	126.00	2	2.0	2.1	47.4
	128.00	7	7.0	7.4	54.7
	130.00	3	3.0	3.2	57.9
	132.00	2	2.0	2.1	60.0
	134.00	7	7.0	7.4	67.4
	136.00	1	1.0	1.1	68.4
	138.00	2	2.0	2.1	70.5
	140.00	6	6.0	6.3	76.8
	142.00	1	1.0	1.1	77.9
	144.00	2	2.0	2.1	80.0
	146.00	2	2.0	2.1	82.1
	150.00	2	2.0	2.1	84.2
	152.00	2	2.0	2.1	86.3
	154.00	4	4.0	4.2	90.5
	156.00	1	1.0	1.1	91.6
	162.00	2	2.0	2.1	93.7
	170.00	1	1.0	1.1	94.7
	172.00	1	1.0	1.1	95.8
	176.00	1	1.0	1.1	96.8
	178.00	1	1.0	1.1	97.9
	190.00	1	1.0	1.1	98.9
	208.00	1	1.0	1.1	100.0
	Total	95	95.0	100.0	
Missing	System	5	5.0		
Total		100	100.0		

The table will look slightly different if there are missing data. To create Table 3.3, we arbitrarily deleted five scores from the 100. Note that the first portion now lists 95 as Valid and 5 as Missing. If you look at the main display, the Frequency and Percent columns look similar to Table 3.2 except that an additional row includes the five missing cases. Note that the Valid Percent column is now different from the Percent column. This is because the valid percentage is computed based on the 95 cases that have data. The Percent column still uses all 100, with 5 or 5% identified as Missing. Next, look at the Cumulative Percent column, and notice that this figure is calculated using only the valid cases. The five missing cases are not included in the cumulative percent.

Although Tables 3.2 and 3.3 are clear and relatively easy to create, they have some important shortcomings. Remember, the primary purpose in creating a table is to visually display data such that readers can more easily comprehend the data. One way to improve these tables is to develop a frequency table that includes **class intervals.** Class intervals are usually equal in length, thereby aiding the comparisons between any two intervals. The number of intervals depends on the number of observations, but in general should range from 5 to 15. With too many class intervals, the data are not sufficiently summarized for a clear visualization of how they are distributed. With too few, the data are over-summarized, and some of the details of the distribution may be lost.

In selecting 5–15 class intervals, we can take several simple steps to determine the appropriate **interval width.** The interval width is the number of units between the upper and lower limits, or **class limits.** For example, if we choose an interval of 90–99 mm, the interval width is 10. If we choose an interval of 90–109 mm, the interval width is 20. To determine an appropriate interval width, the first step is to find the **range**—the difference between the highest and lowest numbers in the data set. Using the data from Table 3.2, you can see that the highest systolic blood pressure is 208 and the lowest is 92, which gives a range of 116. Next, divide 116 by 5 to get 23.2, or 23; and divide 116 by 20 to get 7.7, or 8. What this tells us is that, if we are going to have between 5 and 15 class intervals, the interval width should be between 8 and 23.

The next question becomes: What interval width should we choose? In answering this question, remember that the purpose of a table is to visually display data in a manner that readers can more easily comprehend. Earlier, when we were defining class limits, we used examples of 90–99 mm and 90–109 mm. As you can see if you look ahead to Tables 3.4 and 3.5, interval widths of numbers like 10 and 20 are very easy to understand. The interval widths are calculated using the **class boundaries,** or true limits. Class boundaries are points that demarcate the true upper limit of one class and the true lower limit of the next. For example, the class boundary between classes 90–109 and 110–129 is 109.5; it is the upper boundary for the former and the lower boundary for the latter. The reason the interval width for 90–109 is 20 and not 19 is that the interval width is calculated using the class boundaries. And because the class boundaries

Table 3.4 Systolic Blood Pressures of Subjects from Table 3.1

Class Interval (systolic blood pressure, in mm mercury)	Frequency	Percent	Valid Percent	Cumulative Percent
90–99	5	5.0	5.0	5.0
100–109	10	10.0	10.0	15.0
110–119	19	19.0	19.0	34.0
120–129	20	20.0	20.0	54.0
130–139	16	16.0	16.0	70.0
140–149	12	12.0	12.0	82.0
150–159	9	9.0	9.0	91.0
160–169	3	3.0	3.0	94.0
170–179	4	4.0	4.0	98.0
180–189	0	0.0	0.0	98.0
190–199	1	1.0	1.0	99.0
200–209	1	1.0	1.0	100.0

SOURCE: Data from Honolulu Heart Study.

Table 3.5 Systolic Blood Pressures of Subjects from Table 3.1

Class Interval (systolic blood pressure, in mm mercury)	Frequency	Valid Percent	Cumulative Percent
90–109	15	15.0	15.0
110–129	39	39.0	54.0
130–149	28	28.0	82.0
150–169	12	12.0	94.0
170–189	4	4.0	98.0
190–209	1	1.0	100.0

SOURCE: Data from Honolulu Heart Study.

are 89.5–109.5, the interval width is 20, not 19. When choosing an interval width, a good general rule is to use whole numbers and, when possible, multiples of 5. We are much more accustomed to viewing and counting by 5 than by, say, 4 or 6. Tables 3.4 and 3.5 show completed frequency tables.

3.4 GRAPHING DATA

The second way of displaying data is by use of graphs. Graphs give users a nice overview of the essential features of the data. Although such visual aids are even easier to read than tables, they often do not give the same detail.

Graphs are designed to help users obtain at a glance an intuitive feeling for the data. So it is essential that each graph be self-explanatory—that is, have a

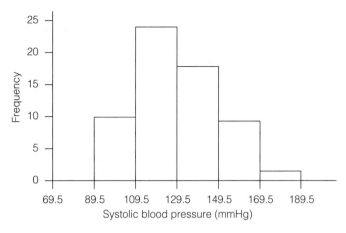

Figure 3.1 Histogram Illustrating the Data of Table 3.5: Systolic Blood Pressure of a Sample of 63 Nonsmokers from the Honolulu Heart Study.

descriptive title, labeled axes, and an indication of the units of observation. An effective graph is simple and clean. It should not attempt to present so much information that it is difficult to comprehend. Seven graphs will be discussed here: histograms, frequency polygons, cumulative frequency polygons, stem-and-leaf displays, bar charts, pie charts, and box-and-whisker plots.

Graphing by hand is often an arduous undertaking, especially for data sets that have more than a few dozen values. The graphs discussed here and other visual representations of data can be easily generated by the computer programs listed at the end of this chapter.

Histograms

Perhaps the most common graph is the **histogram.** A histogram is nothing more than a pictorial representation of the frequency table. It consists of an **abscissa** (horizontal axis), which depicts the class boundaries (not limits), and a perpendicular **ordinate** (vertical axis), which depicts the frequency (or relative frequency) of observations. The vertical scale should begin at zero. A general rule in laying out the two scales is to make the height of the vertical scale equal to approximately three-fourths the length of the horizontal scale. Once the scales have been laid out, a vertical bar is constructed above each class interval equal in height to its class frequency. For our Honolulu Heart Study example, the bar over the first class interval is 10 units high (see Figure 3.1).

Frequencies are represented not only by height but also by the area of each bar. The total area represents 100%. From Figure 3.1, it is possible to measure that 16% of the area corresponds to the 10 scores in the class interval 89.5–109.5 and that 38% of the area corresponds to the 24 observations in the second bar. Because

Table 3.6 Household Income, 1989

Income ($)	Number of Households	Relative Frequency (%)
0–4,999	6,320,400	6.9
5,000–9,999	10,534,000	11.5
10,000–14,999	9,709,600	10.6
15,000–19,999	9,100,000	10.0
20,000–24,999	8,427,200	9.2
25,000–34,999	14,747,600	16.1
35,000–49,999	15,755,200	17.2
50,000–74,999	16,488,000	18.0
75,000 and over	458,000	0.5
Total	91,540,000	100.0

area is proportional to the number of observations, be especially careful when constructing histograms from frequency tables that have unequal class intervals. How this is done is illustrated with the income data shown in Table 3.6.

From Table 3.6 we can see that the first five class intervals are measured in $5000 units while the next two intervals are $10,000 (i.e., two $5000 units) and $15,000 (i.e., three $5000 units), respectively. Because area is an indication of frequency in a histogram, we have to allocate the appropriate amount of area to each bar. The heights of the first five class intervals are their respective relative frequencies—that is, 6.9, 11.5, and so on. The height for the other intervals is obtained using the following formula:

$$\text{Height} = \frac{\text{relative frequency}}{\text{interval width}}$$

The height for the sixth interval is 8.05 (= 16.1/2) and for the seventh, 5.7 (= 17.2/3). For the $50,000–$75,000 interval, the interval will be five times wider than for the $5000 interval [(75,000 − 50,000)/5000 = 5]. Consequently, the height for the last interval will be 3.6 (= 18.0/5).

Using these heights, we can now draw the histogram, as shown in Figure 3.2. From Figure 3.2, we can see that the percent frequencies of households decrease as income increases. Furthermore, we can say that there is a higher percentage of households with low income than with high income. Figure 3.2 is, however, not optimal. Whenever possible, keep the widths of the intervals equal to prevent misleading or awkward-looking histograms.

Frequency Polygons

A second commonly used graph is the **frequency polygon,** which uses the same axes as the histogram. It is constructed by marking a point (at the same height as the histogram's bar) at the **midpoint** of the class interval. These points

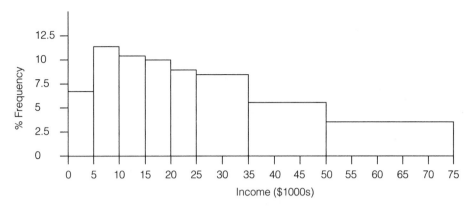

Figure 3.2   Histogram of U.S. Household Income, 1989. (NOTE: The 0.5% of households with income $75,000 and over is not shown.)

are then connected. At the ends, the points are connected to the midpoints of the previous (and succeeding) intervals of zero frequency (see Figure 3.3). Frequency polygons, especially when superimposed, are superior to histograms in providing a means of comparing two frequency distributions. In frequency polygons, the frequency of observations in a given class interval is represented by the area contained beneath the line segment and within the class interval. Frequency polygons should be used to graph only quantitative (numerical) data. Quantitative data have a continuous distribution. Frequency polygons should not be used for qualitative (i.e., nominal or ordinal) data. Qualitative data have an underlying discrete or discontinuous distribution.

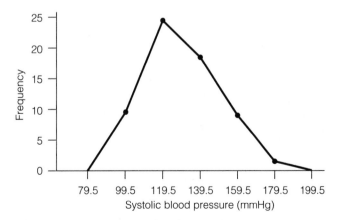

Figure 3.3   Frequency Polygon Illustrating the Data of Table 3.5: Systolic Blood Pressure of a Sample of 63 Nonsmokers from the Honolulu Heart Study.

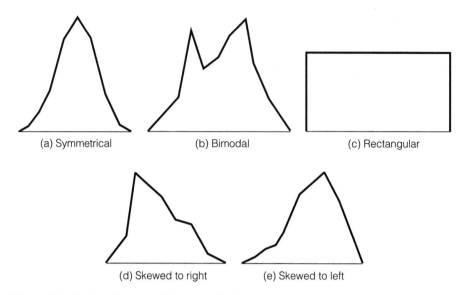

Figure 3.4   Various Shapes of Frequency Polygons.

Frequency polygons may take on a number of different shapes. Some of those most commonly encountered are shown in Figure 3.4. Part (a) of the figure is the classic "bell-shaped" **symmetrical distribution.** Part (b) is a **bimodal** (having two peaks) **distribution** that could represent an overlapping group of males and females. Part (c) is a **rectangular distribution** in which each class interval is equally represented. Parts (a) and (c) are symmetrical, whereas parts (d) and (e) are skewed or asymmetrical. The frequency polygon of part (d) is positively **skewed** because it tapers off in the positive (right-hand) direction, and part (e) is negatively skewed.

Cumulative Frequency Polygons

At times, it is useful to construct a **cumulative frequency polygon,** also called an **ogive,** which is a third type of graph. Although the horizontal scale is the same as that used for a histogram, the vertical scale indicates cumulative frequency or cumulative relative frequency. To construct the ogive, we place a point at the upper class boundary of each class interval. Each point represents the cumulative relative frequency for that class. Note that not until the upper class boundary has been reached have all the data of a class interval been accumulated. The ogive is completed by connecting the points (see Figure 3.5). Ogives are useful in comparing two sets of data—for example, data on healthy and diseased individuals. In Figure 3.5, we can see that 90% of the nonsmokers and 86% of the smokers had systolic blood pressures below 160 mmHg. The ogive gives for each interval the cumulative relative frequency—that is,

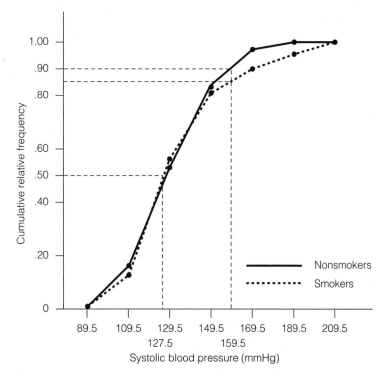

Figure 3.5 Ogives Illustrating the Data on Systolic Blood Pressure of a Sample of 63 Nonsmokers and 37 Smokers from the Honolulu Heart Study.

the percentage of cases having systolic blood pressures in that interval or a lower one.

Percentiles may be obtained from an ogive. The 90th percentile is that observation that exceeds 90% of the set of observations and is exceeded by only 10% of them. Percentiles are readily obtained, as in Figure 3.5. In our example, the 50th percentile, or median, for nonsmokers is a blood pressure of 127.5 mmHg, and the 90th percentile for nonsmokers is 159.5 mmHg.

Stem-and-Leaf Displays

Tukey (1977) suggested an innovative technique for summarizing data that utilizes characteristics of the frequency distribution and the histogram. It is referred to as the **stem-and-leaf display;** in this technique, the "stems" represent the class intervals and the "leaves" are the strings of values within each class interval. Table 3.7 illustrates the usefulness of this technique in helping you develop a better feel for your data. The table is a stem-and-leaf display that utilizes the observations of systolic blood pressures of the 63 nonsmokers of Table 3.1.

Table 3.7 Stem-and-Leaf Display of Data from Table 3.1:
Systolic Blood Pressure of 63 Nonsmokers

Stems (intervals)	Leaves (observations)	Frequency (f)
90–99	2 4 6 8	4
100–109	0 4 6 8 8 8	6
110–119	2 2 4 4 8 8 8 8 8	9
120–129	0 2 2 2 2 4 8 8 8 8 8 8 8 8	15
130–139	0 0 0 2 2 4 4 4 4 4 4 8	12
140–149	0 0 2 4 4 6	6
150–159	2 2 4 4 4 4 6	7
160–169	2 2	2
170–179	0 2	2
180–189		0
Total		63

For each stem (interval), we arrange the last digits of the observations from the lowest to the highest. This arrangement is referred to as the leaf. The leaves (strings of observations) portray a histogram laid on its side; each leaf reflects the values of the observations, from which it is easy to note their size and frequencies. Consequently, we have displayed all observations and provided a visual description of the shape of the distribution. It is often useful to present the stem-and-leaf display together with a conventional frequency distribution. From the stem-and-leaf display of the systolic blood pressure data, we can see that the range of measurements is 92 to 172. The measurements in the 120s occur most frequently, with 128 being the most frequent. We can also see which measurements are not represented.

Bar Charts

The **bar chart** is a convenient graphical device that is particularly useful for displaying nominal or ordinal data—data like ethnicity, gender, and treatment category. The various categories are represented along the horizontal axis. They may be arranged alphabetically, by frequency within a category, or on some other rational basis. We often arrange bar charts according to frequency, beginning with the least frequent and ending with the most frequent. The height of each bar is equal to the frequency of items for that category. To prevent any impression of continuity, it is important that all the bars be of equal width and separate, as in Figure 3.6.

Note that in a bar chart relative frequencies are shown by *heights,* but in a histogram relative frequencies are shown by the *areas* within the bars.

To avoid misleading readers, it is essential that the scale on the vertical axis begin at zero. If that is impractical, you should employ broken bars (or a similar device), as shown in Figure 3.7. Here is an example of what can happen if neither procedure is followed. The public relations department of a West Coast

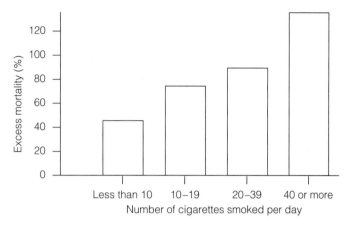

Figure 3.6 Bar Chart of Excess Mortality of Smokers over Nonsmokers According to Number of Cigarettes Smoked. SOURCE: Hammond (1966).

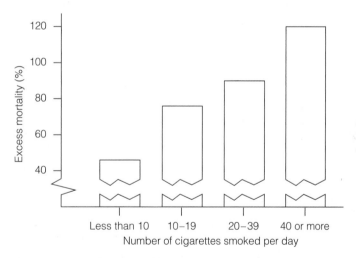

Figure 3.7 Bars Broken to Show Vertical Scale Does Not Begin at Zero. SOURCE: Hammond (1966).

college circulated the graph shown in Figure 3.8a. It gives the clear impression that enrollment doubled between 1986 and 1992. The reason for this is that the bars begin not at zero but at 2000. Persons unskilled in interpreting graphical data may find themselves drawn into one of the many pitfalls that are so well documented in books on the misuse of statistics. Figure 3.8b illustrates the correct way of presenting the same enrollment statistics. This graph makes clear that the enrollment increased by only about 50% over the 7 years.

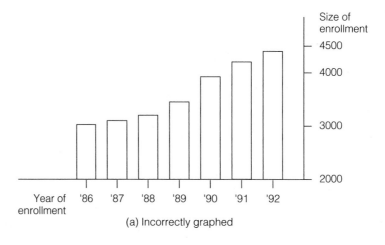

(a) Incorrectly graphed

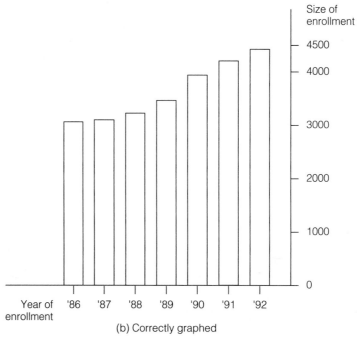

(b) Correctly graphed

Figure 3.8   Size of Enrollment of a West Coast College, 1986–1992.

Pie Charts

A common device for displaying data arranged in categories is the **pie chart** —
a circle divided into wedges that correspond to the percentage frequencies of
the distribution (see Figure 3.9). Pie charts are useful in conveying data that
consist of a small number of categories. Because the area is proportional to the
frequency, pie charts are rarely generated by hand.

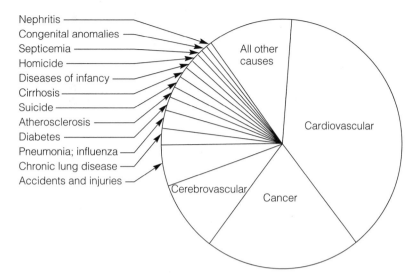

Figure 3.9 Pie Chart of Leading Causes of Death in the United States, 1987. SOURCE: National Center for Health Statistics (1990).

Box-and-Whisker Plots

At times we may wish to graphically examine data such as long-distance telephone charges for different cities to get an idea about the typical customer and the range of the billings. We can do this by using a **box-and-whisker plot.** To do so, we need to determine the median and the quartile statistics.

The **median** is the score that divides a ranked series of scores into two equal halves. If there is an equal number of scores, you will need to obtain the average (mean) of the two middle scores. Half of the scores in each sample are less than the median, and half are larger than the median. To determine the quartiles, we need to first locate the median in the ordered list of observations. The first quartile is then the median of the observations below this median, and the third quartile is the median of the observations above the original median.

In Figure 3.10, we see that we use only five values to summarize the data: the two extremes and the three quartiles. Even with such a considerable condensation, the plot provides interesting information about the sample. The two ends of the box show the range within which the middle 50% of all the measurements lie. The median is the center dot of the sample data, and the ends of the whiskers show the spread of the data.

Computerized Graphing

The graphs presented in this chapter are easily generated by a variety of statistical programs. Each program has slightly different rules and default settings. Standard programs such as those found at www.minitab.com, www.JMP.com,

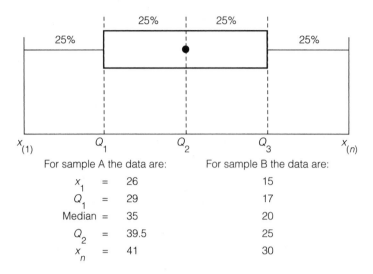

For sample A the data are:	For sample B the data are:
x_1 = 26	15
Q_1 = 29	17
Median = 35	20
Q_2 = 39.5	25
x_n = 41	30

Figure 3.10 Summary of Telephone Charge Data Using a Box-and-Whisker Plot.

and www.spss.com can produce most of these visual representations quite rapidly.

A spreadsheet program such as Microsoft Excel may also be used to generate simple histograms, bar charts, and pie charts, as well as to quickly generate the necessary statistics (quartiles) that are required for box-and-whisker plots. Scientific calculators such as the TI-83 or TI-84 may be used to generate box-and-whisker plots, histograms, and frequency polygons.

Additionally, there is a considerable amount of free software on the Web that can be adapted to generate these types of graphs. Because of the innate fluidity of the Web, we suggest the use of a search engine such as Google to identify numerous freeware sites that can quickly generate the graphs discussed earlier. There are also sites that list freeware sites, such as www.statsci.org/free.html and www.statistics.com.

◆ CONCLUSION

The principles of tabulating and graphing data are essential if we are to understand and evaluate the flood of data with which we are bombarded. By proper use of these principles, statisticians can present data accurately and lucidly. It is also important to know which method of presentation to choose for each specific type of data. Tables are usually comprehensive, but they do not convey the information as quickly or as impressively as do graphs. Remember that graphs and tables must tell their own story and stand on their own.

They should be complete in themselves and require little (if any) explanation in the text.

◆ VOCABULARY LIST

abscissa	frequency polygon	pie chart
bar chart	frequency table	qualitative variable
bimodal distribution	graph	quantitative variable
box-and-whisker plot	grouping variable	range
class boundaries	histogram	ratio scale
class interval	interval scale	rectangular
class limits	interval width	distribution
continuous variable	median	skewed distribution
cumulative frequency	midpoint (class	stem-and-leaf display
polygon (ogive)	midpoint)	symmetrical
cumulative percentage	nominal scale	distribution
discrete variable	ordinal scale	table
figure	ordinate	valid percentage
frequency	percentile	

◆ EXERCISES

3.1 Using the data from Table 3.1, construct a simple frequency table for
  a. serum cholesterol
  b. weight
  c. blood glucose

3.2 Name the variables represented in Table 3.1, and state which type each is.

3.3 State the principal difference between a negatively skewed distribution and a positively skewed one.

3.4 a. From the 83 observations of diastolic blood pressure in Table 2.1, prepare a frequency table that includes class interval and frequency.
  b. Using the same sheet of graph paper, draw a histogram and a frequency polygon for the same data.
  c. Construct an ogive for the same data.
  d. Find the following percentiles from the ogive: 20th, 50th (median), and 90th.
  e. What percentage of the observations are less than 70? 80? 90?

3.5 For the serum cholesterol values of Table 3.1, perform the same operations as suggested in (a) and (b) of Exercise 3.4. Do this by activity status; that is, for those who reported their physical activity as mostly sitting (code 1) or moderate (code 2), make separate frequency tables, histograms, and frequency polygons for the serum cholesterol values.

3.6 Make a bar graph of the educational levels of Table 3.1.

3.7 With each of the variables listed here, two graphical methods are mentioned. Indicate which method is more appropriate. State why one method is more appropriate than the other.
   a. number of dental cavities per person: pie chart, bar graph
   b. triglyceride level: frequency polygon, bar graph
   c. occupational classification: pie chart, histogram
   d. birthrate by year: line graph, histogram

3.8 Prepare a stem-and-leaf display for the weights listed in Table 3.1.
   a. Which are the smallest and the largest weights?
   b. Which is the most frequent weight?

3.9 a. Prepare a stem-and-leaf display for the systolic blood pressure measurements of smokers in Table 3.1. Use the same stems as in Table 3.7, but put the leaves on the left side of the stem.
   b. Combine the stem-and-leaf displays of Exercise 3.9a and Table 3.7 into a back-to-back stem display, and compare the two distributions.

3.10 Prepare a stem-and-leaf display for the heights listed in Table 3.1.
   a. Which is the smallest and which is the largest height?
   b. Which is the most frequent height?

3.11 For the weight data in Table 3.1, do the following:
   a. Construct separate frequency tables for smokers and for nonsmokers. Use six equal class intervals beginning with 45.
   b. Construct a histogram for each group.
   c. Construct a frequency polygon for each group on the same graph.
   d. Compare and discuss the differences in the frequency distributions between smoker and nonsmoker weights.
   e. Construct an ogive for each group. Estimate the 50th percentile, and compare them for the two groups.

3.12 Construct a bar chart of educational level using the data in Table 3.1 for
   a. smokers
   b. nonsmokers
   Compare the two bar charts and comment.

3.13 For the serum cholesterol data in Table 3.1, use equal class intervals of 30, beginning with 130, to construct
   a. a separate frequency table for each of the two subgroups classified on physical activity
   b. a histogram for each subgroup
   c. a frequency polygon for each of the three groups. Compare and discuss the differences in the three frequency polygons.
   d. an ogive for each group. Estimate the 50th percentile and compare the three.

3.14 Prepare a pie chart of the educational level for the entire sample listed in Table 3.1.

3.15 a. Using the income data from Table 3.6, combine the first two and also the third and fourth class intervals, and prepare a histogram similar to Figure 3.2.
   b. Compare your histogram with that of Figure 3.2, and describe your findings.

3.16 The following are weight losses (in pounds) of 25 individuals who enrolled in a 5-week weight-control program:

9	7	10	11	10	2	3	11	5
4	8	10	9	12	5	4	11	
8	3	6	9	7	4	8	9	

a. Construct a frequency table with these six class intervals: 2–3, 4–5, 6–7, 8–9, 10–11, 12–13.

b. Construct a histogram of the weight losses.

c. Construct a frequency polygon and describe the shape of the frequency distribution.

d. What might be a possible interpretation of the particular shape of this distribution?

e. What was the most common weight loss?

3.17 Compare the two frequency distributions that you constructed in Exercise 3.13, and describe them with regard to symmetry, skewness, and modality (most frequently occurring observation).

3.18 Classify the following data as either nominal, ordinal, interval, or ratio.

a. names of students in this class

b. the number of students in this class

c. your ten favorite songs

d. height

e. heads and tails on a coin

3.19 Briefly explain why discrete (discontinuous) variables are treated as continuous variables. Use an example as part of your explanation.

3.20 For the grouped frequency distribution 70–79, 80–89, and 90–99, answer the following questions:

a. What is the class interval?

b. What are the class boundaries for the interval 80–89?

3.21 Determine the median and quartiles necessary to construct a box-and-whisker plot for the following sets of data:

a. 3, 4, 7, 5, 4, 6, 4, 5, 8, 3, 4, 5, 6, 5, 4

b. 18, 14, 17, 22, 16, 26, 33, 27, 35, 28, 44, 40, 31, 53, 70, 73, 62, 74, 93, 103, 75, 86, 84, 90, 79, 99, 73

3.22 Construct the box-and-whisker plots for the data in Exercise 3.21a and b.

3.23 Using the following data from the FBI Uniform Crime Reports, construct a pie chart indicating the weapons used in committing these murders.

11,381 committed with firearms

 3,957 committed with personal weapons such as hands or feet

 <u>1,099</u> committed with knives

16,437 all murders

3.24 Construct a box plot for the sample of $n = 100$ systolic blood pressure readings listed in Table 3.1 separately for smokers and nonsmokers, and provide a written comparison of the two groups based on the box plots.

3.25 Construct a box-and-whisker plot for the weight loss data given in Exercise 3.16.

4 Summarizing Data

CHAPTER OUTLINE

4.1 **Measures of Central Tendency**
Explains why the selection of an appropriate sample has an important bearing on the reliability of inferences about a population

4.2 **Measures of Variation**
Describes several measures of variation or variability including the standard deviation

4.3 **Coefficient of Variation**
Defines the coefficient of variation, useful in comparing levels of variation

4.4 **Measuring and Interpreting Skewness**
Explains how to measure skewness and how to determine if a distribution is symmetrical or skewed

4.5 **Means and Standard Deviations of a Population**
Contrasts the equations for the parameters of a population to the statistics of a sample

✔ LEARNING OBJECTIVES

After studying this chapter, you should be able to

1. Compute and distinguish between the uses of measures of central tendency: mean, median, and mode

2. Compute and list some uses for measures of variation: range, variance, and standard deviation

3. Compare sets of data by computing their coefficients of variation

4. Be able to compute the mean and standard deviation for grouped and ungrouped data

5. Determine if a data set is symmetrical or skewed

6. Understand the distinction between the population mean and the sample mean

4.1 MEASURES OF CENTRAL TENDENCY

Suppose you are considering accepting a new job with a well-known company. Salary is foremost in your mind, so you ask, "What is an employee's typical annual salary?" One person tells you "$54,000"; another, "$45,000." You decide to check further into these inconsistent responses. Finally, you obtain some information you regard as reliable. Specifically, you are interested in knowing the lowest and the highest salaries, the typical salary, and relative frequencies of the various salaries. A small but representative sample of salaries shows them to be $41,000, $45,000, $45,000, $49,000, and $90,000. With this information at hand, you are now prepared to describe the salaries in the company. But to do this, you need to know how to compute statistics that characterize the center of the frequency distribution.

Given a set of data, we invariably wish to find a value about which the observations tend to cluster. The three most common values are the mean, the median, and the mode. They are known as measures of **central tendency**—the tendency of a set of data to center around certain numerical values.

The Mean

The arithmetic mean—or, simply, **mean**—is computed by summing all the observations in the sample and dividing the sum by the number of observations. Because there are other means, such as the harmonic and geometric means, it is essential to designate which type of mean is being used. In this text, we use only the arithmetic mean.

Symbolically, the mean is represented by

$$\bar{x} = \frac{x_1 + x_2 + x_3 + \cdots + x_n}{n} \tag{4.1}$$

or

$$\bar{x} = \frac{\sum_{i=1}^{n} x_i}{n} \tag{4.2}$$

In these expressions, the symbol $\bar{x}$, representing the sample mean, is read "x-bar"; x_1 is the first and x_i the ith in a series of observations. In this text, we use X (uppercase) to denote a random variable and $\bar{x}$ (lowercase) to indicate a particular value of a function. The symbol Σ is the uppercase Greek letter sigma and denotes "the sum of." Thus

$$\sum_{i=1}^{n}$$

indicates that the sum is to begin with $i = 1$ and increase incrementally by one up to and including the last observation, n.

For the sample of the five salaries,

$$\bar{x} = \frac{\$41{,}000 + \$45{,}000 + \$45{,}000 + \$49{,}000 + \$90{,}000}{5} = \$54{,}000$$

The arithmetic mean may be considered the balance point, or fulcrum, in a distribution of observations. It considers the magnitude of each observation and is the point that balances the positive and negative deviations from the fulcrum. The mean is affected by the value of each observation of the distribution. Therefore, large values may distort the mean so that it no longer is representative of the typical values of a distribution.

The Median

In a list ranked according to size—that is, the observations arranged in an array—the **median** is the observation that divides the distribution into equal parts. The median is considered the most typical observation in a distribution. It is that value above which there are the same number of observations as below. In short, it is the middle-most value. In our example of five salaries, the median is $45,000. For an even number of observations, the median is the average of the two middle-most values.

The Mode

The **mode** is the observation that occurs most frequently. In the salary example, the mode is $45,000. It can be read from a graph as that value on the abscissa that corresponds to the peak of the distribution. Frequency distributions like the one displayed in Figure 3.4(b) are bimodal—that is, they have two modes. If all the values are different, there is no mode.

Which Average Should You Use?

With a bit of experience, you can readily determine which measure of central tendency is appropriate to a given situation. The arithmetic mean is by far the most commonly used. Because it considers, for example, the average amount of product consumed by a user, it is indispensable in business and commerce. If, for instance, the average per capita consumption of sugar per year is 25 lb, then the amount of sugar to be sold in a town of 10,000 people would be 250,000 lb. Knowing the mean of a distribution also permits us to compare different frequency distributions.

If you want to know a typical observation in a distribution, particularly if it is skewed, the median proves to be a better measure than the mean. Income is the most common example of a distribution that is typically skewed. Because of the disproportionate weight of a few top-salary jobs, the arithmetic mean for income is nearly always artificially inflated. For income, the median is a good choice because it is not affected by extreme values.

■ **EXAMPLE 1**

Five individuals working for a small firm have annual incomes of $40,000, $55,000, $55,000, $55,000, and $200,000. Find the median, mode, and mean.

The median is $55,000 because it is the middle observation. The mode is the most common observation: $55,000. The mean is

$$\frac{40,000 + (3)55,000 + 200,000}{5} = \frac{405,000}{5} = \$81,000$$

which does not match any of the salaries. ■

Suppose an emergency stock clerk who handles different sizes of crutches wants to know which is the most popular size (the mode) so that he can order enough to meet the demand. By looking at the several measures of central tendency, he can obtain some idea of the shape of the frequency distribution. In a symmetrical distribution (see Figure 4.1), the three measures of central tendency are identical. If a distribution has marked or pronounced asymmetry, that distribution is said to be **skewed.** In an asymmetrical right-skewed distribution (see Figure 4.2), the mode remains located (by definition) at the peak, the mean is off to the right, and the median is in between. Left-skewed distributions are the mirror image of Figure 4.2.

Generally, modes are used for nominal scores, medians for ordinal scores, and means for interval scores.

Let us briefly examine some situations in which you might expect skewed data. Human variables like height and weight tend to be symmetrically distributed *unless* there is some intervening factor such as disease. An example might be systolic blood pressure. If a sample of blood pressures were taken, we would expect the results to be relatively symmetrical. However, you might see numbers such as 160, 170, or even higher, which means there might be some undiagnosed hypertensives in your sample. The net effect is that the mean will be raised and the distribution will be positively (right) skewed. Another variable

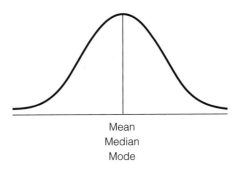

Mean
Median
Mode

Figure 4.1 Symmetrical Frequency Distribution.

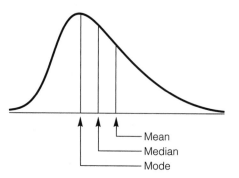

Figure 4.2 Asymmetrical Distribution,
Skewed to the Right.

that tends to be normally distributed is hemoglobin levels. Again, in the absence of disease, we would expect a symmetrical distribution. But what would happen to the distribution if part of the sample had malaria, which tends to lower hemoglobin levels? Those readings would tend to lower the mean and give us a negatively (left) skewed distribution.

4.2 MEASURES OF VARIATION

Knowing a distribution's central tendency is helpful, but it is not enough. It is also important to know whether the observations tend to be quite similar (homogeneous) or vary considerably (heterogeneous). To describe variability, measures of **variation** have been devised. The most common of these are the range, the mean deviation, and the standard deviation.

Range

The **range** is defined as the difference in value between the highest (maximum) and lowest (minimum) observation:

$$\text{Range} = x_{max} - x_{min} \tag{4.3}$$

The range can be computed quickly but is not very useful because it considers only the extremes and does not take into consideration the bulk of the observations.

Mean Deviation

By knowing the range of a data set, we can gain some idea of the set's variability. The **mean deviation** is a bit more sophisticated than the range. It is defined as the average deviation of all observations from the mean. We can compute how far observations deviate from the mean by subtracting the mean from the value of each observation. The mean deviation is the sum of all the **absolute values** of the deviations divided by the number of observations—that is,

$$\text{Mean deviation} = \frac{|x_1 - \bar{x}| + |x_2 - \bar{x}| + \cdots + |x_n - \bar{x}|}{n} \tag{4.4}$$

where $|x_1 - \bar{x}|$ is read as "the absolute value of x sub one minus x-bar." Absolute value ignores the sign of the difference; that is, the mean deviation indicates how much, on average, the observations deviate from the arithmetic mean. The mean deviation is now mainly of historical interest; the measure was more commonly used before the age of calculators and computers.

As an example, consider the percentage of graduates of a medical school who passed their National Boards with honors during a 5-year period (see Table 4.1). Note that some of the deviations are positive, some are negative, and one is zero. In sum, because $\bar{x}$ is the balance point of the observations, they add to zero. By using absolute values, we can eliminate the negative signs and compute a mean deviation:

$$\text{Mean deviation} = \frac{\Sigma|x - \bar{x}|}{n} = \frac{6}{5} = 1.20$$

For the 5-year period, the percentage of graduates earning honors differed, on average, by 1.2 percentage points from the mean of 6%.

Standard Deviation

By far the most widely used measure of variation is the **standard deviation,** represented by the symbol s. It is the square root of the variance of the observations. The **variance,** or s^2, is computed by squaring each deviation from the mean, adding them up, and dividing their sum by one less than n, the sample size:

$$s^2 = \frac{\sum_{i=1}^{n}(x_i - \bar{x})^2}{n - 1} \tag{4.5}$$

Table 4.1 Annual Percentage of Medical School National Board Honorees, 1988–1992

	Year of Graduation				
	1988	1989	1990	1991	1992
Percent of honors graduates (x_i)	4	6	5	8	7
Deviation from mean ($x_i - \bar{x}$)	−2	0	−1	2	1
Absolute value of deviation from mean ($|x_i - \bar{x}|$)	2	0	1	2	1
Squared deviation from mean ($x_i - \bar{x})^2$	4	0	1	4	1

The sample variance may thus be thought of as the mean squared deviation from the mean, and the greater the deviations, the greater the variance.

The variance is readily computed for the data of Table 4.1 as follows:

$$\bar{x} = \frac{30}{5} = 6$$

$$s^2 = \frac{\sum_{i=1}^{n} (x_i - \bar{x})^2}{n - 1}$$

$$s^2 = \frac{4 + 0 + 1 + 4 + 1}{4} = \frac{10}{4} = 2.5$$

The standard deviation is computed by extracting the square root of the variance. Symbolically,

$$s = \sqrt{s^2} \tag{4.6}$$

For our example, $s = \sqrt{2.5} = 1.58$. Equation 4.6 and the mathematically equivalent calculating equation (4.7) are summarized in Table 4.2.

Both the variance and the standard deviation are measures of variation in a set of data. The larger they are, the more heterogeneous the distribution. For example, if we were to compare the National Board scores of graduates of two medical schools, the school with the smaller standard deviation would have students who are more homogeneous in ability than the school with the larger standard deviation. That is, the school with the smaller s will have scores closer to the mean, and the school with the larger s will have scores scattered over a wider range around the mean.

Table 4.2 Equations for Means and Standard Deviations

	Definition Equation		Calculating Equation
		Ungrouped Data	
Mean	$\bar{x} = \dfrac{\sum_{i=1}^{n} x_i}{n}$	(4.2)	Same
Standard deviation	$s = \sqrt{\dfrac{\sum_{i=1}^{n} (x_i - \bar{x})^2}{n - 1}}$	(4.5) and (4.6)	$\sqrt{\dfrac{\sum_{i=1}^{n} x_i^2 - \dfrac{\left(\sum_{i=1}^{n} x_i\right)^2}{n}}{n - 1}}$ (4.7)

Frequently, the symbol SD is used to denote the standard deviation, s, which is usually obtained from s^2. However, SD^2 can also be used to calculate the value of the sample variance if SD is known.

As a measure of variation, standard deviation is much preferred over all other choices. The units of the standard deviation turn out to be the same as the units of the raw data (e.g., inches, millimeters, kilograms), whereas the units of variance are squared. Standard deviation is arithmetically easy to handle and avoids the awkwardness of absolute values. Because the magnitude of the standard deviation depends on the phenomenon being observed, which may be represented by large or small numbers, the standard deviation itself can be large or small. What is a large deviation for one variable may be small for another.

Understanding the sources of variation can help you appreciate the meaning of standard deviation. For example, among subjects, one source of variation may be a personal characteristic such as age or sex. Another source may be individual variation; still another, the varying condition of the subject (i.e., observations obtained before or after dinner, or before or after exercise, may differ). Yet another source of variation is measurement error. Although a certain amount of error is inherent in any observation, scientists strive mightily to keep it to a minimum by use of appropriate experimental designs.

Computing Central Tendency Using SPSS

If you have a data set, you are most likely to use statistical software such as SPSS or Statview. To calculate mean and standard deviation using SPSS, simply go to the menu and choose Analyze. Under Analyze, select Descriptives, and choose the variable(s) you want to analyze. You will see a summary similar to that shown in Table 4.3.

You can also open the dialog box titled Options and select which descriptive statistics you want analyzed and displayed (see Figure 4.3).

If you want additional statistics such as median and mode, you can again use the Analyze selection from the menu. This time, however, you should choose

Table 4.3 Descriptives from SPSS 11.5

	N	Minimum	Maximum	Mean	Std. Deviation
Age	100	46.00	67.00	53.6700	5.10111
Weight	100	47.00	91.00	64.2200	8.61005
Height	100	150.00	175.00	161.8500	5.50918
Glucose	100	58.00	442.00	152.1400	54.75584
Cholesterol	100	134.00	382.00	216.9600	38.85844
SysBP	100	92.00	208.00	130.1000	21.20677
BMI	100	18.30	33.60	24.5275	3.01546
Valid N (listwise)	100				

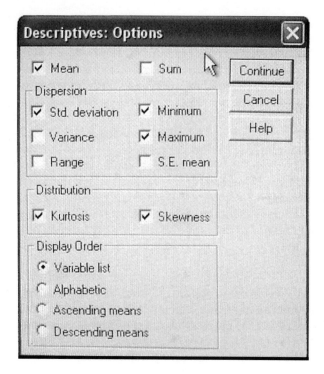

Figure 4.3   SPSS Descriptives Dialog Box.

Reports and then Case Summaries. You will notice a wide range of possible choices including Median and Mode.

4.3   COEFFICIENT OF VARIATION

One important application of the mean and the standard deviation is the **coefficient of variation.** It is defined as the ratio of the standard deviation to the absolute value of the mean, expressed as a percentage:

$$\text{CV} = \frac{100s}{|\bar{x}|}\% \tag{4.8}$$

The coefficient of variation depicts the size of the standard deviation relative to its mean. Because both standard deviation and the mean represent the same units, the units cancel out, and the coefficient of variation becomes a pure number; that is, it is free of the measurement units of the original data. Therefore, it is possible to use it to compare the relative variation of even unrelated quantities. For example, we may wish to know whether the variation of blood glucose readings is greater or less than the variation of serum cholesterol levels. From Table 3.1, we can compute the variation exactly. The coefficient of variation for blood glucose (in milligrams per deciliter) is $54.72/152.14 \times 100 = 36\%$, and for serum cholesterol it is $38.82/216.96 \times 100 = 18\%$. From this, we see that the variation in blood glucose is relatively greater than that in serum cholesterol.

4.4   MEASURING AND INTERPRETING SKEWNESS

You just learned that the mean is the preferred measure of central tendency, assuming the data are symmetrically distributed or at least reasonably close to a symmetrical distribution. However, if the data are skewed, then the preferred measure of central tendency is the median. This leads us to two questions: (1) How do we measure **skewness?** and (2) How do we determine if the distribution is sufficiently skewed that the median becomes the preferred measure of central tendency?

Skewness can be measured using SPSS. Choose Analyze in the menu and Descriptives from the scroll bar. Next, open the dialog box titled Options, and select Skewness. In addition to the data summary displayed in Table 4.3, you will also get the data shown in Table 4.4. Note the two columns under skewness: Statistic and Std. Error. The Statistic column gives the actual measure of skewness, or the **standard error of skewness.** Notice that the standard error of skewness is the same for each variable. The reason for this is that the measure of skewness is based on sample size, and each variable has a sample of 100. A formula that gives a close approximation of the standard error is $\sqrt{\frac{6}{n}} = \sqrt{\frac{6}{100}} = .245$. Notice that .245 is very close to the computer-generated value of .241 from Table 4.4.

The data in Table 3.1 are skewed positively because all the variables under Statistic have a positive number. The key issue is to determine whether the measure of skewness is large enough that the variable can be considered skewed. To determine if the data are significantly skewed, take the standard

Table 4.4 Skewness Descriptive Statistics (SPSS)

	N	Skewness	
	Statistic	Statistic	Std. Error
Age	100	.927	.241
Weight	100	.561	.241
Height	100	.101	.241
Glucose	100	1.815	.241
Cholesterol	100	.923	.241
SysBP	100	.884	.241
BMI	100	.348	.241
Valid N (listwise)	100		

error of skewness, double it, and include + and − values. Using the values from Table 4.4, .241 doubled is .482. Including the + and − gives us values of −.482 to +.482. Any skewness statistic lower than −.482 or greater than .482 would indicate that the data for that particular variable are significantly skewed. Note that age, weight, glucose, cholesterol, and systolic blood pressure are positively skewed. This means that some study subjects are older and heavier, and have sufficiently higher levels of blood glucose, serum cholesterol, and systolic blood pressure. Height and BMI are less than .482 and would therefore be considered reasonably close to being symmetrically distributed.

Why is this information important? At this point, you are just beginning to learn statistics. In Chapter 6, you will be introduced to the concept of the normal distribution. A key factor in determining what statistical procedure to use is to determine whether your data are skewed. If the data are skewed, then the distribution cannot be normal. This means that statistical procedures based on the normal distribution should not be used. If the data are not skewed—that is, if they are symmetrical—then in most cases statistical procedures based on the normal distribution may be used. The term *symmetrical* is not synonymous with *normal*. But in most cases, if biological data are symmetrical, they are probably also close enough to being normally distributed. "However, most biological data are not normally distributed" (Lang, 2003:68).

4.5   MEANS AND STANDARD DEVIATIONS OF A POPULATION

The equations given for the mean and the standard deviation apply to the data of a sample selected from a population. When we have data for an *entire* population, we use similar equations but different symbols. Table 4.3 compares equations used for the two purposes. The **population mean**, μ (lowercase Greek mu), is defined as the sum of the values divided by N, the number of observations for the entire population. The sample mean, $\bar{x}$, is an estimate of μ and is the sum of the values in the sample divided by n, the number of observations in the sample alone. (Convention dictates the use of Greek letters for population parameters and Roman letters for sample statistics.) The population variance, σ^2, is the sum of the squared deviations from the population mean μ divided by N, whereas the sample variance, s^2 (an estimation of σ^2), is the sum of the squared deviations from the sample mean $\bar{x}$ divided by $n − 1$. Dividing by $n − 1$ looks like a peculiarity, but it provides an equation that gives an unbiased sample variance; that is, the mean of all possible samples of a particular sample size gives the correct answer if $n − 1$ is used as a divisor. Therefore, the use of $n − 1$, instead of n, gives a more accurate estimate of σ^2. In Chapter 2, we gave the definitions for a parameter and a statistic. These can now be illustrated with the mean and the standard deviation. Because both μ and σ are characteristics of a population, they are parameters. And because $\bar{x}$ and s are characteristics of a sample, they are statistics. Convention dictates the use of some shorthand to replace more awkward notation. Hence, in subsequent chapters, we will use x instead of x_i and Σ instead of

$$\sum_{i=1}^{n}$$

◆ CONCLUSION

In describing data by use of a summary measure, it is important to select the measure of central tendency that most accurately represents the data. A key factor is to determine if the data are symmetrical or skewed. Data are most commonly represented by two summary measures—one to indicate central tendency and one to indicate variation. The most commonly used pair is the arithmetic mean and the standard deviation.

◆ VOCABULARY LIST

absolute value	mode	standard error of
central tendency	population mean	skewness
coefficient of variation	range	variance
mean	skewed	variation
mean deviation	skewness	
median	standard deviation	

◆ EXERCISES

4.1 Find the mean, median, mode, range, variance, and standard deviation for the data 8, 5, 1, 5, 2, 3. (For variance, use equation (4.5).)

4.2 Using the sample 3, 4, 6, 1, 10, 6,
   a. find the median, mean, and range
   b. compute the standard deviation using equations (4.5) and (4.6)
   c. compute the standard deviation using equation (4.7)
   d. compare the results of (b) and (c)
   Why is the standard deviation in this example larger than that in Exercise 4.1?

4.3 Determine the range, median, and mode for the data in Table 2.1.

4.4 Assuming that Table 2.1 is a population of values, compute the mean, variance, and standard deviation. (Use the equation $\sigma^2 = \Sigma x^2/N - \mu^2$ for the calculation of variance.)

4.5 Compute $\bar{x}$, s^2, and s for the sample of 10 that you took in Exercise 2.1. (Use equation (4.7).) Compare your results with those for Exercise 4.4.

4.6 Determine the mean, variance, and standard deviation of weights in Table 3.1 by using the equations of Table 4.2.

4.7   a. Calculate the coefficient of variation for the heights and weights given in Table 3.1. (Use the results from Exercise 4.6.)

b. Compare the two coefficients. Which one is larger? Approximately how many times larger?

4.8   a. Calculate the mean and the standard deviation for the systolic blood pressure values given in Table 3.1. (*Hint:* Use the equations of Table 4.2.)

b. Calculate $\bar{x} - s$ and $\bar{x} + s$.

c. Calculate $\bar{x} - 2s$ and $\bar{x} + 2s$.

d. Calculate $\bar{x} - 3s$ and $\bar{x} + 3s$.

e. What percentage of the blood pressure observations fall within each of the three intervals you calculated in (b), (c), and (d)?

4.9   a. Find the median age of the sample represented in Table 3.1.

b. What is the age range?

4.10   For the cholesterol values given in Table 3.1, the mean and the standard deviation are, respectively, 216.96 and 38.82. What is the variance?

4.11   If the variance of blood glucose values in Table 3.1 is 2994, what is the standard deviation?

4.12   List some practical uses for standard deviation.

4.13   Describe a situation in which it would be useful to know

a. the mean, median, and mode

b. primarily the median

c. primarily the mean

4.14   a. Refer to Table 3.1. Using equation (4.7), calculate the mean and the standard deviation of systolic blood pressure

i. for those who have had no education (code = 1)

ii. for those who have had intermediate education (code = 3)

b. Compare the standard deviations of the two groups. Which set of values has the larger standard deviation, and by how much?

c. From your computations in (b), draw a conclusion about the relative variation of the observations in the two groups.

4.15   Define:

a. measure of central tendency

b. mean

c. median

d. mode

e. population mean

f. sample standard deviation

g. population variance

h. range

i. deviation

j. coefficient of variation

4.16   Explain what happens to the mean, median, and standard deviation if 10, the fifth observation, is replaced by 2 in Exercise 4.2.

4.17 Explain what these symbols and formulas mean:
  a. Σx
  b. $(\Sigma x)^2$
  c. Σx^2
  Is $(\Sigma x)^2$ always larger than Σx^2?

4.18 Using the results of Exercise 4.8(a) and Exercise 4.10,
  a. compute the coefficient of variation for the systolic blood pressure values
  b. compute the coefficient of variation for the cholesterol values
  c. compare the two coefficients, and specify their units

4.19 What would you consider to be the major distinction between a population variance and a sample variance?

4.20 Describe the characteristics of a frequency distribution if
  a. $\bar{x} = 15$ and the median is 19
  b. $\bar{x} = 19$ and the median is 15
  c. $\bar{x} = 17$ and the median is 17

4.21 a. Why is the standard deviation rather than the variance used more commonly to describe the spread of a distribution?
  b. Why is the sum of the deviations $[\Sigma(x_i - \bar{x})]$ always zero?
  c. Explain how it is possible for a person to drown in a river whose mean depth is 12 inches.
  d. How would you explain the sentence "The average American is a 33-year-old white woman"?

4.22 Using the sample values 1, 2, 3, 4, 4, 5, 6,
  a. find the mean, median, and mode
  b. find the standard deviation
  c. find the coefficient of variation

4.23 What is the standard deviation for a data set that has a mean of 16 and a variance of 144?

4.24 What would be the mean and standard deviation if in Exercise 4.22
  a. each observation is increased by two units
  b. each observation is multiplied by a factor of 2

4.25 Describe the frequency distribution
  a. in which $\bar{x}$ = median = mode
  b. if the median = 10, the mode = 5, and $\bar{x} = 15$

4.26 Explain the basic difference in the formulae of $\bar{x}$ and μ.

4.27 Calculate the mean, median, mode, and standard deviation for *each* of these distributions:

  A (2, 3, 4, 4, 4, 5, 6)

  B (2, 3, 4, 4, 4, 5, 20)

  C (−5, −4, −3, 0, 3, 4, 5)

  a. Which measure of central tendency would be the "best" or most useful measure for each group? Briefly justify your choice.
  b. Which distribution is skewed?

4.28 If there is a large numerical difference between the mean and the median, the distribution is probably _____.

4.29 If you have one or more extreme scores in a data set, which measure of central tendency is most likely to be affected?

4.30 Identify the measure of central tendency that would be most appropriate for the following data sets:
   a. prices of homes in a community
   b. ages of incoming freshmen
   c. number of apples per tree in a commercial orchard
   d. blood pressure readings of college students

◆ COMPREHENSIVE EXERCISES

Using the data in Exercises 4.31–4.33, do the following:
   a. calculate the mean, median and mode
   b. calculate the sample standard deviation and variance
   c. determine if the data are skewed
   d. determine which is the "best" or most appropriate measure of central tendency

4.31 Using the data from Table 3.1, select a random sample of 50 subjects (procedure described in Chapter 2), and then do the computations with the variables age, height, and serum cholesterol level.

4.32 Twenty students were randomly selected for cholesterol screening. Analyze the following data:

260	210	244	233	269
158	221	198	214	246
164	225	254	184	206
209	213	179	257	221

4.33 A certain brand of vitamin C tablets was analyzed for actual vitamin C content. Analyze the following data:

760	790	715	750	785
735	780	760	785	730
740	715	735	770	740
715	770	700	725	785
700	790	735	705	740

5 Probability

CHAPTER OUTLINE

5.1 **What Is Probability?**
Discusses the concept of probability as a measure of the likelihood of occurrence of a particular event

5.2 **Complementary Events**
Demonstrates how to calculate probability when events are complementary

5.3 **Probability Rules**
Solves problems involving the probability of compound events by use of the addition rule or the multiplication rule, or conditional probability

5.4 **Counting Rules**
Explains how to compute the number of possible ways an event can occur by use of permutations and combinations

5.5 **Probability Distributions**
Illustrates the concept of a probability distribution, which lists the probabilities associated with the various outcomes of a variable

5.6 **Lottery Probability and Sampling**
Uses lottery probabilities to illustrate sampling with and without replacement

5.7 **Binomial Distribution**
Describes a common distribution having only two possible outcomes on each trial

✔ LEARNING OBJECTIVES

After studying this chapter, you should be able to

1. Define *probability* and compute it in a given situation
2. State the basic properties of probability

(Continued)

3. Select and apply the appropriate probability rule for a given situation
4. Distinguish between mutually exclusive events and independent events
5. Distinguish between permutations and combinations, and be able to compute them for various events
6. Explain what a probability distribution is, and state its major use
7. State the properties of a binomial distribution
8. Compute probabilities by using a binomial distribution
9. Interpret the symbols in the binomial term

5.1   WHAT IS PROBABILITY?

A pregnant woman wonders about the chance of having a boy or a girl baby. An understanding of probability can throw some light on this question. Any answer must be based on various assumptions. If she assumes that bearing a boy or a girl is equally likely, she will expect one boy baby for every two births—that is, half the time. As another way of estimating her chances of having a boy, she could count the number of boys and girls born in the past year. Vital statistics indicate there are about 1056 live births of boys for every 1000 live births of girls, so she could estimate her probability of having a boy as

$$\frac{1056}{2056} = .514$$

It should be noted that the term *probability* applies exclusively to a future event, never to a past event (even if its outcome is unknown). Therefore, it is really not appropriate to state that the woman's probability of bearing a boy is .514, because, upon conception, the sex of the fetus is already established. It would be more appropriate to discuss the probability *before* the baby is conceived.

Many events in life are inherently uncertain. Probability may be used to measure the uncertainty of the outcome of such events. For example, you may wish to learn the probability of surviving to age 80, of developing cancer, or of becoming divorced. This chapter covers some of the basic concepts of probability and set forth some rules and models that, if followed, can provide quantitative estimates of the occurrence of various events.

Probability statements are numeric, defined in the range of 0 to 1, never more and never less. A probability of 1.0 means that the event will happen with certainty; 0 means that the event will not happen. If the probability is .5, the event should occur once in every two attempts, on average. If the probability is close to 1.0, then the event is more likely to happen, and if the probability is close to 0, it is unlikely to happen.

There are many ways of defining probability. Here is one of the simplest: **Probability** is the ratio of the number of ways the specified event can occur to the total number of **equally likely events** that can occur. This definition was implicit in our example of estimating a woman's probability of bearing a boy baby.

The probability of an event, $P(E)$, can be defined as the proportion of times a favorable event will occur in a long series of repeated trials:

$$P(E) = \frac{n}{N} = \frac{\text{number of favorable outcomes}}{\text{number of possible outcomes}} \tag{5.1}$$

■ **EXAMPLE 1**

One coin: In a toss of a fair coin, there are two possible outcomes, a head (H) or a tail (T); that is, $N = 2$. So the probability of having a head equals

$$P(H) = \frac{1}{2} \blacksquare$$

Note: The word *fair* implies that the coin or dice are not loaded; that is, they will give a fair representation to each outcome in a large number of tosses.

■ **EXAMPLE 2**

Two coins: In a toss of two coins, four outcomes are possible: HT, TH, TT, HH. (HT means heads on the first coin and tails on the second.) There are two helpful ways to ensure that all possible outcomes are listed—the **tree diagram** (see Figure 5.1) and the **contingency table** (see Table 5.1).

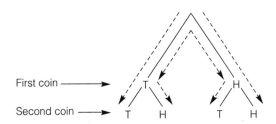

Figure 5.1   Tree Diagram.

Table 5.1 Contingency Table

		Second Coin	
		H	T
First coin	H	HH	HT
	T	TH	TT

Consider the following questions: What is the probability of flipping two heads? At least one head? No heads? One head and one tail? Not more than one tail? We can tabulate the answers as follows:

Probability of an Event	Favorable Events
$P(2H) = \dfrac{1}{4}$	HH
$P(\text{at least } 1H) = \dfrac{3}{4}$	HT, TH, HH
$P(0H) = \dfrac{1}{4}$	TT
$P(1H \text{ and } 1T) = \dfrac{2}{4}$	HT, TH
$P(\text{not more than } 1T) = \dfrac{3}{4}$	HT, TH, HH

■

■ EXAMPLE 3

Dice: In a roll of a fair die, there are six equally possible outcomes ($N = 6$): 1, 2, 3, 4, 5, and 6. You might ask, "What is the probability of rolling a particular number?" And the answer is

$$P(\text{even number}) = \frac{3}{6}$$

$$P(2 \text{ or } 3) = \frac{2}{6}$$

$$P(\text{greater than } 3) = \frac{3}{6} \quad ■$$

Mutually exclusive events, E_i, are events that cannot happen simultaneously; that is, if one event happens, the other event cannot happen. Thus, in the one-coin example, E_1 (heads) and E_2 (tails) are mutually exclusive, and their probabilities add up to 1.

Denoted symbolically, the three basic properties of probability for mutually exclusive events are

$$0 \le P(E_i) \le 1 \tag{5.2}$$

$$P(E_1) + P(E_2) + \cdots + P(E_n) = 1 \tag{5.3}$$

$$P(\text{not } E_1) = 1 - P(E_1) \tag{5.4}$$

where $E_1, E_2, \ldots, E_n$ are mutually exclusive outcomes.

Figure 5.2   Complement of Event *A*.

By perusing our three examples, you can see that (1) the probability of an event is always between 0 and 1 (inclusive), is never negative, and is never greater than 1; (2) the sum of the probabilities of all mutually exclusive outcomes is equal to 1; and (3) the probability of an event E_1 not occurring is equal to 1 minus the probability of E_1.

5.2 COMPLEMENTARY EVENTS

Event $\overline{A}$ is the complement of event *A*, as shown in Figure 5.2. We observe that

$P(A)$ = sum of probabilities of outcomes in A

$P(\overline{A})$ = sum of probabilities of outcomes in $\overline{A}$

and

$P(A) + P(\overline{A}) = 1$

Therefore,

$P(\overline{A}) = 1 - P(A)$

5.3 PROBABILITY RULES

Two indispensable rules help answer the most common questions concerning the probability of compound events (those composed of two or more individual events). These are the multiplication rule and the addition rule.

The Multiplication Rule

Two events are **independent** if the occurrence of one has no effect on the chance of occurrence of the other. The outcomes of repeated tosses of a coin illustrate independent events, because the outcome of one toss does not affect the outcome of any future toss. Note that "independent" and "mutually exclusive" are not the same. The occurrence of one independent event does not affect the chance of another such event occurring at the same time, whereas mutually exclusive events cannot occur simultaneously.

To determine the probability of occurrence of two independent events, we use the multiplication rule. The **multiplication rule** states that the probability of occurrence of two independent events, A and B, is equal to the product of the probabilities of the individual events.
Symbolically,

$$P(A \wedge B) = P(A)P(B) \tag{5.5}$$

where $\wedge$ represents the word *and*.

■ **EXAMPLE 4**

In tossing two coins, what is the probability that a head will occur both on the first coin (H_1) *and* on the second coin (H_2)? The solution:

$$P(H_1 \text{ and } H_2) = [P(H_1)][P(H_2)] = \left(\frac{1}{2}\right)\left(\frac{1}{2}\right) = \frac{1}{4} \quad ■$$

■ **EXAMPLE 5**

Suppose the probability that a typical driver will have an accident during a given year is $\frac{1}{10}$. What is the probability that two randomly selected drivers will *both* have an accident during the year? The solution:

$$P = \left(\frac{1}{10}\right)\left(\frac{1}{10}\right) = \frac{1}{100} \quad ■$$

Conditional Probability Calculating the probability of an event using, in the denominator, a *subset* of all possible outcomes will give a conditional probability. As we will see in Example 6, the probability of stopping smoking during pregnancy is

$$\frac{768}{4075} = .188$$

However, the probability of stopping smoking during pregnancy given that the subgroup consists of those who have 16 years of education is

$$\frac{214}{884} = .242$$

The value .188 is the value of a simple probability, and .242 is the value of a conditional probability. **Conditional probability** is denoted by $P(A \mid B)$. It is the probability that A occurs given that B has occurred, and it is given by the following ratio:

$$P(A \mid B) = \frac{P(A \text{ and } B)}{P(B)} \qquad \text{providing } P(B) \text{ is not equal to zero} \qquad (5.6)$$

The vertical line in $P(A \mid B)$ is read "given."

■ **EXAMPLE 6**

From the data on stopping smoking during pregnancy given in Table 5.2, we can calculate several probabilities. For example, if A is the event of stopping smoking during pregnancy and B is the event that mothers have 16 years of education, then

$$P(A) = \frac{768}{4075} = .188$$

is the probability of selecting a mother who has stopped smoking. The probability of selecting a woman who has 16 years of education is

$$P(B) = \frac{884}{4075} = .2169$$

and the probability of selecting a mother who has both stopped smoking and has 16 years of education is

$$P(A \wedge B) = \frac{214}{4075} = .0525$$

The conditional probability of stopping smoking during pregnancy given that the mother has 16 years of education can be obtained using the formula

$$P(A \mid B) = \frac{P(A \wedge B)}{P(B)} = \frac{.0525}{.2169} = .242$$

Note that the probability obtained using equation (5.6), $P(A \mid B) = .242$, is the same as that obtained directly from the frequencies in Table 5.2, namely,

$$\frac{214}{884} = .242 \ ■$$

Let us consider the difference between $P(A)$ and $P(A \mid B)$. $P(A)$ gives the probability that event A occurs out of all possible outcomes, whereas $P(A \mid B)$

Table 5.2 Number of Mothers of Live-Born Infants Who Stopped Smoking During Pregnancy by Educational Status

| Smoking Status | Years of Education | | | | | | | | | |
	0–11 yrs	%	12 yrs	%	13–15 yrs	%	16 yrs	%	Total	%
Stopped	42	9.7	308	16.9	204	21.8	214	24.2	768	18.8
Did not	390	90.3	1515	83.1	732	78.2	670	75.8	3307	81.2
Total	432	100.0	1823	100.0	936	100.0	884	100.0	4075	100.0

SOURCE: U.S. National Natality Survey, 1980.

gives the probability that event A occurs given that we restrict ourselves to a subset B of all possible outcomes: These two probabilities are not the same unless the two events are independent. The general rule that permits us to make such a statement is

Events A and B are independent if $P(A|B) = P(A)$

From Example 6, we can see that events A and B are not independent because $P(A \mid B) = .242$ does not equal $P(A) = .188$. A modification of Example 3 illustrates how we can check whether events A and B are independent. If A is the event of an even number on the toss of a fair die and B is the event that we consider only the first four numbers, then the two events A and B are independent because their probabilities are equal:

$$P(A) = \frac{3}{6} = \frac{1}{2} \quad \text{and} \quad P(A|B) = \frac{2}{4} = \frac{1}{2}$$

The Addition Rule

To determine the probability that one or another event (but not necessarily both) will occur, we use the addition rule. The **addition rule** states that the probability that event A or event B (or both) will occur equals the sum of the probabilities of each individual event minus the probability of both. Symbolically,

$$P(A \text{ or } B) = P(A) + P(B) - P(A \text{ and } B) \tag{5.7}$$

The reason for subtracting $P(A \text{ and } B)$ is that this portion would otherwise be included twice, as you can see in Figure 5.3a, which is an example of a **Venn diagram.** In such a diagram, circles within a rectangular space represent events, and the relationship between those events is indicated by either a separation or an intersection of the circles. The area excluding A is denoted with a bar over it, $\overline{A}$. The area of not A or not B is denoted as $\overline{A}\,\overline{B}$.

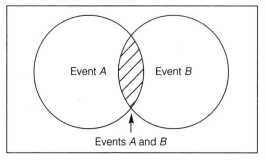

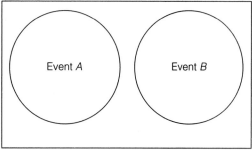

(a) Nonmutually exclusive events   (b) Mutually exclusive events

Figure 5.3   Venn Diagrams of Two Events.

■ **EXAMPLE 7**

In flipping two coins, you may wish to know the probability of having a head on the first coin (H_1), or on the second (H_2), or on both (H_1H_2). To get the answer, use the addition rule:

$$P(H_1 \text{ or } H_2) = \frac{1}{2} + \frac{1}{2} - \frac{1}{4} = \frac{3}{4} \quad ■$$

■ **EXAMPLE 8**

What is the probability that you will obtain a 3 *or* a 4 on one toss of a die? The addition rule gives

$$P(3 \text{ or } 4) = P(3) + P(4) - P(3 \text{ and } 4) = \frac{1}{6} + \frac{1}{6} - 0 = \frac{1}{3} \quad ■$$

Recall that whenever two events are mutually exclusive the probability of both events occurring is zero. By tossing a 3, you have *excluded* the probability of tossing a 4. Likewise, you cannot simultaneously get a head and a tail with one coin flip. Hence, the addition rule is somewhat simplified when the two events are mutually exclusive. The rule then becomes

$$P(A \text{ or } B \text{ or both}) = P(A) + P(B) \tag{5.8}$$

The $P(A$ and $B)$ term of equation 5.7 is zero; it drops out (see Figure 5.3b).

■ **EXAMPLE 9**

At birth, the probability that a U.S. female will survive to age 65 is approximately $\frac{8}{10}$; that is, $P(F_{65}) = \frac{8}{10}$. The probability that a male will survive to age 65 is approximately $\frac{2}{3}$; that is, $P(M_{65}) = \frac{2}{3}$. What is the probability that a U.S. female will die before age 65? Using equation (5.4), we see that the probability of dying before age 65, $P(F_d)$, is computed by subtracting from 1 the probability of surviving to age 65:

$$P(F_d) = 1 - P(F_{65}) = 1 - \frac{8}{10} = .2$$

Carrying the example further, the following probabilities can be computed by appropriately applying the multiplication and addition rules:

1. The probability that both the male and the female will be alive at age 65:

$$P = P(M_{65} \text{ and } F_{65}) = P(M_{65})P(F_{65}) = \left(\frac{2}{3}\right)\left(\frac{8}{10}\right) = .533$$

2. The probability that only the male will be alive at age 65:

$$P = P(M_{65} \text{ and } F_d) = P(M_{65})P(F_d) = \frac{2}{3}\left(1 - \frac{8}{10}\right) = .133$$

3. The probability that only the female will be alive at age 65:

$$P = P(F_{65} \text{ and } M_d) = P(F_{65})P(M_d) = \frac{8}{10}\left(1 - \frac{2}{3}\right) = .267$$

4. The probability that at least one of the two will be alive at age 65:

$$P = P(\text{either one or both will be alive})$$
$$= P(F_{65} \text{ and } M_{65}) + P(M_{65} \text{ and } F_d) + P(F_{65} \text{ and } M_d)$$
$$= .533 + .133 + .267 = .933$$

This answer may also be obtained by finding the probability of the complement of both the male and the female dying; that is,

$$1 - P(M_d \text{ and } F_d) = 1 - \frac{1}{3} \cdot \frac{2}{10} = .933 \ \blacksquare$$

5.4 COUNTING RULES

In computing the probabilities of various events, we first need to know in how many possible ways such events can occur. For example, if we wish to know the probability of having two girls and a boy in a three-child family, it is essential to know the order of their birth. How many different possibilities are there of having two girls and a boy? The number of potential outcomes is eight:

girl girl girl	boy girl girl*
girl girl boy*	boy girl boy
girl boy girl*	boy boy girl
girl boy boy	boy boy boy

Here you can see that the three outcomes marked with asterisks qualify as successes (two girls and a boy).

You may need to know the number of different possibilities of a certain event in order to determine the denominator you need to use to compute a probability. Three general rules are helpful in obtaining counts.

Rule 1: Number of Ways

If event A can occur in n_1 distinct ways and event B can occur in n_2 ways, then the events consisting of A and B can occur in $n_1 \cdot n_2$ ways.

■ EXAMPLE 10

If you had three different diet (D) choices by amount of protein (low, medium, high) and three different choices by amount of fat (low, medium, high), there would be $(n_1)(n_2) = (3)(3) = 9$ different possible diets:

D_1: protein (low), fat (low) D_4: protein (low), fat (medium)

D_2: protein (medium), fat (low) D_5: protein (medium), fat (medium)

D_3: protein (high), fat (low) D_6: protein (high), fat (medium)

D_7: protein (low), fat (high)

D_8: protein (medium), fat (high)

D_9: protein (high), fat (high) ■

Rule 2: Permutations

In determining the number of ways in which you can arrange a group of objects, you must first know whether the *order* of arrangement plays a role. For example, the order of arrangement of a person's missing teeth is important, but the order of selecting a group for a committee is not, because any order results in the same committee.

A **permutation** is a selection of r objects from a group of n objects, taking the order of selection into account. The number of different ways in which n objects may be arranged is given by $n!$. The exclamation mark stands for **factorial,** and the symbol $n!$ (read "n factorial") means $n(n - 1)(n - 2) \cdots 3 \cdot 2 \cdot 1$. Thus, 3! (i.e., three factorial) $= 3 \cdot 2 \cdot 1 = 6$; also, $0! = 1$. This last, $0! = 1$, may seem arbitrary, but it is a mathematically necessary convention that keeps us from multiplying by zero.

■ **EXAMPLE 11**

If we wish to identify vials of a medication by using three different symbols, x, y, and z, how many different ways can the vials be identified? The answer is

$$3! = 3 \cdot 2 \cdot 1 = 6$$

The six different identifications are xyz, xzy, yxz, yzx, zxy, and zyx. ■

Suppose we want to learn the number of ways of selecting r objects from a set of n objects, and order is important. Here we would use the equation

$$P(n,r) = \frac{n!}{(n - r)!} \tag{5.9}$$

■ **EXAMPLE 12**

If there are three effective ways of treating a cancer patient—surgery (S), radiation (R), and chemotherapy (C)—in how many different ways can the patient be treated with two different treatments if the order of treatment is important? The answer is given by

$$P(3,2) = \frac{3!}{(3 - 2)!} = \frac{3 \cdot 2 \cdot 1}{1} = 6$$

or SR, RS, CS, SC, RC, and CR. ■

Rule 3: Combinations

Sometimes we may wish to determine the number of arrangements of a group of objects when order is not important, as in selecting books from a shelf. A **combination** is a selection of a subgroup of distinct objects, with order not being important. The equation for obtaining the number of ways of selecting r objects from n objects, disregarding order, is

$$C(n,r) = \frac{n!}{r!(n - r)!} \tag{5.10}$$

where C denotes the total number of combinations of objects.

■ **EXAMPLE 13**

Suppose that three patients with snakebites are brought to a physician. To his regret, he discovers that he has only two doses of antivenin. The three patients are a pregnant woman (W), a young child (C), and an elderly man (M). Before deciding which two to treat, he examines his choices:

$$C(3,2) = \frac{3!}{2!(3-2)!} = \frac{3 \cdot 2 \cdot 1}{2 \cdot 1} = 3$$

The three choices are WC, WM, and CM. Note that CW, MW, and MC are the same as the first three because order does not matter. ∎

5.5 PROBABILITY DISTRIBUTIONS

A key application of probability to statistics is estimating the probabilities that are associated with the occurrence of different events. For example, we may wish to know the probability of having a family of two girls and one boy or the probability that two out of three patients will be cured by a certain medication. If we know the various probabilities associated with different outcomes of a given phenomenon, we can determine which outcomes are common and which are not. This helps us reach a decision as to whether certain events are significant. A complete list of all possible outcomes, together with the probability of each, constitutes a **probability distribution.**

The outcome of events may be described numerically (e.g., the number of three-boy families). The symbol X usually denotes the variable of interest. This variable, which can assume any number of values, is called a **random variable** because it represents a chance (random) outcome of an experiment. Thus, we can say that a probability distribution is a list of the probabilities associated with the values of the random variable obtained in an experiment. Random variables may be either discrete or continuous. Only discrete variables are discussed in this chapter.

Three examples of probability distribution are illustrated in Table 5.3. As the third example in the table shows, if a three-child family is selected at random, the probability that it is a three-boy family is .125. In this example, the number of boys is the random variable.

From the distributions in Table 5.3, we can again see that the sum of the probabilities of a set of mutually exclusive events always equals 1.

5.6 LOTTERY PROBABILITY AND SAMPLING

State-operated lotteries, with the lure of large cash prizes, are a rapidly expanding activity. In this section, we will show you how to calculate the odds of winning and use these examples to illustrate how probability is determined when you have sampling with and without replacement.

The first example is one that, even if it is not legal in your locale, you have at least heard of: the Powerball. The first five numbers of the Powerball are an

Table 5.3 Examples of Probability Distribution

Toss of Two Coins		Roll of a Die		Sex of Three-Child Family	
E	P(E)	E	P(E)	E	P(E)
HH	$\frac{1}{4}$	1	$\frac{1}{6}$	3 boys*	.125
HT	$\frac{1}{4}$	2	$\frac{1}{6}$	2 boys, 1 girl	.375
TH	$\frac{1}{4}$	3	$\frac{1}{6}$	1 boy, 2 girls	.375
TT	$\frac{1}{4}$	4	$\frac{1}{6}$	3 girls	.125
	1.0	5	$\frac{1}{6}$		1.000
		6	$\frac{1}{6}$		
			1.0		

*For ease of computation, we assume that P(boy) = .5.

example of **sampling without replacement,** which means that once a number has been drawn (or a subject selected) that number may not be drawn again. This means that each time a number is drawn the odds will change. Here's how it works. In the first part of the Powerball, 5 numbers out of 49 are selected. If you have a Powerball ticket, there is a $\frac{5}{49}$ chance that your ticket will have the first number selected. Suppose you were one of the 10% who had the first number (which means 90% of the tickets have no chance at the big prize after the first number). That number cannot be drawn again; in other words, it is not put back in the tank. Now there are 48 numbers left, and you have 4 numbers left on your ticket. The odds of your having the second number are now $\frac{4}{48}$. Now suppose your luck holds out, and you have the second number. What are your chances of having the third number? The first two numbers are now out of use, and there are three numbers left on your ticket. The odds of having the third are $\frac{3}{47}$. Perhaps you can predict the odds of selecting the fourth and fifth numbers. If you said $\frac{2}{46}$ and $\frac{1}{45}$, you are correct. Notice that in sampling without replacement the odds change every time a number is selected.

The next step is to calculate the odds of getting all five numbers *and* the Powerball. As you learned earlier in this chapter, this probability is determined by multiplying the probabilities $\frac{5}{49} \times \frac{4}{48} \times \frac{3}{47} \times \frac{2}{46} \times \frac{1}{45}$. To win the big prize, you not only must get the first five numbers but also must select a sixth number called the Powerball. The Powerballs are numbered 1–42. Your odds of winning the big prize are $\frac{5}{49} \times \frac{4}{48} \times \frac{3}{47} \times \frac{2}{46} \times \frac{1}{45}$ multiplied by the odds of getting the Powerball (sixth number), which is $\frac{1}{42}$. This means that the stated odds of winning the jackpot are 1 in 80,089,128. Two tongue-in-cheek comments about exactly what it means to have a 1 in 80,089,128 chance of winning the Powerball are that (1) your odds of winning are the same regardless of whether you buy a ticket and (2) lotteries are taxes on the mathematically impaired.

A lottery game that illustrates the concept of **sampling with replacement** is called Pick 3. In this game, you have 10 numbers, and you try to pick the three winners. You may pick the same number once, twice, or all three times. You have a $\frac{1}{10}$ chance of picking the first number. That number goes back into the tank, which means that you once again have 10 numbers to choose from, and your odds of selecting the second number are also $\frac{1}{10}$. The same thing happens with the third number; once again, your odds are $\frac{1}{10}$. To calculate your odds of selecting all three numbers, you multiply $\frac{1}{10} \times \frac{1}{10} \times \frac{1}{10}$, which comes to a 1 in 1000 chance of correctly guessing all three numbers. Because the odds are $\frac{1}{10}$ for each number, are your odds "better" if you choose three different numbers? No. Because each number has a $\frac{1}{10}$ chance of occurring with each drawing, the odds of any number appearing three times are the same as any other combination of three numbers.

5.7 BINOMIAL DISTRIBUTION

In practice, we usually work with distributions that are reasonable approximations to theoretical distributions. In constructing a frequency table, we can obtain an estimate of the probability distribution by visualizing the relative frequency associated with each possible outcome. Having this information, we can make statements about how common a given event is.

Various phenomena follow certain underlying mathematical distributions. One of the most useful, the **binomial distribution,** serves as a model for outcomes limited to two choices (e.g., sick or well, dead or alive, at risk or not at risk). For such a dichotomous population, we may wish to know the probability of having a number of r successes on n different attempts, where the probability of success on any one attempt is p.

As an example, let us again consider the probability that a couple planning three children will have two girls and one boy. Suppose we wonder whether the three children will arrive in the sequence GGB. If we assume that the probability of having a girl is .5, then the probability of the sequence GGB occurring is $(\frac{1}{2} \cdot \frac{1}{2}) \cdot \frac{1}{2} = \frac{1}{8}$. However, two girls and a boy may arrive in three different ways—GGB, GBG, BGG—as indicated by $C(3,2) = 3$, where $C(3,2)$ denotes the combination of three things taken two at a time. Because the probability of each sequence is $\frac{1}{8}$, the probability of having two girls and a boy in *any* sequence is

$$3\left(\frac{1}{8}\right) = 3(.125) = .375$$

as indicated in the third probability distribution in Table 5.3.

The probability distribution for this example is obtained algebraically from the expansion of the **binomial term** $(p + q)^n$, where p is the probability of a successful outcome, $q = 1 - p$ is the probability of an unsuccessful outcome, and n

is the number of trials or attempts. The binomial expansion is applicable, provided that

1. Each trial has only two possible outcomes—success or failure
2. The outcome of each trial is independent of the outcomes of any other trial
3. The probability of success, p, is constant from trial to trial

Under these conditions, the probability of the sequence GGB is

$$p \cdot p(1 - p) = p^2 q$$
$$\text{G} \quad \text{G} \quad \text{B}$$

and the probability of any sequence of two girls and a boy is

$$C(3,2)p^2(q) = \frac{3!}{2!(3 - 2)!}\left(\frac{1}{2}\right)^2\left(\frac{1}{2}\right) = 3\left(\frac{1}{2}\right)^3 = .375$$

where $C(3,2)$ becomes the binomial coefficient giving the number of different sequences of three children consisting of two girls and one boy.

In general, the probability of an event consisting of r successes out of n trials is

$$P(r \text{ successes}) = \frac{n!}{r!(n - r)!}p^r q^{n-r} \tag{5.11}$$

where
$n = $ the number of trials in an experiment
$r = $ the number of successes
$n - r = $ the number of failures
$p = $ the probability of success
$q = 1 - p$, the probability of failure

The expression

$$\frac{n!}{r!(n - r)!}p^r q^{n-r}$$

is a term from the binomial expansion. The entire expansion lists the terms for r successes and $(n - r)$ failures from the binomial distribution:

$$(p + q)^3 = q^3 + \frac{3!}{1!(3 - 1)!}pq^2 + \frac{3!}{2!(3 - 2)!}p^2 q + p^3$$

$$= q^3 + 3pq^2 + 3p^2 q + p^3 \tag{5.12}$$

$$= P(3F) + P(1S, 2F) + P(2S, 1F) + P(3S)$$

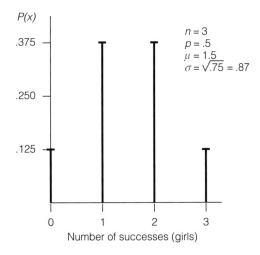

Figure 5.4   Example of Binomial Distribution.

where F = failure and S = success. If a "success" means bearing a girl ($p = .5$), equation 5.12 reduces to

$$(p + q)^3 = \left(\frac{1}{2}\right)^3 + 3\left(\frac{1}{2}\right)\left(\frac{1}{2}\right)^2 + 3\left(\frac{1}{2}\right)^2\left(\frac{1}{2}\right) + \left(\frac{1}{2}\right)^3$$

$$= .125 + .375 + .375 + .125 = 1.000 \tag{5.13}$$

$$= P(3B) + P(1G, 2B) + P(2G, 1B) + P(3G)$$

Equation (5.13) shows that the binomial expansion yields the binomial distribution illustrated initially in the third example in Table 5.3 and visually portrayed in Figure 5.4.

It is essential that you gain a feeling for the meaning of binomial terms so that you will then be able to construct or interpret one for any occasion. Figure 5.5 should enable you to understand the anatomy of the binomial term. Note especially that, in a binomial distribution, r (the number of favorable outcomes) serves as the random variable. Using the probability distribution given in equation (5.11), you can find the following probabilities in a three-child family:

3B	= .125
2G, 1B	= .375

At most 2G (3B; 2B, 1G; 1B, 2G) = .125 + .375 + .375 = .875

At least 1B (3B; 2B, 1G; 1B, 2G) = .125 + .375 + .375 = .875

The probabilities of a binomial term can be obtained by reading them directly from the binomial probability table found in Appendix A. A small portion of this table is reproduced in Table 5.4.

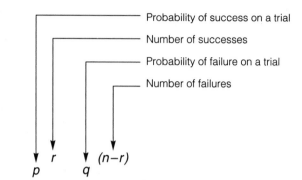

$$\frac{n!}{r!(n-r)!}$$

Number of ways an event can occur

Probability of an event with r successes and $n-r$ failures

Figure 5.5   Identification of the Components of the Binomial Term.

■ **EXAMPLE 14**

What is the probability of having two girls and one boy in a three-child family if the probability of having a boy is .5?

From the calculations in equation 5.13, we can see that

$$P(2G, 1B) = \frac{3!}{2!(3-2)!}\left(\frac{1}{2}\right)^2\left(\frac{1}{2}\right)^1 = 3(.125) = .375$$

Looking at Table 5.4 with $n = 3$, $p = .5$, and $r = 2$, we again find that $P = .375$.

■

The binomial expansion is used to obtain the probability of various events when n is small, say, 30 or less. When n is large, you should use the Gaussian (normal) distribution, discussed in the next chapter, as an approximation. To do this, you need to know the mean and the standard deviation of the binomial distribution, and we will consider these in Chapter 11.

Table 5.4 Portion of Binomial Probability Table

				P	
n	r	.10	.25	1/3	.50
	0	.7290	.4219	.2963	.1250
	1	.2430	.4219	.4444	.3750
3	2	.0270	.1406	.2222	.3750
	3	.0010	.0156	.0370	.1250

◆ CONCLUSION

Probability measures the likelihood that a particular event will or will not occur. In a long series of trials, probability is the ratio of the number of favorable outcomes to the total number of equally likely outcomes. Permutations and combinations are useful in determining the number of outcomes. If compound events are involved, we need to select and apply the addition rule or the multiplication rule to compute probabilities. The outcome of an experiment, together with its respective probabilities, constitutes a probability distribution. One very common probability distribution is the binomial distribution. It presents the probabilities of various numbers of successes in trials where there are only two possible outcomes to each trial.

◆ VOCABULARY LIST

addition rule
binomial distribution
binomial term
combination
conditional probability
contingency table
equally likely events
factorial

independent events
multiplication rule
mutually exclusive
  events
permutation
probability
probability distribution
random variable

sampling with
  replacement
sampling without
  replacement
tree diagram
Venn diagram

◆ EXERCISES

5.1   Two coins are tossed and the results observed. Find the probabilities of observing zero heads, one head, and two heads.

5.2   Take two coins, toss them 20 times, and record the number of heads observed for each toss. Compute the proportion of zero heads, one head, and two heads, and compare the results with the expected results you computed in Exercise (5.1).

5.3   A fair coin is tossed three times and the number of heads observed. Determine the probability of observing
  a. exactly two heads
  b. at least two heads
  c. at most two heads
  d. exactly three heads

5.4   A couple is planning to have three children. Find the following probabilities by listing all the possibilities and using equation (5.1):
  a. two boys and one girl
  b. at least one boy
  c. no girls
  d. at most two girls
  e. two boys followed by a girl
  How does (e) differ from (a)?

5.5   Suppose you observe the result of a throw of a single fair die. How many times would you expect to observe a 1 in 60 throws? How many times would you expect to observe each of the other possibilities (2, 3, 4, 5, 6) in 60 throws?

5.6   Toss a die 60 times and record the frequency of occurrence of 1, 2, 3, 4, 5, and 6. Compare your results with those in Exercise 5.5. In your judgment, is the die you tossed a fair one? (You will learn in Chapter 12 how to apply a statistical test to determine the fairness of a die.)

5.7   On a single toss of a pair of fair dice, what is the probability that
a. a sum of 8 is observed
b. a sum of 7 or 11 comes up
c. a sum of 8 or a double appears
d. a sum of 7 appears and both dice show a number less than 4

5.8   A ball is drawn at random from a box containing 10 red, 30 white, 20 blue, and 15 orange balls. Find the probability that it is:
a. orange or red
b. neither red nor blue
c. not blue
d. white
e. red or white or blue

5.9   In an experiment involving a toxic substance, the probability that a white mouse will be alive for 10 hours is $\frac{7}{10}$, and the probability that a black mouse will be alive for 10 hours is $\frac{9}{10}$. Find the probability that, at the end of 10 hours:
a. both mice will be alive
b. only the black mouse will be alive
c. only the white mouse will be alive
d. at least one mouse will be alive

5.10 If an individual were chosen at random from Table 2.1, what is the probability that that person would be
a. a vegetarian
b. a female
c. a male vegetarian

5.11 Suppose a person is randomly selected from Table 3.1. Find the probability that he or she:
a. has completed high school or technical school
b. is a smoker
c. is physically inactive (code number = 1)
d. is a physically inactive smoker
e. has a serum cholesterol level greater than 250 and systolic blood pressure above 130
f. has a blood glucose level of 100 or less

5.12 In how many ways can five different-colored marbles be arranged in a row?

5.13 In how many ways can a roster of four club officers be selected from 10 nominees so that the first one selected will be president; the second, vice-president; the third, secretary; and the fourth, treasurer?

5.14 Compute
   a. *P*(8,3)
   b. *P*(6,4)

5.15 In how many ways can a committee of five people be chosen out of nine people?

5.16 Calculate
   a. *C*(7,4)
   b. *C*(6,4)
   Compare (b) with Exercise 5.14b. What do you observe?

5.17 In how many ways can 10 objects be split into two groups containing 4 and 6 objects respectively?

5.18 About 50% of all persons age 3 and older wear glasses or contact lenses. For a randomly selected group of five people, and using equation (5.11), compute the probability that
   a. exactly three wear glasses or contact lenses
   b. at least one wears them
   c. at most one wears them

5.19 If 25% of 11-year-old children have no decayed, missing, or filled (DMF) teeth, find the probability that in a sample of 20 children there will be:
   a. exactly 3 with no DMF teeth
   b. 3 or more with no DMF teeth
   c. fewer than 3 with no DMF teeth
   d. exactly 5 with no DMF teeth
   (*Hint:* Refer to the first example in Table 5.3.)

5.20 It is known that approximately 10% of the population is hospitalized at least once during a year. If 10 people in such a community are to be interviewed, what is the probability that you will find
   a. all have been hospitalized at least once during the year
   b. 50% have been hospitalized
   c. at least 3 have been hospitalized
   d. exactly 3 have been hospitalized
   (*Hint:* Refer to the first example in Table 5.3.)

5.21 Seventy-five percent of youths ages 12–17 have a systolic blood pressure lower than 136 mm of mercury. What is the probability that a sample of 12 youths of that age group will include:
   a. exactly 4 who have a blood pressure greater than 136
   b. no more than 4 who have a blood pressure greater than 136
   c. at least 4 who have a blood pressure greater than 136
   (*Hint:* Refer to the first example in Table 5.3.)

5.22 Assuming that, of all persons 17 years and over, half the males and a third of the females are classified as presently smoking cigarettes, find the probability that in a randomly selected group of 10 males and 15 females
   a. exactly 10 smoke (4 males, 6 females)
   b. all smoke
   c. none smoke
   (*Hint:* Refer to the first example in Table 5.3.)

5.23 Define the following:
   a. equally likely events
   b. mutually exclusive events
   c. independent events
   d. probability
   e. conditional probability
   f. probability distribution
   g. random variable

5.24 Define and give an example of the following:
   a. combination
   b. permutation
   c. factorial
   d. addition rule
   e. multiplication rule

5.25 Using the data from Table 5.2, let the event

   A = a mother with less than 12 years of education

   B = a mother who has quit smoking

   a. Calculate $P(A)$.
   b. Calculate $P(B)$.
   c. Calculate $P(B \mid A)$.
   d. Indicate whether events A and B are independent. (*Hint:* Use equations (5.5) and (5.6).)

5.26 a. Define the binomial distribution.
   b. Define the components of a binomial term.

5.27 Using the data from Tables 3.2 and 3.3, prepare a new frequency table of systolic blood pressure for nonsmokers and smokers. Using this new table, let the events

   A = a nonsmoker

   B = a smoker

   C = a systolic blood pressure of 170 or greater

   Find
   a. $P(A)$
   b. $P(B)$
   c. $P(C)$
   d. $P(C \mid A)$
   e. $P(C \mid B)$
   Compare (d) and (e), and comment. Are smoking status and blood pressure level independent events?

5.28 Use Table 5.2 to compute some probabilities you could use in persuading someone that level of education and smoking are inversely related.

5.29 Phenylketonuria (PKU) is a genetic disease that occurs if someone inherits two recessive genes (meaning that this person is unable to metabolize the amino acid phenylalanine into another amino acid, tyrosine). The possible genetic combinations are two dominant genes (no disease), one dominant and one recessive gene (no disease, but a carrier), and two recessive genes (has PKU). Calculate the probability of a child having the disease if:

a. both parents are carriers

b. one parent is a carrier, and the other has two dominant genes

c. one parent has the disease, and the other has two dominant genes

d. both parents have the disease

5.30 Using the information from Exercise 5.29, calculate the probability of a child being a carrier if

a. both parents are carriers

b. one parent is a carrier, and the other has two dominant genes

c. one parent has the disease, and the other has two dominant genes

d. both parents have the disease

5.31 Using the information from Exercise 5.29, calculate the probability of a child having two dominant genes if

a. both parents are carriers

b. one parent is a carrier, and the other has two dominant genes

c. one parent has the disease, and the other has two dominant genes

d. both parents have the disease

5.32 A lottery is created with 35 numbers. You have to pick all five numbers to win the grand prize. If this lottery is an example of sampling without replacement, what are the odds of any one $1 ticket winning? If this is a state lottery, and the grand prize is $250,000, do you expect the state to make money? Explain.

5.33 From Exercise 5.32, calculate the odds of any single ticket winning if the lottery is an example of sampling with replacement.

6 The Normal Distribution

CHAPTER OUTLINE

6.1 **The Importance of Normal Distribution**
Explains why the normal distribution is so important in statistical analysis

6.2 **Properties of the Normal Distribution**
Lists and explains the properties of the normal distribution, so valuable to statistical theory and methodology

6.3 **Areas Under the Normal Curve**
Presents specific examples to demonstrate the interpretation and use of a table of areas that correspond to intervals of the standard score

✔ LEARNING OBJECTIVES

After studying this chapter, you should be able to

1. State why the normal distribution is so important
2. Identify the properties of the normal distribution
3. Interpret the mean and the standard deviation in the context of the normal curve
4. List the differences between the normal and the standard normal distribution
5. Explain the standard score $Z = (x - \mu)/\sigma$
6. Compute the percentage of areas between given points under a normal curve
7. Compute percentiles of specified variables by using a table of standard scores

6.1   THE IMPORTANCE OF NORMAL DISTRIBUTION

Physicians often rely on a knowledge of **normal limits** to classify patients as healthy or otherwise. For example, a serum cholesterol level above 200 mg/dl is widely regarded as indicating a significantly increased risk for coronary heart disease. An accurate determination of such a value, whether or not based on a mathematical model, is critical. The decision may be a matter of life or death, because the physician uses the findings to decide what type of treatment to prescribe for a patient. It would be unfortunate, perhaps tragic, if the "normal limits" were faulty. In that case, some patients might receive an unnecessary treatment, while others might fail to receive a needed treatment.

Serum albumin is the chief protein of blood plasma. For any group of persons, the concentrations of serum albumin tend to follow a **normal distribution.** The normal limits for albumin are calculated by adding and subtracting two standard deviations from the mean of a large set of observations obtained from a group of presumably healthy persons. This calculation provides the limits that contain the middle 95% (the "normal range") of observations but exclude the remaining 5%, of which 2.5% falls in the lower tail and 2.5% in the upper tail. Extreme observations, those in the tails, are considered unusual and may be regarded as presumptive evidence of a health problem. However, not all variables follow a normal distribution. Two well-known counterexamples are urea and alkaline phosphatase. For these, use of the same method would give incorrect "normal limits" that would not include 2.5% of the observations in each tail. In response to this problem, medical statisticians Elveback, Guillier, and Keating (1970) have suggested that "clinical limits" rather than "normal limits" be used. **Clinical limits** are the lower and upper 2.5 percentage points for any distribution, normal or otherwise, of healthy persons. Clinical limits are obtained empirically, not by adding and subtracting two standard deviations from the mean. Use of clinical limits is greatly preferred to use of normal limits, because the term *normal limits* has been grossly misused and has fallen into disrepute.

In Chapter 5, we learned how a distribution of a variable gives an idea of the values of its population. Knowing that a variable is distributed normally can be especially helpful in drawing inferences as to how frequently certain observations are likely to occur.

The normal distribution, perhaps the most important of statistical distributions, was first discovered by the French mathematician Abraham De Moivre in 1733 and was rediscovered and applied to the natural and social sciences by the French mathematician Pierre-Simon de Laplace and the German mathematician and astronomer Carl Friedrich Gauss in the early 19th century. Sir Francis Galton, a cousin of Charles Darwin, first applied the normal curve to medicine.

Scholars like to refer to the normal curve as the **Gaussian distribution.** This preference is in reaction to the tendency of some persons to view anything not "normally" distributed as "abnormal." However, in popular practice, most statisticians and scientists still call it the normal distribution.

There is a legion of reasons the normal distribution plays such a key role in statistics. For one thing, countless phenomena follow (or closely approximate) the normal distribution. Just a few of them are height, serum cholesterol levels, life span of light bulbs, body temperature of healthy persons, size of oranges, and brightness of galaxies. But there are likewise countless phenomena that do *not* follow the normal distribution, ranging from individual annual income to clinical laboratory readings for urea, magnesium, or alkaline phosphatase. Another reason for the normal distribution's popularity is that it possesses certain mathematical properties that make it attractive and easy to manipulate. Still another reason is that much statistical theory and methodology was developed around the assumption that certain data are distributed approximately normally. Normal distribution is the basis for the use of inferential statistics.

6.2 PROPERTIES OF THE NORMAL DISTRIBUTION

The normal distribution has three main properties. First, it has the appearance of a symmetrical **bell-shaped curve** extending infinitely in both directions. It is symmetrical about the mean, μ. Not every bell-shaped curve, however, is a normal distribution.

Second, all normal distributions have a particular internal distribution for the area under the curve. Whether the mean or standard deviation is large or small, the relative area between any two designated points is always the same. Let us look at three commonly used points along the abscissa. In Figure 6.1, we see that 68.26% of the area is contained within $\mu \pm 1\sigma$, 95.45% within $\mu \pm 2\sigma$, and 99.74% within $\mu \pm 3\sigma$ (see Table A, inside back cover).

The amount of area under the normal curve is directly proportional to the percentage of raw scores. For example, if you have .20 of the total area of 1.0, you have .20 or 20% of the raw scores. The total area under the curve in Figure 6.1 equals 1.0. This is a nice feature. Because of it, the area under the curve between any two points can be interpreted as the relative frequency (or probability of occurrence) of the values included between those points.

Third, the normal distribution is a theoretical distribution defined by two parameters: the mean μ and the standard deviation σ. The **exponential equation** for the normal distribution is

$$y = \frac{1}{\sigma\sqrt{2\pi}} \exp\left[-\frac{1}{2}\left(\frac{x - \mu}{\sigma}\right)^2 \right] \tag{6.1}$$

where y is the height of the curve for a given value x, exp is the base of the natural logarithm (approximately 2.71828), and π is the well-known constant (about 3.141519).

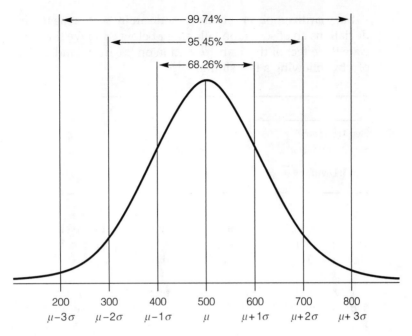

Figure 6.1   Important Divisions of the Normal Distribution of SAT Scores.

6.3   AREAS UNDER THE NORMAL CURVE

Let us assume that the SAT scores of a given population are normally distributed with $\mu = 500$ and $\sigma = 100$. In that case, 68.3% of the SAT scores (rounded up) should fall between 400 and 600 (500 ± 100), as shown in Figure 6.1. Similarly, we would expect approximately 95% of the SAT scores to fall between 300 and 700, 2.5% above 700, and 2.5% below 300. To find the proportion of persons with SAT scores between 550 and 600, we need a table of normal curve areas. But first, let us see how to use such a table.

Because it would be out of the question to tabulate the areas of all possible normal curves, we use the feature that all normal curves are symmetrical and have an area of 1.0. Thus, dealing with one normal curve is like dealing with any other, provided we use a standardized unit. Such a unit is the **standardized score,** Z, which gives the relative position of any observation in the distribution. If a variable is normally distributed, then *any* individual raw score can be converted into a corresponding Z score. Sometimes Z is referred to as **Z score, Z value,** or **standard score.** For the normal curve, the Z score is obtained by

$$Z = \frac{x - \mu}{\sigma} \tag{6.2}$$

Standardized observations provide an indication as to how many standard deviations an observation falls either below or above the mean. You can appreciate the effect of this transformation on the mean and the standard deviation of x by following a few simple steps:

	Variable	Mean	Standard Deviation
Step 1: Start with x	x	μ	σ
Step 2: Subtract μ	$x - \mu$	$\mu - \mu = 0$	σ
Step 3: Divide by σ	$Z = \dfrac{1}{\sigma}(x - \mu) = \dfrac{x - \mu}{\sigma}$	$\left(\dfrac{1}{\sigma}\right)0 = 0$	$\left(\dfrac{1}{\sigma}\right)\sigma = 1$

In step 1, given the variable x, the mean is μ and the standard deviation is σ. In step 2, on subtraction of μ, the mean is shifted from μ to 0, but σ is left unchanged. In step 3, the variable is divided by σ, the mean remains 0, and σ reduces to 1.

The net effect of this so-called Z transformation is to change any normal distribution to the **standard normal distribution,** where $\mu = 0$ and $\sigma = 1$. An example of this transformation is how SAT scores are established. You probably were required to take either the SAT or the ACT prior to admission to your college or university. The population is defined as all those who take the test. All of the scores are tabulated, and a population mean and population standard deviation are calculated. The mean for the math and the verbal portions is given a score of 500 or the 50th percentile. Each standard deviation is established at 100 points. Throughout this chapter, we will use the math portion of the SAT to illustrate how the normal distribution works.

It is this distribution that takes on prominence because of its use in setting confidence limits and tests of hypotheses. Areas for the standard normal distribution are listed in Table A (inside back cover). Here are a few pointers for anyone using it for the first time. Figure 6.2 shows areas under the standard normal curve between various points along the abscissa. The proper use of Table A may be demonstrated by finding the areas between different points along the abscissa. The area under the curve, A, is tabulated in the body of the table; it is that area between zero and some point Z to the right of zero. Z values are given in the left margin. Whole numbers and tenths are read at the left; hundredths along the top, horizontally. Furthermore, because the normal curve is symmetrical, the area between zero and any negative point is equal to the area between zero and the corresponding positive point. Remember that, because the area under the curve is equal to 1 and the curve is symmetrical about zero, the area to the right of Z can be computed by subtracting from .5. Another way of explaining this is that area A (between the mean and Z) plus area B (Z and beyond) *always* equals .5.

Now let us extend our SAT score example to illustrate various uses of Table A.

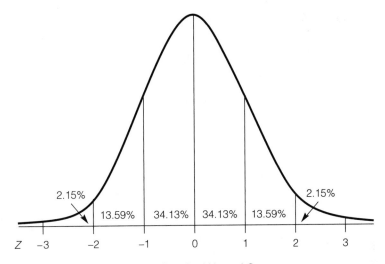

Figure 6.2   Areas Under the Standard Normal Curve.

■ EXAMPLE 1

What is the proportion of persons having SAT math scores between 500 and 650?
    Sketch a curve like the one in Figure 6.3. Shade in the area you wish to find. Transform the SAT variable to a Z score. By equation (6.2), the Z corresponding to $x = 500$ is

$$Z = \frac{x - \mu}{\sigma} = \frac{500 - 500}{100} = 0$$

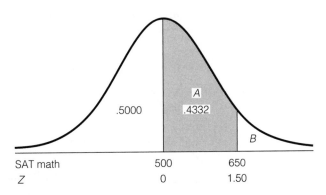

Figure 6.3   Area Corresponding to SAT Scores Between 500 and 650.

and the Z corresponding to $x = 650$ is

$$Z = \frac{650 - 500}{100} = \frac{150}{100} = 1.50$$

By using Table A to find the area for a Z of 1.50, you will find the answer to be .4332. Therefore, the proportion of persons having math SAT scores between 500 and 650 is .4332, about 43%. ■

■ EXAMPLE 2

What proportion of persons has SAT scores greater than 650?
 Again, sketch a curve, this time following the model of Figure 6.4. Because the total area to the right of $Z = 0$ is .50 and the area between $Z = 0$ and 1.50 is .4332, by subtraction you will obtain the area beyond $Z = 1.50$, namely, .5000 − .4332 = .0668. So the answer is that about 7% have SAT scores over 650. ■

■ EXAMPLE 3

What is the proportion of persons with SAT scores between 380 and 620?
 To find the proportion of scores between 380 and 620, you must find the area under the normal curve between Z values that correspond to SAT scores of 380 and 620. The only way to find the area is to convert the raw scores of 380 and 620 to Z scores. Using equation (6.2), we find Z scores of −1.20 and +1.20. Notice that there is exactly the same area between $Z = 0$ and $Z = 1.20$ as there is between $Z = 0$ and $Z = -1.20$, namely, .3849. Adding these two areas gives us a total area of .7698; that is, 77% of the students have math SAT scores between 380 and 620. Figure 6.5 illustrates this solution. ■

 We should point out that a negative Z score means that the corresponding raw score will be lower than the mean. In this example, a raw score of 380 corresponds to a $-Z$ score of −1.20. Notice that the areas between the mean and

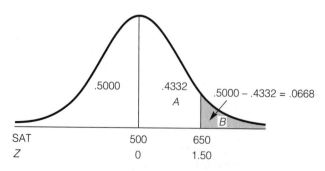

Figure 6.4 Area Corresponding to SAT Scores Above 650.

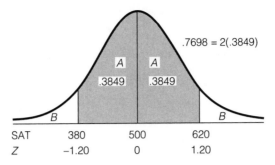

Figure 6.5 Area Corresponding to SAT Scores Between 380 and 620.

$\pm Z$ (both labeled area A) are exactly the same; the only difference is that the positive Z score represents the area above the mean and the negative Z score represents the area below the mean. A Z score of -1.20 means that a raw score of 380 is 1.20 standard deviations *below* the mean and a Z score of 1.20 means that a raw score of 620 is 1.20 standard deviations *above* the mean.

■ **EXAMPLE 4**

What is the proportion of persons with SAT scores between 450 and 670? The corresponding Z scores for the two areas, A_1 and A_2, are

$$A_1: Z = \frac{450 - 500}{100} = \frac{-50}{100} = -.50$$

$$A_2: Z = \frac{670 - 500}{100} = \frac{170}{100} = 1.70$$

Figure 6.6 illustrates the two areas.

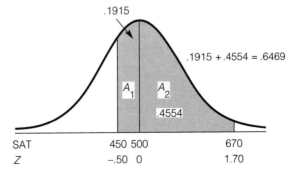

Figure 6.6 Area Corresponding to SAT Scores Between 450 and 670.

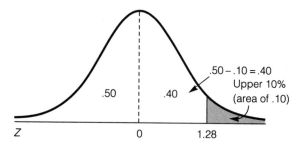

Figure 6.7 *Z* Scores Corresponding to the Upper 10% of SAT Scores.

The area (A_1) between $Z = 0$ and $Z = -.50$ is the same, of course, as that between 0 and +.50. In Table A, we see that A_1 is .1915 and that A_2, between $Z = 0$ and $Z = 1.70$, is .4554. Thus, $A_1 + A_2 = .1915 + .4554 = .6469$. The answer, then, is that about 65% of this population have SAT scores between 450 and 670. ∎

Table A may also be used to determine the Z value that corresponds to any given area, as, for instance, the upper 10% of the curve. Consequently, we can obtain the value on the abscissa that corresponds to the 90th **percentile**, P_{90}.

■ **EXAMPLE 5**

What is the Z value of the normal curve that marks the upper 10% (or 90th percentile) of the area?

The desired Z score is that value corresponding to .40 of the area, as Figure 6.7 illustrates. In Table A, the value is found to be approximately $Z = 1.28$. ∎

■ **EXAMPLE 6**

What is the 90th percentile of SAT scores?

This is the logical extension of Example 5. We just found the Z score of the 90th percentile to be 1.28. But what does this mean in terms of SAT scores? The answer is found by a simple application of equation (6.2).

$$Z = \frac{x - \mu}{\sigma}$$

$$1.28 = \frac{x - 500}{100}$$

Therefore

$$x = \mu + Z\sigma \quad \text{(formula)}$$

$$x = 1.28(100) + 500 = 628 \quad \text{(example)}$$

(6.3)

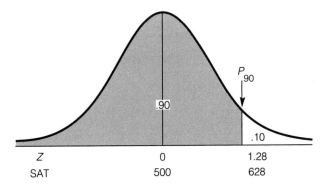

Figure 6.8 90th Percentile of the Distribution of SAT Scores.

Thus, 628 is the 90th percentile of SAT scores, as illustrated in Figure 6.8. ■

■ **EXAMPLE 7**

If 1 million high school students took the SAT, how many would score in the 90th percentile or higher?

   We have already determined in Example 5 that .10 of the area or 10% of the scores are above a Z score of 1.28, and 10% of 1 million is 100,000. We would expect to find 100,000 high school students in the 90th percentile or higher. ■

   Knowing how to compute areas under a normal curve makes it easy to find the proportion (probability) of persons possessing certain cholesterol values, heights, or any other variable that is normally distributed. Knowing the probability of a given event allows us to draw appropriate inferences as to the expected occurrence of that event.

◆ **CONCLUSION**

The normal distribution is an important concept for a number of reasons. It has been used to define "normal limits" for clinical variables. Many variables follow a normal distribution. The assumption of normality proves extremely useful because of the exceptional properties of the distribution. We can quickly reduce any normal distribution to the standard normal distribution by transforming the variable to a Z score. Because these Z scores and the normal curve areas corresponding to them are conveniently tabulated, we are able to compute the probability of occurrence of various events and thus to decide about the degree of uniqueness of those events.

◆ VOCABULARY LIST

bell-shaped curve
clinical limits
exponential equation
normal distribution
 (Gaussian
 distribution)

normal limits
percentile
standard normal
 distribution

standardized score
Z score (Z value;
 standard score)

◆ EXERCISES

6.1 Find the area under the normal curve that lies between the given values of Z.
   a. Z = 0 and Z = 2.37
   b. Z = 0 and Z = −1.94
   c. Z = −1.85 and Z = 1.85
   d. Z = −0.76 and Z = 1.13
   e. Z = 0 and Z = 3.09
   f. Z = −2.77 and Z = −0.96

6.2 Determine the area under the normal curve falling to the right of Z (or to the left of −Z).
   a. Z = 1.73
   b. Z = −2.41 and Z = 2.41
   c. Z = 2.55
   d. Z = −3 and Z = 3
   e. Z = 5

6.3 What Z scores correspond to the following areas under the normal curve?
   a. area of .05 to the right of +Z
   b. area of .01 to the left of −Z
   c. area of .05 beyond ±Z
   d. area of .01 beyond ±Z
   e. area of .90 between ±Z
   f. area of .95 between ±Z

6.4 Find the Z score for
   a. the 95th percentile
   b. the 80th percentile
   c. the 50th percentile
   d. the 30th percentile
   e. the 20th percentile

6.5 The following figure shows the assumed distribution for systolic blood pressure readings of a large male population.
   a. Determine the Z score for the various cutoff points.
   b. Find the equivalent cutoff points in terms of systolic blood pressures if the mean reading is 120 and the standard deviation is 15.
   c. Find the 95th percentile.

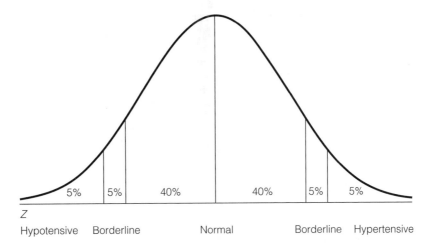

5%	5%	40%	40%	5%	5%

Z

Hypotensive   Borderline   Normal   Borderline   Hypertensive

6.6 If the heights of male youngsters are normally distributed with a mean of 60 inches and a standard deviation of 10, what percentage of the boys' heights (in inches) would we expect to be
a. between 45 and 75
b. between 30 and 90
c. less than 50
d. 45 or more
e. 75 or more
f. between 50 and 75

6.7 An instructor is administering a final examination. She tells her class that she will give an A to the 10% of the students who earn the highest grades. Past experience with the same examination has shown that the mean grade is 75 and the standard deviation is 8. If the present class runs true to form, what grade would a student need in order to earn an A?

6.8 Assume that the age at onset of disease X is distributed normally with a mean of 50 years and a standard deviation of 12 years. What is the probability that an individual afflicted with disease X developed it before age 35?

6.9 a. What is the distinction between a normal distribution and the standard normal distribution?
b. Why do statisticians prefer to work with the standard normal distribution rather than the normal distribution?

6.10 a. Describe the normal distribution.
b. Give two examples of random variables that appear to be normally distributed.
c. What is the probability that the value of a randomly selected variable from a normal distribution will be more than 3 standard deviations from its mean value?

6.11 a. Suppose that 25-year-old males have a remaining mean life expectancy of 55 with a standard deviation of 6. What proportion of 25-year-old males will live past 65?
b. What assumption do you have to make in (a) to obtain a valid answer?

6.12 SAT scores were standardized with a population mean, μ, of 500 and a population standard deviation, σ, of 100 on both the math and verbal portions. The following questions refer to the math portion.

 a. A highly selective school decides that it will consider only applicants with a score in the top 5%. What will be the minimum score (cutoff point) that you must have in order to be considered for admission to this school?

 b. If 1 million students took the SAT, how many of these students would be viable applicants to this school?

 c. Another school targets students between the 60th and 90th percentiles as the most likely applicants. What would be the SAT scores for the 60th and 90th percentiles?

 d. If the school in (c) wants to send out a mass mailing to all students who scored between the 60th and 90th percentiles, and if 1 million students took the SAT, how many pieces of mail would be sent?

 e. What would be the minimum and the maximum SAT scores for the middle 90% of students who took the SAT?

 f. What percentage of students would have math SAT scores of less than 350?

6.13 Explain why "clinical limits" may be more appropriate than "normal limits" in classifying certain clinical values as "abnormal."

6.14 The weights of 18- to 24-year-old women are normally distributed with a mean of 132 pounds and a standard deviation of 27.4. If one randomly selected 150 of these women ages 18–24, how many of them would be expected to weigh 100–150 pounds?

6.15 If blackout thresholds are normally distributed with a mean of 4.7G and a standard deviation of 0.8G, find the probability of randomly selecting a pilot with a blackout threshold that is less than 3.5G.

6.16 Your last statistics quiz had a mean of 30 and a standard deviation of 6. Assume a normal distribution.

 a. What is the median?

 b. What is the Z score of the mean?

 c. In order to get an A, your Z score must be +1.5 or above. What is the minimum raw score necessary?

 d. A Z score of −2.0 and below will be an F. What is that raw score?

 e. If your raw score is 27, what is your Z score?

 f. What raw score would be at the 95th percentile?

Your kind and understanding statistics instructor decides to give everyone in the class an extra point on his or her raw score.

 g. What is the new mean?

 h. If you had a Z score of −1.00 before the extra point, what is your Z score after the extra point?

 i. In order to get an A, you still must have a Z score +1.5 from the mean. What is the minimum raw score necessary?

 j. If your statistics instructor bases his grades on the normal curve (i.e., curves his grades), what effect will the extra point have on your grade?

6.17 Two hundred students took a test. The scores were normally distributed. Your score was in the 60th percentile. How many people scored at or below your score?

6.18 If the mean serum cholesterol level in Table 3.1 is 217 and the variance is 750, determine the probability that a randomly selected person would have a cholesterol value:
   a. between 150 and 250
   b. greater than 250
   c. less than 150

6.19 If adult male cholesterol is normally distributed with $\mu = 200$ and $\sigma = 25$, what is the probability of selecting a male whose cholesterol is:
   a. less than 165
   b. greater than 165
   c. between 165 and 220
   d. greater than 220

6.20 Serum cholesterol levels were taken from a population of college students. The results were normally distributed. Males had a mean of 195 and a standard deviation of 10. Females had a mean of 185 and a standard deviation of 12.
   a. What were the cholesterol levels of the highest 5% of the males?
   b. What were the cholesterol levels of the highest 5% of the females?
   c. What percentage of males would have a cholesterol level of less than 180?
   d. What percentage of females would have a cholesterol level of less than 180?
   e. What percentage of males would have a cholesterol level between 180 and 200?
   f. What percentage of females would have a cholesterol level between 180 and 200?
   g. Concern was expressed by the health educators on a particular college campus of 10,000 that students with serum cholesterol levels above 200 might be at an increased risk of heart disease. If the campus was equally divided between males and females, how many males and how many females on this campus would be at increased risk?

7 Sampling Distribution of Means and Estimation

CHAPTER OUTLINE

✔ LEARNING OBJECTIVES

After studying this chapter, you should be able to

1. Distinguish between the distribution of a population and the distribution of its sample means

2. Explain the importance of the central limit theorem

3. Identify the main parts of the central limit theorem

4. Apply the principles of sampling distributions to predict the behavior of sample means

5. Compute and interpret the standard error of the mean

6. Explain the rationale for degrees of freedom

7. Calculate and interpret confidence intervals

8. Determine when to use a t distribution

7.1 THE DISTRIBUTION OF A POPULATION AND THE DISTRIBUTION OF ITS SAMPLE MEANS

Statisticians are interested in drawing inferences about a population. For example, it would be prohibitively expensive to conduct a health status survey by giving everyone in the United States a standardized comprehensive physical examination. Instead, a statistician would recommend that a sample be examined to estimate the important health parameters of the population. Such estimates, being random variables, would be expected to vary from sample to sample. In fact, if we were to select a large number of samples from a population and tabulate the sample means, the result would be a distribution of sample means. And we might be surprised at the shape of that distribution.

It is of fundamental importance to make a clear distinction between a distribution of sample means and the **population distribution** of observations. A **distribution of sample means** is the set of values of sample means obtained from all possible samples of the same size (n) from a given population; that is, it is the population of all values of that statistic (sample mean in this case).

A distribution of sample means can be readily illustrated by again using the data of blood glucose measurements from the Honolulu Heart Study (see Table 7.1 and Figures 7.1 and 7.2). Figure 7.1 illustrates the distribution of blood glucose values for the entire population of 7683 men. The population mean, μ, is 161.52, and its standard deviation, σ, is 58.15. These parameters are based on all 7683 cases. Suppose you select a sample of size 25 from this population and compute its sample mean $\bar{x}$ and standard deviation s. If, with $n = 25$, you repeat this random sampling scheme a number of times, you will generate a new distribution, that of the means of the samples. This particular random sampling was done 400 times to generate the distribution of sample means shown in the right-hand column of Table 7.1. If it were possible to select all possible samples of size 25 from the population of 7683, the result would be 8.524×10^{71} samples, an overwhelmingly large number! (In practice, of course, we take only one sample.)

As you can see in Figure 7.2, the distribution of sample means is symmetrical, roughly bell-shaped, and centered close to the population mean of 161.52 but with considerably less variation than the distribution of individual glucose values shown in Figure 7.1.

Table 7.1 Distribution of the Population and Distribution of Means from Samples for Blood Glucose Measurements of Men in the Honolulu Heart Study

Blood Glucose (mg/100 ml)	Number of Observations (frequency)	Sample Means ($n = 25$) (frequency)
30.1– 45.0	2	
45.1– 60.0	15	
60.1– 75.0	40	
75.1– 90.0	210	
90.1–105.0	497	
105.1–120.0	977	
120.1–135.0	1073	5
135.1–150.0	1083	62
150.1–165.0	849	201
165.1–180.0	691	109
180.1–195.0	569	23
195.1–210.0	440	
210.1–225.0	343	
225.1–240.0	291	
240.1–255.0	153	
255.1–270.0	115	
270.1–285.0	82	
285.1–300.0	60	
300.1–315.0	38	
315.1–330.0	18	
330.1–345.0	26	
345.1–360.0	19	
360.1–375.0	20	
375.1–390.0	9	
390.1–405.0	13	
405.1–420.0	11	
420.1–435.0	6	
435.1–450.0	5	
450.1–465.0	4	
465.1–480.0	24	
Total	7683	400

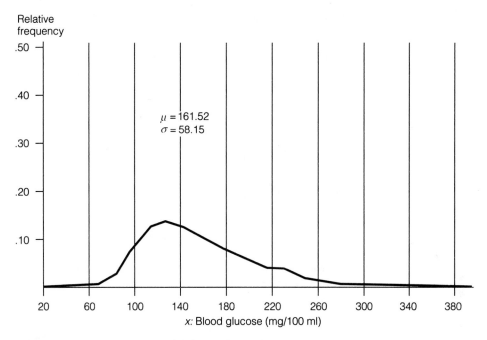

Figure 7.1 Distribution of Blood Glucose Values from the Honolulu Heart Study Population ($N = 7683$).

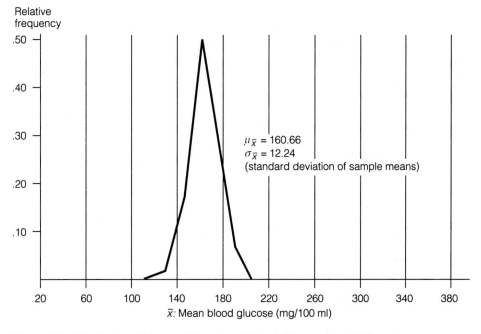

Figure 7.2 Distribution of Means of Samples of Blood Glucose ($n = 25$) from the Honolulu Heart Study.

7.2 CENTRAL LIMIT THEOREM

A quick glance at Figures 7.1 and 7.2 shows one striking similarity and an equally striking difference. The mean of the distribution of sample means is almost identical to the mean of the underlying population. In contrast, the variability of sample means is far less than that of the population. This difference is quite evident from the broad, flat curve of blood glucose readings compared to the narrow, peaked curve of their means. Another noteworthy characteristic is that the distribution of sample means is approximately bell-shaped and symmetrical, whereas the original population distribution was noticeably skewed. This may seem to be unusual, and even paradoxical. Indeed it is! It is one of the most remarkable features of mathematical statistics, called the central limit theorem.

The **central limit theorem** states that for a randomly selected sample of size n (n should be at least 25, but the larger n is, the better the approximation) with a mean μ and a standard deviation σ:

1. The distribution of sample means $\bar{x}$ is approximately normal regardless of whether the population distribution is normal.

From statistical theory come these two additional principles:

2. The mean of the distribution of sample means is equal to the mean of the population distribution—that is, $\mu_{\bar{x}} = \mu$.
3. The standard deviation of the distribution of sample means is equal to the standard deviation of the population divided by the square root of the sample size—that is,

$$\sigma_{\bar{x}} = \frac{\sigma}{\sqrt{n}} \tag{7.1}$$

We illustrate these three principles in Figure 7.3, which shows four very different population distributions. For each, as the sample size n increases, the sampling distribution of the mean approaches normality, regardless of whether the original population distribution was normal. A close scrutiny also reveals that, for any population distribution, the mean of each sampling distribution is the same as the mean (μ) of the population itself. Note also that as the sample size increases the variability of the sampling distribution becomes progressively smaller.

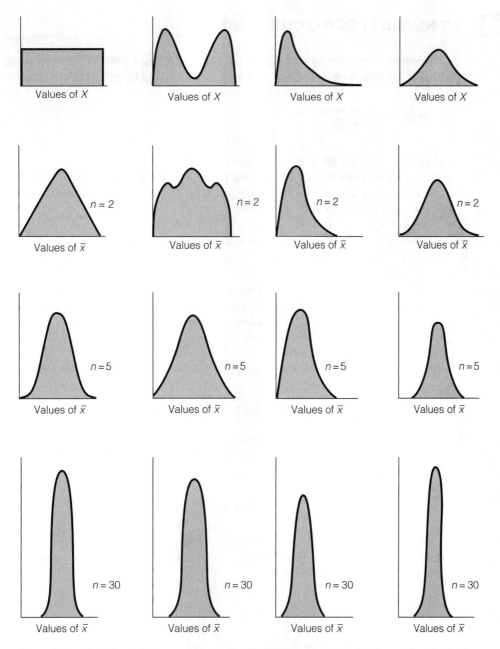

Figure 7.3 The Effect of Shape of Population Distribution and Sample Size on the Distribution of Means of Random Samples.

7.3   STANDARD ERROR OF THE MEAN

The measure of variation of the distribution of sample means, $\sigma/\sqrt{n}$, referred to as the **standard error of the mean,** is denoted as $\text{SE}(\bar{x})$—that is,

$$\text{SE}(\bar{x}) = \sigma_{\bar{x}} = \frac{\sigma}{\sqrt{n}} \tag{7.2}$$

$\text{SE}(\bar{x})$ is a counterpart of the standard deviation in that it is a measure of variation, but variation of sample means rather than of individual observations. It is an important statistical tool because it is a measure of the amount of sampling error. Sampling error differs from other errors in that it can be reduced at will, provided you are willing to increase the sample size. A nearly universal application of the standard error of the mean in medical literature is to specify an interval of $\bar{x} \pm 2\text{SE}(\bar{x})$, which includes the population mean, μ, with about 95% probability.

To prove the central limit theorem requires a considerable mathematical background beyond the level of this book. However, the sampling experiment of Figures 7.1 and 7.2 is in itself convincing evidence of the theorem's truthfulness. In these figures, we can see the following:

1. The mean of the distribution of sample means $\mu_{\bar{x}}$ is nearly identical to the population mean μ.
2. The standard deviation of the sample means computed by use of the traditional formula $\sqrt{\Sigma(\bar{x} - \mu_{\bar{x}})^2/(n-1)}$ is 12.24, very close to the standard error of the mean computed by using $\sigma_{\bar{x}} = \sigma/\sqrt{n} = 11.63$. This is an impressive result; it is now possible to compute the standard error of the mean knowing only the sample size and the population σ or its estimate s.
3. The distribution of sample means is approximately normally distributed.

In practice, σ is seldom known. We estimate it from the sample standard deviation s; consequently, the equation most commonly used for computing the standard error of the mean is

$$s_{\bar{x}} = \frac{s}{\sqrt{n}} \tag{7.3}$$

Note that $s_{\bar{x}}$ is estimated from a sample when σ is unknown.

Often we encounter data that are not normally distributed. This situation may present a problem in statistical analysis, but by working with sample means, we can meet the assumption of normality, provided the sample size is sufficient (about 25 or more).

Because the central limit theorem states that sample means are approximately normally distributed, it is possible to find the area under the curve for the normal distribution of sample means. To find it, we must again use the Z transformation—that is, compute a Z score. For sample means, the equation for Z is

$$Z = \frac{\bar{x} - \mu}{\sigma/\sqrt{n}} \tag{7.4}$$

This computed Z also establishes the relative position of $\bar{x}$ in a distribution of sample means.

7.4 STUDENT'S *t* DISTRIBUTION

All too often, the population standard deviation σ is unknown. Without σ, we are unable to calculate the Z score. We know, however, that when σ is unknown it may be estimated by s, the sample standard deviation. In Chapter 4, we calculated s like this:

$$s = \sqrt{\frac{\Sigma(x - \bar{x})^2}{n - 1}} \quad \text{or} \quad \sqrt{\frac{\sum\limits_{i=1}^{n} x_i^2 - \dfrac{\left(\sum\limits_{i=1}^{n} x_i\right)^2}{n}}{n - 1}}$$

Can this s be used instead of the σ in equation (7.4)? Fortunately, yes. But we no longer have the standard normal distribution. Instead, we have a distribution that was discovered in 1906 and published in 1908 by William S. Gossett, an English chemist and statistician employed by the Guinness Brewery in Dublin. Because the brewery, fearing release of trade secrets, rarely permitted publications by its employees, Gossett published under the pseudonym "Student." So his distribution is commonly referred to as **Student's *t* distribution.** The equation for its *t* score is

$$t = \frac{\bar{x} - \mu}{s/\sqrt{n}} \tag{7.5}$$

This *t* distribution is similar to the standard normal distribution in that it is unimodal, bell-shaped, and symmetrical, and extends infinitely in either direction. Furthermore, although the curve has more variance than the normal distribution, its area still equals 1.0. Areas under the curve, designated as α in Table B (inside back cover), are a function of a quantity called **degrees of freedom** (df), where

$$df = n - 1 \tag{7.6}$$

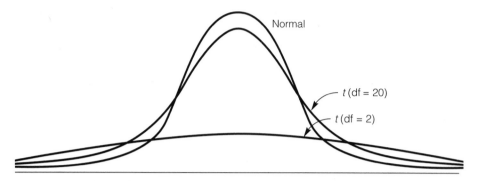

Figure 7.4 Comparison of *t* Distributions and the Normal Distribution.

when estimating the standard deviation from a single sample. Degrees of freedom measure the quantity of information available in a data set that can be
used in estimating the population variance σ^2. Therefore, they are an indication of the reliability of *s*, in that the larger the sample size, the more reliable *s*
will be as an estimate of σ. It follows that the variance of the *t* distribution of
means from large samples is less than that from small samples. Note that when
the sample size exceeds about 30 the *t* distribution so closely approximates the
normal distribution that for practical purposes the normal distribution may be
used. In other words, for large samples, *s* becomes a quite reliable estimate of
σ, as graphically illustrated in Figure 7.4. From the figure, we can see that there
are many *t* distributions, one for each degree of freedom.

   The *t* distribution introduces the concept of infinite degrees of freedom for
large sample sizes. In fact, the *t* distribution for infinite degrees of freedom is
precisely equal to the normal distribution. This equality is readily seen by comparing the critical values for df = ∞ (infinity) of Table B for various values of α
with those of Table A. The approximation is good beginning with 25 df and
nearly identical at 30 df. The percentage points of the *t* distribution in Table B
are given for a limited number of areas. For example, the *t* value for α = .05
with 15 df equals 1.753. It is found by locating df = 15 in the margin and reading the value *t* = 1.753 in the column labeled area = .95. Here α denotes the
area in the tail under the curve.

   When should the *t* distribution be used? Use it when the population standard deviation is not known. If the population standard deviation, σ, is known,
then you should use the normal distribution and Z scores. As the sample size
approaches 50, there is little difference between Z and *t* scores. However, even
with a large sample and an unknown population standard deviation, the technically correct choice is the *t* distribution. Any statistical program, such as SAS
or SPSS, can easily calculate either Z or *t*, but it is the responsibility of the researcher to select the appropriate procedure.

   To summarize, Table 7.2 presents the equations for Student's *t* distribution,
along with other equations introduced in this chapter.

Table 7.2 Characteristics of a Population Distribution and Its Distribution of Sample Means

Characteristic	Population Distribution	Distribution of Sample Means
Mean	μ	$\mu_{\bar{x}} = \mu$
Measure of variation	σ	$\sigma_{\bar{x}} = \dfrac{\sigma}{\sqrt{n}}$
Z score	$Z = \dfrac{x - \mu}{\sigma}$	$Z = \dfrac{\bar{x} - \mu}{\sigma/\sqrt{n}}$
t statistic		$t = \dfrac{\bar{x} - \mu}{s/\sqrt{n}}$

7.5 APPLICATION

Using the blood glucose observations from the entire Honolulu Heart Study population (see Figure 7.1), we find that $\mu = 161.52$ and $\sigma = 58.15$. Suppose we select samples of size 25 from this population: (1) What proportion of sample means would have values of 170 or greater? and (2) What proportion of sample means would have values of 155 or lower?

For question 1, we reduce the problem to Z scores so we can determine the proportion of the area that is beyond Z. On obtaining

$$Z = \frac{170 - 161.52}{58.15/\sqrt{25}} = \frac{8.49}{11.63} = .73$$

we turn to Table A (inside back cover), which shows that the area to the right of $Z = .73$ is $.5 - .2673$, or about 23%.

For question 2, using the same technique, we can find the value of the Z score corresponding to the sample mean 155:

$$Z = \frac{155 - 161.52}{58.15/\sqrt{25}} = \frac{-6.25}{11.63} = -.56$$

Table A reveals that the area below $Z = -.56$ is $.5 - .2123 = .2877$, or about 29%.

7.6 DEGREES OF FREEDOM: A NONMATHEMATICAL EXPLANATION

You have just been introduced to the concept of degrees of freedom. With a one-sample t distribution, you also know that calculating degrees of freedom is simple: $n - 1$. Later, you will see other examples with slightly different formulas for calculating degrees of freedom. But this still does not answer the question that most statistics professors dread: "What exactly are degrees of freedom?" Mathematically, it is not a particularly difficult concept to define, but how do we explain it to students who are not math majors and may not be very adept at math?

Suppose you have 10 people, and they can pick either a positive or a negative number. The only requirement is that the sum of all 10 numbers equal zero. The first 9 people can pick any number between minus infinity (-00) and plus infinity ($+00$). However, after the first 9 numbers are chosen, if the sum of the 10 numbers is going to equal zero, the 10th number must be a specific number. There is no choice or freedom. Because there were 10 samples, the degrees of freedom are $n - 1 = 9$. The degrees of freedom are equal to the number of independent pieces of information used to estimate the parameter. In Chapter 4, you learned to calculate the population variance, σ^2, and sample variance, s^2. As you may recall, the only difference between the two involves whether to divide by N, for the population variance, or $n-1$, for the sample variance. If σ^2 is unknown, then s^2 can be used to estimate the parameter, σ^2. Because σ^2 is estimated by n number of independent scores, the degrees of freedom will equal the number (n) of independent scores minus the number of parameters, or $n - 1$ in the case of the one-sample t distribution. Although this explanation may not be fully satisfactory, it is probably preferable to this mathematical response: "Degrees of freedom are the rank of the quadratic form."

7.7 POPULATION ESTIMATES

Whenever you draw a sample from a population, you eventually want to use the sample statistics to estimate population values or population parameters. There are two ways of estimating population parameters: a point estimate and a confidence interval estimate.

A **point estimate** of the population mean, μ, is the sample mean, $\bar{x}$, computed from a random sample of the population. Because $\bar{x}$ is a statistic, the point estimate varies from sample to sample. In fact, repeating the experiment a number of times would yield a range of $\bar{x}$'s, any one of which would be a point estimate of the same population parameter. A drawback to the point estimate is that it fails to make a probability statement as to how close the estimate ($\bar{x}$) is to the population parameter (μ). In other words, how close does the sample mean come to the population mean? This flaw is remedied by use of a **confidence interval** (CI)—a group of numbers for which we have a specified degree of assurance that the value of the parameter was captured. A confidence interval allows us to estimate the unknown parameter μ and provides a margin for error indicating how good our estimate is. Using only the Z score, we can derive the equation for an interval that has a known probability of including the population mean, μ. With this method, we can be confident that 95% of all sample means fall within ±1.96 standard deviations of the population mean. This formula allows us to calculate what is usually referred to as the 95% confidence interval:

$$\text{95\% CI of } \mu = \pm 1.96(\sigma/\sqrt{n}) \tag{7.7}$$

To calculate the 99% confidence interval, we use

$$\text{99\% CI of } \mu = \pm 2.58(\sigma/\sqrt{n}) \tag{7.8}$$

We can use the data from the one-sample Z test to illustrate point estimates and confidence intervals. From Table 3.1, we determined that for a sample of 100 men we had a mean, $\bar{x}$, blood glucose level of 161.84. If we took another random sample of 100 from the same population, would you expect the mean to again be 161.84? That is highly unlikely. We expect the mean, $\bar{x}$, or point estimate, to vary from sample to sample. In fact, if we were to repeat the sampling a number of times, we would find a range of $\bar{x}$'s, any one of which would be an acceptable point estimate of the population parameter.

■ EXAMPLE 1

To estimate the population mean blood glucose level, μ, from the Honolulu Heart Study, we can calculate the 95% and 99% confidence intervals, using equations (7.7) and (7.8). We already know that $\bar{x} = 161.84$ and $\sigma = 58.15$. From Table 3.1, our sample size is 100. The 95% confidence interval is

$$\text{95\% CI for } \mu = 161.84 \pm 1.96(58.15/\sqrt{100}) = (150.44, 173.24)$$

and the 99% confidence interval is

$$\text{99\% CI for } \mu = 161.84 \pm 2.58(58.15/\sqrt{100}) = (146.84, 176.84)$$

The values 150.44 and 173.24 are the lower and upper **95% confidence limits.** The interval from 150.44 to 173.24 is the 95% confidence interval. Similarly, the values 146.84 and 176.84 are the lower and upper **99% confidence limits,** and the interval from 146.84 to 176.84 is the 99% confidence interval. In this case, we have the luxury of knowing that our population mean, μ, is 160.66, so we can determine that we did indeed capture the population mean with both the 95% and 99% confidence intervals. ■

These confidence intervals are not used very often because they suffer from a major drawback: σ is usually not known. But we have already established that when σ is unknown we can estimate it by s, the sample standard deviation. As before, to construct the interval, we use a t value (with $n - 1$ df) instead of the Z value. By using a procedure parallel to the one employed for equations (7.7) and (7.8), we can obtain the confidence interval when only s (not σ) is known:

$$(1 - \alpha)100\% \text{ CI for } \mu = \bar{x} \pm t \, (s/\sqrt{n}) \tag{7.9}$$

The t value that you use in equation (7.9) will *always* come from Table B (inside back cover) and will *always* be from the two-sided, or two-tailed, column (labeled .95 and .99).

■ EXAMPLE 2

If we wished to estimate the mean VO_2 uptake for a population of joggers from a sample of 25, we could use the 95% confidence interval for μ. Our sample has an $\bar{x}$ of 47.5 ml/kg, and $s = 4.8$ for a sample of 25. In Table B, we find that the t value for 24 df (df $= n - 1$) for .95 (two-sided) is 2.064. The 95% confidence interval is thus

$$95\% \text{ CI for } \mu = \bar{x} \pm 2.064 \, (s/\sqrt{n})$$

$$= 47.5 \pm 2.064 \, (4.5/\sqrt{25})$$

$$= 47.5 \pm 1.98$$

$$= (45.5, 49.5 \text{ ml/kg})$$

The result: Upon many repetitions of this experiment, we would expect 95% of such intervals—$\bar{x} - 2.064(s/\sqrt{n})$ to $\bar{x} + 2.064(s/\sqrt{n})$—to capture the population mean, μ. The values of 45.5 ml/kg and 49.5 ml/kg are the lower and upper 95% confidence limits. The interval 45.5 ml/kg to 49.5 ml/kg is the 95% confidence interval. ■

If we were calculating the 99% confidence interval, we would follow the exact same procedure, except the t value from Table B would come from the .99 (two-sided) column. This number would be 2.797. The 95% confidence interval is used quite commonly, as is the 99% confidence interval. Other percentages may be used, but they are less frequently encountered in practice.

A Cautionary Note About Interpreting Confidence Intervals

We just calculated the 95% (150.44–173.24) and 99% (146.84–176.84) confidence intervals for blood glucose levels. Based on the sample mean, we are trying to determine the population mean. We have either a 95% or a 99% chance of capturing the population mean. This is not the same as saying that 95% or 99% of the individual scores lie between the respective confidence intervals. As evidence, if you sort the blood glucose values from Table 3.1, you will find that 88 and 80 of the 100 scores fall outside the 95% and 99% confidence intervals, respectively. The key point to remember is that the confidence intervals are designed to capture the population mean. The confidence intervals do *not* tell you the percentage of individual scores that fall between the upper and lower limits.

Calculating Confidence Intervals Using SPSS

The calculation of confidence intervals using SPSS is a relatively simple process. Go to the menu and select Analyze. Under Analyze, choose Descriptives and then Explore to open the Explore dialog box. From Table 3.1, you can click any of the variables in the Dependent List. Next, choose Statistics. The 95% confidence interval is the default option. If you want the 99% confidence interval, choose Statistics from the Dialog box, and replace 95 with 99.

7.8 ASSUMPTIONS NECESSARY TO PERFORM *t* TESTS

To perform a test of hypotheses, the following two assumptions need to be met:

1. That the observations are randomly selected
2. That the distribution is a normal distribution

Sometimes the assumptions are not met, and individuals performing the *t* test still obtain valid results because the *t* test has a characteristic referred to as "being robust." In other words, it can handle the violation of the assumptions.

◆ CONCLUSION

A distinction exists between the distribution of a population's observations and the distribution of its sample means. A powerful tool called the central limit theorem gives reassuring results: No matter how unlike normal a population distribution may be, the distribution of its sample means will be approximately normal, provided only that the sample size is reasonably large ($n \geq 30$). The mean of the sampling distribution is equal to the mean of the population distribution. The standard error of sample means equals the standard deviation of the observations divided by the square root of the sample size. In sampling experiments, these results are often applied to determine how unusual a sample mean is.

◆ VOCABULARY LIST

central limit theorem	degrees of freedom	population distribution
confidence interval	distribution of sample	standard error
confidence limits	means	of the mean
(95% and 99%)	point estimate	Student's *t* distribution

◆ EXERCISES

7.1 Suppose samples of size $n = 36$ are drawn from the population of Exercise 6.5. Describe the distribution of the means of these samples.

7.2 If samples of size $n = 25$ are selected from the population of Exercise 6.6, what percentage of the sample means would you expect to be
a. between 57 and 63
b. less than 58
c. 61 or larger

7.3 Repeat Exercise 7.2, but this time use a sample size of 64.

7.4 After completing Exercises 7.2 and 7.3, explain the effect of an increasingly larger sample size on the probabilities you calculated in Exercises 7.2 and 7.3.

7.5 Refer to the population of Exercise 6.8.
a. What is the standard error of the mean for $n = 16$?
b. What is the standard error of the mean for $n = 64$?
c. What is true about the relationship between n and $SE(\bar{x})$?

7.6 Suppose heights of 20-year-old men are approximately normally distributed with a mean of 71 in. and a population standard deviation of 5 in. A random sample of fifteen 20-year-old men is selected and measured. Find the probability that the sample mean $\bar{x}$
a. is at least 77 in.
b. lies between 65 and 75 in.
c. is not more than 63 in.

7.7 If the mean length of newborn infants is 52.5 cm and the standard deviation is 4.5 cm, what is the probability that the mean of a sample of (a) size 10 and (b) size 15 is greater than 56 cm?

7.8 Suppose that the mean weight of infants born in a community is $\mu = 3360$ g and $\sigma = 490$ g.
a. Find $P(2300 < x < 4300)$.
b. Find $P(x \le 2500)$.
c. Find $P(x \ge 5000)$.
What must you assume about the distribution of birth weights to make the answers to (a), (b), and (c) valid?

7.9 Suppose you select a sample of 49 infants from the population described in Exercise 7.8.
a. What are the mean and standard error of this sampling distribution?
b. Find $P(3100 < \bar{x} < 3600)$.
c. Find $P(\bar{x} < 2500)$.
d. Find $P(\bar{x} > 3540)$.
What must you assume about the distribution of birthweights to make the answers to (b), (c), and (d) valid?

7.10 If the mean number of cigarettes smoked by pregnant women is 16 and the standard deviation is 8, find the probability that in a random sample of 100 pregnant women the mean number of cigarettes smoked will be greater than 24.

7.11   a. Describe the three main points of the central limit theorem.
     b. What conditions must be met for the central limit theorem to be applicable?
     c. Explain why the central limit theorem plays such an important role in inferential statistics.

7.12   a. Describe the difference between the distribution of observations from a population and a distribution of its sample means.
     b. What are the differences between the standard deviation and the standard error?
     c. When would we want to use the standard deviation, and when the standard error?

7.13   a. Describe the difference between the Z and the t distributions.
     b. Under what condition is the t distribution equivalent to the Z distribution?
     c. If you had the choice of using the Z distribution or the t distribution, which would you use? Why?

7.14   If the cholesterol level of men in the community is normally distributed with a mean of 200 and a standard deviation of 25, what is the probability that a randomly selected sample of 49 men will have a mean between 190 and 205?

7.15   Compare the critical value ($Z = \pm1.96$) that corresponds to 5% of the tail area of the normal distribution with the critical values of the t distribution for df $= 9, 19, 29$, and ∞. As the degree of freedom increases (which means that the sample size increases), what happens to the value of t compared with the value of Z? Explain why this is occurring.

7.16   If the forced vital capacity of 11-year-old white males is normally distributed with a mean of 2400 cc and $\sigma = 400$, find the probability that a sample of size $n = 64$ will provide a mean
     a. greater than 2500
     b. between 2300 and 2500
     c. less than 2350

7.17   a. Find the standard error in Exercise 7.16.
     b. If you want SE($\bar{x}$) to be one-half its size in Exercise 7.16, how large a sample would you need to have?

7.18   Suppose systolic blood pressure of 17-year-old females is approximately normally distributed with a mean of 118 mmHg and a standard deviation of 12 mmHg.
     a. What proportion of girls would you expect to have blood pressures between 112 mmHg and 124 mmHg?
     b. If you were to select a sample of 16 girls and obtain their mean systolic blood pressure, what proportion of such samples would you expect between 112 mmHg and 124 mmHg?
     c. Compare the results of (a) and (b), and explain the reason for the difference.

7.19   For data that are normally distributed, how much area is included under the normal curve
     a. within $\pm1\sigma$
     b. with ±1 SE($\bar{x}$) for a distribution of sample means
     Compare (a) and (b), and state why the results do or do not surprise you.

7.20 For Table 2.1, $\bar{x} = 73$ and $\sigma^2 = 121$. If a person is chosen at random, what is the probability that she or he would have a diastolic blood pressure
   a. between 80 and 100
   b. less than 70
   c. greater than 90

7.21 The mean blood glucose in Table 3.1 is 152 and $\sigma = 55$. Find the probability that a randomly selected individual would have a glucose value
   a. between 80 and 120
   b. less than 80
   c. greater than 200

7.22 For data that are normally distributed with a mean of 150 and $\sigma = 40$, determine the proportion of individuals who would fall
   a. below 100
   b. between 100 and 200
   c. above 160
   d. below 160

7.23 If you selected a sample of size $n = 100$ from the population given in Exercise 7.22, find the probability of obtaining a value of x below 160.

7.24 Redo Exercise 7.8, but substitute $\sigma = 460$ g for $\sigma = 490$ g.

7.25 If you are sampling an obviously nonnormal population, what other fact can you use to justify performing tests of hypotheses?

7.26 For Table 2.1, $\bar{x} = 73$ and $\sigma = 11$. Calculate the 95% and 99% confidence intervals.

7.27 Using the data from Exercise 7.22, calculate the 95% and 99% confidence intervals. Assume that 150 is the sample mean and the sample size is 100.

7.28 Using the data from Table 3.1, select a random sample of 40 subjects and a random sample of 60 subjects. Use only data that are interval or ratio. Calculate the 95% and 99% confidence intervals.

8

One-Sample Significance Testing, Point Estimates, and Confidence Intervals

CHAPTER OUTLINE

8.10   **Effect of Sample Size on Confidence Intervals**
Offers methods for determining in advance the sample size
needed to design an efficient study

8.11   **P Values and Statistical Significance**
Explains how P values are used to determine statistical
significance

8.12   **Determining Exact P Values from Z Scores**
Demonstrates how to calculate an exact P value from any
Z score

8.13   **One- and Two-Tailed P Values**
Describes the difference between and the appropriate use of
one- and two-tailed P values, including ethical considerations

8.14   **P Values and the t Distribution**
Describes the relationship between P values and hypothesis
testing, and shows the two ways P values are normally
reported in journal articles

8.15   **Type I and Type II Errors**
Discusses two types of errors in the performance of a test
of significance

8.16   **Type I and Type II Errors and Probability Revisited**
Identifies situations that potentially lead to type I and type II
errors, and explains why the term *error* does not necessarily
mean that a mistake has been made

✔ LEARNING OBJECTIVES

After studying this chapter, you should be able to

1. Outline and explain the procedure for a test of significance
2. Explain the meaning of a null hypothesis and an alternative hypothesis
3. Define statistical significance
4. Find the value of Z or t corresponding to a specified significance level, α
5. Distinguish between a one-tailed and a two-tailed test
6. Distinguish between the critical value and the test statistic
7. Determine when to use a Z test and when to use a t test
8. Calculate and interpret a one-sample Z test and a one-sample t test
9. Compute a confidence interval from a set of data for a single population mean

(Continued)

10. Interpret and explain a confidence interval
11. Distinguish between a probability interval and a confidence interval
12. Demonstrate how to narrow the confidence interval
13. Express results in terms of P values
14. Calculate an exact P value for a Z score
15. Determine the sample size required to estimate a variable at a given level of accuracy
16. Explain why it is unethical to choose a one-tailed test after data have been collected and analyzed
17. Explain the meaning and relationship of the two types of errors made in testing hypotheses

8.1   HYPOTHESIS TESTING

One of the principal objectives of research is comparison: How does one group differ from another? Specifically, we may encounter questions such as these: What is the mean serum cholesterol level of a group of middle-aged men? How does it differ from that of women? From that of men of other ages? How does today's level differ from that of a decade ago? Is the latest drug effective in reducing cholesterol levels? What are the effects of various diets on serum cholesterol levels?

These are typical questions that can be handled by the primary tools of classical statistical inference—estimation and hypothesis testing. The unknown characteristic, or **parameter,** of a population is usually estimated from a statistic computed from sample data. Ordinarily, we are interested in estimating the mean and the standard deviation of some characteristic of the population. The purpose of statistical inference is to reach conclusions from our data and to support our conclusions with probability statements. With such information, we will be able to decide whether an observed effect is real or is due to chance. In this chapter, we will use a single sample to explain hypothesis testing, as well as estimation and confidence intervals.

8.2   DEFINITIONS

Before getting into the step-by-step procedure of a test of significance, you will find it helpful to look over the following definitions:

Hypothesis—a statement of belief used in the evaluation of population values.

Null hypothesis, H_0—a claim that there is no difference between the population mean μ and the hypothesized value μ_0.

Alternative hypothesis, H_1—a claim that disagrees with the null hypothesis. If the null hypothesis is rejected, we are left with no choice but to fail to reject the alternative hypothesis that μ is not equal to μ_0. Sometimes referred to as the *research hypothesis.*

Test statistic—a statistic used to determine the relative position of the mean in the hypothesized probability distribution of sample means.

Critical region—The region on the far end of the distribution. If only one end of the distribution, commonly termed "the tail," is involved, the region is referred to as a *one-tailed test;* if both ends are involved, the region is known as a *two-tailed test.* When the computed Z or t falls in the critical region, we reject the null hypothesis. The critical region is sometimes called the *rejection region.* The probability that a test statistic falls in the critical region is denoted by α.

Critical value—The number that divides the normal distribution into the region where we will reject the null hypothesis and the region where we fail to reject the null hypothesis.

Significance level—the level that corresponds to the area in the critical region. By choice, this area is usually small; the implication is that results falling in it do so infrequently. Consequently, such events are deemed unusual or, in the language of statisticians, statistically significant. When a test statistic falls in this area, the result is referred to as *significant* at the α level.

Nonrejection region—the region of the sampling distribution not included in α; that is, the region located under the middle portion of the curve. Whenever a test statistic falls in this region, the evidence does not permit us to reject the null hypothesis. The implication is that results falling in this region are not unexpected. The nonrejection region is denoted by $(1 - \alpha)$.

Test of significance—a procedure used to establish the validity of a claim by determining whether the test statistic falls in the critical region. If it does, the results are referred to as significant. This test is sometimes called the *hypothesis test.*

8.3   BASIS FOR A TEST OF SIGNIFICANCE

To reinforce some of these definitions, let us consider an analogy. In a criminal court, the jury's duty is to evaluate the evidence of the prosecution and the defense to determine whether a defendant is guilty or innocent. By use of the judge's instructions, which provide guidelines for their reaching a decision, the members of the jury can arrive at one of two verdicts: guilty or not guilty. Their decision may be correct, or they could make one of two possible errors: convict an innocent person or exonerate a guilty one.

A court trial and a **test of significance** have a lot in common. With a statistical test of significance, you attempt to determine whether a certain claim is valid. The claim is usually stated as a **null hypothesis,** H_0, which holds that the mean of a certain population is some value, μ_0 (the defendant is innocent). Using the data obtained in the sample (the evidence), you compute a **test statistic** (the jury) and use it to determine whether it supports a population with a mean of μ_0. The basis for finding out whether the test statistic supports the null hypothesis is the **critical region** (judge's instructions). The critical region sets guidelines for rejecting or failing to reject the null hypothesis. If the computed statistic falls in the critical region of the distribution curve, where it is unlikely to occur by chance, the claim is not supported (conviction). If the test statistic falls in the **nonrejection region,** where it is quite likely to occur by chance, the claim is rejected (possible exoneration).

8.4 NULL AND ALTERNATIVE HYPOTHESES

You might legitimately ask, "What does it really mean when researchers 'test' hypotheses or perform 'tests of significance'?" The concept is actually quite simple and direct. We are trying to find out if two (or more) things are the same or if they are different.

Your follow-up question might be, "Can't we just look at the numbers and see if they are the same numerical value or if they are different?" You probably won't be the least bit surprised when we say, "It's not quite that simple."

Let us start our explanation with an example based on probability. What you have is a coin. What you want to do is determine whether heads and tails will appear equally, that is, whether the coin is fair. If the coin is fair and you flip it 10 times, you would expect five heads and five tails. But are you always going to get five heads (H) and five tails (T)? Of course not. If you get 6H and 4T, or 4H and 6T, would you conclude that the coin is not fair? After all, 6H and 4T is different from 5H and 5T. You would probably conclude that 6H and 4T is close enough to 5H and 5T, that the difference is slight and expected. How about 7H and 3T (or 3H and 7T)? You might be a bit suspicious, but it is probably "close enough" that you still believe the coin is fair. Well, what about 8H and 2T? Are your suspicions increasing? You can probably guess what is next: 9H and 1T followed by 10H and 0T. At some point, you start thinking that something is unusual about this coin. Intuitively, you realized that when you start seeing combinations of 8 and 2, 9 and 1, and certainly 10 and 0 the probability of these combinations is fairly low. This is the basis of hypothesis testing. In this chapter, we will show you how statistics can be used to determine whether two numbers are close enough that the difference is not significant or whether the difference is great enough that there really is a significant difference between the numbers.

What actually are null and alternative hypotheses? In this chapter, which is your introduction to hypothesis testing, you will be comparing one sample mean with a population mean μ. The null hypothesis is that there is no difference between the sample and population means. For now, simply remember that the key part of the definition is *no difference*.

The **alternative hypothesis** (or research hypothesis) specifies that there is a difference between the sample mean and the population mean. The alternative or research hypothesis is what the researcher expects to find. This is why the research, and hence the statistical analysis, is being done.

In this chapter, we will statistically test the null hypothesis of no difference. What this means is that, after performing the appropriate statistical test, we must decide whether we will reject or fail to reject the null hypothesis. If we reject the null hypothesis (remember that the null hypothesis means no difference), then we *must* accept the alternative hypothesis, which states that there is a difference between the sample and population means—no exceptions. Conversely, if we fail to reject the null hypothesis of no difference, then we *must* reject the alternative hypothesis—again, no exceptions. There are absolutely no circumstances in which we could either fail to reject both or reject both.

8.5 PROCEDURE FOR A TEST OF SIGNIFICANCE— ONE-SAMPLE Z OR t

In order to perform a test of significance, it is necessary to learn how to set up your hypotheses, compare your calculated and critical values, and draw appropriate conclusions. To complete this task, you will follow the six-step procedure outlined below. The examples in this chapter follow these steps.

1. State one of the following:
   $H_0: \mu = \mu_0$ versus $H_1: \mu \neq \mu_0$ (Figure 8.1a)
   $H_0: \mu \leq \mu_0$ versus $H_1: \mu > \mu_0$ (Figure 8.1b)
   $H_0: \mu \geq \mu_0$ versus $H_1: \mu < \mu_0$ (Figure 8.1c)
2. Choose a significance level α (usually .05 or .01).
3. Compute the test statistic (either Z or t). This is the calculated value that you will later compare with the critical value.

$$Z = \frac{\bar{x} - \mu}{\sigma/\sqrt{n}} \qquad t = \frac{\bar{x} - \mu}{s/\sqrt{n}} \tag{8.1}$$

4. Determine the critical region, as shown in Figure 8.1.
5. Reject the null hypothesis if the test statistic, Z or t, falls in the critical region (tail).
   Fail to reject the null hypothesis if the test statistic falls in the fail-to-reject region.
6. State the appropriate conclusions.

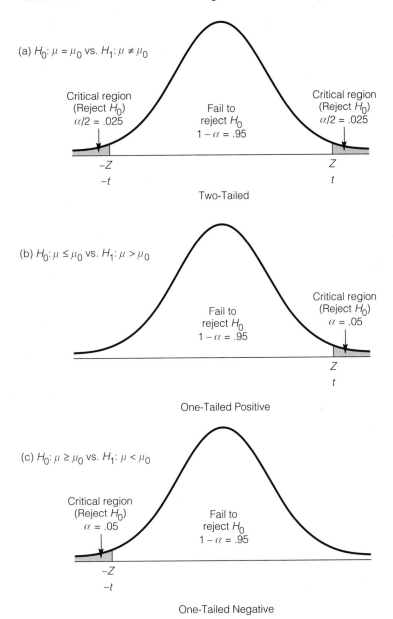

(a) $H_0: \mu = \mu_0$ vs. $H_1: \mu \neq \mu_0$

Critical region
(Reject H_0)
$\alpha/2 = .025$

Fail to
reject H_0
$1 - \alpha = .95$

Critical region
(Reject H_0)
$\alpha/2 = .025$

$-Z$
$-t$

Z
t

Two-Tailed

(b) $H_0: \mu \leq \mu_0$ vs. $H_1: \mu > \mu_0$

Fail to
reject H_0
$1 - \alpha = .95$

Critical region
(Reject H_0)
$\alpha = .05$

Z
t

One-Tailed Positive

(c) $H_0: \mu \geq \mu_0$ vs. $H_1: \mu < \mu_0$

Critical region
(Reject H_0)
$\alpha = .05$

Fail to
reject H_0
$1 - \alpha = .95$

$-Z$
$-t$

One-Tailed Negative

Figure 8.1   Critical Region of Test Statistics *Z* and *t* ($\alpha = .05$).

■ **EXAMPLE 1**

To illustrate the basic concepts of a test of significance, let us again consider the Honolulu Heart Study. Suppose someone claims that the mean age of the population of 7683 individuals is 53.00 years. How can you verify (or reject) this claim? Start by drawing a sample of, say, 100 persons. Suppose the sample mean equals 54.85. Now the question is, What is the likelihood of finding a sample mean of 54.85 in a sample of 100 from a distribution whose true mean, μ, is 53, given that $\sigma = 5.50$? You can determine the answer by examining the relative position of $\bar{x}$ (54.85) on the scale of possible sample means. Using the six-step procedure just outlined, we obtain the following:

1. H_0: $\mu = 53$ versus H_1: $\mu \neq 53$. In this example, we chose a two-tailed hypothesis. The reason for this is that we are asking if the sample mean, $\bar{x}$, is different from the population mean, μ. Different implies that $\bar{x}$ may be higher or lower than μ. We won't know which until we collect the data and calculate the sample mean.

   If you look at $\bar{x} = 54.85$, you might think we should perform a one-tailed test because the sample mean is higher than the population mean. But that would be inappropriate. Your hypotheses are supposed to be written before you collect data, not after. Before the data were collected, we did not know if the sample mean would be higher or lower than the population mean, μ—hence the use of a two-tailed hypothesis in this example.

2. Significance level $\alpha = .05$.

3. Test statistic:

$$Z = \frac{\bar{x} - \mu}{\sigma/\sqrt{n}} = \frac{54.85 - 53}{5.5/\sqrt{100}} = \frac{1.85}{.55} = 3.36$$

4. Critical region: From the normal (Z) distribution (Table A, inside back cover), we find, for a two-tailed test where $\alpha/2 = .025$, the corresponding $Z = \pm 1.96$ (see Figure 8.2). The value ± 1.96 is often referred to as the **critical value**. The critical value is the number that divides the normal distribution into the region where we will fail to reject the null hypothesis and the region where we will reject the null hypothesis.

5. Because the computed test statistic, $Z = 3.36$ (step 3), falls within the critical region (beyond the critical values ± 1.96), we are compelled to reject the null hypothesis that the sample comes from a population with a mean of 53 and accept (fail to reject) the alternative hypothesis that the sample comes from a population with a mean not equal to 53. This result is considered to be significant at the $\alpha = .05$ level because the probability of its occurring by chance is less than .05. The actual probability of obtaining a Z value of 3.36 or larger is much smaller.

6. Rejecting or failing to reject the null hypothesis and therefore determining whether or not the results are significant finish the statistics part of the problem. We still have a little work left. We need to develop meaningful and accurate conclusions based on the statistical analysis. In this case, we rejected our null hypothesis. We would therefore conclude that the mean age of 54.85 is significantly different from (greater than) the popu-

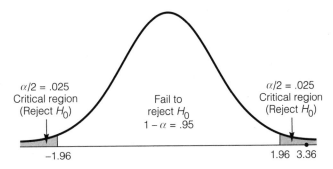

Figure 8.2   Critical Region for Example 1.

lation mean of 53 or that the sample probably came from another population with a mean other than 53. ■

8.6   ONE-TAILED VERSUS TWO-TAILED TESTS

In testing statistical hypotheses, you must always ask a key question: "Am I interested in the deviation of $\bar{x}$ from μ in one or both directions?" The answer is
usually implicit in the way H_0 and H_1 are stated. If you are interested in determining whether the mean age is significantly *different* from a given μ, you
should perform a **two-tailed test,** because the deviation, $\bar{x} - \mu$, could be either
negative or positive. If you are interested in whether the mean age is significantly *larger* than the given μ, you should perform a **one-tailed test.** Likewise,
you should go to the one-tailed test for mean ages *smaller* than μ.

Figure 8.1 illustrates the use of each kind of test. Figure 8.1a indicates that a
two-tailed test is called for in testing the null hypothesis $\mu = \mu_0$ against the alternative hypothesis $\mu \neq \mu_0$. One half of the rejection region α is placed in each
tail of the distribution; that is, we would reject H_0 if the value of the calculated test
statistic fell in either of the outlying regions. Figure 8.1b indicates a one-tailed
test for testing the null hypothesis $\mu \leq \mu_0$ against the alternative hypothesis
$\mu > \mu_0$. Here, the critical region falls entirely in the positive tail; we would reject
H_0 if the test statistic were so large as to fall in the critical region. Figure 8.1c indicates a one-tailed test for testing the null hypothesis $\mu \geq \mu_0$ against the alternative hypothesis $\mu < \mu_0$. Here, the critical region falls entirely in the negative
tail; we would reject H_0 if the calculated statistic were negative and fell in the
critical region.

A one-tailed test is indicated for questions like these: Is a new drug superior
to a standard drug? Does the air pollution level exceed safe limits? Has the death
rate been reduced for those who quit smoking? A two-tailed test is indicated
for questions like these: Is there a difference between the cholesterol levels of
men and women? Does the mean age of a group of volunteers differ from that
of the general population? Notice the difference in the way these questions are

worded. In a potential one-tailed test, you will see words like *exceed, reduced, higher, lower, more,* and *less.* The two-tailed questions are looking for a difference without specifying whether the difference is numerically higher or lower.

We should point out, in the various health science disciplines, there are multiple solutions to the same problem. There often is simply not a clear consensus about which solution will be the best choice. This also is the case when trying to decide whether to use one-tailed (-sided) or two-tailed (-sided) tests. The Food and Drug Administration (FDA) is generally opposed to the use of one-tailed tests (Chow, 2000). With the large number of products being tested that require FDA approval, the FDA has a major impact on what is considered good statistics practice. Chow (2000:247) also pointed out that, "when testing at the 5% level of significance with 80% power, the sample size required increases by 27% for a two-sided test as compared to a one-sided test." Needless to say, the decision to use a two-tailed test can directly affect sample size requirements. Depending on the type of study being done, this can increase both the cost of the study and the difficulty in finding a suitable number of subjects.

If you are not expected or required to use either a one- or a two-tailed test (such as in a study of a product requiring FDA approval), how do you decide? Let us look at the reasons we would use one-tailed tests. Dubey (as cited in Chow, 2000) identified two main contexts in which one-tailed tests would be appropriate: "(a) where there is truly concern for the outcomes in one tail only and (b) where it is completely inconceivable that the results could go in the opposite direction" (247). Regardless of whether you use a one-tailed or a two-tailed test, the choice should be made *before* you collect data and *before* you begin the data analysis. This is generally considered the proper way to conduct scientific research. To collect and partially analyze the data, and then to decide whether the test should be one- or two-tailed, is simply not an appropriate course of action.

8.7 TEST OF SIGNIFICANCE—ONE-SAMPLE *t*

In this section, we will show you how to perform a *t* test in which you compare a sample mean with a population mean, μ. This example and the accompanying data are taken from a *Journal of the American Medical Association* article that appeared in April 1998 (Rosa et al., 1998); if you want to look at the actual data, you can access this Web site: http://www.quackwatch.com.

The article, "A Close Look at Therapeutic Touch," reports on a fourth-grade science fair project conducted by Emily Rosa. She designed a study to determine whether practitioners of touch therapy can actually detect a "human energy field" (HEF) under blind conditions. Practitioners claim to be able to detect the HEF by placing their hands 5–10 cm above the patient and sweeping them over the body from head to feet, "attuning" to the patient's condition by becoming aware of "changes in sensory cues" in the hands. The patient's body is never actually touched.

Figure 8.3 Experimenter Hovering Hand over One of Subject's Hands (draped towel prevents peeking). Based on drawing by Pat Linse, Skeptics Society.

The purpose of the study was to determine whether touch therapists (TT) could detect a human energy field without seeing the patient. Fifteen touch therapists participated in the initial test. A coin was flipped to determine which of each TT's hands would be the target. The experimenter then held her right hand, palm down, 8–10 cm above the TT's hand and said,"Okay." The TT had to determine which of his or her hands was below and nearer to the experimenter's hand. Each TT was given 10 opportunities to select the correct hand (see Figure 8.3).

■ **EXAMPLE 2**

We will again use the steps outlined in Section 8.5, but this time we will be conducting a *t* test instead of a Z test. The reason the *t* test is chosen is that we have sample, rather than population, data. The standard deviation, *s*, will be calculated from the sample, which consisted of 15 touch therapists.

In this example, we have data from the sample, but no population data. In order to calculate *t*, we need a population mean, μ; a sample mean, $\bar{x}$; and a sample standard deviation, *s*. You know how to calculate $\bar{x}$ and *s*; but how do we determine μ? Remember that in statistics we test the null hypothesis. Each TT had 10 chances to select the correct hand. If a HEF does not exist, you would at least expect the TT to be successful 50% of the time. Your population mean would be 50% of 10, or 5. If a HEF does exist, then you would expect a success rate significantly greater than 5. We can now begin the process of answering our question: Can TTs detect a HEF, or are these results explained by chance?

We also need to determine whether this should be a one-tailed or two-tailed hypothesis. Remember that in Example 1 we decided to use a two-tailed hypothesis. In this example, we will choose a one-tailed hypothesis. The main reason is given in the previous paragraph, although you might not have realized it. The key phrase is that if a HEF exists then you would expect a success rate *greater than* 5. Thus, our hypotheses would look like this:

1. H_0: $\mu \leq 5$ versus H_1: $\mu > 5$.

2. $\alpha = .05$.

3. Test statistic: From the sample of 15 TTs we had $\bar{x} = 4.67$ and $s = 1.74$. Using equation (8.1), we get

$$t = \frac{4.67 - 5.0}{1.74/\sqrt{15}} = -.73$$

4. Critical region: When we use the Z distribution for any given α, we will always have the same critical value. In Example 1, we used $\alpha = .05$, two-tailed. Our critical value ± 1.96 will always be the critical value for $\alpha = .05$, two-tailed. If $\alpha = .01$, two-tailed, then our critical value will always be ± 2.58. When we use the t distribution, the critical value is based on the degrees of freedom (df), which we discussed in section 7.4. In this problem, which compares one sample to a population, df $= n - 1$. This is also a one-tailed test, because the alternative hypothesis states that the TT will be able to identify the HEF *more* than the 5 out of 10 times we would expect by chance alone. Turn to Table B (inside back cover) and go to the second line, labeled "Probability Below t Value (One-Sided)." Look for the area .95, which corresponds to $\alpha = .05$. We have 14 ($n - 1$) df. Our critical value is therefore 1.7613, as shown in Figure 8.4.

5. Just as in Example 1, we have to determine whether we will fail to reject or reject the null hypothesis. In this example, we have a calculated t value of $-.73$. In this case, we fail to reject the null hypothesis.

6. As in Example 1, rejecting or failing to reject the null hypothesis is only half the task. We next need to state our conclusions with regard to the problem. Because the touch therapists were unable to locate the human energy field more than what would be expected by chance, Rosa et al. (1998:1005) concluded that their "failure to substantiate TT's most fundamental claim is unrefuted evidence that the claims of TT are groundless and that further professional use is unjustified." This is a stronger statement than you will see in most scientific studies, but nevertheless, com-

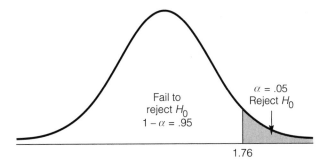

Figure 8.4   Critical Region for Example 2.

pelling data lead us to the conclusion that touch therapists probably cannot detect a human energy field. Before you definitively state that it is a "fact" that touch therapy does not work, however, read sections 8.15 and 8.16 on type I and type II errors. ∎

8.8   POINT ESTIMATES AND CONFIDENCE INTERVALS

Point estimates and confidence intervals were first introduced in the previous chapter. We will use the data from the Honolulu Heart Study and the Touch Therapy Study to illustrate confidence intervals using the Z and t scores, respectively.

   We took one sample of 100 men from the Honolulu Heart Study and found a sample mean age, $\bar{x}$, of 54.85 years. The confidence interval allows us to take a sample statistic, $\bar{x}$, and estimate the unknown parameter, μ. By using equation (8.2), we can be confident that 95% of all sample means, of a given sample size, will fall within ± 1.96 standard deviations of the population mean. By using equation (8.3), we can be confident that 99% of all sample means will fall within ± 2.58 standard deviations of the population mean.

$$95\% \text{ CI of } \mu \ = \bar{x} \pm 1.96(\sigma/\sqrt{n}) \tag{8.2}$$

$$99\% \text{ CI of } \mu \ = \bar{x} \pm 2.58(\sigma/\sqrt{n}) \tag{8.3}$$

∎ EXAMPLE 3

In order to estimate the population mean age, μ, from the Honolulu Heart Study, we can calculate the 95% and 99% confidence intervals, using equations (8.2) and (8.3). We already know that $\bar{x} = 54.85$ years and $\sigma = 5.50$. Our sample size for this example is 100. The 95% confidence interval is thus

$$95\% \text{ CI for } \mu \ = 54.85 \pm 1.96(5.50/\sqrt{100}) = (53.78, 55.93)$$

and the 99% confidence interval is

$$99\% \text{ CI for } \mu = 54.8\overline{5} \pm 2.58(5.50/\sqrt{100}) = (53.43, 56.2\overline{7})$$

   The values 53.78 and 55.93 are the lower and upper 95% confidence limits. The interval from 53.78 to 55.93 is the 95% confidence interval. Similarly, the values 53.43 and 56.27 are the lower and upper 99% confidence limits, and the interval from 53.43 to 56.27 is the 99% confidence interval.

   The 95% confidence interval provides a range that captures the true value of the population mean with 95% probability. However, there is still a 5% chance that the interval does not capture μ. There is a 2.5% chance that μ actually lies above $Z = 1.96$, and there is another 2.5% chance that μ lies below $Z = -1.96$ (see Figure 8.5).

   Similarly, the 99% confidence interval provides a range that captures the true value of the population mean with 99% probability. There is a .5% chance that μ actually lies above $Z = 2.58$, and there is another .5% chance that μ lies below $Z = -2.58$ (see Figure 8.6). ■

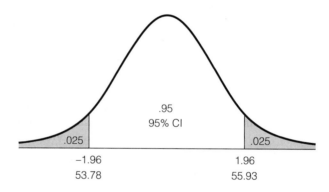

Figure 8.5 95% Confidence Interval for Honolulu Heart Study Data.

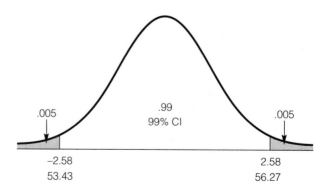

Figure 8.6 99% Confidence Interval for Honolulu Heart Study Data.

Notice that the 99% CI is wider than the 95% CI. Is wider better? Yes, if you want to minimize the possibility of not including the true population mean. There is only a 1% chance that the population mean will not be within the 99% CI. If the interval is too wide, the confidence interval may not provide a useful or practical assessment of the range of possible population means.

Narrow confidence intervals are of the greatest value in making estimates because they allow us to estimate an unknown parameter (population mean) with little room for error. This attribute moves us to consider all possible ways of narrowing confidence intervals. As seen from the confidence interval for the single population mean, μ, the quantities that affect the width of the interval are the sample size, the Z value, and the standard deviation.

A confidence interval can be narrowed by:

1. Increasing the sample size
2. Reducing the confidence level (e.g., instead of using $Z = 2.58$ for 99% confidence, use $Z = 1.96$ for 95% confidence)
3. Increasing precision by reducing measurement (and other nonrandom) errors, thus producing a smaller variance

Unfortunately, there is not an obvious yes or no answer to the question Is wider better? You must look at the data and use your best judgment to determine whether to use a 95% CI or a 99% CI.

8.9 CONFIDENCE INTERVALS AND THE *t* DISTRIBUTION

Calculating the confidence intervals for one-sample *t* tests is similar to calculating them for Z scores, with one key difference. Unlike the Z confidence intervals, which always use 1.96 and 2.58 for the 95% and 99% confidence intervals, respectively, the CI uses a *t* value that will vary depending on the degrees of freedom. The *t* value that you will use in equation (8.4) will *always* come from Table B (inside back cover) and will *always* be from the two-sided, or two-tailed, column (labeled .95 and .99).

$$(1 - \alpha)100\% \text{ CI for } \mu \ = \bar{x} \pm t(s/\sqrt{n}) \tag{8.4}$$

■ EXAMPLE 4

In this example, we will estimate the population of correct choices from the Touch Therapy Study, first introduced in section 8.7. This time, we will use equation (8.4) to calculate the 95% and 99% confidence intervals. We have $\bar{x} = 4.67$ and $s = 1.74$ for a sample of 15. The 95% confidence interval is thus

$$95\% \text{ CI for } \mu \ = \bar{x} \pm 2.1448(1.74/\sqrt{15}) = 4.67 \pm .96 \ = (3.71, 5.63)$$

and the 99% confidence interval is

$$99\% \text{ CI for } \mu = \bar{x} \pm 2.98(1.74/\sqrt{15}) = 4.67 \pm 1.34 = (3.33, 6.01)$$

It is important that we not simply calculate the confidence intervals but also be able to properly interpret them. For the 95% CI, we have a 95% probability of capturing the population mean, μ. This means that we would expect that, if the population of touch therapists were given 10 chances to detect a human energy field, the mean number (μ) of correct responses should range from 3.71 to 5.63. As in Example 3, there is still a 5% chance that the interval does not capture μ. There is a 2.5% chance that μ actually lies above 5.63 and another 2.5% chance that μ lies below 3.71. If we look at the 99% CI, we have a range of 3.33 to 6.01, with only a .5% chance that μ lies below 3.33 and another .5% chance that it lies above 6.01. Once again, there is little reason to believe the therapists' claim that they can reliably detect a human energy field. ■

It is important to note an interesting distinction: These intervals are referred to as *confidence* intervals, not *probability* intervals. Before we actually obtain specific confidence limits based on a sample, the equation is properly referred to as a probability statement. But once the specific confidence limits are calculated, the **a posteriori probability** (i.e., the probability derived from observed facts) is that the interval contains μ or it does not. Therefore, with typical caution, statisticians refer to it as a 95% confidence interval because there is 95% confidence that in the long run the intervals constructed in such a way will indeed contain the population mean.

It would be incorrect to say in Example 3 that the probability is 95% that the true mean, μ, falls between 53.77 and 55.93 years. It either falls or does not fall between these two values. Once the interval is fixed, there is no randomness associated with it, nor is there any probability.

The 95% confidence interval is used quite commonly, as is the 99% confidence interval. Other percentages may be used but are less frequently encountered in practice.

8.10 EFFECT OF SAMPLE SIZE ON CONFIDENCE INTERVALS

Example 3 of 95% and 99% confidence intervals from the Honolulu Heart Study identified the range of possible population means based on a sample size of 100. Let us look at that same data, but this time we will calculate confidence intervals with sample sizes less than 100 (64) and greater than 100 (144), again using equations (8.2) and (8.3).

Again, $\bar{x} = 54.85$ years and $\sigma = 5.50$. For a sample size of 64, we have

$$95\% \text{ CI for } \mu = 54.85 \pm 1.96(5.50/\sqrt{64}) = (53.50, 56.20)$$

and

$$99\% \text{ CI for } \mu = 54.85 \pm 2.58(5.50/\sqrt{64}) = (53.08, 56.62)$$

For a sample size of 144, we have

$$95\% \text{ CI for } \mu = 54.85 \pm 1.96(5.50/\sqrt{144}) = (53.95, 55.75)$$

and

$$99\% \text{ CI for } \mu = 54.85 \pm 2.58(5.50/\sqrt{144}) = (53.67, 56.03)$$

Now let us compare the 95% CI for $n = 64$, $n = 100$, and $n = 144$:

$n = 64$: (53.50, 56.20)
$n = 100$: (53.77, 55.93)
$n = 144$: (53.95, 55.75)

and the 99% CI for $n = 64$, $n = 100$, and $n = 144$:

$n = 64$: (53.08, 56.62)
$n = 100$: (53.43, 56.27)
$n = 144$: (53.67, 56.03)

Notice that, in each instance, as the sample size increases the confidence intervals shrink. This is what you should expect, because as the sample size increases the sample mean should be getting closer and closer to the population mean. The shrinking confidence intervals are evidence of this. One final thought: Remember that whenever we refer to sampling, such as increasing or decreasing the sample size, there is the assumption that the sample is randomly selected; thus, we expect the sample to be representative of the population.

8.11 *P* VALUES AND STATISTICAL SIGNIFICANCE

Research reports often state that the results were **statistically significant** ($P < .05$) or make some similar statement. Such a comment means that the observed difference is too large to be explained by chance alone. The **significance level,** somewhat arbitrarily selected at values of α such as .05, .025, .01, or .001, is a measure of how significant a result is. The significance level α is also the magnitude of error that we are willing to accept in making the decision to reject the null hypothesis. Some investigators prefer to report their results in terms of the *P* value alone and let readers decide whether the information is sufficient to conclude that factors other than chance are operating. Researchers and statisticians generally agree on the following conventions for interpreting *P* **values.**

P Value	Interpretation
$P > .05$	Result is not significant; usually indicated by no asterisk.
$P < .05$	Result is significant; usually indicated by one asterisk.
$P < .01$	Result is highly significant; usually indicated by two asterisks.
$P < .001$	Result is very highly significant; usually indicated by three asterisks.

Some investigators would consider $P < .10$ to be marginally significant. "Statistically significant" means that the evidence obtained from the sample is not compatible with the null hypothesis; consequently, we reject H_0. However, just because a result is "not statistically significant" does not prove that H_0 is true. We may not be able to reject H_0 simply because the sample was too small to provide enough evidence to do so. In that sense, the decision to reject a null hypothesis is stronger than the decision to not reject it. Nor does "statistically significant" imply "clinically significant"; that is, the difference, although technically "significant," may be so small that it has little biological or practical consequence.

8.12 DETERMINING EXACT *P* VALUES FROM *Z* SCORES

■ **EXAMPLE 5**

Using the data from the one-sample *Z* test in Example 1, we can calculate an **exact *P* value.** In that example, we had a sample $\bar{x}$ of 54.85, a population mean μ of 53, and a calculated *Z* score of 3.36. We know that the computed test statistic 3.36 falls exactly 3.36 standard deviations above the mean. What we don't know is the probability of obtaining a *Z* score of 3.36 or higher or how much area is in the tail of the distribution. We can easily determine the area in the tail by using Table A (inside back cover). Observe that because Table A is an abbreviated table we will use a value of 3.09, which is the largest value listed in Table A. We find that the area in the tail is .0010 (.5000 − .4990). If we only use +3.36, we can say that there is an exact *P* value of .001. This means that we expect to obtain a *Z* score of 3.36 or higher .001, or .1%, of the time. This is a relatively rare occurrence and is certainly consistent with our earlier conclusion to reject the null hypothesis when we computed the *Z* score.

The exact *P* value .001 is a one-tailed probability. But, if you recall, we ran the hypothesis test as a two-tailed test. Can you have a two-tailed probability? Yes. It is fairly simple to calculate. Treat the calculated *Z*, 3.36, as ±3.36. This means that you still have .0010 in the positive tail, but you also have .0010 in the negative tail. Add the two numbers together, and you have an exact, two-tailed probability of .002. This means that we expect to find a *Z* score of 3.36 standard deviations above and below the mean .002, or .2%, of the time. Note that the two-tailed probability is twice that of the one-tailed probability (see Figure 8.7).

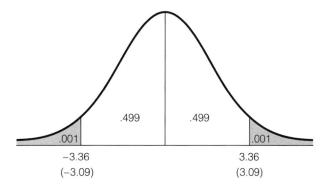

Figure 8.7   Areas Under the Normal Curve for Two-Tailed *P* Value.

The *P* value .002 indicates that the probability of selecting by chance a sample mean that falls as far as or farther than 3.36 standard deviations above or below the population mean of 53 is quite small—that is, less than .002. You might ask yourself, "How could I be so lucky or unlucky as to have obtained such a result?" Your logical conclusion: The sample probably came from another population with a mean other than 53. ∎

From Example 5, we can see that the test is based on how well $\bar{x}$, the estimate of μ, estimates the parameter μ. If H_0 is true, we would expect $\bar{x} - \mu$ to be small. If H_1 is true, we would expect $\bar{x} - \mu$ to be large. By comparing the difference $\bar{x} - \mu$ with SE $(\bar{x})$—that is, computing the test statistic and examining where the test statistic falls on the sampling distribution of computed Z's or t's—we can obtain the probability that this outcome supports H_0 or H_1. This probability is measured by the *P* value. The smaller the *P* value, the stronger the evidence that H_0 is false; the larger the *P* value, the stronger the evidence that H_1 is false. Specifically, we decide that a result is statistically significant if the *P* value is smaller than the value of α chosen to define the critical region.

Within the context of this text, the only exact *P* values you will be able to calculate will be for *Z* scores. You can use Table A for any *Z* score up to ± 3.09. Any other exact *P* values will need to be computer-generated. Example 6 is another illustration of how to determine an exact *P* value from a *Z* score.

■ **EXAMPLE 6**

We have the following data from a study using *Z* scores:

$H_0: \mu \leq 20$
$H_1: \mu > 20$
$\alpha = .05$; critical value $= 1.64$ or 1.65 or 1.645
$Z = 1.86$

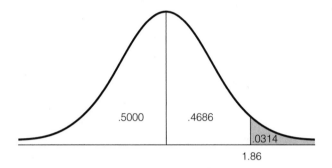

Figure 8.8 Areas Under the Normal Curve for One-Tailed *P* Value.

If we completed the hypothesis test using the above data, we would reject H_0 and fail to reject H_1. The next step is to calculate an exact *P* value. Once again, we are looking at the tail of the distribution, which means we want to find how much area lies beyond a calculated *Z* score of 1.86. Turning to Table A, we find that at $Z = 1.86$, .4686 of the area is between the mean and a *Z* score of 1.86. This leaves .0314 of the area beyond $Z = 1.86$, or .0314 of the area in the tail (see Figure 8.8).

In this example, we have an exact *P* value of .0314. This means that the probability of obtaining a *Z* score of 1.86 or higher is exactly .0314, or about 3%.

Because H_0 was rejected, we know that $P < .05$; that is, the results are significant. The exact *P* value, .0314, tells us exactly how much less than .05 and gives us the specific location of $Z = 1.86$ in the normal distribution. ■

■ EXAMPLE 7

Let us look at one more example to illustrate exact *P* values. In this example, we have the following data:

$H_0: \mu \geq 40$

$H_1: \mu < 40$

$\alpha = .05$; critical value $= -1.64$ or -1.65 or -1.645

$Z = -.57$

This time we fail to reject H_0, which means that there is not a significant difference between the calculated value, $-.57$, and the critical value. To determine the exact *P* value, we again use Table A. This time, we find that the area from $-.57$ and beyond is .2843 (see Figure 8.9). The probability of obtaining a *Z* score of $-.57$ or lower is exactly .2843, or about 28%. Also, because we failed to reject H_0, we know that $P > .05$; that is, the results are not significant. ■

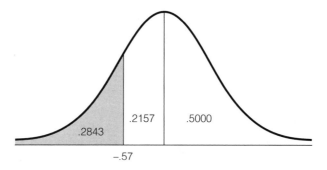

Figure 8.9   Areas Under the Normal Curve for One-Tailed *P* Value.

8.13 ONE- AND TWO-TAILED *P* VALUES

In the previous three examples, we had an example of a **two-tailed *P* value** (Example 5) and two examples of a **one-tailed *P* value** (Examples 6 and 7). Whether to use a one-tailed or a two-tailed exact *P* value is determined by the alternative hypothesis, H_1. If H_1 is two-tailed, then the exact *P* value will also be two-tailed. Conversely, if H_1 is one-tailed, then the exact *P* value will be one-tailed.

Let's treat Example 6 as a two-tailed, rather than a one-tailed, example and calculate an exact *P* value. This time, our example looks like this:

$H_0: \mu = 20$

$H_1: \mu \neq 20$

$\alpha = .05$; critical value $= \pm 1.96$

$Z = 1.86$

We follow the same procedure as in Example 5 to determine the exact *P* value. Again, we have .0314 in the tail. But because this is now a two-tailed hypothesis ($H_1: \mu \neq 20$), we double the area to include both the upper and the lower tail (see Figure 8.10). This gives us an exact *P* value of .0628, or about 6%. Note that we will fail to reject H_0, because our calculated *Z* score, 1.86, is less than our critical *Z* score, ± 1.96. The exact *P* value, .0628, is greater than .05. Our results are not significant.

This example also illustrates a practical advantage of choosing a one-tailed test over a two-tailed test. If—and this can be a very big if—you have reason to believe that one numerical value is going to be either higher or lower, such as in Examples 6 and 7, then it is to your advantage to choose a one-tailed test. The critical value will be lower, therefore, if differences exist; these differences will be more likely to be detected using a one-tailed critical value.

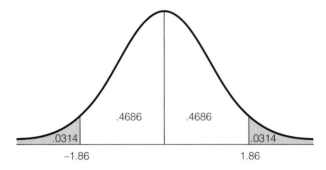

Figure 8.10   Areas Under the Normal Curve for Two-Tailed *P* Value.

There is also a potential ethical issue inherent in this choice. Scientists and researchers generally consider it appropriate to determine the direction of the alternative hypothesis *before* collecting data. In other words, you should not wait until your data are collected and analyzed, and then choose a one-tailed critical value simply because it is "easier" to attain significance. Granted, it is easier to attain significance with a one-tailed critical value, but that should not be the reason for choosing a one-tailed test.

8.14   *P* VALUES AND THE *t* DISTRIBUTION

The determination of exact *P* values using *Z* scores is reasonably straight-forward. A major reason is that the *Z* or normal distribution is based on population parameters. The *t* distribution is based on sample statistics and therefore becomes a family of distributions. To illustrate this point, the critical *Z* scores for $\alpha = .05$ are *always* 1.64 or ± 1.96 for one- and two-tailed tests, respectively. This is not true for the *t* scores, for which the critical value is dependent on the degrees of freedom (df) and thus is directly related to the sample size. The *t* distribution is a series of approximations of the normal distribution, with each df representing a slightly different approximation. Note that as df increases—which means that the sample size is increasing—the approximations get closer and closer to the normal distribution.

The practical implication is that you would need a table (like Table A) for every df in order to calculate an exact *P* value. This is not feasible, but there is an alternative: Let the computer calculate an exact *P* value. An advantage is that the computer can do this quickly and accurately, and for any possible df. At this time, all major statistics programs will display an exact *P* value. The remainder of this section will discuss the interpretation of these *P* values.

Researchers use two basic methods to report *P* values when writing a journal article. The first is to give the calculated *t* value and then indicate, by the

Table 8.1 Characteristics of Health Care Providers

Characteristic	Health Care Provider	*t* Statistic
A Mean (SD)	50 (15.16)	2.02*
B Mean (SD)	55 (12.70)	1.55
C Mean (SD)	2.63 (.85)	2.94**
D Mean (SD)	30.84 (4.72)	4.49***
E Mean (SD)	12.24 (2.11)	−0.31

*$P < .05$
**$P < .01$
***$P < .001$

use of asterisks, the level of significance. Table 8.1 illustrates this technique. In this example, the researcher performed multiple *t* tests; the significance level of each test is given. If there is no asterisk, then the results were not significant—that is, the researcher failed to reject the null hypothesis. The display under "Characteristic" is typical:

A Mean (SD)   followed by   50 (15.16)

The interpretation is that the mean and standard deviation of characteristic A are 50 and 15.16, respectively.

The second method of reporting *P* values is to display the exact *P* values. The interpretation of these values is the same as that of the *P* values in Examples 5–7. For example, a *P* value of .11 is not significant at any level; .03 is significant at .05, but not at .01 or .001; .003 is significant at .05 and .01, but not at .001; finally, .0003 is significant at all three levels.

In a journal article, it is unlikely that the authors will state the null hypothesis. When you see a statistical summary, such as Table 8.1, note the relationship between hypothesis testing and *P* values. If the author indicates that the results are significant at .05, it is equivalent to saying that the null hypothesis was rejected using $\alpha = .05$ but that the author failed to reject the null hypothesis at $\alpha = .01$ or .001.

Occasionally, you may see an exact *P* value of .0000, either on a computer printout or in a journal article. This does not mean that there is absolutely no possibility that this score will occur. What happens is that, because *P* values are computer-generated, the actual *P* value is less than .00005—for example, .00003. However, the computer statistical program may display *P* values to only four decimal places. If you round .00003 to four decimal places, you get .0000. It may appear that there is no probability of obtaining a particular score, but there is, in fact, some probability, albeit remote. The preferred way to report the *P* value in such cases is to indicate $P < .0001$.

8.15 TYPE I AND TYPE II ERRORS

In our analogy between hypothesis testing and a criminal trial, we noted that the jury could make one of two errors: (1) Reject the claim of innocence when the defendant is innocent, or (2) fail to reject the claim of innocence when the defendant is guilty. Likewise, in testing a null hypothesis (H_0), there are two possible decisions:

1. H_0 is false and consequently is rejected; that is, the evidence is that the sample comes from another population than one having $\mu = \mu_0$.
2. H_0 is true, and consequently we fail to reject it. The observed difference between μ and μ_0 is relatively small and may be reasonably ascribed to chance variation.

If your decision is that H_0 is false when indeed it is, you have reached a correct decision. If you decide that H_0 is false when it is actually true, an event likely to occur α proportion of the time, you have committed a **type I error** (also referred to as an **α error**)—rejecting a true hypothesis—which in the court analogy corresponds to convicting an innocent person. If your decision is that H_0 is true when indeed it is, you have also reached a correct decision. If you decide that H_0 is true when it is actually false, an event likely to occur β proportion of the time, you have committed a **type II error** (also referred to as a **β error**)—accepting a false hypothesis—which in the court analogy corresponds to freeing a guilty person. These two errors are summarized in Figure 8.11.

In the test of a null hypothesis, some specific value for the parameter—say, μ_0—is proposed. If this value happens to be correct but we reject it based on the observed sample, we have committed a type I error. If the proposed value happens to be incorrect but we fail to reject it based on the observed sample, we

		TRUE STATE OF NATURE	
		H_0 is true	H_0 is false (H_1 is true)
D E C I S I O N	Accept H_0	Correct decision ($1 - \alpha$)	Type II error (β)
	Reject H_0 (assume H_1 is true)	Type I error (α)	Correct decision ($1 - \beta$)
	Total	1	1

$P\,(\text{Accept } H_0 | H_0 \text{ true}) = 1 - \alpha$

$P\,(\text{Reject } H_0 | H_0 \text{ false}) = 1 - \beta$

Figure 8.11   Possible Errors in Hypothesis Testing.

have committed a type II error. Therefore, we can say that the type I error is the probability of rejecting a true null hypothesis and that the type II error is the probability of failing to reject a false null hypothesis.

Let us apply this test to the Honolulu Heart Study. The mean age for the population was $\mu = 54.36$. If we did not know this but guessed that μ was 53, the upper critical point for the distribution under the null hypothesis of 53 would be 53.90, because, from equation (8.1),

$$1.645 = \frac{\bar{x} - 53}{5.5/\sqrt{100}}$$

reduces to $\bar{x} = 53.90$. Figure 8.12 illustrates that if we had randomly arrived at a value of $\bar{x}$ below 53.90 we would have failed to reject the false H_0 (that $\mu = 53$) β proportion of the time. This β error is represented by the area to the left of $\bar{x} = 53.90$. This area, based on a value of $\bar{x}$ of 53.90 and a value of s of 5.5, using a sample of 100, is equal to the area corresponding to

$$Z = \frac{53.90 - 54.36}{5.5/\sqrt{100}} = \frac{-.46}{.55} = -.84$$

Using Table A (inside back cover), we find that $\beta = .30$.

In Figure 8.12, we see that we would have rejected the false H_0 about 80% of the time $(1 - \beta = .70)$. The quantity $1 - \beta$ is referred to as the **power of a test;** it is the probability of rejecting H_0 when H_0 is indeed false. Generally, statisticians try to design statistical tests that have high power, that is, tests in which β is small—say, .2 or .1. We can infer from Figure 8.12 that this goal could be accomplished either by decreasing the significance level (α) from .01 to .05 or by increasing the sample size.

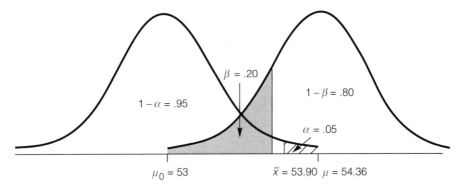

Figure 8.12   Distribution of Sample Means for $\mu_0 = 53$ and $\mu = 54.36$.

From the foregoing discussion, it should be clear that the α level represents the probability of a type I error and β represents the probability of a type II error. A sort of reciprocal relationship exists between the two types of errors. Figure 8.12 suggests that, the smaller you choose α to be, the larger β will be. The reason for this is that, as the critical region moves farther to the right, more β area is generated to the left of the critical point. The only way to reduce both α and β errors is to reduce the overlap—that is, the area common to the two distributions. This can be done by increasing the sample size, which will reduce $s_{\bar{x}} = s / \sqrt{n}$ and thus narrow the sampling distributions.

8.16 TYPE I AND TYPE II ERRORS AND PROBABILITY REVISITED

The situation in the Touch Therapy Study is similar except that this time we failed to reject the null hypothesis. This means that we have the *possibility* of a type II error; that is, we failed to reject the null hypothesis when perhaps we should have rejected the null hypothesis. Is there a chance that touch therapy really does work but that, for some reason, this study failed to recognize its ability to detect a human energy field?

Let us revisit probability and apply it to this situation: If you flip a coin, you have a 50/50 chance of a head or a tail. If you flipped the coin 10 times, analogous to the 10 trials for each touch therapist (TT), you would expect to get five heads and five tails. Certainly, combinations of 6 and 4 or 7 and 3 are also possible. If you are looking at combinations involving 8 and 2, 9 and 1, and 10 and 0, the probability drops to .0439, .0098, and .0016, respectively. In other words, the extremes are possible, although not very likely. This is why most scientists are cautious about drawing firm conclusions from one data set. The TT study consisted of two trials with a total of 28 tests. How many TTs would you expect to have 8 correct trials out of 10? The probability of getting 8 of 10 correct by chance is .0439, that is, about 4% or 1 in 25. Out of 28 trials, you might expect one TT to get 8 correct. Rosa et al. (1998) found 1; no TT got 9 or 10 correct.

So is there a chance that touch therapy works? Yes, that is possible. However, if further studies find similar results, we would undoubtedly conclude that it is ineffective and should not have a place in the health care setting.

One final note involves the use of the word *error* to describe type I and type II errors. The word *error* has the connotation of a mistake. Remember that it is possible for a researcher to have a well-designed study and, regardless of whether the researcher rejects or fails to reject the null hypothesis, *there will always be the possibility of a type I or type II error*, perhaps simply due to chance. Whenever you draw a sample from a population, you expect the sample to be representative of the population. In most cases, that is what happens. It is much like flipping a coin 10 times. You would expect a large number of 3, 4, 5, 6, or 7 heads, but every once in a while (.0016, or .16%, of the time), you will get 10 heads. This is why we usually don't accept something as fact, in scientific terms, until the findings have been replicated. For example, we now accept as fact that smoking during pregnancy leads to lower birth weights. Numerous independent studies have confirmed this to the point that it has become generally accepted as fact. But no matter how well designed a study is, there is always the possibility of a type I or type II error, so replication of research is of crucial importance before we accept any finding as fact.

◆ CONCLUSION

Tests of significance are performed to determine the validity of claims regarding population parameters. From the nature of the claim, we can decide whether the test should be one-tailed or two-tailed. The decision determines how the null and alternative hypotheses are stated, and the manner in which the test is performed. Together with the choice of significance level, this decision defines the critical region. The critical region is the decision-making feature of the test, and the computed test statistic is compared with it. If the value of the test statistic falls in the critical region, we reject the null hypothesis and fail to reject the alternative; if it falls outside the critical region, we fail to reject the null hypothesis and cannot accept the alternative. In the former case, the evidence supports the claim; in the latter, it is insufficient to support the claim. A point estimate represents a "best guess" at a population parameter. A confidence interval gives a range of values to which we can append a probability statement as to whether the population parameter is included. Based on a sample mean, we can determine the 95% and 99% confidence interval or the range of values for the population mean (μ). A randomly selected sample and the resultant calculation of the sample mean, compared with the population mean, can tell us the exact probability that the sample mean differs from the population mean. If we do not wish to define a critical region, it is possible to compute an exact P value, which indicates the probability of the chance occurrence of this or a larger value of the test statistic when the null hypothesis is true. An exact probability can be calculated for Z and t scores. If the P value is smaller than α, we will reject the null hypothesis. If it is larger than α, we will fail to reject the null hypothesis. It is possible to commit one of two types of errors in executing these tests. In rejecting a true null hypothesis, we make a type I error (α error); in failing to reject a false null hypothesis, we make a type II error (β error).

◆ VOCABULARY LIST

a posteriori
   probability
alternative hypothesis
   (research hypothesis)
critical region (rejection
   region)

critical value
exact P value
hypothesis
nonrejection region
null hypothesis
one-tailed P value

one-tailed test
P value
parameter
power of a test
significance level
statistical significance

test of significance   two-tailed P value   type I error (α error)
   (hypothesis test)   two-tailed test   type II error (β error)
test statistic

◆ **EXERCISES**

8.1 For each of the following, state the null (H_0) and alternative (H_1) hypotheses.
   a. Has the mean community level of suspended particulates for the month of August exceeded 30 units per cubic meter?
   b. Does mean age of onset of a certain acute disease for schoolchildren differ from 11.5?
   c. Is the mean IQ of a sample of 60 children significantly above the normal IQ of 100?
   d. Is the average cross-sectional area of the lumen of coronary arteries for men ages 40–59 less than 31.5% of the total arterial cross section?
   e. Is the mean hemoglobin level of a group of high-altitude workers different from 16 g/cc?
   f. Does the mean speed of 50 cars as checked by radar on a particular highway differ from 65 mph?

8.2 Describe the difference between H_0 and H_1.

8.3 In most clinical research studies, would you expect the researcher to use a one- or a two-tailed hypothesis? Explain.

8.4 For each of the following situations, choose an α appropriate to the seriousness of the potential error involved should the null hypothesis be rejected when it is actually true.
   a. You wish to decide whether a new treatment for pancreatic cancer, known to be a usually fatal disease, is superior to the standard treatment.
   b. The claim is made that the mean income for families of size four is greater than $40,000.

8.5 What is the critical value for a test of significance in each of the following situations?
   a. one-tailed test, $\alpha = .05$, σ known, $n = 20$
   b. one-tailed test, $\alpha = .05$, σ unknown, $n = 10$
   c. two-tailed test, $\alpha = .01$, σ unknown, $n = 14$
   d. two-tailed test, $\alpha = .01$, σ known, $n = 25$
   e. two-tailed test, $\alpha = .05$, σ unknown, $n = 35$

8.6 In which of the situations in Exercise 8.5 would you use:
   a. a Z test
   b. a t test
   Why?

8.7 Determine the critical value that would be used to test a hypothesis under the conditions given in each of the following.
   a. $H_0: \mu = 220$ $H_1: \mu \neq 220$ $\alpha = .05$ $n = 20$, σ known
   b. $H_0: \mu \leq 15$ $H_1: \mu > 15$ $\alpha = .01$ $n = 35$, σ known
   c. $H_0: \mu = 70$ $H_1: \mu \neq 70$ $\alpha = .01$ $n = 18$, σ known
   d. $H_0: \mu = 120$ $H_1: \mu \neq 120$ $\alpha = .05$ $n = 25$, σ unknown

e. $H_0: \mu \geq 100$ $H_1: \mu < 100$ $\alpha = .01$ $n = 16$, σ unknown
f. $H_0: \mu \geq 55$ $H_1: \mu < 55$ $\alpha = .05$ $n = 49$, σ unknown

8.8 For each part of Exercise 8.7, decide whether you should reject H_0 or fail to reject H_0 according to the corresponding test statistic.
  a. $Z = -1.79$
  b. $Z = 2.01$
  c. $Z = 3.63$
  d. $t = 2.77$
  e. $t = -2.14$
  f. $t = -1.82$

8.9 Are the 95% confidence intervals narrower or wider than the 99% confidence intervals? Do Exercises 8.10 and 8.11 or Exercise 8.12. The results will either confirm your answer or cause you to change it.

8.10 The standard hemoglobin reading for healthy adult men is 15 g/100 ml with a standard deviation of $\sigma = 2$ g. For a group of 25 men in a certain occupation, we find a mean hemoglobin of 16.0 g.
  a. Obtain a 95% confidence interval for μ, and give its interpretation.
  b. Calculate the 95% confidence interval for the following sample sizes: 36, 49, and 64.
  c. As the sample size increases, do the confidence intervals shrink or widen? Explain. (*Hint:* Recall what you learned about the central limit theorem in Chapter 7.)

8.11 Repeat Exercise 8.10 using a 99% confidence interval instead of a 95% confidence interval.

8.12 Using the following data, calculate the confidence intervals.

Variable	$1 - \alpha$	Sample Mean	n	Standard Deviation	CI
a. Systolic BP	.95	122	61	$s = 11$	_____ to _____
b. Weight (kg)	.99	75	46	$\sigma = 8.4$	_____ to _____
c. Serum cholesterol	.95	177	51	$\sigma = 21$	_____ to _____
d. Age	.95	45	25	$s = 6.2$	_____ to _____
e. Age	.95	45	51	$s = 6.2$	_____ to _____
f. Income (000)	.95	48	91	$\sigma = 12.8$	_____ to _____
g. Income (000)	.99	48	91	$\sigma = 12.8$	_____ to _____

8.13 The mean diastolic blood pressure of 100 individuals in Table 3.1 is 73 mmHg with a standard deviation of $s = 11.6$ mmHg. Construct a 99% confidence interval for μ.

8.14 The mean weight of the sample of 100 men from the Honolulu Heart Study is 64 kg with a standard deviation of $s = 8.61$. Construct a 95% and a 99% confidence interval for μ.

8.15 The standard urine creatinine for healthy adult males is .25–.40 g/6 hr.
  a. If we assume that the range encompasses six standard deviations, what is the estimate of the mean and the standard deviation of the population?
  b. Construct the 99% confidence interval for μ.

8.16 a. Why is a confidence interval not called a probability interval?

b. What is the interpretation of a confidence interval?

c. What factors regulate the length of a confidence interval?

8.17 a. What is the basis for being able to use confidence intervals to perform a test of a hypothesis?

b. What are the rules governing the use of a confidence interval?

8.18 a. What does the type I error tell you?

b. What does the type II error tell you?

c. From the information stated in the problems, are you able to state the type II errors?

d. If in any given problem you should decide to decrease the type I error (say, from .05 to .01), what would happen to the type II error?

e. What is usually done to avoid type II errors?

f. What could you do to reduce both types of error simultaneously?

◆ COMPREHENSIVE EXERCISES

Using the data in Exercises 8.19–8.29, do the following:

a. State the null and alternative hypotheses.

b. Choose the appropriate statistical procedure (Z or t).

c. Identify the level of significance and the corresponding critical value.

d. Calculate Z or t.

e. Determine whether your results are significant.

f. State in one or two sentences your conclusions.

g. Calculate and interpret the confidence intervals.

h. Determine an exact P value if you used a Z test. If you used a t test and are using a computer statistical package, calculate an exact P value.

i. Express your results in terms of P values ($P <$ or $> \alpha$).

j. Explain what the P values tell you about statistical significance.

k. Identify whether there is a possibility of a type I or type II error, and explain what you might do to determine whether a type I or type II error exists.

8.19 The following weights were obtained from a randomly selected sample of 20-year-old, 6-foot-1-inch males from Minnesota. This sample of 25 males had a mean weight of 177 lb. Based on this sample, are Minnesota males heavier than males in general? The mean weight of all U.S. males (6′1″) is 170 lb., and the population standard deviation is 16. Assume a normal distribution. Use $\alpha = .05$.

8.20 Use the same data as in the previous exercise except that the population standard deviation is unknown but the calculated sample standard deviation is 16. Use $\alpha = .05$.

8.21 The mean diastolic blood pressure in Table 3.1 is 73 mmHg with a standard deviation of 11.6 mmHg. For $\alpha = .01$, test whether the mean blood pressure of this group is significantly greater than 70.

8.22 The mean weight of the sample of 100 persons from the Honolulu Heart Study is 64 kg. If the ideal weight is known to be 60 kg, is the group significantly overweight? Assume $\sigma = 10$ kg and $\alpha = .05$.

8.23 A company that cans soup listed the number of milligrams of sodium as 950 mg per serving. A consumers' group is concerned that the soup contains more sodium than what is listed on the can. A sample of 30 cans had a mean sodium content of 975 mg per serving and a sample standard deviation of 60 mg. Do the cans contain more than the 950 mg of sodium per serving listed on the label? Assume a normal distribution. Use $\alpha = .05$ and $\alpha = .01$, and compare your results.

8.24 From Table 3.1, we determined that the 100 subjects have a sample mean serum cholesterol level of 217 and a sample standard deviation of 39. If the desirable serum cholesterol level is set at 200, would you have concerns about elevated serum cholesterol levels in this sample? Use $\alpha = .05$.

8.25 Using the data from Table 3.1, determine whether the systolic blood pressure in the sample is significantly different from the population mean of 120 mmHg. Use $\alpha = .05$.

8.26 The standard serum cholesterol level for adult males is 200 mg/100 ml with a sample standard deviation of 16.67 mg. For a sample of 49 overweight men, the mean reading is 211 mg. Is serum cholesterol elevated in overweight men? Use $\alpha = .05$.

8.27 Boys of a certain age have a mean weight of 85 lb. A complaint is made that in a municipal children's home the boys are underfed. As one bit of evidence, all 25 boys of the given age are weighed and found to have a mean weight of 80.94 lb.
  a. If it is known in advance that the population standard deviation for weights of boys this age is 11.6 lb, what would you conclude regarding the complaint? Use $\alpha = .05$.
  b. Suppose the population standard deviation is unknown. If the sample standard deviation is found to be 12.3 lb, what conclusion regarding the complaint might you draw? Use $\alpha = .05$.

8.28 A researcher wanted to determine whether a program for routine cholesterol screening of college men would identify high serum cholesterol levels. The researcher decided that above 200 would be high. Twenty students were randomly selected for cholesterol screening, and the results are given below. Is there any evidence that asymptomatic college men have elevated serum cholesterol values? Would a large-scale screening program be warranted? Use $\alpha = .05$.

260	210	240	230	260
150	220	190	210	240
160	220	250	180	200
200	210	170	250	220

8.29 Super-Duper Cee Pills were advertised as having 750 mg of vitamin C per pill. A consumers' group believed the amount of vitamin C was less than advertised. Based on the following sample, was this advertisement justified? Use $\alpha = .01$.

700	780	715	720	760
720	710	740	720	725
760	695	755	730	720

8.30 Referring to the previous exercise, would you recommend a larger sample? Explain.

9

Two-Sample Significance Testing, Point Estimates, and Confidence Intervals

✔ LEARNING OBJECTIVES

After studying this chapter, you should be able to

1. Outline and explain the procedure for a test of significance between two sample means

(Continued)

154

2. Determine when to use an independent *t* test and when to use a paired *t* test
3. Calculate and interpret the results of an independent and a paired *t* test
4. List the pros and cons of performing a before-and-after experiment
5. Compute a confidence interval from a set of data for the difference between two population means

9.1 TWO-SAMPLE *t* TESTS

In the previous chapter, you learned how to compare one sample mean with a population mean. In this chapter, you will be comparing two samples. Samples are selected so that they are representative of a population. For example, when we want to measure some variable about a population—men, women, college students, newborn infants, and so on—we rarely have population data. We select a sample and then draw inferences about the population based on the data obtained. In this chapter, we will select two samples from two populations and ask a very basic question: Are they the same, or are they different? Two frequently compared populations are males and females. The researcher will measure one or more variables (e.g., serum cholesterol levels, blood pressure, height, weight, age) and attempt to determine whether there are differences between males and females.

For example, an instructor might want to determine whether there are gender differences in the learning or mastery of statistics. He or she might use test scores (which may or may not measure learning, but let us assume they do) to evaluate how much was learned. The instructor could calculate a mean and a standard deviation for each gender and then compare the scores. Once again, the concept of significant difference is important. If one group had $\bar{x} = 79$ and the other group had $\bar{x} = 80$, is there a difference in mean test scores for the populations represented by the samples? Your immediate response might be yes, but is the difference significant? Almost certainly, the answer is no. The question now becomes, How great must the difference be before we say that the difference is significant? The answer to this question is the basis for this chapter. We will analyze two samples that represent two populations and then determine whether the scores are close enough to allow us to conclude that there is no significant difference. Or we might find the difference to be great enough to lead us to conclude that there is a significant difference between the two samples and hence the two populations.

9.2 INDEPENDENT AND PAIRED *t* TESTS

Two-sample *t* tests may be either **independent** (unpaired) or **paired (dependent).** If the two samples are independent (unpaired), there is no connection between any subject in group 1 and any subject in group 2. A comparison of test scores between males and females is an example of **independent samples.** There is no connection between any female's test score and that of any male. This also means that the samples do not have to have an equal number.

Paired (dependent) samples are exactly what the name implies. In this case, there is a connection between scores in one group and scores in the other. For example, if you wanted to determine how much a student learned in a statistics class, you would do a pre- (before) and post- (after) test. You would have to match each student's pretest with that same student's posttest. It would be of no value to compare one student's pretest with another student's posttest. Another example of a paired sample is matched pair design. In this situation, you identify one or more characteristics and match subject 1, group a, with subject 1, group b; subject 2, group a, with subject 2, group b; and so on. For example, if you wanted to determine whether there are differences in reaction time between males and females, you might match males and females on characteristics such as height, weight, race, gender, and age or even on their condition of health. Subject 1, group a, and subject 1, group b, are similar or matched on one or more characteristics. Thus, in order to use the paired *t* test, the samples must be equal in size.

The reason it is important to identify whether the samples are independent or paired is that there are two different *t* tests, one independent and the other paired, that yield quite different results. Without worrying about the mathematics behind the explanation, note that the paired *t* test factors in an expected correlation between paired scores. For example, in a pre–post design to determine how much learning occurred in a class, you would expect individuals who had relatively high pretest scores to also have relatively high posttest scores. By measuring the difference between each individual pair, you would effectively manage this expected correlation. If you are going to conduct a two-sample *t* test, it is absolutely essential to determine whether the two groups are independent or paired.

9.3 PROCEDURE FOR A TWO-SAMPLE TEST OF SIGNIFICANCE

The procedure for a two-sample test of significance is similar to the process outlined in the previous chapter. This time, we will analyze two samples that represent two populations. We will be trying to determine if the two populations are the same or if the difference between them is great enough that we would find the difference significant.

1. Write the null and alternative hypotheses.
2. Choose a significance level, α (usually .05 or .01).
3. Compute the test statistic. The formula will be given in Examples 9.1 and 9.2.
4. Determine the critical region, using the same procedure you learned in Chapter 8.

5. Reject the null hypothesis if the test statistic, *t*, falls in the critical region (tail). Fail to reject the null hypothesis if the test statistic falls in the fail-to-reject region.
6. Calculate exact *P* values (optional—this can be done only by computer).
7. Express the results in *P* values ($P <$ or $> \alpha$).
8. Calculate confidence intervals, 95% or 99%.
9. State the appropriate conclusions.

We will use the data in Table 9.1 to illustrate a paired and an independent *t* test. We will test the hypothesis that there is an experimental effect on systolic blood pressure in males and females.

Table 9.1 Experimental Effect on Blood Pressure Level (mmHg)

Case	Pre (before)	Post (after)
1—M*	134	134
2—M	103	106
3—M	116	110
4—M	113	115
5—M	124	122
6—M	120	126
7—M	128	130
8—M	122	118
9—M	123	125
10—M	108	110
11—M	134	138
12—M	108	111
13—M	111	115
14—M	125	125
15—M	134	130
16—F*	105	103
17—F	118	120
18—F	97	95
19—F	104	105
20—F	99	104
21—F	131	134
22—F	108	105
23—F	112	110
24—F	97	100
25—F	104	107
26—F	103	100
27—F	114	112
28—F	96	98
29—F	126	127
30—F	109	106

*M = male, F = female

9.4 TEST OF SIGNIFICANCE OF TWO INDEPENDENT SAMPLE MEANS

You learned in Chapter 8 of the frequent need to compare sample means. Because we seldom know the value of σ, we estimate it by its **pooled sample standard deviation,** s_p, and compute the test statistic, with $n_1 + n_2 - 2$ df. Using this test statistic, we compare $\bar{x}_1 - \bar{x}_2$, the difference between the sample means (an estimate of the difference between population means), with $\mu_1 - \mu_2$, the unknown difference between the population means.

■ **EXAMPLE 1**

Using the blood pressure data in Table 9.1, let us test the hypothesis that the preexperiment blood pressure in males is higher than that in females.

1. H_0: $\mu_1 \leq \mu_2$ or $\mu_1 - \mu_2 \leq 0$
   H_1: $\mu_1 > \mu_2$ or $\mu_1 - \mu_2 > 0$

   Note: It doesn't matter whether the males or the females are group 1. What does matter is that, if the males are group 1, then we expect the blood pressure in group 1 to be greater than that in group 2. Conversely, if the females are labeled group 1, then H_1 would look like this:

   H_1: $\mu_1 < \mu_2$ or $\mu_1 - \mu_2 < 0$

2. Significance level: $\alpha = .05$.

3. Test statistic: From Table 9.1, we have the following data:

Group Information for Pretest Blood Pressure (grouping variable: gender)

	Count	Mean	Variance	Standard Deviation	Standard Error
Male	15	120.200	102.029	10.101	2.608
Female	15	108.200	109.886	10.483	2.707

The formula for calculating the independent t statistic is

$$t = \frac{\bar{x}_1 - \bar{x}_2 - (\mu_1 - \mu_2)}{s_p \sqrt{\dfrac{1}{n_1} + \dfrac{1}{n_2}}} \tag{9.1}$$

To compute s_p, we use the following equation:

$$s_p = \sqrt{\frac{s_1^2(n_1 - 1) + s_2^2(n_2 - 1)}{n_1 + n_2 - 2}} \tag{9.2}$$

$$= \sqrt{\frac{102.029(14) + 109.886(14)}{28}} = 10.29$$

Therefore,

$$t = \frac{120.2 - 108.2 - 0}{10.29\sqrt{\dfrac{1}{15} + \dfrac{1}{15}}} = \frac{12}{3.757} = 3.19$$

4. Critical region: We will use Table B (inside back cover) to find the critical value. Because this is a t test, we must first determine the degrees of freedom (df). The df for a two-sample independent t test is $n_1 + n_2 - 2$. We have 15 males and 15 females, so the df is $15 + 15 - 2 = 28$. Turning to Table B, we find 28 df and an area of .95, one-sided, because our alternative hypothesis is one-tailed. The critical value is 1.7011.

5. Because the computed test statistic $t = 3.19$ (step 3) falls within the critical region (beyond the critical value of $+1.70$), we are compelled to reject the null hypothesis of no difference between males and females and to not reject the alternative hypothesis that the males' blood pressures are significantly greater than the females' (see Figure 9.1).

6. Using a computer statistical package (the two most widely used are SPSS and SAS), we calculate a P value of .0035.

7. $P < .05$. We can determine this in two ways. One way is to look at the calculated and critical values (see Figure 9.1). Because the calculated value is in the tail of the distribution, we know that $P < .05$. The other way is simply to look at the exact P value. Because $.0035 < .05$, we conclude that $P < .05$.

8. Next we calculate the confidence interval (CI) using the following formula:

$$95\% \text{ CI for } \mu_1 - \mu_2 = \bar{x}_1 - \bar{x}_2 \pm t_{.05}\left(s_p\sqrt{\frac{1}{n_1} + \frac{1}{n_2}}\right) \qquad (9.3)$$

Using the data from step 3, we know that the blood pressure difference between males and females is 12. We also know the value of $s_p\sqrt{1/n_1 + 1/n_2}$, which is 3.757. The third number we need in order to calculate the confidence interval is the t value. This value always comes

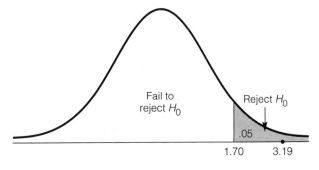

Figure 9.1   Critical Region for Independent t Test.

from Table B and is always two-tailed. Turn to Table B and look at 28 df. The t value is 2.0484. The 95% CI is

$$12 \pm 2.0484(3.757) = 4.30 < \mu < 19.70$$

The interpretation of this CI is that we are 95% sure (or confident) that the population of males' blood pressures ranges from a low of 4.30 points higher to as much as 19.70 points higher than females' blood pressures.

9. Once again, rejecting or failing to reject the null hypothesis, and therefore determining whether the results are significant, finishes the statistics part of the problem. Again, we need to develop meaningful and accurate conclusions based on the statistical analysis. In this example, we rejected our null hypothesis. We can therefore conclude that the systolic blood pressure of males is significantly greater than the systolic blood pressure of females. We could also conclude that the systolic blood pressure of females is significantly lower than the systolic blood pressure of males. ■

9.5   PAIRED (DEPENDENT) t TESTS

Using the data set from Table 9.1, we will now try to determine whether the experimental conditions led to a change in blood pressure. In this investigation, the treatment group will be used as its own control. This technique often generates quite appropriate comparisons, because variability due to extraneous factors is reduced. It is not unusual for extraneous factors to account for many of the differences between means obtained from two independent samples. Use of the treatment group as its own control reduces the variability and gives a smaller standard error, and hence a narrower confidence interval. But we pay a price. First, independence is sacrificed in that we have two samples measured on the same items. Second, we are left with about half the degrees of freedom we would obtain using two independent samples. With fewer degrees of freedom, the t value is larger and, consequently, the confidence interval is wider. We must take these pros and cons into consideration when we plan an experiment. Only then can we tell which procedure—two independent samples or a paired t test—will be more advantageous.

Before we perform the statistical analysis, we have to decide whether we will look at pre- and posttest scores for the entire sample or divide the analysis by gender. We might choose the entire sample if we thought the experimental conditions would affect males and females equally. But, we have just completed an independent t test analysis, and we already know that there is a significant difference between males and females. As in many problems, there might be a "best" choice but not a choice that is unquestionably 100% correct. Without trying to completely resolve the issue, let us assume that there are gender differences in determining whether the systolic blood pressure is significantly changed by the experimental conditions.

■ **EXAMPLE 2**

Using the blood pressure data in Table 9.1, let us test the hypothesis that the preexperiment systolic blood pressure in males is different from the post-experiment systolic blood pressure:

1. H_0: $\mu_1 = \mu_2$ or $\mu_1 - \mu_2 = 0$
   H_1: $\mu_1 \neq \mu_2$ or $\mu_1 - \mu_2 \neq 0$

   Let μ_1 represent the preexperiment blood pressure and μ_2 the postexperiment. In this problem, we will use a two-tailed test because we are trying to determine if the pre- and postexperimental conditions lead to a change in blood pressure without knowing whether the change will lead to a higher or a lower blood pressure.

2. Significance level: $\alpha = .05$.

3. Test statistic: The data are given in Table 9.2.

   The formula for calculating the paired *t* statistic is

$$t = \frac{\bar{d} - 0}{s_d/\sqrt{n}} \tag{9.4}$$

Table 9.2 Experimental Effect on Blood Pressure Level (mmHg)

Case	Pre (before) x	Post (after) y	$d = x - y$	d^2
1—M*	134	134	0	0
2—M	103	106	−3	9
3—M	116	110	6	36
4—M	113	115	−2	4
5—M	124	122	2	4
6—M	120	126	−6	36
7—M	128	130	−2	4
8—M	122	118	4	16
9—M	123	125	−2	4
10—M	108	110	−2	4
11—M	134	138	−4	16
12—M	108	111	−3	9
13—M	111	115	−4	16
14—M	125	125	0	0
15—M	134	130	4	16
	$\Sigma x = 1803$	$\Sigma y = 1815$	$\Sigma d = -12$	$\Sigma d^2 = 174$

$$\bar{x}_1 = 120.2 \qquad \bar{x}_2 = 121.0 \qquad \bar{d} = -.80$$
$$\bar{d} = \bar{x}_1 - \bar{x}_2 \qquad = 120.2 \; - \; 121.0 \quad = -.80$$
$$\bar{d} = \frac{\Sigma d}{n} \qquad\qquad = \frac{-12}{15} \qquad\qquad = -.80$$

*M = male

NOTE: When you are calculating a paired *t* test, *n always* equals the number of pairs.

The value $\bar{d}$ is the mean difference between x (before) and y (after) for each case; s_d is the estimate of the standard deviation of the differences.

To compute s_d, we use the following equation:

$$s_d = \sqrt{\frac{\Sigma d^2 - (\Sigma d)^2/n}{n-1}} \qquad (9.5)$$

Note that in a paired t test n *always* represents the number of pairs.

$$s_d = \sqrt{\frac{174 - (-12)^2/15}{14}} = 3.42678$$

$$t = \frac{-.80}{3.43/\sqrt{15}} = \frac{-.80}{.885} = -.90$$

4. Critical region: We again use Table B to find the critical value. Because this is a paired t test, df $= n-1$ (n = number of pairs). Because we have pre- and posttest scores for 15 males, df $= 15 - 1 = 14$. Turning to Table B, we find 14 df and an area of .95, two-sided, because our alternative hypothesis is two-tailed. The critical value is ± 2.1448.

5. Because the computed test statistic $t = -.90$ (step 3) falls within the fail-to-reject region, we must fail to reject the null hypothesis of no difference between pre- and posttest systolic blood pressure for the male subjects (see Figure 9.2).

6. The exact P value is .3812. Again, this value was computer-generated.

7. $P > .05$. The calculated value is less than the critical value (see Figure 9.2), and the exact P value, .3812, is greater than .05.

8. Next, we calculate the confidence interval (CI) using the following formula:

$$95\% \text{ CI for } (\mu_1 - \mu_2) = \bar{d} \pm t_{.05}\left(\frac{s_d}{\sqrt{n}}\right) \qquad (9.6)$$

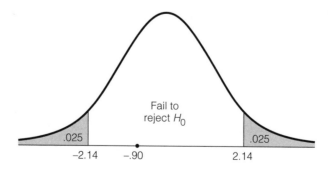

Figure 9.2   Critical Region for Independent t Test.

Using the data from step 3, we know that the pre- and postexperiment blood pressure difference is $-.80$. The value of s_d is 3.43. The third number we need is the t value. Again, this value *always* comes from Table B and is *always* two-tailed. Turn to Table B and look at 14 df (df $= n - 1$, with n representing the number of pairs). The t value is 2.1448. The 95% CI is

$$-.80 \pm 2.1448(.885) = -2.70 < \mu_1 - \mu_2 < 1.10$$

When we have a CI that goes from a negative number to a positive number, the interpretation is a little more difficult. The number -2.70 is fairly easy to interpret. We are 95% sure that systolic blood pressures may be as much as 2.70 points *lower* in the pretest than in the posttest. But what about the number 1.10? The interpretation is that blood pressures may be as much as 1.10 points *higher* in the pretest than in the posttest. Remember that in both the independent and the paired t test the confidence intervals represent the difference between the two means.

9. Our final step is to give meaning to our calculations. When we compared the calculated and critical values, we failed to reject the null hypothesis that there is no significant difference in pre- and posttest blood pressures. As a general rule, when we have a CI that goes from a negative number to a positive number, we will also fail to reject the null hypothesis, because the hypothesized difference is zero, and zero is included in the CI. In this example, this means that the experimental conditions did not lead to a change in systolic blood pressure among the males. ∎

9.6 DETERMINATION OF SAMPLE SIZE

The daily life of a modern statistician involves a lot more than manipulating data and running computer programs. The statistician serves as a resource—sometimes to scientists, sometimes to administrators, almost always to persons less sophisticated in statistics. The statistician has to be prepared to answer many questions, and one of the most commonly heard is "How large a sample size do I need to obtain a statistically meaningful result?"

That is a tough question. It is analogous, in a sense, to "How many runs must we score to win the ball game?" In the ballpark, you could not field that one without more information, so you would have to ask a few questions yourself: "What's the score? What inning? Who's at bat? How many outs?" Similarly, in approaching the sample size question, you first need to ask: "How much error can I live with in estimating the population mean? What level of confidence is needed in the estimate? How much variability exists in the observations?" Once you have the answers to these questions, you can attack the sample-size question.

Arithmetically, the sample size can be obtained by solving for n in the now-familiar equation

$$Z = \frac{\bar{x} - \mu}{\sigma/\sqrt{n}} \tag{9.7}$$

which could be rewritten as

$$Z = \frac{d}{\sigma/\sqrt{n}}$$

where $d = \bar{x} - \mu$ and is a measure of how close we need to come to the population mean μ. Put another way, the estimate should be within d units of the population mean. Solving for n, we obtain

$$n = \left(\frac{Z\sigma}{d}\right)^2 \tag{9.8}$$

■ **EXAMPLE 3**

You need to estimate the mean serum cholesterol level of a population within 10 mg/dl of the true mean. You learn that $\sigma = 20$, and you want to state with 95% confidence that $\bar{x}$ is within 10 units of μ. So you obtain n as follows:

$$n = \frac{[(1.96)(20)]^2}{10^2} = 15.36$$

Because fractional sample sizes are not available, you conservatively round up to the next integer and get busy obtaining a sample of 16. If σ is unknown, you estimate it by s and use the t distribution. ■

Knowing how to determine sample size in advance of an experiment is wise planning, because your financial resources might limit you to, say, only 10 guinea pigs. If 16 are needed to gain significant results, it would be unwise to proceed. Alternatively, you could conserve resources by advance knowledge of the number of animals needed. If 16 guinea pigs would suffice, it would not be cost-effective to do the experiment with 30 animals. Equation (9.8) is the simplest way of estimating sample size. All the approaches underscore an important counsel to researchers: Consult a statistician to determine your sample size.

9.7 SENSITIVITY AND SPECIFICITY

A patient's diagnosis often depends on the outcome of a measurement of a clinical test. Frequently, the measurement has a wide range for both the clinically normal and the diseased states. And because there is no definite dividing line between the normal and the diseased conditions, a patient classified as abnormal could in fact be normal, and a patient classified as normal could in fact be abnormal.

To classify an individual as having or not having a certain condition, we need to compare the value of a clinical test with some given cutoff point that divides individuals into normal or abnormal. A clinical value falling in the abnormal range suggests that the person has the disease; a value falling in the normal range suggests that the person does not have the disease. Here, as with the rejection of H_0, it is possible to make two errors:

1. Classifying a person as diseased when one is not—a **false positive**
2. Classifying a person as not diseased when one has the disease—a **false negative**

We can better understand these terms by looking at the following symbolic representation of the results of classification:

		"True" Patient Condition		
		Diseased	Not Diseased	
Result of Test	Disease Present	a	b	$a + b$
	Disease Absent	c	d	$c + d$
		$a + c$	$b + d$	$a + b + c + d$

The false negatives are represented by c, and the false positives are represented by b.

In comparing the effectiveness of different clinical tests or screening tests, we are interested in knowing what their sensitivities and specificities are. **Sensitivity** is the probability that the clinical test declares those persons positive who have the disease. In terms of the table,

$$\text{Sensitivity} = \frac{a}{a + c}$$

Specificity is the probability that the clinical test declares those persons negative who are without the disease—that is,

$$\text{Specificity} = \frac{d}{b + d}$$

Table 9.3 Outcome of Diabetic Screening Program

	Diabetic	Nondiabetic	
Above 125 mg/100 ml	5	13	18
Below 125 mg/100 ml	1	81	82
	6	94	100

We can see from the table that a relationship exists between these two probabilities and false negatives and false positives; that is, the probability of being a
false negative is 1 minus the sensitivity, and the probability of a false positive
is 1 minus the specificity.

■ **EXAMPLE 4**

A screening program for diabetics used a cutoff point for blood glucose level of
125 mg/100 ml. Those with values above this level were considered diabetics,
and those below were not. Using the results shown in Table 9.3 for 100 individuals, find the sensitivity and the specificity of this screening test.

$$\text{Sensitivity} = \frac{a}{a + c} = 100 \times \frac{5}{6} = 83.3\% \ (16.7\% \text{ false negative})$$

$$\text{Specificity} = \frac{d}{b + d} = 100 \times \frac{81}{94} = 86.2\% \ (13.8\% \text{ false positive})$$

These results indicate that using a blood glucose cutoff point of 125 mg/100 ml
is a procedure with an 83.3% sensitivity and 86.2% specificity; that is, this procedure will declare an average 16.7% of individuals not to be diabetics when
they are diabetics and will declare 13.8% of individuals to be diabetics when
they are not. Because sensitivity and specificity are both binomial proportions,
we can compute for them the standard errors and confidence intervals, as given
in Table 9.4. ■

9.8 SUMMARY TABLE OF INFERENCE FORMULAS

Table 9.4 is a convenient summary of the confidence intervals and test statistics
used in testing hypotheses of specific parameters. The confidence intervals are
discussed in Chapters 8 and 9 for μ and $\mu_1 - \mu_2$ and in Chapter 11 for π and
$\pi_1 - \pi_2$.

Table 9.4 Summary Table of Confidence Intervals and Test Statistics for Various Parameters

Parameter	Confidence Interval	Hypothesis	Test Statistic
μ	$(1 - \alpha)$ 100% CI for μ $= \bar{x} \pm Z\dfrac{\sigma}{\sqrt{n}}$ or $= \bar{x} \pm t\dfrac{s}{\sqrt{n}}$ if σ unknown	$H_0: \mu = \mu_0$	$Z = \dfrac{\bar{x} - \mu_0}{\sigma/\sqrt{n}}$ $t = \dfrac{\bar{x} - \mu_0}{s/\sqrt{n}}$ df $= n - 1$
π^*	$(1 - \alpha)$ 100% CI for π $= p \pm Z\sqrt{\dfrac{p(1 - p)}{n}}$	$H_0: \pi = \pi_0$	$Z = \dfrac{p - \pi_0}{\sqrt{\dfrac{\pi_0(1 - \pi_0)}{n}}}$
δ	$(1 - \alpha)$ 100% CI for δ $= \bar{d} \pm t\dfrac{s_d}{\sqrt{n}}$	$H_0: \delta = 0$	$t = \dfrac{\bar{d} - 0}{s_d/\sqrt{n}}$ df $= n - 1$
$\mu_1 - \mu_2$	$(1 - \alpha)$100% CI for $(\mu_1 - \mu_2)$ $= \bar{x}_1 - \bar{x}_2 \pm Z\sigma\sqrt{\dfrac{1}{n_1} + \dfrac{1}{n_2}}$ or $= \bar{x}_1 - \bar{x}_2 \pm ts_p^{**}\sqrt{\dfrac{1}{n_1} + \dfrac{1}{n_2}}$	$H_0: \mu_1 - \mu_2 = 0$	$Z = \dfrac{\bar{x}_1 - \bar{x}_2 - 0}{\sigma\sqrt{\dfrac{1}{n_1} + \dfrac{1}{n_2}}}$ or $t = \dfrac{\bar{x}_1 - \bar{x}_2 - 0}{s_p\sqrt{\dfrac{1}{n_1} + \dfrac{1}{n_2}}}$ df $= n_1 + n_2 - 2$
$(\pi_1 - \pi_2)^*$	$(1 - \alpha)$ 100% CI for $(\pi_1 - \pi_2)$ $= p_1 - p_2 \pm Z\sqrt{\dfrac{p_1(1 - p_1)}{n_1} + \dfrac{p_2(1 - p_2)}{n_2}}$	$H_0: \pi_1 - \pi_2 = 0$	$Z = \dfrac{p_1 - p_2 - 0}{\sqrt{p'(1 - p')\left(\dfrac{1}{n_1} + \dfrac{1}{n_2}\right)}}$ where $p' = \dfrac{x_1 + x_2}{n_1 + n_2}$

*Discussed in Chapter 11.

$**s_p^2 = \dfrac{s_1^2(n_1 - 1) + s_2^2(n_2 - 1)}{n_1 + n_2 - 2}$

◆ CONCLUSION

You now should be capable of comprehensively solving a two-sample hypothesis problem. It is first necessary to determine whether the samples are independent or paired and whether the test is one- or two-tailed. Next choose a significance level and calculate the t statistic. Then determine whether your results are significant, and identify the resultant P values. Finally, calculate and interpret the confidence intervals. Remember that two-sample confidence intervals represent the difference between the means. You should also be prepared to answer the statistician's toughest and most commonly heard question: "How large a sample do I need?" The answer is both easy and difficult—easy in employing a simple equation, difficult in getting the right input into the equation.

◆ VOCABULARY LIST

false negative	paired (dependent)	pooled sample standard
false positive	samples	deviation
independent samples	paired (dependent)	sensitivity
independent t tests	t tests	specificity

◆ EXERCISES

The exercises in this chapter can be done by calculator or computer program. If you are using SPSS, an excellent (and inexpensive) handbook that shows you how to calculate and interpret t tests is *Ready, Set, Go! A Student Guide to SPSS 9.0 for Windows,* by Pavkov and Pierce (2000).

9.1   a. What assumptions regarding the difference of two means are made in performing the t test?
   b. What is the basis for pooling the sample variances when testing the difference between two population means?

9.2   If you calculated a two-sample t test and found an exact P value of .0000, would it be acceptable to conclude that you are absolutely certain that the difference between the two means is significant? Explain.

9.3   Compute 99% confidence intervals for $\mu_1 - \mu_2$ between males and females if, for 38 males, $\bar{x}_1 = 74.9$ and $s_1^2 = 144$, and, for 45 females, $\bar{x}_2 = 71.8$ and $s_2^2 = 121$.

9.4   The weight gain for a control diet of $n_1 = 10$ individuals is $\bar{x}_1 = 12.78$ and for a treatment diet of $n_2 = 9$ individuals is $\bar{x}_2 = 15.27$. The corresponding variances are $s_1^2 = 13.9$ and $s_2^2 = 12.8$. Compute the 95% confidence interval for $\mu_1 - \mu_2$.

9.5   Do Exercise 9.4 after making the following changes:
   $n_1 = 25, n_2 = 16$.

9.6   Compare the confidence intervals for Exercises 9.4 and 9.5. As the sample size increases, what happens to the confidence intervals? Explain why this occurs.

9.7   The mean serum cholesterol level of 25 men ages 65–74 is 231, with $s_1 = 50$. For 25 women of the same age, the mean is 255, with $s_2 = 49$.

a. What is the 95% confidence interval for the difference in mean serum cholesterol levels between men and women?
b. What is the 99% confidence interval?

9.8 The mean hemoglobin of $n_1 = 16$ white women is $\bar{x}_1 = 13.7$, with $s_1^2 = 2.3$, and for $n_2 = 20$ black women is $\bar{x}_2 = 12.5$, with $s_2^2 = 2.1$.
a. What is the 95% confidence interval for $\mu_w - \mu_b$, the difference between white and black women's hemoglobin?
b. What is the 99% confidence interval for $\mu_w - \mu_b$?

9.9 A hospital administrator wishes to estimate the mean number of days that infants spend in ICUs.
a. How many records should she examine to have 99% confidence that the estimate is not more than .5 day from the mean? Previous records suggest that $\sigma = 1.6$.
b. How many records should she examine if she wants to lower the confidence interval to 95%?

◆ COMPREHENSIVE EXERCISES

Using the data in Exercises 9.10–9.24, do the following:
a. State the null and alternative hypotheses.
b. Choose the appropriate statistical procedure (independent or paired t).
c. Identify the level of significance and the corresponding critical value.
d. Calculate t.
e. If you are using a computer statistical package and the exercise has raw data, calculate an exact P value.
f. Express your results in terms of P values ($P <$ or $> \alpha$).
g. Calculate and interpret the confidence intervals.
h. Determine whether your results are significant.
i. State in one or two sentences your conclusions.
j. Identify whether there is a possibility of a type I or type II error and explain what you might do to determine whether a type I or type II error exists.

9.10 Based on the data from Table 9.1, do the experimental conditions cause a change in the systolic blood pressure of females? Use $\alpha = .05$.

9.11 Again using the data from Table 9.1, determine whether there is a significant difference in posttest systolic blood pressures of males and females. Use $\alpha = .05$.

9.12 Measurements of birth lengths of male and female infants in a small clinic gave the following results:

Group	Sample Size	$\bar{x}$ (cm)	s (cm)
Males	12	52.2	8.6
Females	9	50.7	9.5

Assuming normally distributed populations with equal variances, do these data justify the conclusion, at $\alpha = .05$, that the mean birth length is greater for males than for females?

9.13 A study was conducted using 139 undergraduates at a large private university who volunteered to participate in the research as partial fulfillment of a course requirement. One of the items studied was the maximum daily amount of alcohol consumed in the last month. Based on the data in the following table, are there differences between males and females in the maximum amount of alcohol consumed in any one day in the past month? Use $\alpha = .05$.

Maximum Daily Quantity of Alcohol Consumed in Last Month	
Men	Women
$\bar{x} = 8.2$	$\bar{x} = 5.6$
$s = 5.9$	$s = 5.7$
$n = 54$	$n = 85$

NOTE: These data were extrapolated and are based on Carey and Correia (1997).

9.14 After completing (a)–(j), refer to Chapter 2, "Populations and Samples." What concerns would you have about generalizing these results to all college students? Identify as many concerns as you can.

9.15 Mice of a given strain were assigned randomly to two experimental groups. Each mouse was injected with a measured amount of tumor pulp. The pulp came from a large, suitable tumor excised from another mouse. After the tumor injections, the two groups received different chemotherapy treatments. Forty days after injection, the tumor volumes (in cubic centimeters) were measured as a comparison of the treatments. The data are as follows:

	Chemotherapy Treatment A	Chemotherapy Treatment B
n	27	30
$\bar{x}$	.51 cc	.64 cc
s^2	.010	.045
	$s_p = .17$	

Is there a difference in tumor volume between the two treatments? Use $\alpha = .01$.

9.16 Cholesterol measurements from 54 vegetarians and 51 nonvegetarians yield the following data:

Vegetarians:	115	125	125	130	130	130	130	135	135	140
	140	140	140	145	145	150	150	150	155	160
	160	160	160	160	165	165	165	165	165	165
	165	170	170	170	170	170	170	170	175	175
	175	180	180	180	180	180	185	185	185	200
	215	215	225	230						
Nonvegetarians:	105	110	115	125	125	130	135	145	145	150
	150	160	165	165	165	170	170	170	170	170
	175	175	175	180	180	180	180	185	185	190
	190	190	190	195	200	200	200	200	200	205
	210	210	210	210	215	220	230	230	240	240
	245									

Do vegetarians have lower cholesterol levels than nonvegetarians? Let $\alpha = .01$.

9.17 For Table 2.2, the means and standard deviations of some subgroups of the sample are as shown in the following table:

Subgroup	Mean	Standard Deviation	n
Vegetarians	72.9	11.7	40
Nonvegetarians	73.5	11.4	43
Males	74.9	12.0	38
Females	71.8	11.0	45

Is there a significant difference in the mean diastolic blood pressures, at $\alpha = .05$, between
a. vegetarians and nonvegetarians
b. males and females

9.18 Using the data from the first 50 individuals of the Honolulu Heart Study population in Table 3.1, determine whether there is a difference in the mean systolic blood pressures of smokers and nonsmokers. Use $\alpha = .01$.

9.19 Ten experimental animals were subjected to conditions simulating disease. The number of heartbeats per minute, before and after the experiment, were recorded as follows:

	Heartbeats per Minute				Heartbeats per Minute		
Animal	Before	After	d	Animal	Before	After	d
1	70	115	45	6	120	115	−5
2	84	128	44	7	110	110	0
3	88	146	58	8	67	140	73
4	110	171	61	9	79	131	52
5	105	158	53	10	86	157	71

Do these data provide sufficient evidence to indicate that the experimental condition increases the number of heartbeats per minute? Use $\alpha = .05$.

9.20 Blood samples from 10 persons were sent to each of two labs for cholesterol determinations. Measurements were as follows:

	Serum Cholesterol (mg/ml)	
Subject	Lab 1	Lab 2
1	296	318
2	268	287
3	244	260
4	272	279
5	240	245
6	244	249
7	282	294
8	254	271
9	244	262
10	262	285

Is there a statistically significant difference (at $\alpha = .01$) in the cholesterol levels reported by lab 1 and lab 2?

a. Should you use the independent t test or the paired t test to answer this question?

b. Perform the test you chose for (a) and answer the question.

c. Perform the test you did *not* choose for (a) and compare the result with (b). What do you observe?

9.21 As part of a study to determine the effects of a certain oral contraceptive on weight gain, 12 healthy females were weighed at the beginning of a course of oral contraceptive usage. They were reweighed after 3 months. Do the results suggest evidence of weight gain? Use $\alpha = .05$.

Subject	Initial Weight (lb)	3-Month Weight (lb)
1	120	123
2	141	143
3	130	140
4	162	162
5	150	145
6	148	150
7	135	140
8	140	143
9	129	130
10	120	118
11	140	141
12	130	132

9.22 The resting heart rates were measured in a sample of women smokers and non-smokers at a state university. There were 14 smokers and 18 nonsmokers in the sample. Was there a significant difference in the resting heart rates of the two groups? Use $\alpha = .05$. (Use a two-tailed test.)

Resting Heart Rates			
Smokers		Nonsmokers	
78	85	72	62
100	82	82	66
88	77	62	68
62	91	84	96
94	90	61	58
88	68	68	87
76		72	80
90		64	78
		76	69

9.23 Data were gathered from 558 female Mexican Americans, ages 14–18, from four high schools in the lower Rio Grande Valley region of Texas. Skinfold measurements were taken to assess percent body fat. The females were divided into two groups: (1) athletes who participated in high school sports, and (2) nonathletes, who did not participate. Based on the following data, are there differences between athletes and nonathletes in percent body fat? Use an $\alpha = .05$ and .01, and 95% and 99% confidence intervals.

Skinfold Measurements of Mexican American High School Girls	
Athletes	Nonathletes
$\bar{x} = 35.9\%$	$\bar{x} = 41.4\%$
$s = 11.92$	$s = 17.63$
$n = 186$	$n = 372$

NOTE: These data were extrapolated from Guinn et al. (2002).

9.24 Using the data from Table 3.1, analyze the differences between smokers and nonsmokers using the following variables: weight, blood glucose levels, serum cholesterol levels, and systolic blood pressure.

10 ANOVA

✔ LEARNING OBJECTIVES

After studying this chapter, you should be able to

1. Indicate the circumstances that call for ANOVA rather than a t test
2. Set up an ANOVA table that partitions the total sum of squares into between-group and within-group sums of squares

(Continued)

3. Compute the F ratio and its appropriate degrees of freedom
4. List the two assumptions that need to be made to perform an ANOVA
5. Indicate the type of hypothesis that can be tested with ANOVA
6. Find the critical region for an F-ratio test
7. Indicate the reason for performing a post hoc analysis
8. Apply Tukey's multiple comparison procedure
9. Describe an example of randomized block design

10.1 THE FUNCTION OF ANOVA

In the previous chapter, you learned how to analyze differences between two groups through the use of the t test. At this point, you should be able to determine whether the differences between two groups are significant. But what would you do if you were presented with a problem that had three or more groups, instead of the two groups for which you learned how to perform and interpret the t test? It is possible to take each pair of groups and perform t tests comparing the means of each possible pair, and then to determine which pairs have a significant difference and which do not. This approach presents a number of difficulties: the choice of a proper significance level for "overtesting," the numerous tests needed if many groups are involved, and the lack of one overall measure of significance for the differences among the means.

The analysis of variance, often labeled simply **ANOVA,** is a statistical procedure that is able to handle these difficulties. In actuality, if you were to use the ANOVA formula for calculating a t test, the results would be identical. It is therefore fair to say that ANOVA is a logical extension of the t test when we have data from three or more independent groups. In fact, if you have understood and retained what you learned about hypothesis testing, you should be able to master this chapter on ANOVA.

Let us start by writing our null hypothesis. For two groups, we define

$$H_0:\ \mu_1 = \mu_2 \text{ or } \mu_1 - \mu_2 = 0$$

If we view ANOVA as an extension of the t test, the null hypothesis becomes

$$H_0:\ \mu_1 = \mu_2 = \ldots = \mu_k$$

where k is the number of groups.

Before we write an actual null hypothesis, let us introduce the data set that we will use initially to illustrate the application and interpretation of ANOVA. Suppose a researcher wants to determine whether different brands of cereal lead to different amounts of weight gain. The subjects will be laboratory rats.

The researcher will start with 20 baby rats and four different brands of cereal. When the rats are weaned, the researcher will randomly divide the animals into four groups, with each group having five animals. All four groups will have identical lab conditions, with one exception: the brand of cereal that each group receives during the experimental period.

Now let us go back to the null hypothesis. Remember that the two key words for the null hypothesis are *no difference*, but this time we have four groups rather than two. Symbolically, the null hypothesis being tested, with four groups, is

$$H_0: \; \mu_1 = \mu_2 = \mu_3 = \mu_4$$

The alternative hypothesis, H_1, is that H_0 is not true; that is, either one of the means is not equal to the others or none of them are equal. The theoretical basis for performing ANOVA is the partitioning of the variance of all observations into two sources of variation: variation *between* the group means and variation *within* each group. The sampling distribution used for testing is called the **F distribution** (named in honor of the celebrated R. A. Fisher, who developed the F statistic). Our example is also an example of what is termed a one-way or one-factor ANOVA. The one factor, or variable, is weight change. The data that you will see represent the number of ounces gained during the experimental period.

10.2 THE RATIONALE FOR ANOVA

Analysis of variance is unique in that it compares two different estimates of the population variance to test a hypothesis concerning the population mean. The first of these variances is the **within-group variance,** which is simply the sum of the variances of each group. You learned how to calculate variance, as well as standard deviation, in Chapter 4. Now look at Table 10.1. Note that we have included only the data from cereal A. In this hypothetical experiment, each animal fed cereal A had a mean weight gain of 1 oz. In group A, there is absolutely no variability, so without even performing any calculations you can look at Table 10.1 and see that the within-group variance for group A is zero.

In Table 10.2, the data from cereal B, or group B, is included. You can quickly notice that each animal fed cereal B had a mean weight gain of 7 oz. Once again,

Table 10.1 Weight Gain (oz) of Rats Fed Four Different Brands of Cereal

A	B	C	D
1			
1			
1			
1			
1			

Table 10.2 Weight Gain (oz) of Rats Fed Four Different Brands of Cereal

A	B	C	D
1	7		
1	7		
1	7		
1	7		
1	7		

there is absolutely no variability, which means that the within-group variance for group B is also zero.

If we were to stop here and ask you to analyze the data from groups A and B, you would undoubtedly choose a *t* test for independent means. Without actually performing the *t* test, try to visualize the lab animals. One group has a mean weight gain of 1 oz, while another has a mean weight gain of 7 oz. If you looked at the animals, you would easily see that the group B rats are significantly heavier than the group A rats. The reason you would come to this conclusion is that, even though there is no within-group variance, there is significant (we will measure exactly how much a little later) **between-group variance.** The mean difference, 6 oz, is clearly a significant difference.

Before we finish displaying the data and begin the calculations, it is important that you understand what the within-group variance and between-group variances represent. Recall that at the beginning of the chapter our hypothetical research project was to take 20 rats, divide them equally into four groups, and feed each group a different cereal, keeping all other experimental conditions equal for each animal. If the rats are genetically similar and if their environments are identical, then we should expect to see very little variability in weight during the experiment. In other words, the within-group variance should be minimal. This is what we would normally expect to find in a tightly controlled experiment, although the within-group variance will rarely, if ever, be zero as in this experiment.

Suppose we were studying weight gain (or loss) in a human population. Would you expect a low within-group variance? Probably not, for several reasons. Humans are not all genetically similar; the environment cannot be controlled as in a lab experiment; and, even if the calorie consumption were similar, the types of foods eaten might vary from person to person. Thus, we would expect much more within-group variance. Ideally, researchers want to minimize the amount of within-group variance. Controlling the within-group variance is obviously much easier in lab settings than in natural human settings.

Let us now go back and review the data from Table 10.2. We have already determined that the group B rats gained significantly more weight than the group A rats. Everything being equal, with the important exception of the brand of cereal, what might be the reason for the weight gain difference? The researcher expects the reason to be that there is a treatment difference—that is, cereal B, for whatever reason, caused the group B rats to gain more weight. This is the key feature of between-group variance: Between-group variance measures the treatment effect, which in this example is the weight gain from each different brand of cereal.

Before moving on, we need to introduce some terminology. By convention (agreement among statisticians), within-group variance is denoted by s_w^2. The between-group variance, which measures the variation between the means of the various groups, is denoted by s_b^2. The within-group variance and the between-group variance are also referred to as the **mean squares** or MS. The terms *within-group variance* and *MS within* are interchangeable, as are the terms *between-group variance* and *MS between*. Thus, s_w^2 is the same as MS_w, and s_b^2 is the same as MS_b. Most computer printouts and journal articles use the label MS. The ANOVA tables in this chapter are labeled MS or mean squares.

The comparison of the within-group variance and between-group variance is the basis for the ANOVA statistical procedure. If the between-group variance exceeds the within-group variance, we conclude that there is a treatment effect. In the previous example, this means that one cereal produced greater weight gain than the other. However, if the between-group variance is approximately equal to the within-group variance, we conclude that there is no treatment effect. With this knowledge, we can perform a test of the hypothesis of equality of means by comparing the ratio of the two variance estimates, s_b^2/s_w^2. If the two variances are indeed equal, the ratio s_b^2/s_w^2 should be approximately 1. Because we are dealing with s^2, an estimate of σ^2, the ratio will sometimes be greater and sometimes be smaller than 1 even if the hypothesis of equal means is true. The ratio s_b^2/s_w^2 follows the F distribution and is illustrated in Figure 10.1.

In fact, there is a family of F distributions—one for each pair of degrees of freedom. The F statistic follows a skewed distribution, with two sets of degrees of freedom. The variance estimate s_b^2 has $k - 1$ df (labeled df_b), where k is the number of groups; s_w^2 has $N - k$ df (labeled df_w). Note that in this chapter n represents the number of observations in *each group*, and N is the *total number* of observations. The number of observations per group does not have to be the same. However, in this chapter, the two examples and the end-of-chapter exercises will all have equal n. The table in Appendix B gives critical values for the F distribution. Separate tabulations are provided for $\alpha = .05$ and $\alpha = .01$. For

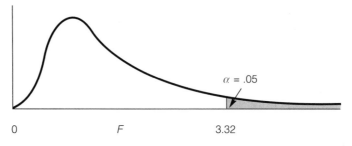

Figure 10.1   Critical Value of $F_{2,30} = 3.32$, $\alpha = .05$.

example, the critical F value for 2 (df_b) and 30 (df_w) df is 3.32 for $\alpha = .05$ (see Figure 10.1) and 5.39 for $\alpha = .01$.

ANOVA CALCULATIONS

Before we show all the data for our example, we need to describe the procedure for computing ANOVA. This procedure may be used for both equal and unequal numbers for any number k groups. The observations within each group are indicated with **double notation,** with the first subscript indicating the group number and the second subscript indicating the observation in that group; for example, x_{12} is the second observation in group 1. By extension, the jth observation in the ith group is indicated by x_{ij} (see Table 10.3). The mean for group 1 is denoted by the familiar $\bar{x}$ and is given by the formula

$$\bar{x}_1 = \sum_{j=1}^{n_1} \frac{x_{1j}}{n_i} = \frac{x_1}{n_1} \tag{10.1}$$

The sum of all observations is given by

$$\sum_{i=1}^{k} \sum_{j=1}^{n_i} x_{ij} \tag{10.2}$$

The overall mean is obtained by dividing the total of all observations of all groups by the total number of observations N, where

$$N = \sum_{i=1}^{k} n_i \tag{10.3}$$

Table 10.3 Symbolic Representation of Data in a One-Way Analysis of k Groups, with Equal Number of Observations per Group

	Group						
	1	2		i		k	
	x_{11}	x_{21}	$\cdots$	x_{i1}	$\cdots$	x_{k1}	
	x_{12}	x_{22}	$\cdots$	x_{i2}	$\cdots$	x_{k2}	
	x_{13}	x_{23}	$\cdots$	x_{i3}	$\cdots$	x_{k3}	
	$\vdots$	$\vdots$		$\vdots$		$\vdots$	
	x_{1j}	x_{2j}	$\cdots$	x_{ij}	$\cdots$	x_{kj}	
	$\vdots$	$\vdots$		$\vdots$		$\vdots$	
	x_{1n_1}	x_{2n_2}	$\cdots$	x_{in_i}	$\cdots$	x_{kn_k}	
Total	Σx_{1j}	Σx_{2j}	$\cdots$	Σx_{ij}	$\cdots$	Σx_{kj}	$\Sigma\Sigma x_{ij}$ (grand total)
Mean	$\bar{x}_1$	$\bar{x}_2$	$\cdots$	$\bar{x}_i$	$\cdots$	$\bar{x}_k$	$\bar{x}$ (grand mean)

The next three formulas give the **between-group sum of squares** (SS_b), the **within-group sum of squares** (SS_w), and the total group sum of squares (SS_t). Because $SS_b + SS_w = SS_t$, any two of the three formulas will allow you to complete the necessary calculations.

$$SS_b = \left[\frac{(\Sigma x_1)^2}{n_1} + \frac{(\Sigma x_2)^2}{n_2} + \cdots \right] - \frac{\left(\sum_{i=1}^{k} \sum_{j=1}^{n} x \right)^2}{N} \tag{10.4}$$

$$SS_w = \sum_{i=1}^{k} \sum_{j=1}^{n} x^2 - \left[\frac{(\Sigma x_1)^2}{n_1} + \frac{(\Sigma x_2)^2}{n_2} + \cdots \right] \tag{10.5}$$

$$SS_t = \sum_{i=1}^{k} \sum_{j=1}^{n} x^2 - \frac{\left(\sum_{i=1}^{k} \sum_{j=1}^{n} x \right)^2}{N} \tag{10.6}$$

10.4 ASSUMPTIONS ABOUT ANOVA

To perform tests of hypotheses, we need to make three assumptions:

1. The observations are independent; that is, the value of one observation is not correlated with the value of another.
2. The observations in each group are normally distributed.
3. The variance of each group is equal to that of any other group; that is, the variances of the various groups are homogeneous, or we have **homogeneity of variances.**

We should point out that ANOVA is a **robust technique,** insensitive to departures from normality and homogeneity, particularly if the sample sizes are large and nearly equal for each group.

10.5 APPLICATION OF ANOVA

Let us now return to the question we posed at the beginning of the chapter: Is there a significant difference in weight gain among the rats that were fed the different brands of cereal? The analysis procedure is as follows:

1. H_0: $\mu_1 = \mu_2 = \mu_3 = \mu_4$
   H_1: One or more means are different from the others.
2. Test statistic: $F = s_b^2 / s_w^2$ or $F = MS_b / MS_w$.

3. Rejection region: We reject H_0 if the computed F statistic is greater than the table value (from Appendix B). When using Appendix B, df_w is $N - k$ and df_b is $k - 1$.

Table 10.4 provides a summary of these calculations and shows where the calculations are placed in a typical ANOVA table.

Now let us complete the data set introduced at the beginning of this chapter and perform the necessary calculations. Table 10.5 shows the data from all four groups. First, we need to calculate Σx^2 and Σx. Table 10.6 illustrates this procedure. Using equation (10.4), we calculate SS_b as follows:

$$SS_b = \left[\frac{(5)^2}{5} + \frac{(35)^2}{5} + \frac{(25)^2}{5} + \frac{(20)^2}{5} \right] - \frac{(85)^2}{20}$$

$$= (5 + 245 + 125 + 80) - 361.25 = 455 - 361.25 = 93.75$$

Table 10.4 One-Way ANOVA Table

Source of Variation	Sum of Squares	df	Mean Squares (s^2)	F Ratio	Critical F	P Value
Between	SS_b	$k - 1$	$MS_b = SS_b/k - 1$	MS_b/MS_w	$F_{k-1, N-k}$	(computer-generated)
Within	SS_w	$N - k$	$MS_w = SS_w/N - k$			
Total	SS_t	$N - 1$				

Table 10.5 Weight Gain (oz) of Rats Fed Four Different Brands of Cereal

A	B	C	D
1	7	9	8
1	7	6	6
1	7	5	4
1	7	3	1
1	7	2	1

Table 10.6 Weight Gain (oz) of Rats Fed Four Different Brands of Cereal

	A	x^2	B	x^2	C	x^2	D	x^2	
	1	1	7	49	9	81	8	64	
	1	1	7	49	6	36	6	36	
	1	1	7	49	5	25	4	16	
	1	1	7	49	3	9	1	1	
	1	1	7	49	2	4	1	1	
Σx	5		35		25		20		= 85
Σx^2		5		245		155		118	= 523

Table 10.7 ANOVA Table for Weight Gain of Rats Fed Four Different Brands of Cereal

Source of Variation	Sum of Squares	df	Mean Squares (s^2)	F Ratio	Critical F	P Value
Between	93.75	3	31.25	7.35	3.24	.0026
Within	68.00	16	4.25			
Total	161.75	19				

Using equation (10.5), we calculate SS_w as follows:

$$SS_w = \Sigma\Sigma x^2 - 455 = 523 \text{ [from Table 10.6]} - 455 = 68$$

The total sum of squares is therefore

$$SS_t = SS_w + SS_b = 68 + 93.75 = 161.75$$

The next step is to calculate the mean squares (the variances). This is done by dividing the sum of squares by the degrees of freedom:

$$MS_b = \frac{93.75 \ (SS_b)}{3 \ (df_b)} = 31.25$$

$$MS_w = \frac{68 \ (SS_w)}{16 \ (df_w)} = 4.25$$

Now we can set up the ANOVA table for our illustration of the effect of the different cereals on weight gain (see Table 10.7). From this table, we can see that the calculated F ratio, 7.35, is greater than the critical value of $F_{3,16} = 3.24$ at $\alpha = .05$. This means that at least one of the means is significantly different from the others (i.e., we have a treatment effect). This conclusion is confirmed by the computer-generated, exact P value of .0026, which is less than our designated α of .05. Because at least one of the cereals leads to greater weight gain, we have to perform an additional analysis, called a **post hoc analysis,** to find this difference. If the results were not significant (i.e., if the calculated F ratio was less than the critical F ratio), then we would not need to perform additional tests. We would automatically know that, because F is not significant, there are no significant differences among any of the pairs.

10.6 POST HOC ANALYSIS

To find out which means are significantly different, we might be tempted to perform a number of multiple t tests between the various pairs of means. Multiple

t tests are inappropriate, however, because the probability of incorrectly reject-ing the hypothesis increases with the number of t tests performed. So, even though we may be performing a test of significance at $\alpha = .05$, the actual α level is, in effect, considerably higher.

A significant F ratio tells us that there are differences between at least one pair of means. The purpose of a post hoc analysis is to find out exactly where those differences are. A variety of different types of post hoc analyses allow us to make multiple pairwise comparisons and determine which pairs are signifi-cantly different and which are not. The interpretation of these analyses is very similar to that of the two-sample t test from Chapter 9. The more popular post hoc procedures include Tukey, Tukey–Kramer, Scheffé, Bonferroni, Dunnett, and Games–Howell. We will show how Tukey's HSD (honestly significant differ-ence) test works.

Tukey's HSD test is used to test the hypothesis that all possible pairs of means are equal. To perform this **multiple comparison test,** we select an overall sig-nificance level, which denotes the probability that one or more of the null hy-potheses is false. Those pairs whose differences exceed the HSD are considered to be significantly different. The formula for computing HSD is

$$HSD = q(\alpha,\ k,\ N - k)\sqrt{\frac{MS_w}{n}} \tag{10.7}$$

Remember the following: n = number of subjects per group ($n = 5$ in our ex-ample); N = total of all subjects in the experiment ($N = 20$ in our example).

■ **EXAMPLE 1**

In the weight gain example, we first determine the difference between each possible pair of means, using the data from Table 10.6. We will subtract the group with the lower mean from the group with the higher mean. Therefore, all of the differences between the means will be positive (see Table 10.8). For example, the mean for group A is 1 and for group B is 7 (7 [higher mean] − 1 [lower mean] = 6).

Table 10.8 Mean Difference for Weight Gain of Each Pair

Pair	Mean Difference
A–B	6
A–C	4
A–D	3
B–C	2
B–D	3
C–D	1

Table 10.9 Mean Difference and Critical Value
for Weight Gain of Each Pair

Pair	Mean Difference	Critical Value
A–B	6*	3.73
A–C	4*	3.73
A–D	3	3.73
B–C	2	3.73
B–D	3	3.73
C–D	1	3.73

*Significant at $\alpha = .05$

Next, we compute the critical value, HSD, from equation (10.7). Using $\alpha = .05$, $k = 4$, and $N - k = 16$, we find from Appendix C that q is 4.05. From Table 10.7, MS_w is 4.25, and from Table 10.6, $n = 5$. Therefore,

$$HSD = 4.05\sqrt{\frac{4.25}{5}} = 4.05(.922) = 3.73$$

We will use this critical value for all six pairs (see Table 10.9).

Because the mean difference for pairs A–B and A–C exceeds the critical value, 3.73, we conclude that there is a significant difference in weight gain between these pairs. Animals fed cereal brands B and C ($\bar{x} = 7$ and $\bar{x} = 5$, respectively) gained significantly more weight than those fed brand A ($\bar{x} = 1$). For the other four pairs, the mean differences were not significant. ∎

We have discussed ANOVA with equal number of observations per treatment. The equations, however, will also accommodate unequal numbers of treatments. So far, we have considered only the one-way ANOVA classification. It is possible to work with two-way, three-way, or multiple-way classifications as well. For example, a two-way ANOVA might consider four treatment groups for each sex group, with the second classification being by sex. This method is discussed in the next section.

10.7 RANDOMIZED BLOCK DESIGN

A **randomized block design** is a design in which homogeneous blocks are divided into experimental units to which the treatments are assigned in a random fashion. The purpose of this design is to remove from the error term the variation due to the blocks. Each block has one experimental unit for each treatment, and each treatment is represented in each block. Table 10.10 shows the layout of the data from a study that used a randomized block design. (Note that here we use double notation, which facilitates the handling of the formu-

Table 10.10 Symbolic Representation of Values for the Randomized Block Design with k Treatments and n Blocks

			Treatments				
Blocks	1	2	3	. . .	k	Total	Mean
1	x_{11}	x_{12}	x_{13}	. . .	x_{1k}	$x_{1\cdot}$	$\bar{x}_{1\cdot}$
2	x_{21}	x_{22}	x_{23}	. . .	x_{2k}	$x_{2\cdot}$	$\bar{x}_{2\cdot}$
3	x_{31}	x_{32}	x_{33}	. . .	x_{3k}	$x_{3\cdot}$	$\bar{x}_{3\cdot}$
$\vdots$	$\vdots$	$\vdots$	$\vdots$		$\vdots$	$\vdots$	$\vdots$
n	x_{n1}	x_{n2}	x_{n3}	. . .	x_{nk}	$x_{n\cdot}$	$\bar{x}_{n\cdot}$
Total	$x_{\cdot1}$	$x_{\cdot2}$	$x_{\cdot3}$	. . .	$x_{\cdot k}$	$x_{\cdot\cdot}$	
Mean	$\bar{x}_{\cdot1}$	$\bar{x}_{\cdot2}$	$\bar{x}_{\cdot3}$	. . .	$\bar{x}_{\cdot k}$		$\bar{x}_{\cdot\cdot}$

las.) There are k **treatment effects** (effects due to some stimulant) and n blocks. Blocks can be homogeneous subgroups stratified on age, weight, SES (socio-economic status), or other factors. One of the first things usually done is to observe what the treatment and block means are. They are computed in the following fashion. The mean for the first treatment is given by

$$\bar{x}_{1\cdot} = \sum_{j=1}^{n} \frac{x_{ij}}{n} = \frac{x_{1\cdot}}{n}$$

and the mean for the first block is given by

$$\bar{x}_{\cdot1} = \sum_{i=1}^{k} \frac{x_{i1}}{n} = \frac{x_{\cdot1}}{k}$$

The sum of all the observations is given by

$$\sum_{i=1}^{k} \sum_{j=1}^{k} x_{ij} = x_{\cdot\cdot}$$

Note that we are assuming we have a balanced design; that is, each block has k treatments, and each treatment has n blocks.

■ **EXAMPLE 2**

Let us look at the relationship between maternal smoking and infant birth weight, taking the mother's weight into account. We will look at three treatment groups: mothers who did not smoke, those who smoked up to 1 pack/day, and those who smoked 1+ pack/day. The six weight groups, in increments of 5 kg, are the six blocks. Technically, this design assumes that the smoking "treatment level" was assigned randomly to the pregnant women in a particular block (weight group). Such an assignment, however, was not the case. The data are shown in Table 10.11.

Table 10.11 Infant Birth Weight (grams) and Means Classified by Maternal Smoking Status and Prepregnancy Weight Group

Blocks Group (kg)	Treatments			Total	Mean
	None	1 Pack/Day	1+ Pack/Day		
45–49	3,175	2,750	1,730	7,655	2,552
50–54	3,232	2,835	2,466	8,533	2,844
55–59	3,240	3,062	2,509	8,811	2,937
60–64	3,420	3,076	2,608	9,104	3,035
65–69	3,459	3,340	2,778	9,577	3,192
70–74	3,515	3,416	2,920	9,851	3,284
Total	20,041	18,479	15,011	53,531	
Mean	3,340	3,080	2,502		2,974

From the means in the table, we can see that there is an inverse relationship between maternal smoking and infant birth weight; that is, the means for the three smoking groups decrease with an increased level of smoking. There is also a direct relationship between prepregnancy weight and infant birth weight; that is, birth weight increases as the mother's weight increases. To determine whether there is a significant treatment (smoking) effect after we remove the variation due to blocks (prepregnancy weight), we need to prepare an ANOVA table. In the two-way ANOVA, the total sum of squares can be partitioned into three parts: the effect due to blocks, that due to treatment, and a residual part similar to the within term we saw before—that is,

$$SS_t = SS_b + SS_{tr} + SS_r$$

The formulas for these are

$$SS_t = \Sigma\Sigma(x_{ij} - \bar{x}..)^2 = \Sigma\Sigma x_{ij}^2 - CT$$

$$SS_b = \Sigma\Sigma(\bar{x}_{i.} - \bar{x}..)^2 = \Sigma\Sigma \bar{x}_{i.}^2 - CT$$

$$SS_{tr} = \Sigma\Sigma(\bar{x}_{.j} - \bar{x}..)^2 = \Sigma\Sigma \bar{x}_{.j}^2 - CT$$

$$SS_r = \Sigma\Sigma(x_{ij} - \bar{x}_{.j} - \bar{x}_{i.} + \bar{x}..)^2$$

where CT, the "correction term," is given by

$$CT = \frac{(\Sigma x_{ij})^2}{kn} = \frac{x_{..}^2}{kn}$$

We can apply these formulas to the data in Table 10.11 and obtain

$$CT = \frac{\Sigma\Sigma x_{..}^2}{kn} = \frac{(53,531)^2}{3(6)} = \frac{2,865,567,961}{18} = 159,198,220$$

$$SS_t = \sum_{i=1}^{k} \sum_{j=1}^{n} x_j^2 - CT$$

$$= 162{,}716{,}841 - 159{,}198{,}220 = 3{,}518{,}621$$

$$SS_b = \sum_{i=1}^{k} \sum_{j=1}^{n} x_{i \cdot}^2 - CT = k(\bar{x}_{1 \cdot}^2 + \cdots + \bar{x}_{6 \cdot}^2) - CT$$

$$= 3(2552^2 + \cdots + 3284^2) - CT$$

$$= 3(53{,}411{,}754) - 159{,}198{,}220$$

$$= 1{,}037{,}042$$

$$SS_{tr} = \sum_{i=1}^{k} \sum_{j=1}^{n} \bar{x}_{\cdot j}^2 - CT = n(\bar{x}_{\cdot 1}^2 + \bar{x}_{\cdot 2}^2 + \bar{x}_{\cdot 3}^3) - CT$$

$$= 6(3340^2 + 3080^2 + 2502^2) - CT$$

$$= 6(26{,}902{,}004) - 159{,}198{,}220$$

$$= 2{,}213{,}804$$

$$SS_r = SS_t - SS_b - SS_{tr}$$

$$= 3{,}518{,}621 - 1{,}037{,}042 - 2{,}213{,}804$$

$$= 267{,}775$$

The degrees of freedom are also partitioned, as follows:

Total = blocks + treatments + residual

$$kn - 1 = (n - 1) + (k - 1) + (n - 1)(k - 1)$$

For our example, these would be

$$18 - 1 = (6 - 1) + (3 - 1) + (6 - 1)(3 - 1)$$

$$17 = 5 + 2 + 10$$

The layout for the ANOVA table for the randomized block design is shown in Table 10.12.

Because we are interested in knowing whether there is a treatment (maternal smoking) effect on infant birth weight after removing the variation due to prepregnancy weight, we proceed as follows:

1. State H_0: There is no treatment (smoking) effect.
2. We calculate the F ratio using the formula from Table 10.12. If H_0 is true, both $MS(SS_{tr})$ and $MS(SS_r)$ are estimates of σ^2. Therefore, the F ratio should be about 1.0.

Table 10.12 ANOVA Table for the Randomized Complete Block Design

Source of Variation	Sum of Squares	df	MS	F Ratio
Treatments	SS_{tr}	$k - 1$	$\dfrac{SS_{tr}}{k - 1}$	$\dfrac{MS(SS_{tr})}{MS(SS_r)}$
Blocks	SS_b	$n - 1$	$\dfrac{SS_b}{n - 1}$	
Residual	SS_r	$(k - 1)(n - 1)$	$\dfrac{SS_r}{(k - 1)(n - 1)}$	
Total	SS_t	$kn - 1$		

3. If H_0 is true, the quantity

$$\frac{MS(SS_{tr})}{MS(SS_r)}$$

should follow an F distribution with $(k - 1)$ and $(k - 1)(n - 1)$ degrees of freedom. If the computed value of F is greater than the critical value from the F table, we reject H_0.

We can now prepare the ANOVA table and reach a decision:

Source	SS	df	MS	F
Treatments	2,213,804	2	1,106,902	41.3
Blocks	1,037,042	5	207,408	
Residual	267,775	10	26,776	
Total	3,518,621	17		

Our computed value of $F = 41.3$ is greater than the critical 1% $F_{2,10} = 7.56$, so we reject the H_0 of no treatment (smoking) effect at the $\alpha = .01$ level. To find out which pairs of means are significant, we could apply Tukey's HSD test. ∎

To perform the test of H_0, we need to make the following assumptions:

1. The observations, x_{ij}, are normally distributed.
2. The treatment effects, the block effects, and the residuals ($x_{ij} - x_{i.} - \bar{x}_{.j} + \bar{x}_{..}$) are independent and have the same variances.

The ANOVA technique is quite robust to any violations of these assumptions. Therefore, the results are still valid even when the assumptions are not strictly met. If the violations are considerable, we can frequently remedy the situation by transforming the values of x_{ij} by taking a log, square root, or reciprocal of them.

Because this is an introductory text, the presentation of the ANOVA technique is necessarily brief. If you are using SPSS, an excellent companion book is *Ready, Set, Go! A Student Guide to SPSS 11.0 for Windows,* by Pavkov and Pierce (2003).

◆ CONCLUSION

The analysis of variance is so named because the ANOVA test procedure is based on a comparison of the estimate of the between-group variance with the estimate of the within-group variance. These two estimates of σ^2 are obtained by partitioning the overall variance. An F statistic is used to determine the critical region for the test. If the computed F ratio falls in the critical region, we conclude that at least one of the means is significantly different from the others. To determine which specific pairs of means are significant, we utilize a multiple comparison test, not multiple t tests. To test the hypothesis, we must assume independence of observations, normality of each group, and homogeneous variances. An important interpretation of ANOVA is that it tests whether there is a treatment effect, where the treatment is drug dosage, smoking exposure, or some other factor.

In this chapter, we focused on the one-way classification of variance. To be able to account for the many possible sources of variation in a particular experiment, you may wish to perform a two-way or a three-way ANOVA.

◆ VOCABULARY LIST

ANOVA	homogeneity	robust technique
between-group sum	of variances	treatment effects
of squares	mean squares	Tukey's HSD test
between-group	multiple comparison test	within-group sum
variance	post hoc analysis	of squares
double notation	randomized block	within-group variance
F distribution	design	

◆ EXERCISES

10.1 You obtained a calculated F of -4.50. Under what circumstances would you calculate a $-F$ ratio? Explain.

10.2 a. Describe the differences between a one-way and a two-way ANOVA.
b. What are the assumptions made when you perform an ANOVA?
c. What H_0 is usually tested with a one-way and a two-way ANOVA?

10.3   What are the following critical F values for the $\alpha = .05$ level?

a. $F_{1,16} = $ _____; $F_{3,16} = $ _____; $F_{3,36} = $ _____

b. What are these critical values for $\alpha = .01$?

10.4   a. Why might you use a multiple comparison test such as Tukey's HSD rather than a t test?

b. How would your results differ if you were to use the t test rather than Tukey's HSD test?

10.5   a. What are the degrees of freedom for between, within, and total treatments for a one-way ANOVA with four treatments and 10 subjects in each treatment?

b. What are the degrees of freedom for each of the components of a randomized complete block design with five treatments and three blocks?

10.6   Complete the following ANOVA table:

Source	SS	df	MS	F
Between	360			
Within	450	15		
Total		19		

Is the F ratio significant at the $\alpha = .05$ level?

10.7   Complete the following ANOVA table:

Source	SS	df	MS	F
Treatment	160	4		
Blocks		5		
Error	200			
Total	600	29		

What is your conclusion regarding the significance of the treatment effect?

◆ COMPREHENSIVE EXERCISES

Using the data from Exercises 10.8–10.15, do the following:

a. State the null hypothesis.

b. Construct an ANOVA table. (Only include exact P value if the analysis is done by computer.)

c. Determine whether your results are significant.

d. Do a post hoc analysis, if necessary.

e. State your conclusions in one or two sentences.

10.8   A survey was done in a community in which residents were asked if they felt that family planning counseling was needed in the community. The tabulation in the accompanying table gives the opinions and the number of children of the respondents. Determine whether there is a difference in mean number of children of respondents.

	Great Need	Some Need	No Need	
	0	10	17	
	1	5	10	
	3	7	9	
	4	3	3	
Number of children	2	9	15	
	1	8	10	
	3	7	11	
	0	9	10	
	1	10	9	
	2	9	8	
Σx	17	77	102	196 (grand total)
$\bar{x}$	1.7	7.7	10.2	6.53 (grand mean)

10.9 Five samples were taken randomly from each blood type, and the white cell counts were noted to be as follows:

	Blood Type				
	A	B	AB	O	
	5,000	7,000	7,000	5,325	
White cell counts	5,500	8,000	7,125	7,985	
	8,000	5,000	9,000	6,689	
	10,000	9,900	9,235	9,321	
	7,735	6,342	7,699	6,666	
Σx	36,235	36,242	40,059	35,986	148,522 (grand total)
$\bar{x}$	7,247.0	7,248.4	8,011.8	7,197.2	7,426.1 (grand mean)

Are the four blood types the same with respect to white cell counts?

10.10 Seven samples of individuals were selected randomly from three communities. The ages of the persons were as tabulated:

	Community A	Community B	Community C	
	16	65	45	
	15	43	30	
	25	77	22	
Age	30	90	66	
	39	82	47	
	20	69	33	
	16	73	50	
Σx	161	499	293	953.00 (grand total)
$\bar{x}$	23	71.29	41.86	45.38 (grand mean)

Is there a significant difference in the ages?

10.11 Measurements on cumulative radiation dosage were made on workers at an atomic weapons plant over a 6-month period. The following table presents data for workers whose dosage was assessed at three different locations. Determine whether there was a significant difference in the mean dosage level among the three locations.

	Location A	Location B	Location C	
	11	29	37	
	27	41	51	
	19	19	42	
Cumulative	21	39	28	
radiation	31	24	35	
dosage	14	35	48	
	28	46	75	
	22	64	49	
	18	52	61	
	10	23	52	
Σx	201	372	478	1,051 (grand total)
$\bar{x}$	20.1	37.2	47.8	35.03 (grand mean)

10.12 An investigator wants to determine whether there is a significant difference between three different smoking cessation programs in terms of recidivism. He also wants to learn whether being part of a different weight group plays a role in earlier recidivism. He conjures up a study to see how many days a person was smoke-free during the first 30 days. Following are his data:

	Program		
Weight Groups	A	B	C
121–140	30	25	21
141–160	25	23	20
161–180	27	20	22
181–200	25	19	16
201–220	20	18	14
220+	22	14	18

10.13 A researcher wanted to determine if different cereals had varying effects on growth and weight gain. A laboratory experiment was designed so that each of five groups of newly weaned rats was fed a diet of a particular brand of cereal. Each group had 7 rats for a total of 35 rats. At the end of the experimental period, the animals were weighed, and their weight in ounces was recorded in the following table. Determine whether weight gain was affected by brand of cereal.

	Brand				
	A	B	C	D	E
	9	5	2	6	3
Weight	7	4	1	5	8
gain	8	6	1	5	9
(ounces)	9	5	3	5	2
	6	6	2	6	5
	8	7	2	7	7
	9	2	3	8	1

10.14 Determine whether there is a significant difference in birth weight (grams) among three groups of infants classified by the smoking status of the mother, based on the following data:

	Smoking Status		
Subject	None 1	1 Pack/Day 2	1+ Pack/Day 3
1	3515	3444	2608
2	3420	3827	2509
3	3175	3884	3600
4	3586	3515	1730
5	3232	3416	3175
6	3884	3742	3459
7	3856	3062	3288
8	3941	3076	2920
9	3232	2835	3020
10	4054	2750	2778
11	3459	3460	2466
12	3998	3340	3260

10.15 In an effort to match the availability of emergency health care with expected demand for emergency services, a broad area was divided into four zones of approximately equal numbers of residents. The number of emergency calls per zone (labeled A, B, C, and D) was tabulated over 10 randomly selected time periods. The results were as follows:

A	B	C	D
8	10	23	11
7	12	14	10
3	7	16	11
9	7	13	9
8	16	15	12
5	12	18	15
7	13	10	11
10	13	10	8
6	11	21	7
5	9	16	12

If you were responsible for allocating resources, what would you recommend?

11

Inferences Regarding Proportions

CHAPTER OUTLINE

✔ LEARNING OBJECTIVES

After studying this chapter, you should be able to

1. Compute the mean and the standard deviation of a binomial distribution
2. Compute Z scores for specific points on a binomial distribution
3. Perform significance tests of a binomial proportion and of the difference between two binomial proportions
4. Calculate confidence intervals for a binomial proportion and for the difference between two proportions

11.1 INFERENCES WITH QUALITATIVE DATA

Is there a significant difference in the risk of death from leukemia for males and females? Is the proportion of persons who now smoke less than it was at the time of publication of the Surgeon General's Report on the hazards of smoking? These are typical questions that cannot easily be answered using the methods discussed in the previous chapters. Why not? The methods previously discussed are applicable to *quantitative* data such as height, weight, and blood pressure for which a mean and standard error can be computed. The new questions deal with *qualitative* data—data for which individual quantitative measurements are not available but that relate to the presence or absence of some characteristic, such as smoking. For these data, we have a new statistic, p, the estimate of the true proportion, π, of individuals who possess a certain characteristic. Previously, we dealt with $\bar{x}$, the mean value of some characteristic for a group of individuals.

This chapter focuses on (1) the mean and the standard deviation of x, the number of successful events in a binomial experiment, and (2) the mean and the standard error of p, the proportion of successful events observed in a sample. To best understand the difference between the distribution of binomial events (x) and the distribution of the **binomial proportion** (p), try comparing these distributions with those in the approximate analogous quantitative situation. Roughly speaking, the x's of a binomial distribution correspond to the quantitative x's in a distribution with a mean μ and a standard deviation σ. The p's of the binomial distribution correspond to the $\bar{x}$'s in a distribution with a mean $\mu_{\bar{x}}$ and a standard error $\sigma/\sqrt{n}$.

This chapter considers the tests of significance for proportions and the differences between two proportions, and the confidence intervals for both.

11.2 MEAN AND STANDARD DEVIATION OF THE BINOMIAL DISTRIBUTION

In Chapter 5, you learned that the probability of x successful outcomes in n independent trials is given by

$$\binom{n}{x} P^x (1 - P)^{n-x}$$

where P is the probability of a success in one individual trial. To be consistent in using Greek letters to designate unknown parameters, in this chapter we use π to designate the probability of x successful outcomes.

Using mathematical statistics, we can show that in a binomial distribution the mean for the number of successes, x, is

$$\mu = n\pi \tag{11.1}$$

and the standard deviation is

$$\sigma = \sqrt{n\pi(1 - \pi)} \tag{11.2}$$

11.3 APPROXIMATION OF THE NORMAL TO THE BINOMIAL DISTRIBUTION

The normal distribution is a reasonable approximation to the binomial distribution when n is large. Therefore, we can find the point on the Z distribution that corresponds to a point x on the binomial distribution by using

$$Z = \frac{x - n\pi}{\sqrt{n\pi(1 - \pi)}} \tag{11.3}$$

In Chapter 5, we showed that, when the number of trials or cases is greater than 30, it would be quite cumbersome to evaluate the binomial expansion to find the exact probability of the occurrence of a certain event. Mathematical statisticians have demonstrated that the continuous normal distribution is a good approximation to the discrete binomial, providing the following relationships are satisfied:

$$n\pi \geq 5 \quad \text{and} \quad n(1 - \pi) \geq 5$$

Hence, with the use of the well-known equations for the mean and the standard deviation of the binomial distribution, shown in Figure 5.4, it is a simple task to approximate the probability of a binomial event.

■ **EXAMPLE 1**

A group of physicians treated 25 cases of chronic leukemia, a disease for which the 5-year survival rate was known to be .20. They observed that 9 of their patients had survived for 5 years or more. They wanted to know whether such an event was unusual. What is the probability, out of 25 cases, of observing 9 or more "successes" (i.e., survival for 5 or more years)?

First, we compute the mean and the standard deviation:

$$\mu = n\pi = (25)(.2) = 5$$
$$\sigma = \sqrt{n\pi(1 - \pi)} = \sqrt{25(.2)(.8)} = 2$$

Then we compute the Z score:

$$Z = \frac{x - n\pi}{\sqrt{n\pi(1 - \pi)}} = \frac{9 - 5}{\sqrt{25(.2)(.8)}} = \frac{4}{2} = 2.0$$

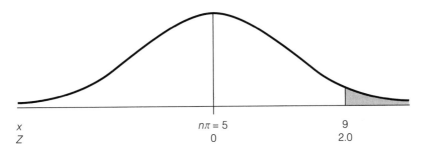

Figure 11.1   Approximation to the Binomial Distribution for Example 1.

The result: Observing nine 5-year survivals on the binomial distribution corresponds to a Z score of 2.0 on the normal distribution, as shown in Figure 11.1. The area beyond $Z = 2.0$ is .023. Therefore, the probability of 5-year survival for at least 9 of 25 patients is .023, whereas the probability of 5-year survival for 1 patient is .20. ∎

Because we are using a normal (continuous) distribution to approximate a discrete one, we may apply the **continuity correction** to achieve an adjustment. This correction is made by subtracting ½ from the absolute value of the numerator; that is,

$$Z = \frac{|x - n\pi| - 1/2}{\sqrt{n\pi(1 - \pi)}}$$

$$= \frac{|9 - 5| - 1/2}{\sqrt{25(.2)(.8)}} = \frac{3.5}{2} = 1.75$$

and $P(Z > 1.75) = .0401$, a result nearly two times that obtained without the correction. The continuity correction will not make a large difference when n is large.

When n is very large and π is very small, another important distribution, the **Poisson distribution,** is a good approximation to the binomial. It deals with discrete events that occur infrequently.

11.4   TEST OF SIGNIFICANCE OF A BINOMIAL PROPORTION

The previous section considered the distribution of the binomial event x. This section considers the distribution of the binomial proportion p, which is similar to considering the distribution of $\bar{x}$ for quantitative data.

The mean of the distribution of a binomial proportion p is given by the population parameter

$$\pi = \frac{x}{n} = \frac{\text{number of successes in population}}{\text{number of cases in population}} \tag{11.4}$$

and the standard error of p is given by

$$\text{SE}(p) = \sqrt{\frac{\pi(1 - \pi)}{n}} \tag{11.5}$$

Because p appears to be normally distributed, providing n is reasonably large, we can find the Z score corresponding to a particular p and perform a test of significance.

■ **EXAMPLE 2**

There were 245 deaths from leukemia in California one year. Of these, 145 were males,

$$p = \frac{145}{245} = .59$$

and 100 were females,

$$1 - p = \frac{100}{245} = .41$$

Is .59, the observed proportion of male deaths, significantly different from the expected .49, the proportion of males in the California population?

$$\pi = .49 \qquad 1 - \pi = .51 \qquad n = 245$$

$$\text{SE}(p) = \sqrt{\frac{\pi(1 - \pi)}{n}} = \sqrt{\frac{(.49)(.51)}{245}} = .032$$

Using the steps of a test of a hypothesis, we get the following results:

1. H_0: $\pi = .49$; there is no sex difference in the proportion of deaths.
2. $\alpha = .05$.
3. Test statistic:

$$Z = \frac{p - \pi}{\text{SE}(p)} = \frac{.59 - .49}{.032} = \frac{.10}{.032} = 3.12 \tag{11.6}$$

4. Critical region: From the Z distribution (Table A, inside back cover), we find that Z is ± 1.96 (see Figure 11.2).

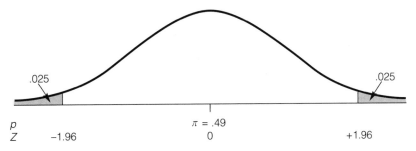

Figure 11.2 Critical Region for Example 2.

5. The computed Z score of 3.12 is greater than the critical value of 1.96, so we reject the null hypothesis that the proportion of deaths from leukemia is the same for both sexes and conclude that the risk of dying from this disease is greater for males than for females. If we apply the continuity correction in this example, we will have

$$Z = \frac{|.59 - .49| - 1/2n}{.032}$$

$$= \frac{.10 - .002}{.032} = \frac{.098}{.032} = 3.06$$

which actually makes very little difference in the result. ∎

11.5 TEST OF SIGNIFICANCE OF THE DIFFERENCE BETWEEN TWO PROPORTIONS

In practice, you will seldom have a convenient population proportion for comparison. More commonly, you will be called upon to compare proportions from two different samples—possibly one from a control group (baseline data) and the other after some type of treatment or intervention. To do this, you must first assume that the proportions are equal—that is, $\pi_1 = \pi_2$—in estimating $SE(p_1 - p_2)$. You want to learn if p_1, the proportion with the given characteristic in one sample, differs significantly from p_2, the proportion with the same characteristic but in the second sample. To determine if the proportions are significantly different, you need to know three things: (1) the distribution of the differences $(p_1 - p_2)$, (2) the mean, μ, and (3) the standard error (SE) of this distribution. Statisticians have shown that $p_1 - p_2$ follows a nearly normal distribution. The mean is

$$\mu = p_1 - p_2 \tag{11.7}$$

The standard error is estimated by

$$SE(p_1 - p_2) = \sqrt{\frac{p'q'}{n_1} + \frac{p'q'}{n_2}} \qquad (11.8)$$

where

$$p' = \frac{x_1 + x_2}{n_1 + n_2} \quad \text{and} \quad q' = 1 - p' \qquad (11.9)$$

and

$$p_1 = \frac{x_1}{n_1} \qquad (11.10)$$

and

$$p_2 = \frac{x_2}{n_2} \qquad (11.11)$$

Knowing the mean and the standard error of the distribution of differences, we can calculate a Z score:

$$Z = \frac{p_1 - p_2 - (\pi_1 - \pi_2)}{SE(p_1 - p_2)} \qquad (11.12)$$

If $\pi_1 \neq \pi_2$, the formula for $SE(p_1 - p_2)$ is

$$\sqrt{\frac{\pi_1(1 - \pi_1)}{n_1} + \frac{\pi_2(1 - \pi_2)}{n_2}}$$

■ EXAMPLE 3

For patients who are bedridden, pressure ulcers can have a devastating impact, in terms of both significant physical discomfort and increased health care costs. Often these ulcers develop during prolonged hospital stays. The term used to describe this is a *nosocomial incidence,* which refers to new cases of pressure ulcers that develop during prolonged hospitalization. Coloplast Corporation, Skin Health Division developed a protocol and skin care products to reduce or prevent the nosocomial incidence of pressure ulcers. Baseline data were collected at a regional tertiary hospital in 2000 (Cole and Nesbitt, 2003). The researchers found that, of 84 patients who met the eligibility requirements for this study, 15 (17.9%) developed nosocomial pressure ulcers. In 2001, the new treatment protocol was initiated. Of the 77 patients eligible for inclusion, 4 (5.2%) developed pressure ulcers. The key question is to determine if the reduction in the proportion from .179 to .052 is statistically significant. Using the procedure just described, we can calculate the following statistics:

$$p_1 = \frac{15}{84} = .179 \quad p_2 = \frac{4}{77} = 0.052 \quad p' = \frac{15 + 4}{84 + 77} = \frac{19}{161} = 0.118$$

$$SE(p_1 - p_2) = \sqrt{\frac{(.118)(.882)}{84} + \frac{(.118)(.882)}{77}}$$

$$= \sqrt{.002591} = 0.0509$$

Next, we apply the steps for a hypothesis test:

1. $H_0: \pi_1 - \pi_2 \leq 0$ (no reduction in the nosocomial incidence of pressure ulcers)

   $H_0: \pi_1 - \pi_2 > 0$ (a reduction)
2. $\alpha = .05$ and $\alpha = .01$.
3. Test statistic:

$$Z = \frac{p_1 - p_2 - 0}{SE(p_1 - p_2)} = \frac{.179 - .052}{0.0509} = \frac{.127}{0.0509} = 2.50$$

4. Critical region: From Table A (inside back cover), the critical values are 1.64 for $\alpha = .05$ and 2.33 for $\alpha = .01$.
5. The computed Z score of 2.50 exceeds the critical value for $\alpha = .05$ and $\alpha = .01$. The respective critical values are 1.64 and 2.33. Based on this sample, we reject the null hypothesis that the protocol developed by Coloplast does not lead to a reduction in nosocomial pressure ulcers and conclude that there is a statistically significant reduction in the incidence of these ulcers. ∎

11.6 CONFIDENCE INTERVALS

Although hypothesis testing is useful, we often go a step further to learn (1) the true proportion (e.g., of the nosocomial incidence of pressure ulcers in 2000 and 2002) and (2) the true difference in the proportion between the baseline data and the revised data (e.g., the original data in 2001 and the new prevention program in 2001). To answer these questions, we compute confidence intervals for π and for $\pi_1 - \pi_2$ by employing a method parallel to the one used for computing confidence intervals for μ and $\mu_1 - \mu_2$.

Confidence Interval for π

In Chapter 8, we found the confidence interval for μ to be

$$\bar{x} \pm Z \frac{\sigma}{\sqrt{n}}$$

Similarly, the confidence interval for π is

$$p \pm Z \sqrt{\frac{\pi(1 - \pi)}{n}}$$

This expression presents a dilemma: It requires that we know π, which is unknown. The way out of this dilemma is to have a sufficiently large sample size, permitting the use of p as an estimate of π. The expression then becomes

$$p \pm Z \sqrt{\frac{p(1 - p)}{n}} \tag{11.13}$$

The solution for small sample sizes is known but is derived from the binomial distribution. Some statistical textbooks feature it.

■ EXAMPLE 4

In Example 3, we determined that the baseline nosocomial incidence of pressure ulcers was 0.179. Because this finding was based on a sample of 84, we might also want to determine the confidence interval to bracket the true value of π. The 95% CI is calculated as follows:

$$95\% \text{ CI for } \pi = p \pm 1.96 \sqrt{\frac{p(1 - p)}{n}}$$

$$= 0.179 + 1.96 \sqrt{\frac{(.179)(.821)}{84}}$$

$$= 0.179 \pm 0.082$$

$$= (0.097, \ 0.261)$$

We can now state, with 95% confidence, that the true proportion of nosocomial pressure ulcers (at the baseline reading) was between 0.097 and 0.261. ■

Confidence Interval for $\pi_1 - \pi_2$

The confidence interval for the difference of two means is

$$\text{CI for } \mu_1 - \mu_2 = \bar{x}_1 - \bar{x}_2 \pm Z[SE(\bar{x}_1 - \bar{x}_2)]$$

The confidence interval for the difference of two proportions is similar:

$$\text{CI for } \pi_1 - \pi_2 = p_1 - p_2 \pm Z\sqrt{\frac{p_1(1 - p_1)}{n_1} + \frac{p_2(1 - p_2)}{n_2}} \qquad (11.14)$$

■ EXAMPLE 5

To find the confidence interval of the true difference between the baseline incidence of nosocomial pressure ulcers and the incidence after the new treatment/prevention protocol, we perform the following calculation:

$$95\% \text{ CI for } \pi_1 - \pi_2 = p_1 - p_2 \pm 1.96\sqrt{\frac{p_1(1 - p_1)}{n_2} + \frac{p_2(1 - p_2)}{n_2}}$$

$$= 0.179 - 0.052 \pm 1.96\sqrt{\frac{.179(.821)}{84} + \frac{.052(.948)}{77}}$$

$$= 0.127 \pm 0.096$$

$$= (0.031, \ 0.223)$$

We can now state, with 95% confidence, that the revised protocol led to a reduction in the nosocomial incidence of pressure ulcers of between 0.031 and 0.223. This means that the revised protocol may lead to a reduction of between 3.1% and 22.3% in new cases of pressure ulcers. ■

◆ CONCLUSION

The normal approximation to the binomial distribution is a useful statistical tool. It helps answer questions regarding qualitative data involving proportions where individuals are classified into two categories. The mean and the standard deviation are, respectively, $\mu = n\pi$ and $\sigma = \sqrt{n\pi(1 - \pi)}$, giving a Z score of $(x - n\pi)/\sqrt{n\pi(1 - \pi)}$. With an understanding of the distribution of the binomial proportion p and of the distribution of the difference between two proportions $p_1 - p_2$, we can perform tests of significance and calculate confidence intervals.

◆ VOCABULARY LIST

binomial proportion   continuity correction   Poisson distribution

◆ EXERCISES

11.1 For the Honolulu Heart Study data of Table 3.1, compute
   a. the proportion of individuals in each education category
   b. the proportion of smokers and nonsmokers
   c. the proportion for each physical activity level

11.2 Using your results from Exercise 11.1b, calculate estimates of the mean and the standard deviation of the proportion of smokers.

11.3 Given that the proportion of smokers in the United States is .31, test to see if the proportion of smokers in Honolulu is significantly different from the national proportion. Use $\alpha = .05$.

11.4 What is the 95% confidence interval for the proportion of smokers in Honolulu for 1969? Refer to Exercise 11.1b.

11.5 In a study of hypertension and taste acuity, one variable of interest was smoking status. Of the 7 persons in the hypertensive group, 4 were smokers. The control group of 21 normotensive persons included 7 smokers. Is there a difference in the proportion of smokers in the two groups at the .05 level of significance?

11.6 Construct a 90% confidence interval for the difference in the proportions of smokers in the hypertensive and normotensive groups of Exercise 11.5.

11.7 In a study of longevity in a village in Ecuador, 29 persons in a population of 99 were age 65 or older. If it is also known that 20% of the U.S. population is 65 or older, does it appear that the proportion of Ecuadorian villagers surviving to 65 and beyond exceeds that of people in the United States? Use $\alpha = .01$.

11.8 Calculate a 99% confidence interval for the proportion of Ecuadorians (Exercise 11.7) who are age 65 or older.

11.9 Of 186 participants in a program to control heart disease, it was discovered that 102 had education beyond secondary school. Does this indicate that the program is attracting a more highly educated group of people than would be expected, given that 25% of the U.S. population has education beyond secondary school? Use $\alpha = .01$.

11.10 In a study of drug abuse among adults, 55 of 219 "abusers" and 117 of 822 "nonusers" stated that they started smoking cigarettes at age 12 or younger. Do these data indicate that there is a significant difference in the proportions of abusers and nonusers who took up smoking at an early age?

11.11 In a dental study of a tie between infant occlusion and feeding methods, there were 27 breast-fed and 60 bottle-fed infants. It was noted that 7 of the breast-fed babies and 26 of the bottle-fed babies developed a related open-bite gum pad in the first 4 months of life. Would you conclude that the bottle-fed group showed a higher proportion of the open-bite gum pad problem? Use $\alpha = .05$.

11.12 Compute the following confidence intervals for the difference in proportions, $\pi_1 - \pi_2$:
   a. 99% CI for Exercise 11.10
   b. 95% CI for Exercise 11.11

11.13 a. What are the mean and the standard deviation of x, the number of successes in a binomial distribution?
b. What is the difference between p and π?
c. What are the mean and the standard deviation of the binomial proportion p?
d. Under what condition is the normal distribution a reasonable approximation to the binomial distribution?

11.14 Public health officials found that, in a random sample of 100 men in a small community, 13 were infected with AIDS.
a. Obtain an estimate of the proportion of men infected with AIDS in that community.
b. Calculate the 95% CI for π, the true proportion of men infected with AIDS.

11.15 A random check of drivers on a busy highway revealed that 60 out of 100 male drivers and 70 out of 100 female drivers were wearing their seat belts.
a. Obtain estimates of the proportion of male and female drivers who wear seat belts.
b. Construct a 99% CI for $\pi_1 - \pi_2$, the true difference in wearing seat belts between males and females.
c. Is the observed difference between males and females significant at the $\alpha = .01$ level?

11.16 A survey of 100 women and 100 men indicated that 49 of the women and 35 of the men said they were trying to lose weight.
a. Estimate the difference in the proportion desiring to lose weight between men and women.
b. Perform a test of significance to determine whether this difference is significant at the $\alpha = .05$ level.
c. Calculate a 95% CI for $\pi_1 - \pi_2$.
d. Do the results from (b) and (c) support or contradict each other? Why?

11.17 A nationwide survey of medical complaints indicated that 43 out of 100 people in the Southwest and 22 out of 100 people in the region close to the nation's capital suffered from allergies. Is this a chance difference? Are the data consistent with the hypothesis that geography plays a role? (Use $\alpha = .01$.)

11.18 A fitness survey found that 35 out of 100 women and 25 out of 100 men did not exercise. Is this likely to be a real difference, or can it be explained by chance? Construct a 95% CI for the difference, and state your conclusion.

11.19 A random sample of 100 industrial workers found that 13 of them were exposed to toxic chemicals routinely on their job. Prepare a report that will provide management with information regarding the magnitude of this problem. What statistic or statistics would you include in your report?

11.20 As of September 1996, 14 states had lowered the legal blood alcohol limit from 0.10% to 0.08%. A "study was undertaken to assess whether, relative to nearby states, states adopting a 0.08% legal limit experienced a reduction in the proportion of fatal crashes involving (1) fatally injured drivers with blood alcohol levels of 0.08% or higher and 0.15% or higher, and (2) any driver with a blood alcohol level of 0.08% or higher and 0.15% or higher" (Hingson et al., 1996:1297–1299). Two comparison states were Oregon (0.08%) and Washington.

	Before 0.08% Law		After 0.08% Law	
	Fatally Injured Drivers	Drivers at 0.08% or Higher	Fatally Injured Drivers	Drivers at 0.08% or Higher
Oregon (0.08%)	1275	4455	1023	4186
Washington	1735	6184	1582	5390

NOTE: These data were extrapolated and based on the study by Hingson et al. (1996).

a. First, calculate a proportion for each state, before and after the 0.08% law went into effect. You will calculate a total of four proportions.

b. Following the procedure explained in section 11.5, including Example 3, calculate a test of significance for the difference before and after the new law for Oregon, and then do the same for Washington.

c. Are your results significant for either state? Explain the importance of your findings. Remember that Oregon changed to 0.08% and Washington did not.

11.21 In 2003, Coloplast Corporation, Skin Health Division developed a refined protocol for reducing the incidence of nosocomial pressure ulcers. With 100 patients, the nosocomial incidence was .20. Using the data introduced in section 11.5, conduct a test of significance and calculate intervals for the 2000 and 2003 data, and for the 2001 and 2003 data.

12 The Chi-Square Test

CHAPTER OUTLINE

✔ LEARNING OBJECTIVES

After studying this chapter, you should be able to

1. Indicate the kinds of data and circumstances that call for a chi-square test
2. Compute the expected value for a chi-square contingency table
3. Compute a chi-square statistic and its appropriate degrees of freedom
4. Explain the meaning of degrees of freedom
5. Indicate the type of hypothesis that can be tested with chi-square
6. Find the critical region for a chi-square test
7. Compute two different measures of the strength of association of factors reported in 2 × 2 tables

---

12.1 RATIONALE FOR THE CHI-SQUARE TEST

Although the t test is popular and widely used, it may not be appropriate for certain health science problems that call for tests of significance. Because the t test requires data that are quantitative, it is simply not applicable to qualitative data. In other chapters, whenever means or standard deviations were computed, we worked with measurement data. With such data, we were able to record a specific value for each observation. These represented quantitative variables such as height, weight, and cholesterol level. But we are often obliged to classify persons into categories such as male or female, hypertensive or normotensive, and smoker or nonsmoker, and to count the number of observations falling into each category. The result is **frequency data.** In addition, we often have to deal with **enumeration data,** because we enumerate the number of persons in each category; **categorical data,** because we count the number of persons falling into each category; and, as mentioned earlier, **qualitative data,** because we group the categories according to some quality of interest.

Categorical data are not used to quantify blood pressure levels, for example, but rather to classify persons as hypertensive or normotensive. The classification table used to do this is called a **contingency table.** Its use, though, does not permit us to determine whether there is a relationship between two variables by means of a correlation coefficient, because we do not have quantitative x and y observations for each person. Instead, we could perform a **chi-square test** to determine whether there is some association between the two variables. This chapter considers various chi-square tests to deal with such cases involving frequency data.

12.2   THE BASICS OF A CHI-SQUARE TEST

For a given phenomenon, the chi-square test compares the **observed frequencies** with the **expected frequencies.** The expected frequency is calculated from some hypothesis. To illustrate, let us take the simple example of trying to determine whether a coin is fair.

Suppose you toss a coin 100 times and observe that heads (H) comes up 40 times and tails (T) 60 times. If you hypothesize that the coin is fair, you would expect heads and tails to occur equally—that is, 50 times each. In comparing the observed frequency (O) with the expected frequency (E), you need to determine whether the *deviations* ($O - E$) are significant. As you can see in Table 12.1, if you were to sum the deviations, the total would equal zero, as indicated in column 3.

To avoid this problem, you might first square each deviation, as in column 4. But this approach has a problem, too: The same value is obtained for equal deviations regardless of magnitude. For instance, consider $O - E$ for two possibilities: $60 - 50 = 10$ and $510 - 500 = 10$. Arithmetically, the deviations are identical, but they are far from identical in meaning; although a deviation of 10 from an expected 50 is impressive, the same deviation from an expected 500 is hardly noticeable. The best way of overcoming this problem is to look at the proportional squared deviations, $(O - E)^2/E$. Here, the two possibilities become $(60 - 50)^2/50 = 2.0$ and $(510 - 500)^2/500 = 0.2$. Now the deviations offer a more meaningful statistical perspective. From column 5 of Table 12.1, we can see that for the coin problem the sum of the proportional squared deviations is equal to 4.

The next question is whether the value we have just calculated,

$$\sum \frac{(O - E)^2}{E} = 4$$

Table 12.1 Observed and Expected Frequencies and Their Deviations for 100 Tosses of a Coin

	(1)	(2)	(3)	(4)	(5)
	O	E	$O - E$	$(O - E)^2$	$\dfrac{(O - E)^2}{E}$
H	40	50	-10	100	2
T	60	50	10	100	2
Total	100	100	0	200	4

can occur easily by chance or whether it is an unusual event that is unlikely to occur by chance except in rare instances, say, less than 5% of the time. To resolve this question, we need to know how the quantity, designated as χ^2 (chi-square), is distributed; that is, we have to determine the probability distribution for the statistic

$$\chi^2 = \sum \frac{(O - E)^2}{E} \tag{12.1}$$

Mathematical statisticians have shown that this quantity is approximated quite well by the **chi-square distribution** if the sample sizes and the expected numbers are not too small. This distribution is positively skewed, beginning at zero. By figuring out the area beyond 4 on a chi-square distribution, we can determine a P value and either accept or reject the hypothesis.

There is, in fact, a family of chi-square distributions. The correct one to use depends, as in the t distribution, on a quantity called the degrees of freedom. For chi-square, degrees of freedom are determined by the number of *independent* deviations (each $O - E$) in the contingency table. A two-cell table (e.g., Table 12.1) has 1 df. Wherever you can determine expected frequencies from your hypothesis, the degrees of freedom are one less than the number of categories. The coin problem has two categories, heads and tails, so there is 1 df. If you were trying to determine whether a six-sided die was unbiased, you would have $6 - 1 = 5$ df.

In Figure 12.1, you can see the shapes of several chi-square distributions. For each, the upper 5% of the area is shaded. Note that, as the degrees of freedom increase, so does the critical value needed to reject a null hypothesis. Intuitively, this sounds right: Because the degrees of freedom are proportional to the number of independent categories, you would expect the critical chi-square value to increase with more categories.

Table 12.2 gives the critical values for the chi-square distribution for various degrees of freedom. Here, you can see that the upper 5% chi-square value for 1 df is 3.84, for 4 df is 9.49, and for 6 df is 12.59.

Back to our original question: "Is the coin fair?" Recall that the χ^2 sum was 4. For 1 df, this falls within the upper 5% critical region. Therefore, you would reject the H_0 that the coin is fair; that is, you would not expect to observe a deviation as large as (or larger than) this to occur by chance alone. Your conclusion: The coin is probably unbalanced or loaded, or was not properly thrown. A point to note is that the chi-square test, unlike some others, is a one-tailed test. The rationale for this is that we are almost always concerned only about whether the deviations are too large, seldom about whether they are too small. For example, we would worry about a dangerously high level of air pollution, but certainly not about too low a level.

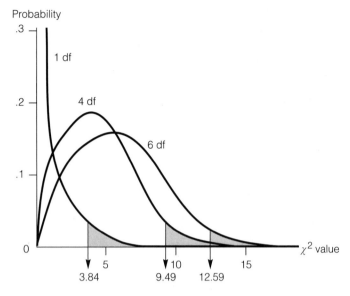

Figure 12.1   The Chi-Square Distribution for Varying Degrees of Freedom.

Table 12.2 The Probability of Exceeding the Chi-Square Value in the Chi-Square Distribution

df	.99	.95	.90	.50	.10	.05	.01	.001
				α				
1	.00157	.00393	.0158	.455	2.706	3.841	6.635	10.827
2	.0201	.103	.211	1.386	4.605	5.991	9.210	13.815
3	.115	.352	.584	2.366	6.251	7.815	11.345	16.226
4	.297	.711	1.064	3.357	7.779	9.488	13.277	18.467
5	.554	1.145	1.610	4.351	9.236	11.070	15.806	20.515
6	.872	1.635	2.204	5.348	10.645	12.592	16.812	22.457
7	1.239	2.167	2.833	6.346	12.017	14.067	18.475	24.322
8	1.646	2.733	3.490	7.344	13.362	15.507	20.090	26.125
9	2.088	3.325	4.168	8.343	14.684	16.919	21.666	27.877
10	2.558	3.940	4.865	9.342	15.987	18.307	23.209	29.588
11	3.053	4.575	5.578	10.341	17.275	19.675	24.725	31.264
12	3.571	5.226	6.304	11.340	18.549	21.026	26.217	32.909
13	4.107	5.892	7.042	12.340	19.812	22.362	27.688	34.528
14	4.660	6.571	7.790	13.339	21.064	23.685	29.141	36.123
15	5.229	7.261	8.547	14.339	22.307	24.996	30.578	37.697
20	8.260	10.581	12.443	19.337	28.412	31.410	37.566	43.315
30	14.953	18.493	20.599	29.336	40.256	43.773	50.892	59.703
40	22.164	26.509	29.051	39.335	51.805	55.759	63.691	73.402
50	29.707	34.764	37.689	49.335	63.167	67.505	76.154	86.661
60	37.485	43.188	46.459	59.335	74.397	79.082	88.379	99.607

12.3 TYPES OF CHI-SQUARE TESTS

In real-life contexts, you will often encounter problems involving two variables. Specifically, you may employ chi-square tests to determine the following:

1. Whether the two variables are independent
2. Whether various subgroups are homogeneous
3. Whether there is a significant difference in the proportions in the subclasses among the subgroups

We will discuss each of these tests.

12.4 TEST OF INDEPENDENCE BETWEEN TWO VARIABLES

Kuzma and Kissinger (1981) published a study of the effects that maternal use of alcohol during pregnancy has on the newborn. Some of their data regarding smoking and drinking are shown in Table 12.3. Here, you can see that 30.5% of the nondrinking women and 67.3% of the heaviest drinkers smoked during their pregnancies. We might wonder whether drinking and smoking are dependent variables or whether the relationship is explainable by chance. A way to approach this question is to test the null hypothesis that there is no relationship between smoking and drinking during pregnancy. To do this, we need to know the expected values before we can compute a χ^2 statistic. Expected values can be generated from the null hypothesis, which states that there is no relationship between drinking and smoking during pregnancy.

For purposes of this discussion, we set up a special notation, in which the eight cells of Table 12.3 are identified as $E_{11}, \ldots, E_{24}$, as shown in Table 12.4. The probability multiplication rule states that the probability of two independent events A and B is $P(A \text{ and } B) = P(A)P(B)$.

We are testing the hypothesis that the two variables are independent. Therefore, we can apply the multiplication rule to obtain the frequencies expected if the hypothesis of independence is indeed true. That is, from the data in

Table 12.3 Number and Percentages of 11,127 Pregnant Women by Alcohol and Drinking Status

Smoking Status	Alcohol Consumption				
	None	Low	Medium	High	Total
Smokers	1,880 (30.5%)	2,048 (45.7%)	194 (53.0%)	76 (67.3%)	4,198 (37.7%)
Nonsmokers	4,290 (69.5%)	2,430 (54.3%)	172 (47.0%)	37 (32.7%)	6,929 (62.3%)
Total	6,170 (55.5%)	4,478 (40.2%)	366 (3.3%)	113 (1.0%)	11,127 (100.0%)

Table 12.4 Notation for Expected Frequencies of a Two-Variable Table

Smoking Status	Alcohol Consumption				
	None	Low	Medium	High	Total
Smokers	E_{11}	E_{12}	E_{13}	E_{14}	T_s
Nonsmokers	E_{21}	E_{22}	E_{23}	E_{24}	T_{ns}
Total	T_{nd}	T_{ld}	T_{md}	T_{hd}	T

Table 12.3, the probability of a woman's being in the smoking group (A) *and* in the nondrinking group (B) is

$$P(A)P(B) = \left(\frac{4,198}{11,127}\right)\left(\frac{6,170}{11,127}\right) = (.377)(.555) = .2092$$

$$= \left(\frac{T_s}{T}\right)\left(\frac{T_{nd}}{T}\right)$$

where T_s = total smokers and T_{nd} = total nondrinkers. Therefore, the expected number of smokers who are also nondrinkers is

$$E_{11} = 11,127(.2092) = 2327.8$$

The meaning of E_{11} is what you would expect, assuming the null hypothesis to be true—that 2328 of the smokers will be nondrinkers. Continuing in the same way, we can obtain expected frequencies for all cells: for low, medium, and high alcohol consumption, and for the nonsmoking categories. Thus,

$$E_{12} = (.37728)(.40244)(11,127) = 1689.4$$
$$E_{13} = (.37728)(.03289)(11,127) = 138.1$$
$$E_{24} = (.62272)(.010155)(11,127) = 70.4$$

Although it may seem absurd to compute expected values to a fraction of a person, this is often done in order to avoid round-off error and ensure that "expected" and "observed" row totals are identical. All expected frequencies are shown in Table 12.5. Now we can proceed to compute the χ^2 statistic:

$$\chi^2 = \sum \frac{(O - E)^2}{E} = \frac{(1880 - 2327.8)^2}{2327.8} + \frac{(2048 - 1689.4)^2}{1689.4}$$

$$+ \frac{(194 - 138.1)^2}{138.1} + \frac{(76 - 42.7)^2}{42.7} + \frac{(4290 - 3842.2)^2}{3842.2}$$

$$+ \frac{(2430 - 2788.5)^2}{2788.5} + \frac{(172 - 227.9)^2}{227.9} + \frac{(37 - 70.4)^2}{70.4} = 338.7$$

Table 12.5 Observed and Expected Frequency of Alcohol Consumption and Smoking During Pregnancy for 11,127 Women

| | \multicolumn{8}{c|}{Alcohol Consumption} |
| Smoking Status | \multicolumn{2}{c}{None} | \multicolumn{2}{c}{Low} | \multicolumn{2}{c}{Medium} | \multicolumn{2}{c}{High} |
	O	E	O	E	O	E	O	E
Smokers	1880	2327.8	2048	1689.4	194	138.1	76	42.7
Nonsmokers	4290	3842.2	2430	2788.5	172	227.9	37	70.4
Total	6170		4478		366		113	

Is a χ^2 of 338.7 significant? To find out, we check Table 12.2 for the critical value. But first we need to know the number of degrees of freedom. In the case of our example, where we do not know the expected frequencies **a priori** (i.e., by deductive reasoning) but have obtained them from the data, the degrees of freedom are equal to $(c - 1)(r - 1)$, where c is the number of columns and r the number of rows. Here, we have 4 columns and 2 rows; therefore, df $= (4 - 1)(2 - 1) = 3$.

From Table 12.2, we find the critical 5% value for 3 df to be 7.8. Because the computed χ^2 of 338.7 falls well into the critical region, we reject the hypothesis of independence between drinking and smoking during pregnancy. This suggests that there is an association between smoking and drinking among pregnant women.

The preceding discussion should help you understand the meaning of degrees of freedom. Note that the expected values for each category add up to the total observed value for that category. Note also that we could have computed expected values for only three of the eight cells, with the others obtained by subtraction. These three cells represent the three "independent" quantities—that is, the 3 df. The other five quantities are not "independent" because they can be obtained by subtracting the first three from column or row totals.

12.5 TEST OF HOMOGENEITY

It is often important to determine whether the distribution of a particular characteristic is similar for various groups. To do this, we can perform a chi-square test called a test of homogeneity.

■ EXAMPLE 1

From the alcohol–pregnancy study of Kuzma and Kissinger (1981), we have data on the distribution of drinkers by ethnic group. As shown in Table 12.6, among Caucasians, 51.2% were abstainers, 43.6% light drinkers, 3.9% medium drinkers, and 1.2% heavy drinkers. The percentage distribution is fairly similar among the

Table 12.6 Drinking Status During Pregnancy, by Ethnic Group

	None		Light (<1.0 oz*)		Medium (1.0–2.99 oz)		Heavy (≥3.00 oz)		Total	
Ethnicity	n	%	n	%	n	%	n	%	n	%
Black	411	60.4	253	37.2	12	1.8	5	0.7	681	6.3
Hispanic	1,459	64.0	757	33.2	53	2.3	10	0.4	2,279	21.2
Caucasian	3,732	51.2	3,179	43.6	284	3.9	90	1.2	7,285	67.7
Other	322	61.6	187	35.8	10	1.9	4	0.8	523	4.9
Total	5,924	55.0	4,376	40.6	359	3.3	109	1.0	10,768	100.0

*Equivalent ounces of absolute alcohol per day.

ethnic groups, except that the Caucasian group includes fewer abstainers and more drinkers in all categories. Is this difference real or no greater than would be expected by chance? That is, can we assume that groups of pregnant women of various ethnicity tend to have essentially the same drinking patterns?

To test for homogeneity, we again need to establish the expected frequencies, this time basing them on a somewhat different rationale than the probability argument used in section 12.4. Nevertheless, the equations used to obtain expected frequencies are the same. For example, the expected number of abstainers among Caucasian women is computed as

$$E_{31} = \left(\frac{5,924}{10,768}\right)\left(\frac{7,285}{10,768}\right)(10,768) = 4007.8$$

The other expected frequencies are obtained similarly and are shown in parentheses in Table 12.7. Having the expected frequencies, we can now proceed with the test of significance as follows:

1. H_0: The several ethnic groups are homogeneous in their drinking patterns.
   H_1: The several groups are not homogeneous in their drinking patterns.

2. $\alpha = .05$.

3. Critical region: The critical region for χ^2 with $(c - 1)(r - 1) = (4 - 1)(4 - 1) = 9$ df (denoted as χ_9^2) is shown in Figure 12.2 to be 16.92.

4. Test statistic:

$$\chi^2 = \sum \frac{(O - E)^2}{E}$$

$$= \frac{(411 - 374.7)^2}{374.7} + \frac{(253 - 276.8)^2}{276.8} + \cdots + \frac{(4 - 5.3)^2}{5.3}$$

$$= 146.3$$

Table 12.7 Observed and Expected Frequencies of Alcohol Intake During Entire Pregnancy, by Ethnic Group

Ethnicity	\multicolumn{2}{Alcohol Consumption None}		Light		Medium		Heavy		Total
	O	E	O	E	O	E	O	E	Total
Black	411	(374.7)	253	(276.8)	12	(22.7)	5	(6.9)	681
Hispanic	1,459	(1,253.8)	757	(926.2)	53	(76.0)	10	(23.1)	2,279
Caucasian	3,732	(4,007.8)	3,179	(2,960.5)	284	(242.9)	90	(73.7)	7,285
Other	322	(287.7)	187	(212.5)	10	(17.4)	4	(5.3)	523
Total	5,924		4,376		359		109		10,768

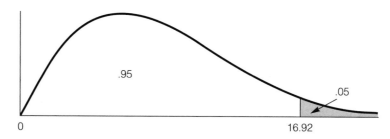

Figure 12.2 Critical Region for χ^2_9.

5. The computed χ^2 of 146.3 falls in the critical region, so we conclude that the deviations in drinking patterns among the various ethnic groups are not homogeneous; that is, the various ethnic groups do not appear to be homogeneous in their drinking patterns. ∎

12.6 TEST OF SIGNIFICANCE OF THE DIFFERENCE BETWEEN TWO PROPORTIONS

Another application of the chi-square test is in learning whether the proportion of successes in a treated group differs significantly from the proportion in a control group. It can be considered an alternative to the Z test for a 2 × 2 table.

■ **EXAMPLE 2**

For some years, there has been a lively medical controversy over the efficacy of vitamin C in preventing the common cold. Several studies concluded that vitamin C was no more effective than a placebo. In Table 12.8, which presents some

Table 12.8 Number and Frequencies of Children Developing Colds, by Vitamin C and Placebo Groups

Status	Vitamin C Group		Placebo Group		Total
Children free of colds	21	(37%)	11	(24%)	32
Children developing colds	36	(63%)	35	(76%)	71
Total	57	(100%)	46	(100%)	$n = 103$

unpublished data from one such study, we find that 63% of the children treated with vitamin C and 76% of the placebo group caught colds. Does the number developing colds differ between the two groups?

The expected frequencies for Table 12.8 are

$$E_{11} = \frac{(32)(57)}{103} = 17.7$$

By subtraction, the remaining expected frequencies are $E_{12} = 14.3$, $E_{21} = 39.3$, and $E_{22} = 31.7$. The value of the test statistic is

$$\chi^2 = \sum \frac{(O - E)^2}{E}$$

$$= \frac{(21 - 17.7)^2}{17.7} + \frac{(11 - 14.3)^2}{14.3} + \frac{(36 - 39.3)^2}{39.3} + \frac{(35 - 31.7)^2}{31.7}$$

$$= .61 + .76 + .28 + .34$$

$$= 1.99$$

As before, there are $(c - 1)(r - 1)$ df. In this example, $(c - 1)(r - 1) = 1$. The critical χ^2 at the 5% level for 1 df is 3.84.

The resulting χ^2 of 1.99 is not within the critical region; therefore, we fail to reject the hypothesis that the percentage with colds in both groups is the same. So we could logically conclude that, for this size sample, the observed difference of children free of colds between the groups, 37% − 24% = 13%, could well have occurred by chance. ■

12.7　TWO-BY-TWO CONTINGENCY TABLES

Perhaps the most common chi-square analysis used in health research involves data presented in a 2 × 2 (fourfold) table in which there are two groups and two possible responses. Table 12.9 is a generalized representation of such a table. The observed frequencies are represented symbolically by the letters *a*, *b*,

Table 12.9 Schematic Representation for 2 × 2 Contingency Table

Response	Treatment	Control	Total
Yes	a	b	$a + b$
No	c	d	$c + d$
	$a + c$	$b + d$	$a + b + c + d = n$

c, and d. With such data, it is possible to compute the χ^2 statistic directly, avoiding the need to compute expected frequencies:

$$\chi^2 = \frac{n(ad - bc)^2}{(a + c)(b + d)(a + b)(c + d)} \tag{12.2}$$

Thus, using the data on vitamin C in Example 2, we obtain the same result as in that example:

$$\chi^2 = \frac{103[(21)(35) - (11)(36)]^2}{(57)(46)(32)(71)} = 1.99$$

The equations we use to compute χ^2 result in approximations to the chi-square distribution. They are quite close for many degrees of freedom, not too close for a few, and not as good for 1 df. Just as we always use discrete observations to approximate a statistic that is continuously distributed, it is desirable to apply a correction for this. A frequently used solution is the **Yates continuity correction** for chi-squares with 1 df. However, Grizzle (1967) has shown that, because the correction is too conservative in that it leads too often to nonrejection of the null hypothesis, many practicing statisticians do not recommend its use.

■ **EXAMPLE 3**

A survey on the use of seat belts found that 24 out of 60 males with a high school education and 30 out of 40 male college graduates wore seat belts regularly. Is there evidence suggesting an association between education and seat belt use? Table 12.10 presents the data in a 2 × 2 contingency table.

Using equation (12.2) to compute χ^2, we have

$$\chi^2 = \frac{n(ad - bc)^2}{(a + c)(b + d)(a + b)(c + d)}$$

$$= \frac{100[(24)(10) - (36)(30)]^2}{(54)(46)(60)(40)}$$

$$= 11.8$$

Table 12.10 A 2 × 2 Contingency Table of Seat Belt Use and Education of a Sample of 100 Men

Education	Used Seat Belt		
	Yes	No	Total
High School Graduate	24	36	60
College Graduate	30	10	40
Total	54	46	100

Because the computed χ^2 of 11.8 is larger than the critical χ^2 of 3.84, with 1 df, we would reject the H_0 of independence; that is, we would suspect that there is an association between education and seat belt use. ■

For those who insist on the use of the Yates correction, which was proposed by Yates in 1934, to subtract one-half of the total number of observations from the absolute value of $ad - bc$, we illustrate it with the data from this example.

$$\chi^2_{(corrected)} = \frac{n(|ad - bc| - .5n)^2}{(a + c)(b + d)(a + b)(c + d)}$$

$$= \frac{100(|24 \times 10 - 36 \times 30| - .5 \times 100)^2}{54 \times 46 \times 60 \times 40}$$

$$= \frac{62,410,000}{5,961,600} = 10.5$$

As you can see, the difference between the two results is not important.

12.8 McNEMAR'S TEST FOR CORRELATED PROPORTIONS

The chi-square test we just considered tests the hypothesis that the proportions estimated from two independent samples are equal. In this section, we present a chi-square test for the situation when samples are matched, that is, are not independent. Investigators frequently use a before-and-after design in which they are trying to test whether there has been a significant change between the before-and-after situations. The features of such a design are illustrated with an example of data on seat belt use before and after a driver was involved in an auto accident. This design, with the data, is shown in Table 12.11.

The appropriate test statistic to use to test the H_0 that there is no change in seat belt use from the period before the accident occurred to that after the accident occurred is **McNemar's chi-square test:**

$$\chi^2 = \frac{(b - c)^2}{b + c}$$

Table 12.11 A 2 × 2 Table of Seat Belt Use *Before* and *After* Involvement in an Auto Accident for a Sample of 100 Accident Victims

		Wore seat belt regularly after the accident		
		Yes	No	
Wore seat belt regularly before the accident	Yes	$a = 60$	$b = 6$	66
	No	$c = 19$	$d = 15$	34
Total		79	21	100

Using the data from Table 12.11, we find that the test shows that

$$\chi^2 = \frac{(6 - 19)^2}{6 + 19} = \frac{169}{25} = 6.76$$

Because the computed $\chi^2 = 6.76$ is larger than the critical value, $\chi^2 = 3.84$, for $\alpha = .05$ with 1 df, we reject the H_0 of no change and conclude that there is a possible increase in seat belt use after involvement in an auto accident. Note that we use only the drivers who have changed their seat belt use (b and c) in computing McNemar's test.

12.9 MEASURES OF STRENGTH OF ASSOCIATION

A popular measure of the strength of an association between two variables is **relative risk** (RR). Relative risk is widely used in research by clinicians and epidemiologists, largely because it is easy to calculate and interpret.

Relative risk is defined as the ratio of the incidence rate for persons exposed to a risk factor to the incidence rate for those not exposed to the risk factor:

$$\text{Relative risk (RR)} = \frac{\text{incidence rate among exposed}}{\text{incidence rate among unexposed}}$$

Some also call it the risk ratio. We can use a generalized 2 × 2 table to represent frequencies for each of the four cells in a table (see Table 12.12). Relative risk can be computed using the following equation:

$$\text{RR} = \frac{a/(a + b)}{c/(c + d)} \tag{12.3}$$

Table 12.12 A 2 × 2 Table for Measuring Relative Risk

Risk Factor	Disease Present	Disease Absent	Total
Present	a	b	$a + b$
Absent	c	d	$c + d$

Another commonly used measure of strength of association is the **odds ratio** (OR). The odds ratio, sometimes called relative odds, receives wide use in case-control studies and is defined as the ratio of a/b to c/d. Although the OR is not based on disease rates, it is a valid measure of strength of association.

■ **EXAMPLE 4**

In a group of retirees, a community health survey revealed the relationship shown in Table 12.13 between smoking and presence of heart disease. Using the notation of Table 12.12, the relative risk (RR) of developing heart disease is

$$RR = \frac{a/(a + b)}{c/(c + d)} = \frac{25/35}{14/65} = 3.3$$

Based on the results of this survey, smokers have approximately 3.3 times the risk of developing heart disease as nonsmokers. ■

Table 12.13 A 2 × 2 Table of Smoking History and Heart Disease

Risk Factor	Heart Disease Present	Absent	Total
Smoker	25	10	35
Nonsmoker	14	51	65
Total	39	61	100

■ **EXAMPLE 5**

In a controversial study of the relationship between coffee consumption and pancreatic cancer, MacMahon et al. (1981) interviewed 369 cancer patients and 644 controls. Their findings, in part, showed that the patients were much more likely than the controls to have been heavy coffee drinkers. The data are shown in Table 12.14.

The relative odds ratio is computed, using the data from Table 12.14, as

$$OR = \frac{ad}{bc} = \frac{(60)(32)}{(82)(9)} = 2.6$$

Table 12.14 A 2 × 2 Table for Measuring Relative Odds

Coffee Drinking (cups per day)	Male Pancreatic Cancer Patients	Male Controls
≥5	$a = 60$	$b = 82$
0	$c = 9$	$d = 32$

We would estimate from these results that habitual heavy coffee use increased the risk of pancreatic cancer in men by a factor of 2.6 relative to men who did not drink coffee. (This finding has not been confirmed by other studies.) ∎

We use relative odds when we have two binomial variables obtained from prospective (but not retrospective) studies. Relative odds is a highly useful concept because it provides a quantitative measure relating a stimulus variable (e.g., coffee use) to an outcome variable (e.g., pancreatic cancer).

A relative odds of 2.0 would indicate that heavy coffee use is associated with a twofold (100%) increase in the risk of pancreatic cancer, so coffee may be an important etiologic factor in that type of cancer. It is thus clear why relative risk is so popular. It serves as a quantitative measure of risk, a means of drawing inferences of clinical significance, given the important provision that statistical significance has been established.

12.10   LIMITATIONS IN THE USE OF CHI-SQUARE

We previously mentioned that the techniques suggested in this chapter produce values that follow the continuous chi-square distribution. We use discrete data to approximate a continuous distribution. The closeness of the approximation also depends on the frequency size in the various cells of the contingency table. To ensure that the approximation is adequate, we follow a basic rule: The expected frequencies must not be too small. What is "small"? Its definition can vary by the type of chi-square test being performed. However, a general, well-accepted rule is that no expected frequency should be less than 1 and not more than 20% of the cells should have an expected frequency of less than 5. If a contingency table violates this rule, a good technique is to merge ("collapse") some rows or columns to increase the frequencies of some of the cells. If the expected frequencies are too small, we should use Fisher's exact test, described in section 14.8.

The chi-square test is very popular because it is easy to perform. Also, it has a wide variety of applications in the health and medical sciences. Sometimes, however, its frequency of use leads to misuse. A common misapplication, for example, is to compute a χ^2 statistic for data that do not represent independent observations. This happens when one person is included more than once, when a before-and-after experiment is involved, or when multiple responses are recorded for the same person, as in measuring the frequency of decayed or missing teeth. In the last case, there is obviously a lack of independence, because adjacent teeth in someone's mouth are more likely to be affected than are teeth from different mouths. In such a case, independence would be ensured by counting the number of individuals and classifying them according to the number of decayed or missing teeth rather than by simply counting the number of teeth.

If you suspect that your data are suffering from lack of independence, it would be wise to consult an advanced statistics textbook or obtain help from a statistician. Advanced statistics includes a variety of appropriate methods that can solve almost any problem.

◆ CONCLUSION

Qualitative data may be analyzed by use of a chi-square test. The object of the test is to determine whether the difference between observed frequencies and those expected from a hypothesis are statistically significant. The test is performed by comparing a computed test statistic, χ^2, with a one-tailed critical value found in a chi-square table. The critical value depends on the selected α and on the number of degrees of freedom, the latter reflecting the number of independent differences as computed from the data. The test statistic is computed as the sum of the ratios of squared differences to expected values. As in other tests of significance, if the computed test statistic exceeds the critical value, the null hypothesis is rejected.

◆ VOCABULARY LIST

a priori	expected frequency	qualitative data
categorical data	frequency data	relative risk
chi-square distribution	McNemar's chi-square	Yates continuity
chi-square test	test	correction
contingency table	observed frequency	
enumeration data	odds ratio	

◆ EXERCISES

12.1   From the Honolulu Heart Study data in Table 3.1, we can develop a number of chi-square tests of association between two factors. The contingency table for one such test is as follows:

Educational Level	Smoker	Nonsmoker	Total
None	4	16	20
Primary	15	17	32
Intermediate	12	12	24
Senior high	1	8	9
Technical school	0	10	10
Total	32	63	95

a. Using $\alpha = .05$, perform the test and determine whether there is an association between the two variables.

b. Observe that the limitations of the test, as discussed in section 12.10, were violated, thus invalidating the conclusion of a significant association. To correct the problem of small numbers, combine the senior high and technical school groups to make a 2 × 4 table and repeat the test. Does collapsing the groups change the conclusion?

12.2   As in Exercise 12.1, use Table 3.1 as a source for contingency tables. Test them for associations between the following variables:

a. Activity status (levels 1 and 2) and smoking status (smokers and nonsmokers). Use $\alpha = .01$.

b. Activity status (levels 1 and 2) and systolic blood pressure (classify as less than 140 mmHg for group 1 and greater than or equal to 140 mmHg for group 2). Test at $\alpha = .05$. (*Hint:* Use equation (12.2).)

12.3   A study of diet and age at menarche yielded the following information:

Age of Menarche	Egg Consumption			
	Never	Once per Week	2–4 Times per Week	Daily
Low	5	13	8	4
Medium	4	20	14	0
High	11	18	15	0

a. Test, at $\alpha = .05$, the hypothesis of independence of the two variables. (*Hint:* Use equation (12.1).)

b. Because the expected values indicate a violation of the small numbers limitation of the test, recompute by collapsing the two categories "2–4 times per week" and "daily" into a new category: "2–7 times per week." Does the result change your conclusion?

12.4   Perform chi-square tests for significant difference between the two proportions for the following exercises:

a. 11.5

b. 11.10

c. 11.11

12.5   One of the variables considered in Heartbeat (a coronary risk reduction program) was age. An important question emerged: Was the age distribution of the participants different from that of the population in the metropolitan statistical area (MSA) where Heartbeat was conducted? Perform a chi-square test to answer the question. Use the MSA population age distribution to compute the expected values.

Age Interval	Heartbeat Participants	MSA Population (1970)
25–34	18	140,195
35–44	33	125,363
45–54	54	120,826
55–64	48	98,884
65 and over	35	125,884
Total	188	611,152

12.6 a. How are degrees of freedom (df) computed for a chi-square table?
  b. What is the meaning of degrees of freedom in the context of a contingency table?
  c. What is a typical H_0 for a contingency table?

12.7 a. What is the basis for computing the expected frequencies in a contingency table?
  b. How are the expected frequencies computed?

12.8 What circumstances call for the use of McNemar's test for correlated proportions rather than a typical χ^2 test?

12.9 Compute the relative odds ratio (OR) for the data in Table 12.13, and interpret it.

12.10 The following table presents data on 100 pregnant women and their smoking status before and after pregnancy. Determine whether there is a relationship between pregnancy and smoking status.

A 2 × 2 Table of Smoking Status Before and After Pregnancy

Before Pregnancy	After Pregnancy		Total
	Smoker	Nonsmoker	
Nonsmoker	5	55	60
Smoker	20	20	40
Total	25	75	100

12.11 A public health screening survey provided the following data on the relationship between smoking and lung cancer:

Smoking Status	Lung Cancer		Total
	Present	Absent	
Nonsmoker	1	6,700	6,701
Smoker	20	3,279	3,299
Total	21	9,979	10,000

Determine the strength of the association between smoking and lung cancer by computing the relative risk (RR) of a smoker's developing cancer.

12.12 Prepare a contingency table for the data on allergies and geographic region given in Exercise 11.17.

    a. At the $\alpha = .01$ level, determine whether there is an association between the rate of allergy complaints and geographic region.

    b. Compare the conclusion reached in (a) with the one from Exercise 11.17. Why are they the same or different?

12.13 A survey of 100 men and 100 women revealed that 15 of the men and 36 of the women were more than 20% overweight. Prepare a contingency table and test the hypothesis that the two gender groups are homogeneous with respect to being overweight. (Use $\alpha = .05$.)

12.14 Prepare a contingency table for the data on gender and exercise given in Exercise 11.18.

    a. Determine whether there is an association between gender and fitness at $\alpha = .05$.

    b. Compare your conclusion with that reached in Exercise 11.18.

12.15 Prepare a contingency table for the data on seat belt use and gender given in Exercise 11.15.

    a. Determine whether the proportion of seat belt users is the same for both sexes by performing the test of homogeneity.

    b. How do your conclusions differ from those reached in Exercise 11.15?

    c. Compute χ^2, using both the equation that requires expected frequencies (equation (12.1)) and the one that does not (equation (12.2)). How do the results differ?

12.16 A study was done to examine predictors of readiness to change smoking behavior in a predominantly African American community. Barriers to quitting smoking were examined for associations between races. One of the barriers examined was boredom. Residents in the community were asked whether boredom would be a problem, and therefore a barrier to quitting, should the respondent quit smoking. The respondents were divided into two groups—African Americans and whites/others—and the results are shown in the 2 × 2 table that follows. Based on these data, is there a relationship between race and boredom as a barrier to quitting smoking?

Boredom Would Be a Problem If Stopped Smoking	Ethnicity	
	African American N = 268	White/Other N = 111
Yes	75	51
No	193	60

NOTE: These data were extrapolated and based on the study by Tessaro et al. (1997).

12.17 A study investigated the differences between incarcerated juveniles from alcoholic families and those from nonalcoholic families. Three variables examined were substance abuse, family violence, and child neglect. The following three tables were compiled from the data obtained from incarcerated juveniles. Based on these three 2 × 2 tables, analyze the data.

Substance Abuse

	High	Low
Alcoholic Family	28	12
Nonalcoholic Family	13	15

Family Violence

	Police Called to Home One or More Times	No Police Calls
Alcoholic Family	25	15
Nonalcoholic Family	6	22

Neglect

	Left Alone for Long Periods	Not Left Alone for Long Periods
Alcoholic Family	5	35
Nonalcoholic Family	8	20

NOTE: These data were extrapolated and based on McGaha and Leoni (1995).

12.18 A study investigated dietary differences between low-income African American women and low-income white women. One dietary practice examined was the consumption of mutagen-containing meats (defined as a serving of any meat that has been smoked, grilled, or fried). Based on the following table, is there any reason to believe that there are differences between low-income African American women and low-income white women with respect to their consumption of mutagen-containing meats?

	Mutagen-Containing Meats		
Race	0–1 Servings per Day	2–3 Servings per Day	4 or More Servings per Day
African American	68	36	11
White	73	18	4

NOTE: These data were extrapolated and based on Cox (1994).

12.19 A study was conducted to assess the relationship between syphilis and HIV infection in injection drug users in the Bronx, New York. One part of the study examined the relationship between the incidence and prevalence of syphilis and whether the drug user was involved with "paid sex." A 2 × 2 table was developed as shown here.

	Syphilis Cases	
Paid Sex	Positive	Negative
Yes	16	137
No	19	618

NOTE: These data were extrapolated and based on Gourevitch et al. (1996).

a. Based on the data in this table, calculate the odds ratio.
b. After calculating the odds ratio, explain the results.

13

Correlation and Linear Regression

CHAPTER OUTLINE

✔ LEARNING OBJECTIVES

After studying this chapter, you should be able to

1. Distinguish between the basic purposes of correlation analysis and regression analysis
2. Plot a scatter diagram
3. Compute and explain the meaning of a correlation coefficient in terms of
   a. the kind of data it may be used for
   b. the kind of relationship it can measure
   c. its limitations
4. Compute and interpret a regression equation
5. Perform a test of significance of a correlation coefficient and a regression coefficient
6. Find the confidence limits for ρ and β

13.1 RELATIONSHIP BETWEEN TWO VARIABLES

Some of our most intriguing scientific questions deal with the relationship between two variables. Is there a relationship between underground nuclear explosions and the increased frequency of earthquakes? Does a relationship exist between use of oral contraceptives and the incidence of thromboembolism? What is the relationship of a mother's weight to her baby's birth weight? These are typical of countless questions we pose in seeking to understand the relationship between two variables.

Whenever an unusual event occurs, people speculate as to its cause. There is an all-too-human tendency to attribute a **cause-and-effect relationship** to variables that *might* be related. Innumerable variables appear to be related to other variables but fail as plausible explanations of causal relationships. For instance, there is a significant association between a child's foot size and handwriting ability, but we would hesitate to claim that a large foot *causes* better handwriting. A more logical explanation is that foot size and handwriting ability both increase with age; thus, the relationship is not causal but direct and age-dependent. As another example, one investigator reported a high degree of association between increased washing machine sales and admissions to mental institutions. It would require a rather convoluted argument to demonstrate a causal relationship between these two variables.

Spurious associations between variables have so vexed scientists that one of them, Everett Edington of the California Department of Education, composed a clever essay, "Evils of Pickle Eating" (see Figure 13.1), in which he satirizes

Evils of Pickle Eating

Pickles are associated with all the major diseases of the body. Eating them breeds war and Communism. They can be related to most airline tragedies. Auto accidents are caused by pickles. There exists a positive relationship between crime waves and consumption of this fruit of the cucurbit family. For example . . .

Nearly all sick people have eaten pickles. The effects are obviously cumulative.

- 99.9% of all people who die from cancer have eaten pickles.
- 100% of all soldiers have eaten pickles.
- 96.8% of all Communist sympathizers have eaten pickles.
- 99.7% of the people involved in air and auto accidents ate pickles within 14 days preceding the accident.
- 93.1% of juvenile delinquents come from homes where pickles are served frequently. Evidence points to the long-term effects of pickle eating.
- Of the people born in 1839 who later dined on pickles, there has been a 100% mortality.

All pickle eaters born between 1849 and 1859 have wrinkled skin, have lost most of their teeth, have brittle bones and failing eyesight—if the ills of pickle eating have not already caused their death.

Even more convincing is the report of a noted team of medical specialists: rats force-fed with 20 pounds of pickles per day for 30 days developed bulging abdomens. Their appetites for WHOLESOME FOOD were destroyed.

In spite of all the evidence, pickle growers and packers continue to spread their evil. More than 120,000 acres of fertile U.S. soil are devoted to growing pickles. Our per capita consumption is nearly four pounds.

Eat orchid petal soup. Practically no one has as many problems from eating orchid petal soup as they do with eating pickles.

EVERETT D. EDINGTON

Figure 13.1 An Example of Spurious Associations Between Variables.   SOURCE: "Evils of Pickle Eating," by Everett D. Edington, originally printed in *Cyanograms.*

such relationships. To see how easily you might be deceived into believing that a cause-and-effect relationship, however ridiculous, exists, simply substitute "milk," "candy," or "bread" for "pickle" in Edington's lampoon.

How, then, can we demonstrate the existence of an actual causal relationship? What statistical methods are available to measure the relationship between two variables?

In this chapter, we consider the relationship of two variables, *x* and *y*. Such pairs are referred to as **bivariate data.** In the health sciences, these pairs of data are most commonly obtained from human subjects. Examples include height and weight, fat consumption and cholesterol level, and daily cigarette consumption and age at death. We discuss methods of measuring the relationships of bivariate data, determining the strength of the relationships, and making inferences about the population from which the sample was drawn.

13.2 DIFFERENCES BETWEEN CORRELATION AND REGRESSION

The two most common methods used to describe the relationship between two quantitative variables (x and y) are **linear correlation** and **linear regression.** The former is a statistic that measures the *strength* of a bivariate association; the latter is a **prediction equation** that estimates the value of y for any given x.

When should you use correlation and when regression? Your choice depends on the questions raised and the kind of assumptions you make about the data. For example, you may address questions such as "Is there a relationship between IQ and grade point average?" or "Is there a relationship between the concentration of fluoride in drinking water and the number of cavities in children's teeth?" Such questions are approached by means of the **correlation coefficient,** which is a measure of the strength of the relationship between the two variables, provided the relationship is linear. As we will see in section 13.4, it is appropriate to compute a correlation coefficient for such data because both x and y may be viewed as random variables (i.e., variables that fluctuate in value according to their distribution).

Certain conventions apply to bivariate data. Almost universally, x refers to the **independent** (or **input**) **variable,** because its outcome is independent of the other variable; and y refers to the **dependent** (or **outcome**) **variable,** because its response is dependent on the other variable. Suppose you ask, "What change will occur in one's blood pressure after one reduces salt intake?" Here, you would use the regression method, because you are interested in the *degree* of relationship between two variables. Blood pressure would be represented by y, the dependent variable, and salt intake by x, the independent variable. You can see from this example that the investigator may arbitrarily select the values of the independent variable and then observe the results of the experiment in terms of the dependent variable y for various levels of x.

To further illustrate the methods of correlation and regression, let us suppose you are interested in studying the relationship of the prepregnancy weights of a group of mothers to their infants' birth weights. "How strong," you might ask, "is the association between the mother's weight and her infant's birth weight?" The method of choice is to calculate a correlation coefficient as a measure of the strength of association between these two variables.

On the other hand, if you were to ask, "What would be an infant's predicted birth weight for a mother possessing a known prepregnancy weight?" you would employ linear regression analysis.

13.3   THE SCATTER DIAGRAM

An ever-popular graphical method used to display the relationship between two variables is the **scatter diagram** (or **scattergram**). The scatter diagram plots the value of each pair of bivariate observations (x, y) at the point of intersection of the vertical line through the x value on the abscissa and of the horizontal line through the y value on the ordinate. For instance, let us use data from the Loma Linda Fetal Alcohol Syndrome Study (Kuzma and Sokol, 1982), displayed in Table 13.1. We can make a scatter diagram of these data by plotting on a graph each point corresponding to an (x, y) value (see Figure 13.2). Take case 13, for example. The mother's prepregnancy weight was 61.2 kg, and she delivered a baby weighing 3062 g. The point appears on Figure 13.2 where the lines for these values intersect. The diagonal line is called the **regression line** $(\hat{y})$ or, sometimes, the **line of best fit**. From this line, we expect women weighing 61.2 kg (prepregnancy) to bear babies weighing about 3400 (precisely 3387) g.

Table 13.1 Prepregnancy Weights of Mothers and Birth Weights of Their Infants (based on sample size 25)

Case Number	x Mother's Weight (kg)	y Infant's Birth Weight (g)
1	49.4	3515
2	63.5	3742
3	68.0	3629
4	52.2	2680
5	54.4	3006
6	70.3	4068
7	50.8	3373
8	73.9	4124
9	65.8	3572
10	54.4	3359
11	73.5	3230
12	59.0	3572
13	61.2	3062
14	52.2	3374
15	63.1	2722
16	65.8	3345
17	61.2	3714
18	55.8	2991
19	61.2	4026
20	56.7	2920
21	63.5	4152
22	59.0	2977
23	49.9	2764
24	65.8	2920
25	43.1	2693

SOURCE: Kuzma and Sokol, 1982.

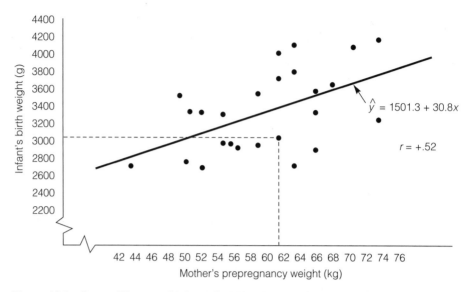

Figure 13.2   Scatter Diagram of Infants' Birth Weights Relative to Mothers' Prepregnancy Weights.

But we also expect random variation—and, of course, it happens. Case 13's baby weighed 3062 g, 325 g less than would be expected solely on the basis of the mother's weight. This difference is called the **residual.** We will further examine the subject of regression later.

In examining the data of Figure 13.2, you will notice that there is some sort of a relationship between the mother's prepregnancy weight and the infant's birth weight. Although the relationship is subtle, mothers of low prepregnancy weight generally bear infants of low birth weights, whereas mothers of high prepregnancy weight generally bear heavier infants. Is the relationship linear? An easy way to tell is to examine its scatter diagram to see if the trend roughly follows a straight line. How strong is the relationship? To find out, you need to compute an appropriate statistic, such as the correlation coefficient.

13.4   THE CORRELATION COEFFICIENT

As we noted earlier, the sample correlation coefficient, r, is a measure of the strength of the linear association between two variables, x and y. The population value is given by ρ (Greek rho). The correlation coefficient is often referred to as Pearson's product-moment r. It has some unique characteristics: It may take on values between -1 and $+1$, and it is a pure number and nondimensional; that is, it has no units such as centimeters or kilograms. A correlation coefficient of zero represents no relationship between the variables. The closer the coefficient comes to either $+1$ or -1, the stronger the relationship is and the more nearly it approximates a straight line. A **positive correlation** implies a direct relationship between the variables, and a **negative correlation** implies an inverse relationship.

The sample correlation coefficient is defined by

$$r = \frac{\Sigma(x - \bar{x})(y - \bar{y})}{\sqrt{[\Sigma(x - \bar{x})^2][\Sigma(y - \bar{y})^2]}} \tag{13.1}$$

In computing, we more often use

$$r = \frac{\Sigma xy - \dfrac{(\Sigma x)(\Sigma y)}{n}}{\sqrt{\left[\Sigma x^2 - \dfrac{(\Sigma x)^2}{n}\right]\left[\Sigma y^2 - \dfrac{(\Sigma y)^2}{n}\right]}} \tag{13.2}$$

Another formula, mathematically equivalent but easier to remember because it is defined in terms of the means and standard deviations of x and y and S_{xy}, the **sample covariance** of x only, is

$$r = \frac{\Sigma xy - n\bar{x}\bar{y}/(n - 1)}{S_x S_y} = \frac{S_{xy}}{S_x S_y} \tag{13.3}$$

Figure 13.3 illustrates six quite different sets of data and the ways in which they are summarized by r. Figure 13.3a illustrates the case of $r = +1.0$, a perfect positive correlation in which all the points fall on a straight line. It is positive because the values of y increase with increases in x. Figure 13.3b is a perfect negative correlation of $r = -1.0$. All the points again fall on a straight line, but as x increases, y decreases.

In real life, there are always random variations in our observations; hence, a perfect linear relationship is extremely rare. Examples of positive relationships are height and weight, education and income, and dietary fat and serum cholesterol levels. In positive relationships, as one of the variables numerically *increases,* the other variable also numerically *increases.* Examples of negative relationships include cigarette consumption and age at death, exercise and weight, and postmenopausal age and bone density. In negative relationships, as one of the variables numerically *increases,* the other variable numerically *decreases.*

Although it is no longer 1.0, the correlation coefficient remains high when the points cluster fairly closely around a straight line (see Figure 13.3c). The coefficient becomes smaller and smaller as the distribution of points clusters less closely around the line (see Figure 13.3d), and it becomes virtually zero (no correlation between the variables) when the distribution approximates a circle (see Figure 13.3e). Figure 13.3f illustrates one drawback of the correlation coefficient: It is ineffective for measuring a relationship that is not linear. In this case, we observe a neat curvilinear relationship whose linear correlation

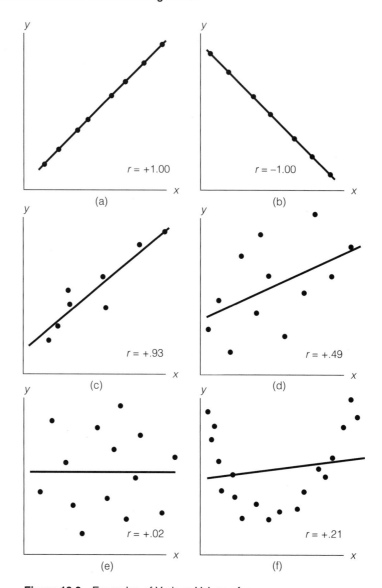

Figure 13.3   Examples of Various Values of r.

coefficient is quite low. This situation occurs because linear correlation tells its user how closely the relationship follows a straight line.

It is useful to know that the value of r does not change if the units of measurement of a particular variable change. For example, the value of r remains the same whether the measurements are inches and pounds or centimeters and kilograms. Also, r^2 provides an estimate of the proportion of the total variation in the variable y that is explained by the variation in the variable x.

To illustrate the computation of a correlation coefficient, we can apply the data of Table 13.1. Using equation (13.2), we obtain

$$r = \frac{\Sigma xy - \dfrac{(\Sigma x)(\Sigma y)}{n}}{\sqrt{\left[\Sigma x^2 - \dfrac{(\Sigma x)^2}{n}\right]\left[\Sigma y^2 - \dfrac{(\Sigma y)^2}{n}\right]}}$$

$$= \frac{5,036,414 - \dfrac{(1494)(83,530)}{25}}{\sqrt{\left[90,728 - \dfrac{(1494)^2}{25}\right]\left[284,266,104 - \dfrac{(83,530)^2}{25}\right]}} = .51615$$

A correlation coefficient of .51615 seems to be of moderate magnitude. But to interpret it, we need to answer two questions: (1) What inferences can we make regarding its true value? and (2) Is the correlation statistically significant?

Curvilinear Relationships

If the scatter diagram indicates that the data do not fit a linear model, then the relationship may be **curvilinear,** as shown in Figure 13.3f. It would not make much sense to try to fit a least-squares line in such a situation. One possible solution would be fitting a linear regression to a transformed set of variables such as $\sqrt{y}$. If the error terms are smaller using $\sqrt{y}$, then we have gained some in keeping a simple straight-line model to explain the relationship. A number of different transformations could be used, such as y^2, $\frac{1}{y}$, or log y. The object is to obtain a better linear relationship than that given by the original data. However, there are no precise ways to determine which transformation you should use.

Coefficient of Determination

A definition for r^2, the **coefficient of determination,** is $r^2 = 1 - (\text{SSE}/\text{SST})$, where SST represents the total sum of squares and SSE is the sum of squares $\Sigma(y - \bar{y})^2$, which represents the overall variability of the response variable y.

We should note the following characteristics about r^2:

1. It is always between 0 and 1. At the extreme value of 0, the regression line is horizontal; that is, $b_1 = 0$.
2. The closer r^2 is to 1, the "better" the regression line is in the sense that the residual sum of squares is much smaller than the total sum of squares. For this reason, r^2 is usually reported as an overall "figure of merit" for regression analysis.

We can interpret r^2 as the fraction of the total variation in y (SST) that is accounted for by the regression relationship between y and x.

Table 13.2 Characteristics of 15 Babies Measured Within 3 Hours of Birth

Weight (oz)	Height (in.)	Daily Cigarette Consumption of Mother	Daily Caffeine Consumption of Mother (mg)	Daily Alcohol Intake of Mother (oz)
81	17.0	50	55	5.0
83	17.3	45	70	5.2
86	17.5	40	160	4.5
88	17.2	0	250	4.0
88	18.1	20	190	0
95	18.0	40	55	1.4
98	19.4	0	30	3.6
101	18.7	30	65	2.5
102	18.8	20	100	0
106	19.0	5	125	0.5
112	18.2	0	65	1.0
118	20.0	15	225	1.2
118	20.5	10	300	1.0
120	20.5	0	255	0.7
125	19.7	0	60	1.1

Multiple Correlations

The Pearson correlation (r) technique is especially useful if you have two or more different variables and want to examine the relationship but not necessarily make predictions about them. Using the data set in Table 13.2, we will show how to analyze these variables and create a correlation matrix. In section 13.5, we will describe the process of interpreting correlation coefficients.

Given the data in Table 13.2, a researcher might choose to use a Pearson correlation to analyze *all* possible pairs of variables. If you are using a calculator, you would still use equation (13.2), arbitrarily labeling one of the variables x and the other y. This means that you would analyze 10 possible pairs, each time using equation (13.2). Most researchers would put the data into a spreadsheet and have the computer create what is commonly referred to as a **correlation matrix**. A matrix analyzing all pairs was created using Statview (SPSS would yield a similar matrix). The resulting matrix is shown in Table 13.3. The handbook *Ready, Set, Go! A Student Guide to SPSS 11.0 for Windows,* by Pavkov and Pierce (2003), illustrates an example of the Pearson correlation using SPSS.

13.5 TESTS OF HYPOTHESES AND CONFIDENCE INTERVALS FOR A POPULATION CORRELATION COEFFICIENT

As you might expect, the correlation coefficient r is a simple value. It is an estimate of the population correlation coefficient ρ in the same sense that $\bar{x}$ is an estimate of the population mean μ. We are most often interested in drawing inferences from a sample to the general population, so it is logical to perform a

Table 13.3 Correlation Matrix Created by Statview

Correlation Matrix

	Wt	Ht	Cig	Caf	Alc
Wt	1.000	.888	−.678	.271	−.672
Ht	.888	1.000	−.608	.379	−.624
Cig	−.678	−.608	1.000	−.327	.513
Caf	.271	.379	−.327	1.000	−.255
Alc	−.672	−.624	.513	−.255	1.000

15 observations were used in this computation.

test of significance on the population correlation coefficient and estimate a confidence interval for it.

If you wish to test the null hypothesis that $\rho = 0$ (i.e., x and y are not linearly correlated) against the alternative hypothesis that $\rho \neq 0$, you can use the following procedure. The only needed assumptions: The pairs of observations (x_1, y_1), $(x_2, y_2), \ldots, (x_n, y_n)$ must have been obtained randomly, and both x and y must be normally distributed. The test statistic to use is

$$t = \frac{r - 0}{\sqrt{(1 - r^2)/(n - 2)}} \tag{13.4}$$

with $n - 2$ df, where n is the number of paired observations.

For example, the correlation between birth weight and maternal cigarette consumption is −.678.

$$t = \frac{-.678}{\sqrt{[1 - (-.678)^2]/(15 - 2)}} = -3.33$$

which (by reference to Table B, inside back cover) represents a correlation significantly different ($\rho < .01$) from zero. Our conclusion: There appears to be an association between a child's birth weight and the mother's prepregnancy consumption of cigarettes. Very often, in a journal article, the researchers will have performed multiple correlations. The correlations will then be displayed in a correlation matrix. Table 13.4 is an abbreviated version of an actual correlation matrix created by Windle and Windle (1996). The complete matrix included all possible correlations from 15 variables. The original matrix had a total of 105 correlation coefficients! For each of the correlation coefficients, we have used a computer to compute a t test for significance. This matrix is a typical display of the correlation coefficients, with asterisks to indicate which correlations are significant at .05 and .01.

Notice in Table 13.4 that the correlation of variable 1 and variable 8 yields a correlation coefficient of .08. This correlation is significant at .05. Under just about

Table 13.4 Example of Correlation Matrix

Variable	1	2	3	4	5	6	7	8
1	—							
2	.07	—						
3	.27**	.16**	—					
4	.23**	.34**	.35**	—				
5	.03	−.11**	.33**	.16**	—			
6	−.05	−.07	.15**	.11**	.32**	—		
7	.05	.36**	−.11**	.16**	−.22**	−.03	—	
8	.08*	−.07	.30**	.22**	.30**	.12**	−.19**	—
N = 733	*p < .05	**p < .01						

NOTE: These data were copied and the table abbreviated from Windle and Windle (1996).

any conceivable circumstance, .08 is a very low correlation, yet in this study, it was found to be significant. How is it possible that such a low correlation could be significant? The answer has to do with the sample size. When a sample is large (733 is a large sample), using equation (13.4) will almost always give a significant correlation. Note what happens to the calculated t with a correlation coefficient of .08 and an N of 733:

$$t = \frac{.08}{\sqrt{[1 - (.08)^2]/731}} = 2.17$$

The calculated t of 2.17, compared with a critical t of ± 1.97 (200 df from Table B), yields a statistically significant correlation. The inescapable conclusion is that you must be careful in interpreting the meaning of a significant correlation when the sample size is large.

Where did the t statistic of equation (13.4) come from? Mathematical statisticians are able to make a comparatively simple derivation from other equations, as you will see in section 13.8.

Computing a confidence interval for ρ involves an equation much more complex than the corresponding one for the population mean. In consequence, tables giving confidence intervals have been prepared for the convenience of the user. Figure 13.4 illustrates 95% confidence intervals for different sample sizes. Suppose you wanted to find the 95% confidence interval for the population correlation coefficient ρ from the mother–child example ($r = .52, n = 25$). It is quite simple to do this using Figure 13.4. Find the r of $+.52$ on the abscissa and sketch a vertical line through it. The points given by the intersection of that line and the intervals for $n = 25$ give the upper and lower 95% confidence limits. Use the curves that correspond to your sample size, or visually interpolate. The limits are read on the ordinate—approximately, $+.10$ and $+.75$. If we can safely assume that our data for the 25 mother–child pairs (see Table 13.1) represent a random sample of all the pairs in the study, then the 95% confidence interval for the true population ρ is indeed .10–.75. Regardless of the true

Scale of *r* (= sample correlation coefficient)

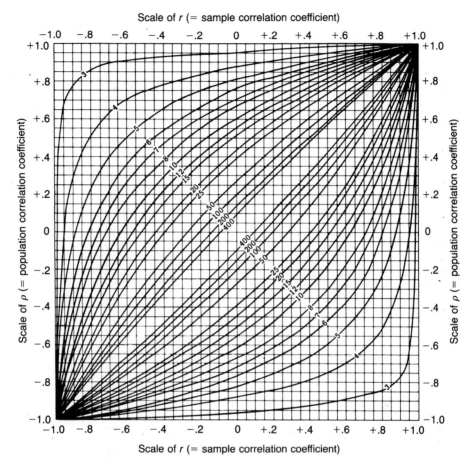

Figure 13.4 Confidence Intervals for the Correlation Coefficient $(1 - \alpha = .95)$. Source: Reprinted with permission from *Handbook of Tables for Probability and Statistics*, ed. William H. Beyer (Boca Raton, Fl.: CRC Press, 1966). Copyright CRC Press, Inc., Boca Raton, Fl.

value of the population correlation coefficient, we can draw the inference, with 95% confidence, that it is captured by the range .10–.75. Furthermore, the test of H_0: $\rho = 0$ at the $\alpha = .01$ level indicates that ρ is significantly different from zero because zero falls below the interval .10–.75.

Understanding the Correlation Matrix

Now let us return to the characteristics of the 15 babies (see Table 13.2) and create and interpret a correlation matrix. Performing a computer analysis yields the data in Table 13.5. Included are the 10 correlation coefficients, along with an exact *P* value and the 95% confidence interval for each coefficient.

Table 13.5 Correlation Analysis of Table 13.2
Created by Statview

Correlation Analysis

	Correlation	P Value	95% Lower	95% Upper
Wt, Ht	.888	<.0001	.690	.963
Wt, Cig	−.678	.0043	−.883	−.253
Wt, Caf	.271	.3355	−.280	.688
Wt, Alc	−.672	.0048	−.881	−.244
Ht, Cig	−.608	.0146	−.854	−.138
Ht, Caf	.379	.1671	−.165	.746
Ht, Alc	−.624	.0113	−.861	−.164
Cig, Caf	−.327	.2396	−.719	.223
Cig, Alc	.513	.0494	.001	.812
Caf, Alc	−.255	.3664	−.679	.296

15 observations were used in this computation.

If a researcher were publishing these data, the final correlation matrix would look something like Table 13.6. Notice how this matrix differs from the original computer-generated version (see Tables 13.3 and 13.5). Correlation coefficients are normally reported to two decimal places, rather than the three decimal places generated by a computer. The third decimal place is almost always irrelevant. Another difference is that each correlation coefficient is usually, but not always, reported only once, not twice as in the computer-generated version. Table 13.6 shows all the coefficients above the diagonal row of 1.00 coefficients.

You may also see the coefficients displayed as shown in Table 13.7. You still have the same 10 correlation coefficients, but now they are displayed below the

Table 13.6 Pearson Correlation of Characteristics of 15 Babies Measured Within 3 Hours of Birth: Version 1

Variable	Weight (oz)	Height (in.)	Daily Cigarette Consumption of Mother	Daily Caffeine Consumption of Mother (mg)	Daily Alcohol Intake of Mother (oz)
Wt (oz)	1.00	.89***	−.68**	.27	−.67**
Ht (in.)		1.00	−.61*	.38	−.62*
Cig			1.00	−.33	.51*
Caf				1.00	−.26
Alc					1.00

$N = 15$ *$p < .05$ *$p < .01$ ***$p < .001$

Table 13.7 Pearson Correlation of Characteristics of 15 Babies Measured Within 3 Hours of Birth: Version 2

Variable	Weight (oz)	Height (in.)	Daily Cigarette Consumption of Mother	Daily Caffeine Consumption of Mother (mg)	Daily Alcohol Intake of Mother (oz)
Wt (oz)	—				
Ht (in.)	.89***	—			
Cig	−.68**	−.61*	—		
Caf	.27	.38	−.33	—	
Alc	−.67**	−.62*	.51*	−.26	—
N = 15	*p < .05	**p < .01	***p < .001		

diagonal line. Notice also that the diagonal line is different. In Table 13.6, the diagonal is a series of 1.00 correlations, and in Table 13.7, it is a series of dashes. Either form is acceptable. The 1.00 is a "dummy" correlation; it is what you get if you correlate a series of numbers with that same series. If you correlate weight with weight, height with height, and so on, you will always get a perfect positive correlation for the simple reason that the data sets are identical. Finally, notice the P values. The various asterisks tell you which correlations are significant and at which level, with the most common levels (α) being .05, .01, and .001. These values were derived from the exact P values displayed in Table 13.5.

13.6 LIMITATIONS OF THE CORRELATION COEFFICIENT

As we mentioned, one limitation of the correlation coefficient is that, though it measures how closely the two variables approximate a straight line, it does not validly measure the strength of a nonlinear relationship. We also have to equivocate a bit as to the reliability of the correlation when n is small (say, fewer than about 50 pairs of observations). Furthermore, it is always useful to plot a scattergram (e.g., Figure 13.2) to see if there are any **outliers**—that is, observations that clearly appear to be out of range of the other observations. Outliers have a marked effect on the correlation coefficient, often suggest erroneous data, and are likely to give misleading results. Perhaps the most important drawback of the correlation coefficient is that a high (or statistically significant) correlation can so easily be taken to imply a cause-and-effect relationship. Use caution: Do not take it as proof of such a relationship.

With all these reservations, you may be puzzled as to how major decisions in public policy can be based on correlation analysis. For instance, in the Surgeon General's Report (U.S. Department of Health, Education, and Welfare, 1971), we see an important public document that includes a good deal of correlation analysis and concludes that smoking causes lung cancer. In reaching

Table 13.8 Correlation Between Increased Smoking and Increased Death Rate

Number of Cigarettes Smoked	Mortality Ratio of Smokers to Nonsmokers	Excess in Death Rate of Smokers over Nonsmokers (%)
<10	1.45	45
10–19	1.75	75
20–39	1.90	90
40 or more	2.20	120

their conclusions, the Surgeon General's blue-ribbon panel of experts (which included leading statisticians) relied heavily on the consistency of the results of a large number of population and laboratory studies. In essence, their conclusion was based not on a single correlation coefficient, but on an overwhelming body of evidence:

1. The death rate for cigarette smokers was about 70% higher than for nonsmokers.

2. Death rates increased with increased smoking (see Table 13.8).

3. The death rates of heavy smokers were more than two times larger than those of light smokers.

4. The mortality ratio of cigarette smokers to nonsmokers was substantially higher for those who started smoking before age 20 than for those who started smoking after age 25. The mortality ratio increased with more years of smoking.

5. The mortality of smokers who inhaled was higher than that of those who did not.

6. Persons who stopped smoking had a mortality ratio 1.4 times that of persons who never smoked, while current smokers had a ratio of 1.7.

7. In prospective studies, it was found that for all causes of death smokers experienced 70% greater mortality than nonsmokers, but for respiratory system causes, the percentage was even higher. For lung cancer, it was 10 times higher; for bronchitis and emphysema, it was 6.1 times higher.

13.7   REGRESSION ANALYSIS

We are indebted to Sir Francis Galton for coining the term *regression* during his study of heredity laws. He observed that physical characteristics of children were correlated with those of their fathers. He noted in particular that the heights of sons were less extreme than those of their fathers. Specifically, he found that tall fathers tended to have shorter sons, whereas short fathers tended to have

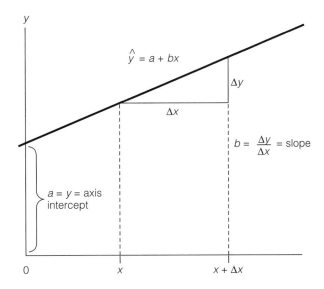

Figure 13.5   Equation of a Straight Line.

taller sons, a phenomenon he called "regression toward the mean." In plotting median heights of sons and fathers, he found that there was a positive association and that the relationship was roughly linear.

   Subsequently, statisticians used means, not medians, and embraced the term *regression line* to describe a linear relationship between two variables. The regression line also indicates prediction of the value of a dependent (outcome) variable (y) from a known value of an independent variable (x), as well as the expected change in a dependent variable for a unit change in an independent variable. For any two variables, there is a linear equation that best represents the relationship between them. It is often useful to find an estimate of the true equation that describes the straight-line regression. Such an estimate is given by

$$\hat{y} = a + bx \tag{13.5}$$

That is, the dependent variable $\hat{y}$ can be estimated in terms of a constant, a, plus another constant, b, times the independent variable x. Note the important distinction between $\hat{y}$, the predicted value (which falls on the regression line), and y, the observed value (which usually does not fall on the line). The constants a and b are estimates of the two parameters of the true regression equation that define the location of the line. Their specific meaning is illustrated in Figure 13.5. The constant a represents the value of y when $x = 0$, while b is the slope (or gradient) of the line. The slope can be more precisely defined as the amount of change, Δy, in the dependent variable for a given change, Δx, in the independent variable. Thus, the slope, often referred to as the **regression coefficient,** gives a good indication of the relationship between the variables x and y.

Equation (13.5) is an estimate of the following equation, which describes the population regression of y on x:

$$y = \beta_0 + \beta_1 x + \epsilon$$

where β_0 is the **y-axis intercept** and corresponds to a of equation (13.5); β_1 is the slope of the population regression line and corresponds to b of equation (13.5); and ϵ is the error in the observed value of y for a specified value of x. The error, the residual, is estimated by $y - \hat{y}$, the difference between the observed and the predicted value.

Certainly, you strive to solve regression problems with some equation that provides the "best fit" to the data. But how do you do this? There is a mathematical procedure that minimizes the estimated error $(y - \hat{y})$, known as the **least-squares method.** This procedure uses equations that estimate β_0 and β_1 by the following equations for a and b. The equation for estimating β_1 is

$$\hat{\beta}_1 = b = \frac{\Sigma(x - \bar{x})(y - \bar{y})}{\Sigma(x - \bar{x})^2} = r_{xy}\frac{s_y}{s_x} \tag{13.6}$$

and the equation for estimating β_0 is

$$\hat{\beta}_0 = a = \bar{y} - b\bar{x} \tag{13.7}$$

Again using our data on mothers' and infants' weights (see Table 13.1), we can now compute the slope. For convenience, we use the following mathematically identical computation equations:

$$
\begin{aligned}
b &= \frac{\Sigma xy - [(\Sigma x)(\Sigma y)]/n}{\Sigma x^2 - [(\Sigma x)^2]/n} \\
&= \frac{5,036,414.1 - (1493.7)(83,530)/25}{90,728.45 - (1493.7)^2/25} = 30.794
\end{aligned}
\tag{13.8}
$$

and

$$a = \bar{y} - b\bar{x} = 3341.2 - 30.794\,(59.748) = 1501.32 \tag{13.9}$$

Now that we know the values of the two constants, we can write the equation for the best-fitting line of regression:

$$\hat{y} = 1501.32 + 30.794x$$

Symbolically, $\hat{y}$ is the predicted value for a given value of x. It is actually the estimated mean of all y's that could be observed for a specific value of x.

To illustrate further: Women with a prepregnancy weight of 70.3 kg would be expected from the preceding equation to bear infants weighing an average of 3666 g. But case 6, a subject who weighed 70.3 kg, bore a baby weighing 4068 g.

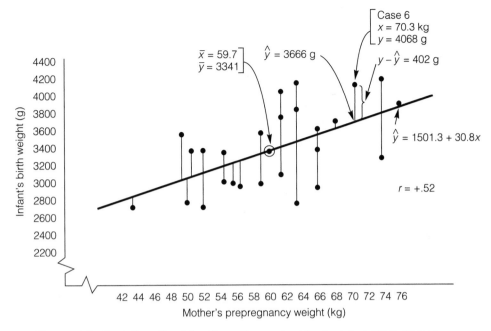

Figure 13.6   Deviations About the Linear Regression Line for Infants' Birth Weights Relative to Mothers' Prepregnancy Weights.

The difference, $y - \hat{y} = 4068 - 3666 = 402$ g, represents the deviation, or residual, of the observed value from the value predicted by the least-squares regression line. The residuals are shown as the vertical lines in Figure 13.6.

The regression line always passes through the means of x and y—that is, through $(x = \bar{x}, y = \bar{y})$. Hence, it is simple to superimpose it on the scattergram. A characteristic of a least-squares regression line is that the sum of the deviations about the line is equal to zero, and the sum of the squared deviations is a minimum; that is, there is no other line for which it could be less. That is why it is referred to as the line of best fit in the sense of "least squares." Table 13.9 helps verify this. It shows that the sum of the residuals above the regression line equals the sum of those below the line; that is, $\Sigma(y - \hat{y}) = 0$, or actually 0.14, which is a tiny round-off error.

An indication of just how precisely the regression line describes the relationship between x and y is the variance of the deviations $(y - \hat{y})$ about the line. This variance is denoted $s_{y \cdot x}^2$. It is an estimate of the true error of prediction $\sigma_{y \cdot x}^2$. Underlying this estimate is an assumption of homogeneity—namely, that $\sigma_{y \cdot x}^2$ remains constant for all y's distributed about each x along the regression line.

The last column of Table 13.9 is used to compute $s_{y \cdot x}^2$, the equation being

$$s_{y \cdot x}^2 = \frac{\Sigma(y - \hat{y})^2}{n - 2} \tag{13.10}$$

Table 13.9 Prepregnancy Weights of Mothers and Birth Weights of Their Infants—Deviations About the Linear Line of Regression

Case Number	x Mother's Weight (kg)	y Infant's Actual Birth Weight (g)	$\hat{y}$ Infant's Expected Birth Weight (g)*	$y - \hat{y}$ Residual (g)	$(y - \hat{y})^2$ Squared Residual (g)^2
1	49.4	3515	3022.54	492.46	242,516.85
2	63.5	3742	3456.73	285.27	81,378.97
3	68.0	3629	3595.31	33.69	1,135.02
4	52.2	2680	3108.76	−428.76	183,835.13
5	54.4	3006	3176.51	−170.51	29,073.66
6	70.3	4068	3666.13	401.87	161,499.49
7	50.8	3373	3065.65	307.35	94,464.02
8	73.9	4124	3776.99	347.01	120,415.94
9	65.8	3572	3527.56	44.44	1,974.91
10	54.4	3359	3176.51	182.49	33,302.60
11	73.5	3230	3764.67	−534.67	285,872.00
12	59.0	3572	3318.16	253.84	64,434.75
13	61.2	3062	3385.91	−323.91	104,917.68
14	52.2	3374	3108.76	265.24	70,352.26
15	63.1	2722	3444.42	−722.42	521,890.65
16	65.8	3345	3527.56	−182.56	33,328.15
17	61.2	3714	3385.91	328.09	107,643.04
18	55.8	2991	3219.62	−228.62	52,267.10
19	61.2	4026	3385.91	640.09	409,715.21
20	56.7	2920	3247.33	−327.33	107,144.92
21	63.5	4152	3456.73	695.27	483,400.37
22	59.0	2977	3318.16	−341.16	116,390.14
23	49.9	2764	3037.93	−273.93	75,037.64
24	65.8	2920	3527.56	−607.56	369,129.15
25	43.1	2693	2828.54	−135.54	18,371.09
	$\bar{x} = 59.7480$	$\bar{y} = 3341.20$	—	$\Sigma(y - \hat{y}) = 0.14$	$\Sigma(y - \hat{y})^2 = 3,769,490.74$

*$\hat{y} = 30.794x + 1501.32$

where $n - 2$ represents the degrees of freedom. From Table 13.9, we compute $s^2_{y \cdot x}$ as $3,769,490.7/23 = 163,890.9$. Alternatively, the same variance can be obtained directly without computing predicted values ($\hat{y}$) by substituting $\alpha + bx$ for y, which gives

$$s^2_{y \cdot x} = \frac{\Sigma(y - a - bx)^2}{n - 2} \tag{13.11}$$

After some algebraic manipulations, we can rewrite this as

$$s^2_{y \cdot x} = \frac{\Sigma y^2 - a\Sigma y - b\Sigma xy}{n - 2} \tag{13.12}$$

The square root of $s^2_{y \cdot x}$ is referred to as the **standard error of estimate.** Once you have obtained the equation for a linear regression line, you would probably like to know how reliable the line is for predicting dependent variables. To find out, you need to use the standard error of estimate in a test of significance or obtain confidence intervals for β_1, the slope of the population regression line.

13.8 INFERENCES REGARDING THE SLOPE OF THE REGRESSION LINE

Thus far, we have assumed that (1) the means of each distribution of y's for a given x fall on a straight line and (2) the variances, $\sigma^2_{y \cdot x}$, are homogeneous for each distribution of y's for a given x. To perform tests of significance or compute confidence intervals, we will need one more assumption: The distribution of y's is normal for each value of x.

We noted earlier that the slope, b, computed from sample data is an estimate of some true value, β_1, for the population regression line, which is defined by

$$y = \beta_0 + \beta_1 x + \epsilon \tag{13.13}$$

We now wish to determine (1) how useful the regression line obtained from sample data is in predicting the outcome variable and (2) whether the slope b differs significantly from $\beta_1 = 0$. To do this, we need to perform a hypothesis test for β much as we did for μ. The first step is to compute the standard error of b. Mathematical statisticians have shown that

$$SE(b) = \sqrt{\frac{s^2_{y \cdot x}}{\Sigma(x - \bar{x})^2}} \tag{13.14}$$

which simplifies to

$$SE(b) = \frac{s_{y \cdot x}}{s_x \sqrt{n - 1}}$$

For our data on mothers' weights and infants' birth weights (see Table 13.9), this computes to

$$SE(b) = \frac{\sqrt{163,890.9}}{\sqrt{90,728.45 - 1493.7^2/25}} = \frac{404.834}{38.51} = 10.512$$

Using this value, we can now perform the following hypothesis test:

1. H_0: $\beta_1 = 0$ (slope of 0 means that there appears to be no relationship between x and y) versus H_1: $\beta_1 \neq 0$.
2. $\alpha = .05$.

3. The test statistic (with $n - 2$ df) is

$$t = \frac{b - 0}{SE(b)}$$

$$= \frac{30.794}{10.512} \tag{13.15}$$

$$= 2.93$$

4. The critical region for t with 23 df for $\alpha = .05$ is $t = 2.07$.

5. We reject H_0 because a t of 2.93 falls in the critical region.

6. We conclude that the slope differs significantly from zero; consequently, a regression line estimated from our data can, with reasonable reliability, predict dependent variables for given values of x.

From the test statistic for the regression coefficient b, it is a simple matter to describe the confidence interval for the true regression coefficient β_1:

$$\text{CI for } \beta_1 = b \pm t[SE(b)] \tag{13.16}$$

again based on $n - 2$ df.

The confidence interval corresponds to the central $(1 - \alpha)$ proportion of the area. Assuming only that our data for 25 mother–infant pairs represent a random sample of all such pairs, the 95% confidence interval for β_1, the true slope, is

$$\text{CI} = 30.794 \pm 2.07(10.512)$$

$$= 30.794 \pm 21.760$$

$$= 9.03 \text{ to } 52.55$$

Therefore, we can say (with 95% confidence) that β_1 is unlikely to be less than 9.03 or greater than 52.56.

We can show that the t statistic of equation (13.4) can be derived from testing the null hypothesis that β, the slope of the line of regression, is zero. The equation to use is

$$t = \frac{b}{SE(b)}$$

where b represents a sample estimate of β. Testing whether β equals zero is functionally equivalent to testing for ρ equals zero.

◆ CONCLUSION

Correlation analysis and regression analysis have different purposes. The former is used to determine whether a relationship exists between two variables and how strong that relationship is. The latter is used to determine the equation that describes the relationship and to predict the value of y for a given x. An aid to visualizing these concepts is the scatter diagram.

A correlation coefficient (r) can take on values from -1 to $+1$. The closer r approaches -1 or $+1$, the stronger the linear relationship between x and y; the closer r approaches zero, the weaker the relationship. It is important to keep in mind that a high correlation merely indicates a strong association between the variables; it does not imply a cause-and-effect relationship. A correlation coefficient is valid only where a linear relationship exists between the variables. After computing the correlation coefficient r and the regression coefficient b, we are obliged to test their significance or set up confidence limits that encompass the population values they estimate.

◆ VOCABULARY LIST

bivariate data
cause-and-effect
    relationship
coefficient of
    determination
correlation coefficient
correlation matrix
curvilinear
    relationship
dependent variable
    (outcome variable)

independent variable
    (input variable)
least-squares method
linear correlation
linear regression
negative correlation
outlier
positive correlation
prediction equation
regression coefficient
    (slope, gradient)

regression line
    (line of best fit)
residual
sample covariance
scatter diagram
    (scattergram)
standard error of
    estimate
y-axis intercept

◆ EXERCISES

13.1   A correlation coefficient r consists of two parts: a sign and a numerical value.
   a. What is the range of possible values for r?
   b. What does the sign tell you about the relationship between variables x and y?
   c. What information do you derive from the value of r regarding x and y?
   d. What does r tell you about the ability of the regression line to predict values of y for given values of x?
   e. For any given set of data, would the correlation coefficient and the regression coefficient necessarily have the same sign? The same magnitude?

13.2   Give examples of variables that would be suitable for computing a
   a. correlation coefficient
   b. regression line

13.3   What is the meaning of
   a. r
   b. r^2
   c. a and b in a regression line
   d. least-squares regression line

13.4 What are the limitations of a correlation coefficient?

13.5 What are the assumptions that you need to make in
a. testing H_0: $\rho = 0$
b. testing H_0: $\beta = 0$ or computing the CI for β

13.6 You obtained a Pearson r of -1.04. What does this tell you about the relationship between the two variables correlated?

13.7 You obtained a Pearson r of .45. How many pairs of subjects or scores must you have for this correlation to be considered significant? Assume that this is a one-tailed test.

13.8 Which of these correlations is the strongest? The weakest? Explain.
a. $-.71$ b. .08   c. .62   d. $-.12$

13.9 You obtained a Pearson r of .60.
a. With an n of 25, 50, and 100, what are the confidence intervals?
b. Why do the confidence intervals become narrower as the sample size increases?

13.10 The correlation matrix from which Table 13.4 is derived actually had 105 correlations from 15 variables. If there were absolutely no significant correlations between any of the variables, at a .05 level of significance, how many correlations would you expect to be significant? (*Hint:* This is directly related to the possibility of a type I or type II error.)

13.11 You obtained the following correlation matrix:

A.	1.00	.48	−.06	.87	
B.		1.00	.17	−.71	$N = 32$
C.			1.00	−.40	
D.				1.00	

a. Which correlations are significant at .05 (two-tail)?
b. Which correlations are significant at .01 (two-tail)?

13.12 The correlation matrix below was taken directly from an article by Lee et al. (1999).

Variable	1	2	3	4	5	6	7	8	9
1	1.00	.21***	.84***	.13*	−.03	.42***	.04	.16**	.37***
2	.21***	1.00	.47***	.11	.02	.22***	.02	.12	.27***
3	.84***	.47***	1.00	.21***	.09	.54***	.02	.27***	.37***
4	.13*	.11	.21***	1.00	.30***	.28***	.27***	.36***	.22***
5	−.03	.02	.09	.30***	1.00	.25***	−.15*	.33***	.03
6	.42***	.22***	.54***	.28***	.25***	1.00	−.02	.39***	.46***
7	.04	.02	.02	.27***	−.15*	−.02	1.00	.07	.00
8	.16**	.12	.27***	.36***	.33***	.39***	.07	1.00	.25***
9	.37*	.27***	.37***	.22***	.03	.46***	.00	.25***	1.00

a. There is one mistake in the matrix. Can you identify it? (*Hint:* Although the mistake is relatively minor, it is "significant.")
b. Which of the correlations is strongest? Weakest? Explain.

13.13 The American Heart Association has provided the following regression equations for computing a person's ideal weight ($\hat{y}$) based on a person's height (x) in feet. For females, it is given by $\hat{y} = 100 + 4.0x$; for males, it is given by

$\hat{y} = 110 + 5.0x$. Use the appropriate equation to determine your ideal weight, and compare it with your actual weight to determine whether you are over- or underweight.

◆ COMPREHENSIVE EXERCISES

Using the data from Exercises 13.14–13.19, do the following:
a. Compute a Pearson r.
b. Test H_0: $\rho = 0$ at $\alpha = .05$.
c. Compute r^2 and explain what it means.
d. Obtain the 95% confidence interval for ρ.

13.14 In a study of systolic blood pressure (SBP) in relation to whole blood cadmium (Cd) and zinc (Zn) levels, the following data were obtained:

Cd (ppm/g ash)	68	63	56	48	96	70	66	45	50	60	53	47	36	65
Zn (ppm/g ash)	127	118	78	76	181	134	122	87	80	107	116	103	64	123
SBP (mmHg)	166	162	116	120	160	120	182	134	130	116	108	134	116	96

e. Make a scatter diagram of cadmium and systolic blood pressure, using the latter as the dependent variable.
f. Judging from the diagram, would you be justified in using linear regression analysis to determine a line of best fit for cadmium and blood pressure? Why or why not?
g. Using zinc as the dependent variable, plot a scatter diagram of cadmium and zinc.
h. Does the diagram in (g) provide justification for using regression analysis to determine a line of best fit? Why or why not?
i. Calculate the equation of the line of best fit for the relationship between zinc and cadmium, and draw the line on the scatter diagram for (g).
j. If it were determined that a patient had a whole blood cadmium level of 80, what would you expect that patient's zinc level to be?
k. Would you be justified in stating that there is a cause-and-effect relationship between cadmium and zinc? Why or why not?

13.15 The following are data for 12 individuals' daily sodium intake and their systolic blood pressure readings.

Person	Sodium	BP	Person	Sodium	BP
1	6.8	154	7	7.0	166
2	7.0	167	8	7.5	195
3	6.9	162	9	7.3	189
4	7.2	175	10	7.1	186
5	7.3	190	11	6.5	148
6	7.0	158	12	6.4	140

A research investigator is interested in learning how strong the association is between these variables and how well we can predict blood pressure from sodium intake.

  e. Calculate the regression equation for the data.
  f. Test $H_0: \beta = 0$ at the $\alpha = .01$ level.
  g. What would be a likely blood pressure for a person with a sodium intake of 6.3? Of 7.6?

13.16 Richard Doll, a British investigator of the relationship between smoking and lung cancer, compiled the following information on per capita cigarette consumption in 1930 and lung cancer 20 years later (in 1950) for a number of countries, as shown below:

Country	Cigarette Consumption in 1930	Deaths per 100,000 in 1950
USA	1300	20
Great Britain	1100	46
Finland	1100	35
Switzerland	510	25
Canada	500	15
Holland	490	24
Australia	480	18
Denmark	380	17
Sweden	300	11
Norway	250	9
Iceland	230	6

  e. Construct a scatter diagram and describe the relationship between cigarette consumption in 1930 and lung cancer in 1950.

13.17 The authors of the touch therapy article (described in Chapter 8) collected data on the number of correct choices and the therapists' years of experience. Is there any relationship between the number of correct responses and the number of years of experience?

Initial Test Results (Number of Correct Choices Out of 10)

	Correct Choices	Years of Experience
CMT* 1	4	4
CMT 2	3	4
CMT 3	6	3
CMT 4	3	2
CMT 5	3	5
Layperson 1	4	3
Layperson 2	5	6
LPN**	5	6
Medical Assistant	4	8
RN*** 1	3	17
RN 2	2	3
RN 3	7	15
RN 4	6	12
RN 5	8	7
RN 6	7	17

*CMT = certified massage therapist
**LPN = licensed practical nurse
***RN = registered nurse

Follow-Up Test Results (Number of Correct Choices Out of 10)

	Correct Choices	Years of Experience
CMT 2	3	6
CMT 6	3	5
CMT 7	5	12
Chiropractor	5	7
LPN	3	8
Phlebotomist	5	27
RN 2	7	7
RN 3	3	15
RN 4	4	13
RN 5	4	7
RN 6	5	23
RN 7	1	8
RN 8	5	1

In this exercise, treat the initial and follow-up results as two separate correlations. Then combine them and treat them as one correlation. After analyzing each, explain the differences. These data can be obtained from the following Web site: http://www.quackwatch.com

13.18 Characteristics of 20 males who died of heart disease were measured, and their age at death was determined. What is the relationship between each of these variables? In addition to parts (a)–(d), create a correlation matrix. See Tables 13.6 and 13.7 for examples of a correlation matrix.

Age at Death	Height	Pounds Overweight (+) or Underweight (−)	Cholesterol Level	Systolic Blood Pressure
46	5′10″	+40	195	158
46	6′1″	+29	265	157
49	5′9″	+30	312	157
49	6′6″	+6	246	160
50	5′11″	+18	278	131
51	5′7″	+16	301	138
53	5′4″	0	212	160
54	6′2″	+13	248	122
57	6′4″	+1	257	123
58	5′11″	+12	183	122
59	6′	+14	198	134
59	6′5″	+1	200	157
62	5′11″	+2	235	150
62	6′3″	+3	218	117
64	5′7″	+1	192	126
65	5′9″	0	242	109
68	6′4″	+1	185	120
69	5′11″	−3	197	111
71	5′9″	−5	185	107
74	5′7″	−1	223	119

13.19 Using the data from Table 3.1 (Honolulu Heart Study), create a correlation matrix and complete parts (a)–(d). See Tables 13.6 and 13.7 for examples of a correlation matrix. Use these variables: weight, height, age, blood glucose level, serum cholesterol level, systolic blood pressure, and body mass index. If you are doing this problem by computer (this problem will take forever if you aren't), divide the group by smoking status and compare the results.

e. Calculate the equation of the regression line for the relationship between blood glucose (x) and serum cholesterol (y). Perform a test of significance of $H_0: \beta_1 = 0$ at $\alpha = .01$.

f. Calculate the equation of the regression line for the relationship between body mass index (x) and systolic blood pressure (y). Perform a test of significance of $H_0: \beta_1 = 0$ at $\alpha = .05$.

14 Nonparametric Methods

CHAPTER OUTLINE

✔ **LEARNING OBJECTIVES**

After studying this chapter, you should be able to

1. Distinguish between
   a. parametric and nonparametric methods
   b. rank-sum tests and signed-rank tests
   c. Pearson and Spearman correlation coefficients
2. List the advantages and disadvantages of nonparametric methods
3. Give the equation for the sum of the first n integers
4. List the assumptions necessary to perform hypothesis tests by nonparametric methods
5. Be able to apply the sign test to paired data
6. Know when and how to use Fisher's exact test

14.1 RATIONALE FOR NONPARAMETRIC METHODS

In the preceding chapters, we discussed several methods that enable us to determine whether there is a significant difference between two sample means. The most popular of these involve the normal and the t distributions. We also learned about the correlation coefficient, which measures the amount of linear association between two variables. Underlying such test statistics were assumptions of normality, homogeneity of variances, and linearity. Whenever we dealt with measurement data used in test statistics, we also were interested in obtaining some estimate of the population parameter—that is, μ or ρ.

All these statistical techniques are collectively referred to as **parametric methods.** In contrast to these are the **nonparametric methods,** which have been developed for conditions in which the assumptions necessary for using parametric methods cannot be made. Nonparametric methods are sometimes referred to as **distribution-free methods** because it is not necessary to assume that the observations are normally distributed. A nonparametric method is appropriate for dealing with data that are measured on a nominal or ordinal scale (discussed in Chapter 3) and whose distribution is unknown. Because of the many advantages of nonparametric methods, their use has been increasing rapidly. But, like most methods, they also have disadvantages.

14.2 ADVANTAGES AND DISADVANTAGES OF NONPARAMETRIC METHODS

Nonparametric methods have three main advantages:

1. They do not have restrictive assumptions such as normality of the observations. In practice, data are often nonnormal or the sample size is not large enough to gain the benefit of the central limit theorem. At most, the distribution should be somewhat symmetrical. This gives nonparametric methods a major advantage.

2. Computations can be performed speedily and easily—a prime advantage when a quick preliminary indication of results is needed.

3. They are well suited to experiments or surveys that yield outcomes that are difficult to quantify. In such cases, the parametric methods, although statistically more powerful, may yield less reliable results than the nonparametric methods, which tend to be less sensitive to the errors inherent in ordinal measurements.

There are also three distinct disadvantages of nonparametric methods:

1. They are less efficient (i.e., they require a larger sample size to reject a false hypothesis) than comparable parametric tests.

2. Hypotheses tested with nonparametric methods are less specific than those tested comparably with parametric methods.

3. They do not take advantage of all of the special characteristics of a distribution. Consequently, these methods do not fully utilize the information known about the distribution.

In using nonparametric methods, you should be careful to view them as complementary statistical methods rather than attractive alternatives. With a knowledge of their advantages and disadvantages, and some experience, you should be able to determine easily which statistical test is the most appropriate for a given application.

An inherent characteristic of many nonparametric statistics is that they deal with ranks rather than values of the observations. The observations are arranged in an array, and ranks are assigned from 1 to n. Consequently, computations are simple; you deal only with positive integers: 1, 2, 3, . . . , n. When working with ranks, we often need to compute the sum of the numbers 1 through n, which, we recall from algebra, equals $n(n + 1)/2$. For example, the sum of the first 10 integers is $10(10 + 1)/2 = 55$.

Though there are numerous nonparametric methods, we will limit ourselves to those that correspond to parametric t tests for single samples, independent samples, dependent or paired samples, and correlation coefficients. We also present Fisher's exact test, which is appropriate when the χ^2 test would not be valid to use. These techniques are the Wilcoxon rank-sum test/Mann–Whitney U test, the Spearman rank-order correlation coefficient, the Kruskal–Wallis one-way ANOVA, and the sign test. Figure 14.1 lists the parametric tests and their nonparametric equivalents.

	Parametric Test	**Nonparametric Test**
One Sample	One-sample *t* test	One-sample sign test
Two Independent Samples	Two-sample independent *t* test	Wilcoxon rank-sum test Mann–Whitney U test
Two Dependent Samples	Two-paired *t* test	Wilcoxon signed-rank test Sign test
Correlation	Pearson *r*	Spearman rank-order correlation
Multiple Groups, One Factor	One-way ANOVA	Kruskal–Wallis one-way ANOVA

Figure 14.1   Parametric Tests and Corresponding Nonparametric Equivalent.

14.3 WILCOXON RANK-SUM TEST AND MANN–WHITNEY U TEST

The **Wilcoxon rank-sum test** and the **Mann–Whitney U test** are mathematically equivalent procedures. Regardless of which computer statistical program you use, p values generated by the Wilcoxon rank-sum test and the Mann–Whitney U test will be equal. In other words, the two procedures will yield the same results. Both procedures are used to test the null hypothesis that there is no difference in the two population distributions. Based on the ranks from two independent samples, they correspond to the t test for two independent samples, except that no assumptions are necessary regarding normality or equality of variances. These tests are excellent alternatives to the t test if your data are significantly skewed.

To carry out these two tests, we proceed as follows:

1. Combine the observations from both samples and arrange them in an array from the smallest to the largest.
2. Assign ranks to each of the observations.
3. List the ranks from one sample separately from those of the other.
4. Separately sum the ranks for the first and second samples.

Given the hypothesis that the average of the ranks is approximately equal for both samples, the test statistic W_1 (the sum of the ranks of the first sample) should not differ significantly from W_e (the expected sum of the ranks).

Accordingly, we can show that the expected sum of the ranks for the first sample is

$$W_e = \frac{n_1(n_1 + n_2 + 1)}{2} \tag{14.1}$$

We have shown that, if we obtain W_1s from repeated samples of lists of ranks, the standard error, σ_w, is

$$\sigma_w = \sqrt{\frac{n_1 n_2 (n_1 + n_2 + 1)}{12}} \tag{14.2}$$

We have further shown that, regardless of the shape of the population distribution, the sampling distribution for the sum of a subset of ranks is approximately normal. Consequently, we have what we need to perform a test of significance regarding the equality of the distributions, namely,

$$Z = \frac{W_1 - W_e}{\sigma_w} = \frac{W_1 - W_e}{\sqrt{n_1 n_2 (n_1 + n_2 + 1)/12}} \tag{14.3}$$

Utilizing the data of Table 14.1, we can compute the Z statistic, which compares W_1, the sum of the sample ranks, with W_e, the value that would be expected if the hypothesis were true.

This test assumes that, if the first sample has primarily smaller observations than the second sample, then the rank values obtained from the combined

Table 14.1 Wilcoxon Rank-Sum Test for Two Independent Samples: Number of Prenatal Care Visits for Mothers Bearing Babies of Low and of Normal Birth Weight

Mothers Bearing Low-Birth-Weight Babies			Mothers Bearing Normal-Birth-Weight Babies		
No.	X (Number of Visits)	R (Rank)	No.	X (Number of Visits)	R (Rank)
1	3	5.5*	1	4	7.5*
2	0	1.5*	2	5	9
3	4	7.5*	3	6	10
4	0	1.5*	4	11	15
5	1	3	5	7	11
6	2	4	6	8	12
7 ($= n_1$)	3	5.5*	7	10	14
			8 ($= n_2$)	9	13
		$W_1 = 28.5$			$W_2 = 91.5$
		$\bar{R}_1 = 4.1$			$\bar{R}_2 = 11.4$

*Two-way tie.

sample will be small, giving a small W_1. This implies that the values of the first distribution will be located on the lower end of the combined distribution—which, of course, is contrary to the H_0 that the two distributions are equal.

In attempting to rank the data in Table 14.1, we notice that we have three two-way ties—for zero, three, and four visits. Traditionally, the procedure is to assign the average of the ranks to each tie. For example, the two zeros rank first and second, so we assign them both the average rank of 1.5.

To compute the Z statistic, we will need the expected rank sum. To obtain it, we use equation (14.1):

$$W_e = \frac{n_1(n_1 + n_2 + 1)}{2} = \frac{7(7 + 8 + 1)}{2} = 56$$

To determine whether there is a significant difference between the observed sum of 28.5, obtained from Table 14.1, and the expected value of 56, we use equation (14.3):

$$Z = \frac{W_1 - W_e}{\sqrt{n_1 n_2 (n_1 + n_2 + 1)/12}}$$

$$= \frac{28.5 - 56}{\sqrt{7(8)(15 + 1)/12}}$$

$$= \frac{-27.5}{\sqrt{74.67}} = \frac{-27.5}{8.6} = -3.2$$

From this, we see that the mothers with the low-birth-weight infants had a rank sum of 28.5, considerably lower than the expected rank sum of 56. In fact, the observed rank sum falls 3.2 standard errors below the mean of a normal distribution of rank sums. So our conclusion, based on rank sums, is that the mothers bearing low-birth-weight infants had a significantly lower number of prenatal visits than the mothers bearing normal-birth-weight infants. This conclusion is not surprising, as we can see from comparing the average rankings of the prenatal care visits of the two groups of mothers: $\bar{R}_1 = 4.1$ versus $\bar{R}_2 = 11.4$.

We are able to perform this Z test because W is approximately normally distributed. This situation holds if we have at least six cases in each of the groups. Can we perform exact tests if we have smaller sample sizes? Yes. For such methods, with accompanying tables, see an advanced text such as Brown and Hollander (1977).

As mentioned earlier, the rank-sum test parallels the t test for two independent samples, but it is less powerful. Its power efficiency is greater than 92%, measured by the performance of repeated rank-sum tests on normally distributed data.

14.4 WILCOXON SIGNED-RANK TEST

In previous chapters, we also considered the paired t test for matched observations. The counterpart nonparametric test to this is the **Wilcoxon signed-rank test.** With this test, we assume that we have a series of pairs of dependent observations. We wish to test the hypothesis that the median of the first sample equals the median of the second—that is, that there is no tendency for the differences between the outcomes before and after some condition to favor either the before or the after condition.

The procedure is to obtain the differences (d) between individual pairs of observations. Pairs yielding a difference of zero are eliminated from the computation; the sample size is reduced accordingly.

To perform the test, we rank the absolute differences by assigning ranks of 1 for the smallest to n for the largest. If ties are encountered, they are eliminated from the analysis. The signs of the original differences are restored to each rank. We obtain the sum of the positive ranks, W_1, which serves as the test statistic. If the null hypothesis is true, we would expect to have about an equal mixture of positive and negative ranks; that is, we would expect the sum of the positive ranks to equal that of the negative ranks.

Using the data in Table 14.2 on pregnancy and smoking, we see that, because each pair of observations is on the same woman, we have *dependent* samples; therefore, the Wilcoxon signed-rank test is the appropriate one to perform. The column denoted by d represents differences (before and after pregnancy); the

Table 14.2 Wilcoxon Signed-Rank Test: Number of Cigarettes Usually Smoked per Day, Before and After Pregnancy

| Subject | Number of Cigarettes Smoked per Day | | $d = x_a - x_b$ | $\|d\|$ | r_d |
	x_b: Before Pregnancy	x_a: After Pregnancy			
1	8	5	-3	3	$3(-)$
2	13	15	$+2$	2	$2(+)$
3	24	11	-13	13	$9(-)$
4	15	19	$+4$	4	$4(+)$
5	7	0	-7	7	$7(-)$
6	11	12	$+1$	1	$1(+)$
7	20	15	-5	5	$5(-)$
8	22	0	-22	22	$10(-)$
9	6	0	-6	6	$6(-)$
10	15	6	-9	9	$8(-)$
11	20	20	0	—	—

$$\Sigma r_d = \frac{n(n+1)}{2} = \frac{10(11)}{2} = 55 \qquad \Sigma r_{d(+)} = W_1 = 7$$

$$W_e = \frac{\Sigma r_d}{2} = \frac{55}{2} = 27.5 \qquad \Sigma r_{d(-)} = W_2 = 48$$

column labeled r_d is the rank by size of the absolute difference. Rank 1 is assigned to the smallest and n (here, 10) to the largest. Now we can obtain W_1 and W_2, the sums, respectively, of the positive and negative ranks. Recall that the sum of all ranks is $n(n + 1)/2$. Under the null hypothesis, we assume that the sum of the ranks of the positive d's is equal to the sum of the ranks of the negative d's; that is, each will be half of the total sum of the ranks. Algebraically, the expected sum of the ranks will be

$$W_e = \left(\frac{1}{2}\right) \frac{n(n + 1)}{2} \tag{14.4}$$

which, for the data in Table 14.2, is $10(11)/4 = 27.5$. The test statistic is the smaller of the sums, namely, $W_1 = 7$.

Because W_1 is approximately normally distributed with a mean of W_e and a standard deviation of σ_w, we are able to perform a Z test for the difference between the sums of the matched ranks by using the following equation:

$$
\begin{aligned}
Z &= \frac{W_1 - W_e}{\sigma_w} \\
&= \frac{W_1 - W_e}{\sqrt{(2n + 1)W_e/6}} \\
&= \frac{7 - 27.5}{\sqrt{[2(10) + 1]27.5/6}} \\
&= \frac{-20.5}{\sqrt{96.25}} = -2.09
\end{aligned}
\tag{14.5}
$$

At $\alpha = .05$, the two-tailed critical value is ± 1.645. This result indicates that the difference between the observed and expected rank sums is significant ($p < .05$). Thus, it leads us to reject the H_0 that there is no difference between smoking status before and after pregnancy. The implication: There is a significant reduction in the smoking habit consequent to pregnancy. The Z score of -2.09 can also be converted into an exact P value, using the procedure outlined in Chapter 9. From Table A (inside back cover), -2.09 yields an exact, two-tailed P value of .0366, which is less than $\alpha = .05$.

The Wilcoxon signed-rank test has a power efficiency of 92% as compared with paired t tests, which satisfies the assumption of normality. Note that this technique is somewhat less sensitive than the parametric one in that the ranks do not directly describe the amount of reduction in smoking.

The assumption of normality for the sum of the signed-rank test is appropriate, provided you have at least eight pairs. For a smaller sample size, you will need an exact test. Tables for such a test are available in more advanced textbooks, such as Brown and Hollander (1977), which also includes confidence intervals for the Wilcoxon tests.

A natural question arises here: Does a nonparametric procedure exist for making comparisons of more than two groups? That is, is there a parallel nonparametric ANOVA test? There is; it is called the Kruskal–Wallis test.

14.5 KRUSKAL–WALLIS ONE-WAY ANOVA BY RANKS

The **Kruskal–Wallis test** is the nonparametric equivalent of the one-way ANOVA. This technique is an alternative to the one-way ANOVA when you have three or more groups, the groups are independent, and the populations from which the samples are selected are not normally distributed or the samples do not have equal variances. It can also be used when you have ordered outcomes—that is, ordinal data rather than the interval or ratio data necessary to use an ANOVA. For example, suppose the rows represent three or more pain relievers and the columns represent distinct, ordered responses. These responses might be no relief, mild relief, moderate relief, strong relief, and complete relief (Mehta, 1994). The example used in this chapter will start with ratio data and the assumption that the one-way ANOVA is not the appropriate procedure, for one of the reasons just described.

To use the Kruskal–Wallis technique, you combine the observations of the various groups. After arranging them in order of magnitude from lowest to highest, you then assign ranks to each of the observations and replace them in each of the groups. What you have done is convert the original ratio data into ordinal or ranked data. If you started with ordinal data, this conversion would not be necessary.

Next, the ranks are summed in each of the groups, and the test statistic H is computed. The ranks assigned to observations in each of the k groups are added separately to give k rank sums.

The test statistic is computed using

$$H = \frac{12}{N(N+1)} \sum_{j}^{k} \frac{R_j^2}{n_j} - 3(N+1)$$

$$= 12 \sum_{j}^{k} \frac{R_j^2}{n_j} - 3(N+1)$$

(14.6)

In this equation

k = the number of groups

n_j = the number of observations in the jth group

N = the number of observations in all groups combined

R_j = the sum of the ranks in the jth group

Let us look at performance scores of three different types of teachers:

	Teacher Type	
A	B	C
96	68	115
128	124	149
83	132	166
61	135	147
101	109	—

The table of corresponding ranks is shown here:

	Teacher Type	
A	B	C
4	2	7
9	8	13
3	10	14
1	11	12
5	6	—
$R_1 = 22$	$R_2 = 37$	$R_3 = 46$

Using an example from Siegal (1956:3), we can now calculate statistic H:

$$H = \frac{12}{14(14 + 1)} \sum \frac{R_j^2}{n_j} - 3(N + 1) = \frac{12}{14(15)}\left(\frac{22^2}{5} + \frac{37^2}{5} + \frac{46^2}{4}\right) - 3(14 + 1) = 6.4$$

When we refer to Appendix F, it shows that, when the n_j's are 5, 5, and 4, $H \geq 6.4$ has probability of occurrence under the null hypothesis of $p < .049$. Because the probability is smaller than $\alpha = .05$, our decision in this study is to reject H_0, and we conclude that the three groups of educators differ in their scores. If this same analysis is done by a computer, an exact P value of .0406 is obtained. Because this probability is smaller than $\alpha = .05$, our decision is still to reject H_0 and conclude that the three groups of educators differ in their scores.

Tied Observations

When two or more scores are tied, each score is given the mean of ranks for which it is tied. Because H is somewhat influenced by ties, you may wish to correct for ties in computing H. To correct for the effect of ties, H is computed from equation (14.7) and divided by

$$1 - \frac{\Sigma T}{N^3 - N}$$

where T is the number of tied observations in a tied group of scores.

The effect of correcting for ties is to increase the value of H and thus make the result more significant than it would be if H remained uncorrected. In most cases, the effect of correction is negligible. With even 25% of observations involved in ties, the probability associated with an H computed without the correction for ties is rarely changed by more than 10% when the correction of ties is made. (See Mehta, 1994.)

14.6 THE SIGN TEST

The **sign test** is one of the simplest of statistical tests. It focuses on the median rather than the mean as a measure of central tendency. The only assumption made in performing this test is that the variables come from a continuous distribution.

It is called the sign test because we use pluses and minuses as the new data in performing the calculations. We illustrate its use with a single sample and a paired sample. The sign test is useful when we are not able to use the t test because the assumption of normality has been violated.

Single Sample

In the case of a single sample, we wish to test the H_0 that the sample median is equal to the population median m. To do this, we assign $+$ to observations that fall above the population median and $-$ to those that fall below. A tie is given a zero and is not counted. If the H_0 is true—the medians are the same—we expect an equal number: 50% pluses and 50% minuses.

We can use the binomial distribution to determine if the number of positive signs deviates significantly from some expected number. Instead of using the binomial equation, however, we can use the table in Appendix D. This table shows the probability of having the observed number of pluses when we expect 50%.

■ EXAMPLE 1

In an anesthetic used for major surgery, the median number of hours it takes for the anesthesia to wear off is 7. A new agent has been suggested that supposedly provides recovery much sooner. In a series of 12 surgeries using the new anesthetic, the following times for recovery were observed:

Recovery time:	4	4	5	5	5	6	6	6	7	7	8	9
Sign:	−	−	−	−	−	−	−	−	0	0	+	+

H_0: The median recovery time for the new anesthetic is 7 hours.

Because the suggestion is made that the new anesthetic is better, we have a one-tailed test. We can see that eight outcomes are less than the median of the standard anesthetic and two are more. We exclude the two with a score of 7 hours because they are equal to the median of 7. Thus, we observe two pluses when we expected five pluses under the null hypothesis.

To determine the probability that the two pluses occur randomly, we can use the binomial distribution formula or the table of critical values for the sign test in Appendix D. From this table, we can see, for $n = 10$ and for $\alpha = .05$, one-sided, that $q = 1$ or 9. Therefore, for this sample to have a significantly better recovery time than 7 hours would require nine minuses or one plus. We observed eight minuses, so we cannot reject H_0; that is, we find no statistically significant difference between the recovery time from the sample and the population median. ■

Paired Samples

The sign test is also suitable for experiments with paired data such as before and after, or treatment and control. In this case, we need to satisfy only one assumption—that the different pairs are independent; that is, only the direction of change in each pair is recorded as a plus or minus sign. We expect an equal number of pluses or minuses if there is no treatment effect. The H_0 tested by the paired samples sign test is that the median of the observations listed first is the same as that of the observations listed second in each pair.

■ EXAMPLE 2

Ten blood samples were sent to two labs for cholesterol determinations. The results from the two labs are as follows:

Serum Cholesterol Determinations Obtained from Two Labs on the Same Samples

Patient	1	2	3	4	5	6	7	8	9	10
Lab A	296	268	244	272	240	244	282	254	244	262
Lab B	318	287	260	279	245	249	294	271	262	285
Sign of difference	−	−	−	−	−	−	−	−	−	−

H_0: The median serum cholesterol determination of both labs is equal.

We can see that all 10 observations are minuses. What are the chances of obtaining such a result by chance? From the table in Appendix D, we can see that for $n = 10$ the critical value of q is either 1 or 9 for $\alpha = .05$, two-sided. Consequently, because our result was 10, we conclude that there is a significant difference in the way the two labs determine cholesterol levels. ■

14.7   SPEARMAN RANK-ORDER CORRELATION COEFFICIENT

In Chapter 13, we discussed in detail the Pearson correlation coefficient, which describes the association between measurement variables x and y. In this section, we discuss an association between two ranked variables. With the **Spear-**

man rank-order correlation coefficient, we obtain perfect correlation (±1) if the ranks for variables x and y are equal for each individual. Conversely, lack of association is measured by examining the differences in the ordered ranks, $d_i = x_i - y_i$. The Spearman rank-order correlation coefficient, r_s (s is for Spearman), can be derived from the Pearson correlation coefficient, r. The equation is

$$r_s = 1 - \frac{6\Sigma d_i^2}{n(n^2 - 1)} \tag{14.7}$$

where d_i is the difference between the paired ranks and n is the number of pairs. Like the Pearson correlation coefficient, the Spearman rank-order correlation coefficient may take on values from -1 to $+1$. Values close to ±1 indicate a high correlation; values close to zero indicate a lack of association. The minus or plus sign indicates whether the correlation coefficient is negative or positive.

To illustrate the use of the Spearman rank-order correlation coefficient, let us consider a situation that is all too familiar to any college student. The work of 12 students is observed independently by two faculty evaluators, who rank their performance from 1 to 12 (see Table 14.3). As before, ties in rank are handled by averaging the ranks. Note that observer C had a three-way tie for first place. The x and y columns of Table 14.3 are the ranks, the d_i column is the difference between the ranks, and the final column is d_i^2. Using equation (14.7), we obtain

$$r_s = 1 - \frac{6\Sigma d_i^2}{n(n^2 - 1)}$$

$$= 1 - \frac{6(55.50)}{12(144 - 1)} = .81$$

Table 14.3 Ranking of Students' Performance by Two Independent Observers

Student No.	Observer B: Rank Order (x)	Observer C: Rank Order (y)	$d_i = x_i - y_i$	$d_i^2 = (x_i - y_i)^2$
1	2.5*	5	−2.5	6.25
2	2.5*	2**	0.5	0.25
3	9	8	1.0	1.00
4	5.5*	7	−1.5	2.25
5	12	12	0	0
6	7.5*	11	−3.5	12.25
7	1	2**	−1.0	1.00
8	10	6	4.0	16.00
9	4	2**	2.0	4.00
10	5.5*	4	1.5	2.25
11	7.5*	10	−2.5	6.25
12	11	9	2.0	4.00
				$\Sigma d_i^2 = 55.50$

*Two-way tie
**Three-way tie

To determine whether this coefficient differs significantly from zero, we need to assume that x and y represent randomly selected and independent pairs of ranks. We can use the same test procedure as for the Pearson r. It provides a good approximation if the sample size is at least 10. The equation for the test statistic is

$$t = \frac{r_s\sqrt{n-2}}{\sqrt{1-r_s^2}} \qquad (14.8)$$

with $n - 2$ df. Using the data from Table 14.3, we find that

$$t = \frac{.81\sqrt{10}}{\sqrt{1-.66}} = \frac{(.81)(3.16)}{.58} = 4.41$$

Because the computed t of 4.41 is greater than the critical $t_{.95}$ of 2.23 for 10 df, we reject H_0 and conclude that the correlation differs significantly from zero.

Whenever you are able to meet the assumptions for the Pearson r, use it. It is preferable to the Spearman r_s because the power of the latter is not as great as that of r. The Spearman r_s is most appropriate when you have either ordinal data or data that are sufficiently skewed that the Pearson r assumptions are not met.

■ EXAMPLE 3

In this example, an instructor was asked to rate 12 students from the most capable or best statistics student to the least capable or weakest. This ranking was then compared with the actual grades of the students. Table 14.4 lists the rank and the final grade for each student.

Before we actually analyze the data, look closely at Table 14.4. Would you expect a positive correlation (i.e., the higher the rank, the better the final grade) or a negative correlation (i.e., the lower the rank, the higher the final grade)? Even at a quick glance, without doing a statistical analysis, it clearly looks as if, the higher the rank, the better the final grade. The correlation appears to be a strong, positive one.

To do this analysis using SPSS, enter these numbers into the spreadsheet, choose Analyze from the menu, go to Correlate, select Bivariate, and then choose Spearman. However, when you do this, the Spearman correlation reads $-.965$. Remember that a negative correlation, either Spearman or Pearson, implies an inverse relationship—that is, as one variable increases, the other decreases. But in this example, you would expect a positive correlation: the higher the ranking by the instructor, the higher the final grade. Before we explain things, see if you can determine why we got a negative correlation when we clearly expected a positive one. (This situation actually occurred: One of our colleagues expected a strong positive correlation, conducted the analysis, and instead found a strong negative correlation.)

Table 14.4 Instructor Ranking
and Final Grades

Instructor Rank Order	Final Grade (%)
1	98
2	95
3	96
4	91
5	89
6	81
7	85
8	82
9	77
10	74
11	61
12	71

Were you able to figure out what happened? Is there a positive correlation between the instructor's subjective evaluation of the students and their final grades? Yes. The "better" the student, the higher the grade. Then why is there a negative correlation? A computer will analyze only the numbers that are entered into it. In this case, we used the number 1 to designate the highest or "best" ranking and the number 12 to designate the lowest or "worst" ranking. However, the computer will read 12 as the highest score because the number 12 is the highest number in the instructor ranking column, and the number 1 will be read as the lowest score. Apparently, the higher the ranking, numerically speaking, the lower the final grade—hence the negative correlation when we really have a positive correlation. The key point to remember is that the computer does not have any way of knowing that number 1 is "first" or "highest" or "best." The computer reads the number 1 as the lowest rank simply because 1 is the lowest number.

Should you encounter this situation, how might you handle it? A simple solution is to give the highest ranking the most points. What you would do is to say that whatever subject is ranked the highest of the 12 subjects gets the most points or the highest score. The highest-ranked student would therefore get a score of 12, the second highest 11, the third highest 10, and so on. The analysis would then yield the expected positive correlation of .965. ■

14.8　FISHER'S EXACT TEST

The chi-square test described in Chapter 12 has a limitation. It is not appropriate for a situation in which the sample size is small, yielding small expected frequencies. There should be no expected frequencies less than 1, and not more than 20% of the expected frequencies should be less than 5. For a situation with a small sample size, we should consider using **Fisher's exact test,** which computes directly the probability of observing a particular set of frequencies in a 2×2 table. It is calculated using the following formula:

$$P = \frac{(a + b)!\,(c + d)!\,(a + c)!\,(b + d)!}{N!\; a!\; b!\; c!\; d!} \tag{14.9}$$

where a, b, c, and d are the frequencies of a 2×2 table and N is the sample size.

■ **EXAMPLE 4**

An infant heart transplant surgeon had nine infant patients who needed a heart transplant. Only five suitable donors were identified. A follow-up of the nine patients was done a year later to see if there was a difference in the survival rates of those with and without heart transplants. The following results were found:

Heart Transplant Candidates

Surgery Performed	Alive 12 Months Later?		Total
	Yes	No	
Yes	$a = 4$	$b = 1$	5
No	$c = 1$	$d = 3$	4
Total	5	4	9

The probability of observing this particular set of frequencies is

$$P = \frac{5!\,4!\,4!\,5!}{9!\,4!\,1!\,1!\,3!} = \frac{5 \cdot 4 \cdot 3 \cdot 2 \cdot 4}{6 \cdot 7 \cdot 8 \cdot 9} = \frac{20}{126} = .159$$

However, to compute the P value, we need to find the probability of obtaining this or a more extreme result while keeping the marginal totals in the table fixed. A more extreme result would be, for example, if all of the infants without a heart transplant were dead a year later. To do this, we reduce by 1 the smallest frequency that is greater than zero while holding the marginal totals constant in the table on heart transplant candidates. This gives the following 2×2 table:

5	0	5
0	4	4
5	4	9

The probability of obtaining this set of frequencies is

$$P = \frac{5!\,4!\,4!\,5!}{9!\,5!\,0!\,0!\,4!} = \frac{5!\,4!}{9!} = \frac{4 \cdot 3 \cdot 2 \cdot 1}{6 \cdot 7 \cdot 8 \cdot 9} = \frac{1}{126} = .008$$

Thus, the probability of observing this particular frequency of successful transplants or a more extreme frequency is $.159 + .008 = .167$. This P value is for a one-tailed test. An estimate of the P value for a two-tailed test is obtained by multiplying the value by 2: $2 \times .167 = .334$. Based on this outcome, we would fail to reject the H_0 that there is no difference in the survival rate between infants with or without a heart transplant.

Although this result may be difficult to accept, it is the best we can do with such a small sample. There has been some controversy as to whether it is appropriate to use Fisher's exact test in the health sciences because the model requires that the marginal totals in the 2×2 table be fixed—and they seldom are in actual health science settings. Nevertheless, some statisticians use this test anyway because the test results tend to give conservative values of P; that is, the true P value is actually less than the computed one. ∎

◆ CONCLUSION

There are nonparametric methods that correspond to parametric methods such as the t test, paired t test, and correlation coefficient. The primary advantage of these methods is that they do not involve restrictive assumptions such as normality and homogeneity of variance. Their major disadvantage is that they are less efficient than the corresponding parametric methods of five methods described here—the Wilcoxon rank-sum test, the Wilcoxon signed-rank test, Kruskal–Wallis test, the Mann–Whitney U test, the sign test, the Spearman rank-order correlation coefficient, and Fisher's exact test. These are the nonparametric methods used most frequently in the health sciences.

◆ VOCABULARY LIST

Fisher's exact test
Kruskal–Wallis test
nonparametric methods
   (distribution-free
   methods)

Mann–Whitney U test
parametric methods
sign test
Spearman rank-order
   correlation coefficient

Wilcoxon rank-sum test
Wilcoxon signed-rank
   test

◆ EXERCISES

14.1   To learn whether babies who were breast-fed had a better dental record than those who were not, 13 children were picked at random to see at what age they acquired their first cavities. The results were as follows:

Subject	Breast-Fed	Age at First Cavity
1	No	9
2	No	10
3	Yes	14
4	No	8
5	Yes	15
6	No	6
7	No	10
8	Yes	12
9	No	12
10	Yes	13
11	No	6
12	No	20
13	Yes	19

a. State the null hypothesis.
b. State the alternative hypothesis.
c. Do a Wilcoxon rank-sum test.

14.2 Refer to Table 2.1. Compute a Wilcoxon rank-sum test to determine whether there is a significant difference in diastolic blood pressure between
a. vegetarian males and nonvegetarian males
b. vegetarian males and vegetarian females

14.3 Two communities are to be compared to see which has a better dental record. Town A has fluoride in the water; town B does not. Ten persons are randomly picked from each town, and their dental cavities are counted and reported. The data are as follows:

	Person									
	1	2	3	4	5	6	7	8	9	10
Town A	0	1	3	1	1	2	1	2	3	1
Town B	3	2	2	3	4	3	2	3	4	3

a. State the null hypothesis.
b. State the alternative hypothesis.
c. Do a Wilcoxon rank-sum test.

14.4 There are two methods of counting heartbeats: (1) by counting the pulse at the wrist and (2) by counting the pulse on the neck. An investigator wishes to know the degree of correlation between the two methods. The data are as follows:

	Person									
	1	2	3	4	5	6	7	8	9	10
Neck Pulse	73	99	77	63	50	80	83	73	66	82
Wrist Pulse	74	103	77	61	51	81	82	74	66	83

a. State the null hypothesis.
b. State the alternative hypothesis.
c. Obtain the Spearman rank-order correlation coefficient. (*Hint:* Rank the neck pulse from highest to lowest; do the same for the wrist pulse.)

14.5 Two health inspectors rate 11 hospitals on cleanliness, as shown in the tabulation that follows. Determine whether their rankings are comparable.

	Hospital										
	1	2	3	4	5	6	7	8	9	10	11
Inspector 1	2	3	2	3	1	4	5	3	1	3	4
Inspector 2	1	3	3	2	2	5	4	2	1	4	3

a. State the null hypothesis.
b. State the alternative hypothesis.
c. Perform the appropriate test.

14.6 a. What is meant by nonparametric methods?
b. What are their advantages?
c. What are their disadvantages?

14.7 Describe the conditions that call for using each of the following tests:
a. Wilcoxon rank-sum test
b. Wilcoxon signed-rank test
c. Spearman rank-order correlation coefficient

14.8 A group of 11 hypertensive individuals were determined to find out if they could lower their systolic blood pressure through a systematic physical fitness program. They observed their blood pressure before they began their program and then again 6 months later. The following results were found:

	Case										
	1	2	3	4	5	6	7	8	9	10	11
Before	156	130	142	155	174	140	148	152	156	136	126
After	148	124	135	146	169	145	140	156	161	133	123

a. State H_0 and H_1.
b. Perform the Wilcoxon signed-rank test at the $\alpha = .05$ level.

14.9 a. Calculate a Spearman rank-order correlation coefficient for the data from Exercise 14.8.
b. State H_0 and H_1, and perform a test of significance at the $\alpha = .01$ level.

14.10 For the data in Exercise 9.19, determine whether the experimental condition increases the number of heartbeats per minute.
a. State H_0 and H_1.
b. Perform the appropriate test of significance at the $\alpha = .05$ level.

14.11 An investigator observed the following responses to two different dental treatments:

	Treatment A	Treatment B	Total
Favorable	4	2	6
Not favorable	1	4	5
Total	5	6	11

a. Determine whether the differences in response rates between treatments A and B are significant at $\alpha = .05$.
b. What was the H_0 that you tested in (a)?

14.12 a. Using the data of Exercise 14.8, perform a sign test. Indicate the H_0 you are testing and whether you would reject it at the $\alpha = .05$ level.
b. Using the data of Exercise 14.4, perform a sign test. Indicate the H_0 you are testing and whether you would reject it at the $\alpha = .05$ level.

14.13 A study investigated dietary differences between low-income African-American women and low-income white women. One dietary practice examined was the daily servings of meat (1 serving = 3 oz edible portion of meat). Based on the following table, is there any reason to believe that there are differences between low-income African-American women and low-income white women with respect to their consumption of meat?

	Number of servings												
African-American	0	0	1	1	1	2	2	3	3	3	3	3	5	6
White	0	0	0	1	2	2	2	2	3	3	4			

NOTE: These data were extrapolated and based on Cox (1994).

a. State the null hypothesis.
b. State the alternative hypothesis.
c. Do a Wilcoxon rank-sum test.

14.14 Exercise 14.13 is based on an actual study conducted by Ruby Cox. In her study, there were 115 African-American women and 95 white women sampled. When she used the Wilcoxon procedure, she found a significant difference in the daily meat consumption of the two groups of women (African-American women consumed more). If you calculated your statistics correctly for Exercise 14.13, you did not find a significant difference. This illustrates a weakness of the Wilcoxon rank-sum test. What is that weakness?

14.15 Nurses are often expected to subjectively evaluate a patient's comfort level. A nurse researcher wanted to determine whether the subjective ranking done by two nurses (working with the same patients) of comfort levels of 15 patients were similar. Based on the following data, is there a relationship between the rankings of the two nurses?

| Patient | Comfort Rank | |
	Nurse 1	Nurse 2
A	2	1
B	4	3
C	12	14
D	1	2
E	15	11
F	8	8
G	3	6
H	6	4
I	11	13
J	9	10
K	5	5
L	14	15
M	10	9
N	7	7
O	13	12

14.16 Xerosis is a common skin condition of diabetics. Moisturizers are widely recognized as an effective method of controlling xerosis; however, satisfactory control is elusive. In 1999, Coloplast Corporation (a leading manufacturer of skin care products) conducted a multisite, double-blind study to determine if a moisturizer containing 10% urea (a humectant) and 4% lactic acid (an exfoliant and humectant) would achieve better control of xerosis of the foot than moisturizers now routinely used. For each patient, one foot received the new product while the other foot received a currently accepted moisturizer. Use a Wilcoxon signed-rank test to determine whether the new product (treatment) produced greater control of xerosis than current moisturizers (control). The following data come from one of the sites. The numbers represent the researchers' evaluation of each patient's improvement from the beginning to the end of the study.

Patient	Treatment	Control
1	0	1
2	1	1
3	3	2
4	5	3
5	3	1
6	4	2
7	2	1
8	3	0
9	4	2
10	5	4

14.17 An "expert" was asked at the beginning of the season to rate the 10 basketball teams in a college conference. At the end of the season, the number of wins for each team was recorded. Is there a correlation between the expert's ranking and the number of wins? Before you analyze the data, ask yourself: Does it look as if our expert was able to accurately predict the number of wins? That is, does it look like a strong positive correlation?

Predicted Rank Order	Final Number of Wins
1	17
2	16
3	11
4	13
5	9
6	8
7	5
8	4
9	6
10	1

14.18 Using the data from Table 3.1, first identify those variables that have interval or ratio data, and then determine whether the data are significantly skewed. Using smoking status as the grouping variable, perform the appropriate nonparametric test to determine if there are significant differences between smokers and nonsmokers. Test at both $\alpha = .05$ and $\alpha = .01$.

15

Vital Statistics and Demographic Methods

CHAPTER OUTLINE

✔ LEARNING OBJECTIVES

After studying this chapter, you should be able to

1. Distinguish among rates, ratios, and proportions, and among measures of morbidity, mortality, and fertility
2. Compute and understand the meaning of various vital measures
3. State the reasons measures are adjusted
4. Compute an adjusted rate by the direct method

15.1 VITAL STATISTICS AND DEMOGRAPHICS

Decision making in the health sciences, especially public health, is continually becoming more quantitative. Demographic data and **vital statistics** have emerged as indispensable tools for researchers, epidemiologists, health planners, and other health professionals. To determine the health status of a community, to decide how best to provide a health service, to plan a public health program, or to evaluate a program's effectiveness, it is essential to use these tools knowledgeably.

Demographic variables describe a population's characteristics—for instance, its size and how that changes over time; its composition by age, sex, income, occupation, and utilization of health services; and its geographic location and density. Once you possess demographic data and information about **vital events** (births, deaths, marriages, divorces), you can tackle a remarkable variety of problems regarding a community's status at a particular time or its trends over time. Together with measures of illness and disease, demographic data are invaluable in program planning and disease control. Such data also go a long way toward providing research clues as to the often-unexpected associations between a population's health practices and its disease experience.

A wide array of methodological tools is available to deal with such data. In this chapter, we consider vital rates, ratios, proportions, measures of fertility and morbidity, and adjustment of rates. But first, we discuss some of the sources of demographic data and vital statistics.

15.2 SOURCES OF VITAL STATISTICS AND DEMOGRAPHIC DATA

The three main sources of demographic data, vital statistics, and morbidity data are the census, registration of vital events, and morbidity surveys. These are usually given for defined populations such as cities, states, and other political areas. Traditionally, hospital and clinic data have also been major sources of morbidity data. Although the latter are useful, their populations of reference may be difficult to define.

The Census

The United States has conducted a **decennial census** of the population since 1790. In a census, each household and resident is enumerated. Information obtained on each person includes his or her sex, age, race, marital status, place of residence, and relationship to or position as the head of household. A systematic sample of households then provides more information, such as income, housing, number of children born, education, employment status, means of transportation to work, and occupation. Census tables are published for the entire United States, for each state, for **Metropolitan Statistical Areas (MSAs),** for counties, and for cities, neighborhoods (census tracts), and city blocks. The MSAs are urbanized areas. An area qualifies as an MSA if it has one or more cities of at least 50,000 residents and there is a social and economic integration of the cities with the surrounding rural areas. In the 1990 census, there were 332 MSAs (including 5 in Puerto Rico).

Census results are published in the *Decennial Census of the United States* about 2 years after the census is taken. They are also made available on magnetic tape for computerized analysis. A good deal of census information is summarized annually in the *Statistical Abstract of the United States*. The importance of census data is universally recognized. More than four-fifths of the world's population is counted in some kind of census at more or less regular intervals.

Annual Registration of Vital Events

As noted earlier, vital events are births, deaths, marriages, and divorces. In the United States, state laws require that all vital events be registered. Registration is now quite complete and reliable. Birth certificates serve as proof of citizenship, age, birthplace, and parentage; death certificates are required as burial documents and in the settlement of estates and insurance claims. In the United States, **death registration** began in Massachusetts in 1857; was extended to 10 states, the District of Columbia, and several other cities by 1900; and has been conducted nationwide since 1933. **Birth registration** began in 1915, encompassing 10 states and the District of Columbia. By 1933, all states had been admitted to the nationwide birth and death registration system. A great deal of information is recorded on birth and death certificates. Some of the key elements are the following:

Birth certificate	Death certificate
Name	Name
Sex	Date and time of death
Date and time of birth	Race
Weight and length at birth	Age
Race of parents	Place of birth
Age of parents	Names of decedent's parents
Birth order	Name and address of survivor (or informant)
Occupation of father	Marital status
Place of birth	Occupation
Residence of mother	Place of residence
Physician's (or attendant's) certification	Cause(s) of death
	Place of death
	Burial data
	If death due to injury: accident, suicide, or homicide
	Physician's (or coroner's) certification

The National Center for Health Statistics collects a systematic sample of 10% of the births and deaths in each state. From this, it publishes the *Monthly Vital Statistics Report.* Annually, it issues the four-volume set *Vital Statistics of the United States,* which includes many detailed tables on vital events for all sorts of demographic characteristics and for major geographical subdivisions. Data on marriages and divorces are similarly collected and published in a separate volume of *Vital Statistics of the United States.*

The federal government has been instrumental in getting the various states to adopt standard birth and death certificates. This enables researchers to collect more standardized information. All states now compile computerized death certificate data, or "death tapes," which are computer-readable extracts of the most important data appearing on death certificates. Since 1979, the National Center for Health Statistics has prepared *The National Death Index,* a nationwide, computerized index of death records compiled from tapes submitted by the vital statistics offices of each state. These tapes contain a standard set of identifying data for each decedent. The index (National Center for Health Statistics, 1981) permits researchers to determine if persons in their studies have died; for each such case, the death certificate number is available, along with the identity of the state where the death occurred and the date of death. Given these **mortality data,** researchers can order a copy of the death certificate from the state's vital statistics office.

One of the tasks performed by the National Center for Health Statistics is to classify deaths into various numerical categories. This very complex task is performed by nosologists who use the two current volumes on how to classify a particular cause of death (COD). This classification is then used to tabulate data according to various codes.

Morbidity Surveys

Morbidity data (i.e., data on the prevalence of disease) are far more difficult to gather and interpret than are mortality data. Whereas death registration is now estimated to be 99% complete, cases of communicable disease are all too often underreported.

Reporting of communicable diseases is a time-honored, if flawed, method of gathering morbidity data. In 1876, Massachusetts tried voluntary case reporting; the first compulsory reporting began in Michigan in 1883 (Winslow et al., 1952). But even now, more than a century later, there are wide gaps in the data. California, for example, has 52 reportable diseases; other states have fewer. Various surveys have concluded that the more serious diseases are well reported. But whereas virtually every case of cholera, plague, yellow fever, rabies, and paralytic polio is promptly brought to the attention of health authorities, the common childhood diseases are notoriously underreported.

Each local health department tallies the number of cases of reportable communicable disease within its area and forwards its count to the state health department, where a cumulative total is made and sent to the Centers for Disease

Control in Atlanta for publication in *Morbidity and Mortality Weekly Reports (MMWR)*.

Because of chronic underreporting, a number of novel systems have been developed to allow researchers to make better estimates of morbidity data. In the following partial list of these systems, note that many of them go far beyond communicable-disease reporting to include data on noninfectious, occupational, and chronic diseases.

1. Reportable diseases
2. National Health Survey
3. Hospital records data
4. Industrial hygiene records
5. School nurse records
6. Medical care subgroups (most often: prepaid medical plans)
7. Chronic-disease registries (most often: tumor registries)
8. Insurance industry data

The **National Health Survey** is worthy of special note. Originated by an Act of Congress in 1956, it provides for an annual nationwide survey of a representative sample of 40,000 persons. A number of subprograms are included, the most notable of which are the National Health Interview Survey, National Health and Nutrition Examination Survey (HANES), National Hospital Discharge Survey, National Ambulatory Medical Care Survey, and National Nursing Home Survey. The results are published in *Vital and Health Statistics*, sometimes referred to (due to its colorful covers) as the "rainbow series." Published results encompass a vast spectrum of medical care data including incidence or prevalence rates for many diseases, length of hospital stays, hospitalizations by cause, number of days of disability, and patterns of ambulatory care service.

Hospital and clinic records are a fair source of morbidity data. However, except for prepaid medical plans, the population served by a hospital is difficult to define. The Professional Activity Study of Battle Creek, Michigan, provides a uniform reporting system that is used by over 2000 hospitals nationwide. Researchers use this system to make morbidity estimates for population studies. Hospital administrators find this and other resources to be invaluable for planning strategies of health care delivery.

Chronic-disease registries are rapidly taking on a major role in the understanding of morbidity data. Most such registries are cancer-oriented (and are therefore known as cancer, or tumor, registries), although some are specialized for diseases such as cardiovascular disease, tuberculosis, diabetes, and psychiatric disease. A cancer registry is defined as a "facility for the collection, storage, analysis, and interpretation of data on persons with cancer." Some such registries are hospital-based; that is, they work within the walls of a hospital or group of hospitals. Others are population-based, in that they serve a population of defined composition and size. Among the best-known of the latter are the tumor registries of Connecticut and Iowa, each serving the entire state (Muir and Nectoux, 1977).

Although we have focused on data for the United States, similar data are available for most of the developed world. They may be found in the annual *Demographic Yearbook* (United Nations, 1990).

15.3 VITAL STATISTICS RATES, RATIOS, AND PROPORTIONS

The field of vital statistics makes some special applications of rates, ratios, and proportions. A **rate** is an expression of the form

$$\left[\frac{a}{(a+b)t}\right]c \tag{15.1}$$

where

> a = the number of persons experiencing a particular event during a given period

> $a + b$ = the number of persons who are at risk of experiencing the particular event during the same period

> t = the total time at risk

> c = a multiplier, such as 100, 1000, 10,000, or 100,000

The purpose of the multiplier, also referred to as the **base,** is to avoid the inconvenience of working with minute decimal fractions; it also helps users comprehend the meaning of a given rate. We usually choose c to give a rate that is in the tens or hundreds.

Three kinds of rates are commonly used in vital statistics: crude, specific, and adjusted. **Crude rates** are computed for an entire population. They disregard differences that usually exist by age, sex, race, or some category of disease. **Specific rates** consider the differences among subgroups and are computed by age, race, sex, or some other variable. **Adjusted** (or **standardized**) **rates** are used to make valid summary comparisons between two or more groups possessing different age (or other) distributions.

A **ratio** is a computation of the form

$$\left(\frac{a}{d}\right)c \tag{15.2}$$

where a and c are defined as for rates, and d is the number of individuals experiencing some event different from event a during the same period. Quite commonly used is the sex ratio; by convention, it places males in the numerator and females in the denominator. A ratio of 1.0 would describe a population with an equal number of males and females.

A **proportion** is an expression of the form

$$\left(\frac{a}{a + b}\right)c \tag{15.3}$$

where a, $a + b$, and c are defined as for rates.

15.4 MEASURES OF MORTALITY

A wide variety of rates, ratios, and proportions is based on numbers of deaths. Each rate is a measure of the relative frequency of deaths that occurred in a given population over a specific period. If we know the population and **time at risk,** we can compute a mortality rate. Unfortunately, these figures are sometimes difficult to obtain. A convention is used to define population size: the population at midyear (July 1). The figure obtained serves as a reasonable estimate of the **population at risk** $(a + b)$ over the time (t) of one year. If this convention cannot be met, the calculation should preferably be termed a "proportion" rather than a "rate."

In the health sciences, the fine distinctions among rates, ratios, and proportions are often ignored. Consequently, you may find that some sources erroneously call certain ratios "rates"; the most common of these are starred (*) in the discussion that follows. Some proportions are similarly misnamed "rates"; these also are starred.

Annual Crude Death Rate

The annual crude death rate is defined as the number of deaths in a calendar year divided by the population on July 1 of that year, with the quotient multiplied by 1000.

■ **EXAMPLE 1**

California, 1987—population: 27,663,000; deaths: 210,171.

$$\text{Crude death rate} = \frac{210,171}{27,663,000} \times 1000$$

$$= 7.6 \text{ deaths per 1000 population per year } ∎$$

The annual crude death rate is universally used. It is indeed crude—a generalized indicator of the health of a population. In our example, the rate of 7.6 deaths per 1000 is a bit less than the overall U.S. death rate of 8.7. But it is often unwise to make such a comparison, especially when the two populations are known to differ on important characteristics such as age, race, or sex. More appropriate comparisons are made by use of adjusted rates. The process of adjustment is a bit involved; we will deal with it later. In the meantime, there is another way of making fair comparisons between groups—by use of *specific* rates. Death rates may be specific for age, for sex, or for some particular cause of death.

Age-Specific Death Rate

The age-specific death rate is defined as the number of deaths in a specific age group in a calendar year divided by the population of the same age group on July 1 of that year, with the quotient multiplied by 1000.

■ EXAMPLE 2

United States, 1987—age group: 25–34 years; population: 43,513,000; deaths: 57,701.

$$\text{Age-specific death rate} = \frac{57,701}{43,513,000} \times 1000$$

$$= 1.3 \text{ deaths per 1000 population per year}$$
$$\text{for age group 25–34} \ ■$$

Cause-Specific Death Rate

The cause-specific death rate is defined as the number of deaths assigned to a specific cause in a calendar year divided by the population on July 1 of that year, with the quotient multiplied by 100,000.

■ EXAMPLE 3

United States, 1987—cause: accidents; population: 243,827,000; deaths: 94,840.

$$\text{Cause-specific death rate} = \frac{94,840}{243,827,000} \times 100,000$$

$$= 38.9 \text{ accidental deaths per 100,000 population}$$
$$\text{per year} \ ■$$

Cause-/Race-Specific Death Rate

The cause-/race-specific death rate is one of many possible examples of how the idea of specific death rates may be extended simultaneously to cover two characteristics.

■ EXAMPLE 4

United States, 1987—cause: accidents; white male population, 100,589,000; nonwhite male population, 17,942,000.

Table 15.1 Cause-/Race-Specific Death Rate, United States, 1987

	White Males	Nonwhite Males
Population	100,589,000	17,942,000
Deaths assigned to accidents	53,936	10,880
Cause-/race-specific death rate per 100,000	53.6	60.6

The data for this example are given in Table 15.1. Note the difference in the death rate between the two racial groups. The underlying explanation for the difference, however, may be something other than race. What other factor might explain the difference? ■

*Proportional Mortality Ratio

The **proportional mortality ratio** is defined as the number of deaths assigned to a specific cause in a calendar year divided by the total number of deaths in that year, with the quotient multiplied by 100.

■ **EXAMPLE 5**

United States, 1987—total deaths from all causes: 2,123,000; deaths assigned to malignant neoplasms: 476,927.

$$\text{Proportional mortality ratio} = \frac{476,927}{2,123,000} \times 100$$

$$= 22.5\% \text{ of total deaths per year from malignant neoplasms} \blacksquare$$

■ **EXAMPLE 6**

United States, 1987—persons 15–24 years old: 38,481,000; persons age 65 or over: 29,835,000.

From the data for this example in Table 15.2, you can see that this ratio is useful as a measure of the relative importance of a specific cause of death. But

Table 15.2 Cause-Specific Death Rate, United States, 1987

	Persons Ages 15–24	Persons Age 65 and Over
Population	38,481,000	29,835,000
Deaths—all causes		
Number	38,023	1,509,686
Death rate per 100,000	98.8	5,060.1
Deaths—accidental causes		
Number	18,695	25,838
Death rate per 100,000	48.6	86.2
Proportional mortality—accidental causes (%)	49.2%	1.7%

though it is quite simple to compute, it should be used with caution because it is also quite easy to misinterpret. For instance, the proportional mortality for accidental death here is much greater for young adults than for elderly persons. Nevertheless, the death rate from accidents is higher for the elderly. This apparent dilemma disappears when you realize the numerical impact of the large number of deaths from all causes among the elderly. ■

Proportional mortality is particularly useful in occupational studies as a measure of the relative importance of a specific cause of death. It suffers from not having a population base in the denominator. Although it does not provide a reliable population estimate as does the cause-specific death rate, it is valuable in making preliminary assessments when denominator data are not available.

The next five measures are concerned with events involved in pregnancy, birth, and infancy. Most are based on the number of live births.

*Maternal Mortality Ratio

The **maternal mortality ratio** is defined as the number of deaths assigned to puerperal causes (i.e., those related to childbearing) in a calendar year divided by the number of live births in that year, with the quotient multiplied by 100,000.

■ **EXAMPLE 7**

United States, 1987—deaths assigned to puerperal causes: 253; live births: 3,829,000.

$$\text{Maternal mortality ratio} = \frac{253}{3,829,000} \times 100,000$$

$$= 6.6 \text{ maternal deaths per 100,000 live births per year} ■$$

Note that this ratio has an inherent problem: It includes maternal deaths in the numerator but only live births in the denominator. Fetal deaths are not represented. Consequently, this practice tends to inflate the ratio slightly. A second problem derives from multiple births. They inflate the denominator but do not affect the numerator. Because such events are comparatively rare, the net effect would be a minor change to a ratio based on an otherwise large population.

Infant Mortality Rate

The **infant mortality rate** is defined as the number of deaths of persons of age 0–1 in a calendar year divided by the number of live births in that year, with the quotient multiplied by 1000.

■ **EXAMPLE 8**

California, 1987—live births: 494,053; infant deaths: 4546.

$$\text{Infant mortality rate} = \frac{4546}{494,053} \times 1000$$

$$= 9.2 \text{ infant deaths per 1000 live births per year} \quad \blacksquare$$

This rate has an inherent problem in those populations that are experiencing rapidly changing birthrates. As you can see from our example, the numerator includes some infants who died in 1987 but were born in 1986, and some of the infants born in 1987 would die in 1988. In a population with a stable birthrate (e.g., that of the United States or Canada), such differences are likely to cancel out; this is not the case in a population undergoing a significant change in its birthrate.

Neonatal Mortality Proportion

The **neonatal mortality proportion** is defined as the number of deaths of neonates (i.e., infants less than 28 days of age) that occurred in a calendar year divided by the number of live births in that year, with the quotient multiplied by 1000.

■ EXAMPLE 9

California, 1987—deaths at age less than 1 year: 4546; deaths at age less than 25 days: 2780; live births: 494,053.

$$\text{Neonatal mortality proportion} = \frac{2780}{494,053} \times 1000$$

$$= 5.6 \text{ neonatal deaths per 1000 live births} \quad \blacksquare$$

Because this example shows that 61.1% [(2780/4546) × 100] of all infant deaths were neonatal, it underscores the importance of neonatal mortality: The great bulk of infant deaths occur in a relatively short period following birth.

Fetal Death Ratio

A fetal death is defined as the delivery of a fetus that shows no evidence of life (no heart action, breathing, or movement of voluntary muscles) if the 20th week of gestation has been completed or if the period of gestation was unstated.

The **fetal death ratio** is defined as the number of fetal deaths in a calendar year divided by the number of live births in that year, with the quotient multiplied by 1000. Note that this ratio applies only to fetal deaths that occur in the second half of pregnancy. No reporting is required for early miscarriages.

■ EXAMPLE 10

California, 1987—fetal deaths: 3477; live births: 494,053.

$$\text{Fetal death ratio} = \frac{3477}{494,053} \times 1000$$

$$= 7.0 \text{ fetal deaths per 1000 live births} \quad \blacksquare$$

Regrettably, fetal deaths tend to be grossly underreported, so every fetal death ratio is an underestimate (McMillen, 1979).

Perinatal Mortality Proportion

The **perinatal mortality proportion** is defined as the number of fetal plus neonatal deaths divided by the number of live births plus fetal deaths, with the quotient multiplied by 1000.

■ EXAMPLE 11

California, 1987—fetal deaths: 3477; neonatal deaths: 2780; live births: 494,053.

$$\text{Perinatal mortality proportion} = \frac{3477 + 2780}{3477 + 494,053} \times 1000$$

$$= 12.6 \text{ perinatal deaths per 1000 fetal deaths}$$
plus live births ■

15.5 MEASURES OF FERTILITY

Measures of fertility are indispensable when approaching population control problems. They are particularly useful in planning maternal and child health services. These measures also help school boards plan their future needs for facilities and teachers. The two most common measures of fertility are the crude birthrate and the general fertility rate.

Crude Birthrate

The **crude birthrate** is defined as the number of live births in a calendar year divided by the population on July 1 of that year, with the quotient multiplied by 1000.

■ EXAMPLE 12

California, 1987—live births: 494,053; population: 27,663,000.

$$\text{Crude birthrate} = \frac{494,053}{27,663,000} \times 1000$$

$$= 17.9 \text{ live births per 1000 population per year } ■$$

The crude birthrate, though quite commonly used, is a none-too-sensitive measure of fertility because its denominator includes both men and women. Strictly speaking, this measure cannot be a rate because only a fraction of the population is capable of bearing children. A more sensitive measure is the general fertility rate.

General Fertility Rate

The **general fertility rate** is defined as the number of live births in a calendar year divided by the number of women ages 15–44 at midyear, with the quotient multiplied by 1000.

■ **EXAMPLE 13**

United States, 1987—live births: 3,829,000; number of women ages 15–44: 58,012,000.

$$\text{General fertility rate} = \frac{3,829,000}{58,012,000} \times 1000$$

$$= 66.0 \text{ live births per 1000 women ages 15–44 per year} \quad ■$$

This rate is more sensitive than the crude birthrate because its denominator includes only women of childbearing age.

Other measures of fertility are age-specific fertility rates and age-adjusted fertility rates. Both can be used to make valid comparisons between different population groups.

15.6 MEASURES OF MORBIDITY

At best, mortality data provide indirect means of assessing the health of a community. The **underlying cause of death** hardly provides an adequate picture of the countless illnesses and other health problems that exist in any community. Because morbidity is less precisely recorded than mortality, such data are difficult to analyze, but they are nonetheless useful in program planning and evaluation. Many measures exist. We will discuss here three that deal with the frequency, prevalence, and seriousness of disease.

Incidence Rate

The **incidence rate** is defined as the number of newly reported cases of a given disease in a calendar year divided by the population on July 1 of that year, with the quotient multiplied by a convenient factor, usually 1000, 100,000, or 1,000,000.

■ **EXAMPLE 14**

California, 1987—new cases of AIDS reported to the State Health Department: 4878; population: 27,663,000.

$$\text{Incidence rate} = \frac{4878}{27,663,000} \times 100,000$$

$$= 17.6 \text{ new cases of AIDS per 100,000 population per year} \quad ■$$

*Prevalence Proportion

The **prevalence proportion** is defined as the number of existing cases of a given disease at a given time divided by the population at that time, with the quotient multiplied by 1000, 100,000, or 1,000,000.

■ EXAMPLE 15

United States, 1988—number of men alive with AIDS: 27,598; population: 120,203,000 men.

$$\text{Prevalence proportion} = \frac{27,598}{120,203,000} \times 100,000$$

$$= 23.0 \text{ AIDS cases per } 100,000 \text{ men } ■$$

*Case-Fatality Proportion

The **case-fatality proportion** is defined as the number of deaths assigned to a given cause in a certain period divided by the number of cases of the disease reported during the same period, with the quotient multiplied by 100.

■ EXAMPLE 16

United States, 1988—reported number of male AIDS cases: 27,598; deaths from the disease: 13,886.

$$\text{Case-fatality proportion} = \frac{13,886}{27,598} \times 100$$

$$= 50.3\% \text{ mortality among reported cases} \\ \text{of AIDS } ■$$

This proportion uses the relative number of deaths as an indicator of the seriousness of a disease. It is often used as a means of showing the relative effectiveness of various methods of treatment.

15.7 ADJUSTMENT OF RATES

Crude rates can be used to make approximate comparisons between different populations. But the comparisons are invalid if the populations are dissimilar with respect to an important characteristic such as age, sex, or race. As we know so well, many diseases have quite different impacts on different groups: on men and women, on old and young persons, on blacks and whites. We would therefore hesitate to compare the death rate for Alaska, with its young population, to that of Florida, with its relatively old population. We can see in Table 15.3 that the crude death rate for Alaska is much lower than that for

Table 15.3 Population Distribution and Age-Specific Death Rates for Alaska and Florida, 1987

Age Group	Alaska Number of Deaths	Population Persons	Population %	Deaths per 100,000 Persons	Florida Number of Deaths	Population Persons	Population %	Deaths per 100,000 Persons
0–4	163	60,000	11.45	271.7	2,271	812,000	6.75	279.7
5–24	152	173,000	33.01	87.9	2,296	3,093,000	25.73	74.2
25–44	376	193,000	36.83	194.8	6,958	3,450,000	28.70	201.7
45–64	518	79,000	15.08	655.7	20,524	2,528,000	21.03	811.9
65+	845	19,000	3.63	4,447.4	95,141	2,139,000	17.79	4,447.9
Total	2,054	524,000	100.00	392.0	127,190	12,022,000	100.00	1,058.0

SOURCE: *1990 Statistical Abstracts of the United States.*

Florida. The real explanation for this is that Alaska has many more young people than does Florida, and the death rate for a younger group is low. A good way to handle the comparison is to examine the corresponding age-specific death rates for the two states. However, comparing a long series of age-specific rates is often quite cumbersome, especially if more than two populations are involved. To solve this, an *adjusted*, or *standardized*, rate is used to make the comparison valid. Statistically, the adjustment removes the difference in composition with respect to age.

There are two methods of adjustment: direct and indirect. The type of data available dictates the method to be used. But keep in mind that an adjusted rate is artificial in that it is a rate applied to a population with a hypothetical distribution. Such rates do not at all reflect the actual rates of a population. They have real meaning only as relative comparisons. The numerical values of the adjusted rates depend in large part on the choice of the standard population.

The Direct Method

The **direct method of adjustment** applies a standard population distribution to the death rates of two comparison groups. The sum of the expected deaths for the two groups is then used to compute the adjusted death rate (dividing the expected deaths by the total of the standard population). With the direct method, it is essential to have both the age-specific death rates for the populations being adjusted and the distribution of the standard population by age (or by whatever other factor is being adjusted).

■ **EXAMPLE 17**

In Table 15.3, we see that the 1987 crude death rate per 100,000 population for Alaska was 392.0 and for Florida, 1058.0. But a close look at the age distribution discloses that Alaska had a higher percentage of its population in the younger

Table 15.4 Age-Adjusted Death Rates per 100,000 Population for Alaska and Florida, 1987, Using the Direct Method and Based on the 1987 U.S. Standard Million

Age Group	(1) 1987 U.S. Standard Million	(2) Alaska Age-Specific Death Rates	(3) Alaska Expected Deaths with U.S. Standard Million	(4) Florida Age-Specific Death Rates	(5) Florida Expected Deaths with U.S. Standard Million
0–4	75,080	271.7	204.0	279.7	210.0
5–24	216,113	87.9	190.0	74.2	160.4
25–44	400,170	194.8	779.5	201.7	807.1
45–64	186,091	655.7	1220.2	811.9	1510.9
65+	122,546	4447.4	5450.1	4447.9	5450.7
Total	1,000,000		7843.8		8139.1

age groups. This finding makes it essential to adjust the death rates of the two states in order to make a valid comparison. With the direct method, we can figure out what the death rate would be for each state if the age distributions of both populations were identical. An efficient way to make this calculation is to apply the U.S. standard population to both states and then compute the expected number of deaths for each state as if its population distribution were indeed the same as for the U.S. standard.

To carry out this method, we use the **U.S. standard million.** This is a population of 1 million persons that identically follows the age distribution for the entire United States, as shown in column 1 of Table 15.4.

The specific steps involved in calculating the age-adjusted rate are as follows:

1. Compute the expected number of deaths for the standard population by applying the age-specific death rates of the state. For Alaska, multiply column 1 by column 2, divide the product by 100,000, and enter the result in column 3. For Florida, multiply column 1 by column 4, divide the product by 100,000, and enter the result in column 5.

2. Total the expected deaths in columns 3 and 5. You can see that, if Alaska's population were distributed the same as the U.S. standard million, the expected number of deaths (given Alaska's known age-specific death rates) would be 7843.8. Similarly, the expected number of deaths for Florida would be 8139.1.

3. Compute the age-adjusted death rate per 1000 by dividing the total expected deaths by 1000. For Alaska, the adjusted rate is 7.84, and for Florida, it is 8.14. Remember that the crude death rates per 1000 were 3.92 for Alaska and 10.58 for Florida (Table 15.3).

The striking result: Florida's crude death rate was much higher than Alaska's. However, based on a comparable population, the age-adjusted death rates were nearly the same for both states! ■

The choice of the standard population affects the values of the adjusted rates. Therefore, in comparing adjusted rates between different states or countries, you should know which standard population was used because different standards will yield different results.

The Indirect Method

The **indirect method of adjustment** is somewhat different from the direct method. It is utilized when age-specific death rates are not available for the populations being adjusted but the age-specific death rates for the standard population are known. With this method, we compute a **standard mortality ratio (SMR)** (i.e., observed deaths divided by expected deaths) and use it as a standardizing factor to adjust the crude death rates of the given populations. The SMR increases or decreases a crude rate in relation to the excess or deficit of the group's composition as compared to the standard population. Both this method and the direct method are as applicable to ratios and proportions as they are to rates.

◆ CONCLUSION

Public health decision making is a quantitative matter. The health of a population is assessed by use of its vital statistics and demographic data. Information about demographic characteristics is obtainable from census data, registration of vital events, and morbidity surveys. Such data are used to calculate vital rates and other statistics that are used to indicate the magnitude of health problems.

Vital rates, ratios, and proportions are classified into measures of mortality (death), fertility (birth), and morbidity (illness). These measures may be crude or specific, the latter referring to calculations for subgroups selected for a common characteristic such as age, sex, race, or disease experience. Comparisons of vital rates, ratios, or proportions among different populations should be made with care and be validated by use of specific or adjusted measures. The choice of the adjustment method depends on the type of data available.

◆ VOCABULARY LIST

adjusted rate
  (standardized rate)
base
birth registration
case-fatality proportion
crude birthrate
crude rate
death registration
decennial census
demographic variables

direct method of
  adjustment
fetal death ratio
general fertility rate
incidence rate
indirect method
  of adjustment
infant mortality rate
maternal mortality
  ratio

Metropolitan Statistical
  Area (MSA)
morbidity data
mortality data
National Health Survey
neonatal mortality
  proportion
perinatal mortality
  proportion
population at risk

prevalence proportion	ratio	underlying cause of
proportion	specific rate	death
proportional mortality	standard mortality ratio	U.S. standard million
ratio	(SMR)	vital events
rate	time at risk	vital statistics

◆ EXERCISES

Note: For all these exercises, use as appropriate the sources referred to in section 15.2.

15.1 Find the size of the U.S. population (including those in the armed forces) for 1970, 1980, and 1990.

15.2 What was the population of New York State in 1970? In 1980?

15.3 In 1987, how many Iowans were
a. under 5 years old?
b. 65 or more years old?

15.4 What was the percentage of blacks living in 1987 in Minnesota? In Georgia?

15.5 In 1987, what were the birth and death rates for Alaska? For Kansas?

15.6 For the United States during 1987, what were the five leading causes of death?

15.7 What were the maternal mortality ratios for U.S. whites and nonwhites in 1950? In 1980?

15.8 What were the death rates from cirrhosis of the liver by sex and race (white and nonwhite) for the United States in 1987?

15.9 What were the numbers of total deaths, infant deaths, and neonatal deaths, by place of residence, for two California counties, Riverside and San Bernardino, in 1987?

15.10 a. For 1987, compute the crude birthrates for Alaska and for Arizona.
b. What do you observe about the birthrates of these two states? What are some possible explanations?

15.11 Find the death rates for Hawaii and for Nevada. Which state had the highest birthrates and fertility rates in 1993?

15.12 Obtain the sex-specific death rates from cirrhosis of the liver for males and females in 1993 for the United States.

15.13 Obtain the cause-specific death rates for Michigan, Utah, Tennessee, and the United States for cancer, heart disease, accidents, and diabetes in 1993.

15.14 Obtain the population size and number of deaths due to cancer in Tennessee for 1980 and 1990.

15.15 Find the states with the three highest HIV death rates in 1993.

16 Life Tables

✔ LEARNING OBJECTIVES

After studying this chapter, you should be able to

1. Distinguish among the three types of life tables
2. Identify and be able to compute the components of a current life table
3. Compute measures of mortality and longevity from a life table
4. Construct a follow-up life table

16.1   GENERAL USES OF LIFE TABLES

Life tables have been in use for centuries. The first systematic, if inexact, life table was developed by British astronomer Edmund Halley (of Halley's comet fame) to describe the longevity of residents of 17th-century Breslau. In 1815, Joshua Milne published the first mathematically accurate life table, which described the mortality experience of a city in northern England (Shyrock and Siegel, 1973).

Life tables are now in general use and have many important applications. For instance, they are used by demographers to measure and analyze the mortality or longevity of a population or one of its segments, by insurance companies to compute premiums, and by research workers to determine whether the differences in mortality or longevity of two groups are significant. They are employed to predict survival or the likelihood of death at any time. A life table analysis can be fundamental to the solution of many public health and medical problems.

Three types of life tables are in general use. They are the current life table; the cohort, or generation, life table; and the follow-up, or modified, life table. Current and follow-up life tables are the most common and will be discussed in some detail.

The **current life table** illustrates how age-specific death rates affect a population. Such a table considers mortality rates for the entire population for a given period. For instance, a 1979–1981 life table considers the mortality of the various age groups over 3 years. It does not follow the mortality experience of a single age group throughout its life. Three years are used in preference to 1 year because this span tends to stabilize the death rates, which otherwise would be unduly sensitive to year-by-year fluctuations.

By contrast, the **cohort life table** follows a defined group—a **cohort**—from birth (or some other measurable point in time) until the last person in the group has died, which is why it is also known as a **generation life table.** The key difference between the current life table and the cohort life table is that the former generates a fictitious pattern of mortality whereas the latter presents the historical record of what actually occurred.

Because there are usually major differences in the patterns of mortality among various subgroups of a population, life tables are quite commonly constructed for specific groups: by race, sex, occupation, or specific diseases.

An interesting extension of the life table idea has come into general use in recent years. Life tables may be employed for studies wherein the outcome variable is an event other than death. For example, an outcome could be recurrence of coronary heart disease, contraceptive failure, or time from driver's license issuance to first reported accident. An illustration of the recurrence of cancer as an outcome variable appears in Kuzma and Dixon (1966). Furthermore, the **follow-up,** or **modified, life table** has been used recently by medical researchers. They have adopted its use to determine the survival experience of patients with a particular condition.

16.2 CURRENT LIFE TABLES

To demonstrate the many applications of a current life table, we will use an **abridged life table** for the 1987 U.S. population. Table 16.1 illustrates what would have happened to a hypothetical population of 100,000 persons as it passed through time—that is, how many persons would have died and how many would have survived in each particular age group—if they had spent their entire lifetimes exposed to the 1987 mortality rate. The table also indicates the probability of dying during any age interval, the probability of surviving to a particular age, and the average life expectancy. The table is abridged for convenience, with most of the age intervals covering 5-year periods. A **complete life table** would have a separate entry for each year.

By systematically dissecting a life table, we can gain some valuable insights into what it means and how it works. We will discuss the several columns of Table 16.1.

Age Interval [x to $(x + n)$]

The **age interval** is the period between the two exact ages stated. For example, 35–39 means the 5-year span that includes the 35th to 39th birthdays.

Age-Specific Death Rate ($_nm_x$)

The symbol $_nm_x$ denotes the average annual age-specific death rate for the age interval stated; that is, x denotes the beginning of the interval, and n denotes the width. The numerator for this rate is the average number of deaths per year in a 3-year period (1986–1988), divided by the July 1 average population for 1986, 1987, and 1988. For example, the age-specific death rate for age group 35–39, $_5m_{35}$, is .0018554, or about 1.9 per 1000.

Correction Term ($_na_x$)

We need a correction term for a very simple reason. Among tiny infants, most deaths occur early in the first year, whereas among adults, deaths are fairly uniformly distributed throughout the year. The correction term defines and adjusts for the maldistribution. The $_na_x$ column shows the average fraction of the age interval lived by persons who die during that interval. Notice that $_5a_{35}$ is .54, a shade more than half a year. Values for $_na_x$ are computed by use of a complex equation discussed in advanced treatments of this topic, such as in Chiang (1984).

Table 16.1 Abridged Life Table for the Total U.S. Population, 1987

| Age Interval | Proportion Dying | | | Of 100,000 Born Alive | | Person-Years Lived | | Average Remaining Lifetime |
| | Uncorrected | Correction Term | Corrected | | | | | |
Period of Life Between Two Exact Ages Stated x to (x + n)	Average Annual Age-Specific Death Rate $_n m_x$	Fraction of Last Age Interval Lived $_n a_x$	Proportion Dying During Age Interval $_n q_x$	Number Living at Beginning of Age Interval l_x	Number Dying During Age Interval $_n d_x$	In the Age Interval $_n L_x$	In This and All Subsequent Age Intervals T_x	Average Number of Years of Life Remaining at Beginning of Age Interval $\mathring{e}_x$
<1	.0101724	.10	.0100801	100,000	1,008	99,093	7,510,914	75.11
1–4	.0005149	.39	.0020570	98,992	204	395,472	7,411,821	74.87
5–9	.0002404	.46	.0012012	98,788	119	493,620	7,016,349	71.02
10–14	.0002877	.56	.0014375	98,669	142	493,035	6,522,729	66.10
15–19	.0008659	.57	.0043214	98,527	426	491,720	6,029,694	61.20
20–24	.0011492	.49	.0057292	98,101	562	489,070	5,537,974	56.45
25–29	.0012114	.50	.0060753	97,539	593	486,215	5,048,904	51.76
30–34	.0014645	.52	.0072968	96,946	707	483,035	4,562,689	47.06
35–39	.0018554	.54	.0092375	96,239	889	479,150	4,079,654	42.39
40–44	.0025259	.54	.0127201	95,350	1,213	473,960	3,600,504	37.76
45–49	.0038527	.54	.0190943	94,137	1,797	466,550	3,126,544	33.21
50–54	.0062165	.53	.0306349	92,340	2,829	455,050	2,659,994	28.81
55–59	.0097092	.52	.0474405	89,511	4,246	437,365	2,204,944	24.63
60–64	.0152116	.52	.0733790	85,265	6,257	411,310	1,767,579	20.73
65–69	.0223704	.52	.1061527	79,008	8,387	374,910	1,356,269	17.17
70–74	.0342433	.51	.1579639	70,621	11,156	325,775	981,359	13.90
75–79	.0511817	.51	.2273943	59,465	13,522	264,195	655,584	11.02
80–84	.0795990	.48	.3297506	45,943	15,150	190,325	391,389	8.52
85+	.1531499	—	1.0000000	30,793	30,793	201,064	201,064	6.53

Source: *Monthly Vital Statistics Report* (National Center for Health Statistics), 1986–1988.

Corrected (Estimated) Death Rate ($_n\hat{q}_x$)

The symbol $_n\hat{q}_x$ denotes the proportion of those persons who are alive at the beginning of the age interval but die during that interval. For example, the probability that a 35-year-old will die before reaching age 40 is $_5\hat{q}_{35} = .0092$. The computing formula for $_n\hat{q}_x$ is

$$_n\hat{q}_x = \frac{n \cdot {_nm_x}}{1 + (1 - {_na_x}) \cdot n \cdot {_nm_x}}$$

Number Living at Beginning of Age Interval (l_x)

We use l_x to indicate the number of persons, starting with the original cohort of 100,000 live births, who survive to the exact age marking the beginning of each interval. Each l_x value is computed by subtracting the $_nd_x$ (number dying during interval) for the previous age interval from the l_x for that interval—that is,

$$l_{x+n} = l_x - d_x \tag{16.1}$$

Thus

$$l_{35} = l_{30} - {_5d_{30}} = 96,946 - 707 = 96,239$$

Number Dying During Age Interval ($_nd_x$)

The number of persons of the original 100,000 who die during each successive age interval is denoted by $_nd_x$. It is calculated by multiplying the proportion dying ($_n\hat{q}_x$) during the interval by the number alive (l_x) at the beginning of the interval.

$$_nd_x = (l_x)(_n\hat{q}_x) \tag{16.2}$$

For example,

$$_5d_{30} = (l_{30})(_5\hat{q}_{30}) = 96,946(.0072968) = 707$$

Person-Years Lived in Interval ($_nL_x$)

The symbol $_nL_x$ designates the totality of years lived by the survivors of the original 100,000 (l_x) between the ages x and $(x + n)$. For example, $_5L_{30} = 483,035$ is the number of **person-years** lived by the 96,946 (l_{30}) alive at the beginning of the 30th year. It is computed by the equation

$$_nL_x = n[l_{x+n} + (_na_x)(_nd_x)] \tag{16.3}$$

for all intervals except the last, for which

$$_nL_x = \frac{_nd_x}{_nm_x} \tag{16.4}$$

So

$$_5L_{30} = 5[l_{35} + (_5a_{30})(_5d_{30})]$$
$$= 5[96{,}239 + (.52)(707)]$$
$$= 483{,}033$$

Sometimes the $_nL_x$ column of the life table is termed the **stationary population.** Given the hypothetical assumption that the number of births and deaths remains constant each year, the number of person-years would, in fact, be unchanging, hence the term. This idea is useful in certain applications to studies of population structure.

Total Number of Person-Years (T_x)

The symbol T_x denotes the total number of person-years lived by the l_x survivors from year x to death. It is obtained by cumulating the person-years lived in the intervals ($_nL_x$):

$$T_0 = {}_1L_0 + {}_4L_1 + {}_5L_5 + \cdots + {}_5L_{80} + {}_5L_{85} = 7{,}510{,}914$$

Expectation of Life ($\hat{e}_x$)

Because of its general usefulness, $\hat{e}_x$ may be the most valuable feature of the life table. It denotes **life expectation,** the average number of years of life remaining to those who survive to the beginning of the age interval. It is calculated by dividing the number of person-years lived after a given age (T_x) by the number who reached that same age (l_x):

$$\hat{e}_x = \frac{T_x}{l_x} \tag{16.5}$$

The future life expectancy for a 35-year-old, for example, is calculated by $\hat{e}_{35} = T_{35}/l_{35} = 4{,}079{,}654/96{,}239 = 42.4$ years; that is, on average, persons reaching age 35 may expect to live to $35 + 42.4 = 77.4$ years.

A life table enables us to compute some special measures of mortality that are real improvements over the use of general rates. One of these measures is the expectation of life at age 1, which removes the considerable impact that infant mortality has on life expectation from birth. Another is the expectation of life at age 65, which zeros in on the mortality of the older ages, when most deaths occur. Still another is the probability of surviving from birth to age 65, which is defined as

$$_{65}P_0 = \frac{l_{65}}{l_0}$$

An interesting measure is the **median age at death,** which is the age to which precisely half of the cohort survives. It corresponds to the age x at which $l_x = 50{,}000$ in a life table based on a cohort of 100,000 persons. By interpolation from Table 16.1, we would estimate the median age at death as 78.5 years.

A commonly used survival rate in population studies is

$$_nP_x = \frac{l_{x+n}}{l_x} \tag{16.6}$$

the probability of surviving from year x to year $x + n$. For example, using Table 16.1, we can calculate the proportion of newborn babies who will reach their tenth birthday:

$$_{10}P_0 = \frac{l_{10}}{l_0} = \frac{98{,}669}{100{,}000} = .98669$$

Similarly, the proportion of newborns who will reach their first birthday is

$$_1P_0 = \frac{l_1}{l_0} = \frac{98{,}992}{100{,}000} = .98992$$

and the probability that a 25-year-old will survive 10 more years is

$$_{10}P_{25} = \frac{l_{35}}{l_{25}} = \frac{96{,}239}{97{,}539} = .98667$$

Not surprisingly, we can follow the same pattern to compute probabilities of death. The probability that a 25-year-old will die before reaching age 30 is

$$_5q_{25} = \frac{_5d_{25}}{l_{25}} = \frac{593}{97{,}539} = .00608$$

Note that l_x may be thought of as a cumulation of the age-specific death rates up to (but not including) age x. In other words, it shows the net effect of all death rates up to that age, whereas life expectation, $\hat{e}_x$, shows the effect of the age-specific death rates after that age.

We already mentioned that the current life table considers a hypothetical cohort. The assumption is that the cohort is subject throughout its existence to those age-specific mortality rates that were observed for one particular period. However, specific rates actually vary with time. Although little variation occurs from one year to the next, significant changes are common over long periods. Table 16.2 illustrates the point for U.S. white males for the years 1900–1980. Note that most of the improvement in longevity has occurred under age 65, and especially in the first year of life.

Table 16.2 Changes in the Mortality of U.S. White Males According to Various Life Table Measures, 1900–1980

Measure	Base Period for Life Table*						
	1900	1910	1920	1930	1940	1950	1980
Expectation of life at birth	48.2	50.2	56.3	59.1	62.8	66.3	73.6
Expectation of life at age 1	54.6	56.3	60.2	62.0	65.0	67.1	73.6
Expectation of life at age 65	11.5	11.3	12.2	11.8	12.1	12.8	16.4
Probability of surviving from birth to age 65	.39	.41	.51	.53	.58	.64	.77
Median age at death of initial cohort	57.2	59.3	65.4	66.4	68.7	70.7	77.1

*Life tables for periods before 1929–1931 relate to those states that required death registration.

Demographers make an important distinction between **life span** and life expectation. A life span of "four score years and ten" has been well known from time immemorial. Although inexact, life span is the age that persons are likely to reach, given optimum conditions. Life span could be defined as that age reached by the longest-lived 0.1% of the population, which would currently be quite close to 100 years (Shyrock and Siegel, 1973). Life expectation has increased not so much by virtue of a longer life span as by reduction of infant mortality and thus an increase in the average years of life.

16.3 FOLLOW-UP LIFE TABLES

"How long do I have?" is often the first question a patient asks the physician when told that he or she is suffering from a life-threatening chronic disease. The follow-up life table (or modified life table) provides a basis for answering this difficult question. Chronic-disease registries, especially cancer registries, make regular use of the follow-up table to track the survival of patients over time. In this connection, life tables are often used to evaluate the relative effectiveness of alternative modes of treatment by computing the probability of survival of patients treated using each mode.

The follow-up table is particularly useful because it utilizes the experience of each person for the entire time he or she was in the study; that is, the method considers the period of exposure in terms of person-years or other appropriate units.

Life tables may be calculated for a cohort in which all the members start the study at the same time or for one in which the members are admitted to the study at different times over a period of years. In either case, the data are handled identically, provided that (1) death rates do not change materially over time and (2) exposure to the disease prior to treatment is not increasing with time.

Construction of a Follow-Up Life Table

To construct a follow-up life table, you need to know the period of follow-up after some event, such as a heart attack, diagnosis of cancer, or surgery. To ensure accuracy, you need well-defined starting and end points. Given a known period of observation for each patient, you can then tally how many survive, how many die, and how many are lost to follow-up during the first and subsequent years of the study.

The construction of such a table is illustrated in Table 16.3 with data from a cancer follow-up study. A total of 356 (l_0) patients began the study. During the first year of follow-up, 60 (d_0) patients died. Thus, the probability of surviving the first year was $\hat{p}_1 = (356 - 60)/356 = .8315$. During the second year, of the 296 patients remaining, 47 died; 1 was lost to follow-up. By convention, it is assumed that a person who is lost to follow-up (f_x) or who withdraws from the study alive (w_x) lives through half the interval. Consequently, the effective number exposed to the risk of dying is here estimated as $l'_x = 296 - .5 = 295.5$. The probability of surviving the second year of follow-up is then estimated as

$$\hat{p}_2 = \frac{l'_2 - d_2}{l'_2} = \frac{295.5 - 47}{295.5} = .8409 \tag{16.7}$$

The probabilities of surviving successive years are computed similarly. The equation for the effective number exposed to the risk of dying may be summarized as

$$l'_x = l_x - .5(w_x + f_x) \tag{16.8}$$

Having found the probabilities of survival for each individual year, we can now easily compute the probability of surviving several years. For example, the probability of surviving the first 2 years is $P_{02} = (p_1)(p_2)$, and the probability of surviving the first 5 years is $P_{05} = (p_1)(p_2)(p_3)(p_4)(p_5)$.

The **5-year survival rate** is commonly used in cancer research as a measure of a treatment's effectiveness. Differences between survival rates of two groups are tested by means of a t test, which implies the need to know standard errors. For a detailed discussion of two different methods of preparing a life table, see Kuzma (1967).

Some special problems in calculating survival rates occur when persons are lost to follow-up or withdraw alive (i.e., persons are known to be alive at the beginning of the time interval, but their fate is unknown at the end). Numerous suggestions have been offered on how to handle these problems. For instance, if the proportion of such cases is small, the assumption is made that each case was lost or withdrew at the middle of the last known interval. Thus, the convention is that such cases are considered to be alive for half of the last interval during which they were observed.

Table 16.3 Follow-Up Life Table: Classification of Cases and Survival Rates of Cancer Patients

Interval in Years x to $(x+1)$	Alive at Beginning of Interval l_x	Died During Interval d_x	Lost to Follow-Up f_x	Withdrawn Alive w_x	Effective No. Exposed to Risk of Dying l'_x	Proportion Dying $\hat{q}_x$	Proportion Surviving $\hat{p}_x$	Survival Rate P_{0x}
0-1	356	60	0	0	356	0.1685	.8315	.8315
1-2	296	47	1	0	295.5	0.1591	.8408	.6992
2-3	248	29	5	0	245.5	0.1181	.8818	.6166
3-4	214	24	20	25	191.5	0.1253	.8746	.5393
4-5	145	11	13	50	113.5	0.0969	.9032	.4871
5-6	71	4	0	57	42.5	0.0941	.9057	.4412

Clinical trials frequently utilize life tables to estimate survival rates. It is often necessary to determine whether there is a statistically significant difference between P'_{0x}, the xth-year survival rate of a treatment group, and P_{0x}, the xth-year survival rate of a control group. The equation used is

$$Z = \frac{P'_{0x} - P_{0x}}{\sqrt{SE(P'_{0x})^2 + SE(P_{0x})^2}} \tag{16.9}$$

where $SE(P'_{0x})$ and $SE(P_{0x})$ are standard errors for the two groups and Z is the normal score.

A rigorous justification for the standard-error equation is beyond the scope of this book. However, an approximation suggested by M. Greenwood, as described in Cutler and Ederer (1958), is as follows:

$$SE(P_{0x}) = P_{0x} \sqrt{\sum \frac{d_x}{(l_x - \frac{1}{2} w_x)(l_x - d_x - \frac{1}{2} w_x)}} \tag{16.10}$$

where x is summed from $x = 0$ to $x = n$, that is, through the interval prior to that containing P_{0x}.

We illustrate the computation of the standard error of P_{05} using the data from Table 16.3:

$$SE(P_{05}) = .4412 \sqrt{\frac{60}{(356)(296)} + \frac{47}{(296)(249)} + \frac{29}{(248)(215)} + \frac{24}{(214)(189.5)} + \frac{11}{(145)(109)}}$$

$$= .4412 \sqrt{.0005693 + .0006376 + .0005438 + .0005918 + .0006959}$$

$$= .4412 \sqrt{.0030384} = .4412(.055122)$$

$$= .02432$$

Using the value of the standard error, it is now possible to compute the Z statistic.

◆ CONCLUSION

Life tables provide excellent means for measuring mortality and longevity. The current life table shows the effects of age-specific death rates on a group. From this table, measures of mortality and life expectation can be computed. Whereas the current life table presents a hypothetical picture of the effects of present mortality rates, the cohort life table is an actual historical record of the mortality of a group followed through life. The follow-up life table considers the experiences of persons from event to event during the period of a study.

◆ VOCABULARY LIST

abridged life table	current life table	life table
age interval	5-year survival rate	median age at death
cohort	follow-up life table	person-years
cohort life table	(modified life table)	stationary population
(generation life table)	life expectation	
complete life table	life span	

◆ EXERCISES

16.1 Table 16.4 is an incomplete abridged life table for the U.S. population (1980). Complete the table by filling in the blanks.

16.2 A distinguished citizen is celebrating his 75th birthday. Use Table 16.1 to compute the probability that he will live to celebrate his 80th.

In Exercises 16.3–16.9, use your completed life table from Exercise 16.1.

16.3 Calculate the probability at birth of living to be 80.

16.4 Compute the following proportions:
   a. all persons dying between birth and the first birthday
   b. all persons dying between birth and the fifth birthday
   c. babies born alive dying between birth and the fifth birthday

16.5 Find the proportion of
   a. all persons dying between the ages of 35 and 45
   b. 35-year-olds dying between the ages of 35 and 45

16.6 What is the probability that a person age 20 will survive until age 65?

16.7 Find the expectation of life at birth, at 1 year, at 35 years, and at 75 years of age.

16.8 Find the proportion of 70-year-olds dying between the ages of 70 and 75. Compare this figure with that found in Exercise 16.4c, and explain the difference.

16.9 Why are the results of (b) and (c) of Exercise 16.4 the same and the results of (a) and (b) of Exercise 16.5 different?

Table 16.4 Abridged Life Table for the Total U.S. Population, 1980

| Age Interval | Proportion Dying | | | Of 100,000 Born Alive | | Person-Years Lived | | Average Remaining Lifetime |
| | Uncorrected | Correction Term | Corrected | | | | | |
Period of Life Between Two Exact Ages Stated x to $(x + n)$	Average Annual Age-Specific Death Rate $_n m_x$	Fraction of Last Age Interval Lived $_n a_x$	Proportion Dying During Age Interval $_n \hat{q}_x$	Number Living at Beginning of Age Interval l_x	Number Dying During Age Interval $_n d_x$	In the Age Interval $_n L_x$	In This and All Subsequent Age Intervals T_x	Average Number of Years of Life Remaining at Beginning of Age Interval $\hat{e}_x$
<1	.0127445	.10	.0126000	100,000	1,260	98,866	7,361,560	73.62
2–4	.0006510	.39	.0025999	98,740	257	394,334	7,262,690	73.55
5–9	.0003403	.46	.0016999	98,483	167	491,964	6,868,360	69.74
10–14	.0003002	.56	.0015000	98,316	147	491,255	6,376,390	64.86
15–19	.0010222	.57	.0050998	98,168	501	489,766	5,885,140	59.95
20–24	.0013647	.49	.0067998	97,668	664	486,645	5,395,370	55.24
25–29	.0013646	.50	.0067998	97,004	660	483,369	4,908,730	50.60
30–34	.0014651	.52	.0072998	96,344	703	480,032	4,425,360	45.93
35–39	.0017873	.54	.0088999	95,641	851	476,246	3,945,330	41.25
40–44	.0028181	.54	.0139998	94,790	1,327	470,896	3,469,080	36.60
45–49	.0045062	.54	.0222999	93,463	2,084	462,519	2,998,180	32.08
50–54	.0072412	.53	.0356002	91,378	3,253	449,247	2,535,660	27.75
55–59	.0111928	.52	.0545000	88,125	4,803	429,099	2,086,420	23.68
60–64	.0169420	.52	.0814002	83,322	6,782	400,334	1,657,320	19.89
65–69	.0246352	.52	.1163000	76,540	8,902	361,336	1,256,980	16.42
70–74	.0363293	.51	.1668000	—	—	—	—	—
75–79	.0608562	.51	.2648000	—	—	—	—	—
80–84	.0894622	.48	.3629000	—	—	—	—	—
85+	.1536440	—	1.0000000	26,397	26,397	171,806	171,806	6.51

17

The Health Survey and the Research Report

CHAPTER OUTLINE

17.1 **Planning a Health Survey**
Presents an outline for a survey with a brief discussion of the steps involved

17.2 **Evaluating a Research Report**
Lists and discusses steps for evaluating a medical report

✔ LEARNING OBJECTIVES

After studying this chapter, you should be able to
1. Prepare an outline for a health survey
2. Critically evaluate a medical report

17.1 PLANNING A HEALTH SURVEY

So far in this book, we have discussed statistical topics generally covered by most introductory statistics textbooks. In this chapter, we consider the survey, one of two research tools that are indispensable to persons who deal with data and statistics. We also discuss the second tool, the evaluation of research articles. The coverage of both topics is all too brief—each could itself be the subject of a good-size book.

Health surveys are conducted for a number of reasons, but most often they are undertaken to determine the health needs of a community. Subjects of a health survey are members of the general public, all of whom are, to some degree, users of health services. In the same sense that people consume gasoline, stockings, and corn flakes, they are regarded as **consumers** of health services.

What constitutes a health survey? Many things. For instance, health surveys may entail inquiries into the consumer's knowledge, attitudes, and practices; utilization of health services; disease experience in the past; and satisfaction (or dissatisfaction) with health service delivery. Or they may involve research directed ultimately toward elucidating the etiology of a disease or evaluation of a program's success. All these points are generally focused in one direction: toward aiding the decision-making process of health service (or public health) managers.

The goal of most researchers is to conduct a survey that clearly and accurately describes some health-related phenomenon. But caution is advised; a health survey can be a tricky business. Unless it follows a prescribed stepwise procedure (like the one we outline here), a survey could produce faulty information leading to unfortunate (possibly grave) consequences. An example of a report with an intriguing finding—that left-handed people have a shortened life expectancy—was reported in the *New England Journal of Medicine*. With time, we will learn how well it stands up to careful scientific scrutiny.

Immediately after the following outline, we will describe each step briefly.

*Outline for Planning a Health Survey**

1. Make a written statement of the purpose of the survey.
2. Write out the objectives and hypotheses.
3. Specify the target population.
4. List the variables to be measured.
5. Review existing pertinent data.
6. Outline the methods of data collection.

---

*Credit for this outline goes to Dr. David Abbey, a survey statistician who developed it for a course on Health Survey Methods.

7. Establish the time frame.
8. Design the questionnaire.
9. Pretest the questionnaire.
10. Obtain informed consent.
11. Select subjects for the sample.
12. Collect the data.
13. Edit, code, and enter the data on a computer, and verify the data entry.
14. Analyze the data.
15. Report the findings.

Step 1: Make a Written Statement of the Purpose

The purpose of your survey should be well thought out, carefully defined, and clearly stated in two or three sentences. This step will aid your own thinking and will help you in carrying out the subsequent steps. Without it, a survey is doomed to failure.

Step 2: Formulate Objectives and Hypotheses

A descriptive survey seeks to estimate one or more characteristics of a population. That, quite simply, is its specific objective. An analytical survey seeks to examine relationships among some specified characteristics. To carry it out, you need to define the hypotheses to be tested.

Step 3: Specify the Target Population

The **target population** is that group of people from whom inferences are to be drawn. This population may well be restricted to one from which you can feasibly draw a sample. To test your research hypothesis, it is essential that you estimate certain key characteristics of individual members of the target population. In statistical sampling, an individual member of a population is often referred to as an **element.** But in health surveys, the element may be a person, a mother–child pair, or some logical group of persons such as a household. Measurements are taken on the element. The population can be defined as the collection of all elements.

Step 4: List the Variables

Once your target population is defined and elements are identified, list the variables that are to be assessed on each element. For example, a target population might be all the students enrolled in a college course who successfully stopped smoking during the past 12 months. The element would be each member of the class possessing that characteristic; variables measured might be age, sex, amount of smoking, and number of years of smoking before quitting.

There is an endless list of potential variables that you may wish to measure. In general, you should focus on personal characteristics of individual members of the target population. Such characteristics could be weight, blood pressure, age, race, and smoking status. The variables considered should be potentially measurable on each person. In a health survey, you usually want to collect information both on outcome variables and on concomitant variables. The latter are those covariables that, although themselves uncontrollable, may well affect the outcome. All variables should be clearly defined during the planning stages.

Step 5: Review Existing Data

It is important to review current literature on the topic being surveyed so that you can determine the state of the art, current hypotheses, those variables regarded as pertinent, and the likely success of your chosen strategy. It is often advisable to use standardized questions for which ample documentation of validity and reliability exists. And by using the wording of standardized questions, you will be able to compare your results with those of well-known studies.

Step 6: Decide How to Collect Data

In collecting data, there are numerous methods to choose from, each of which has certain advantages and disadvantages. The **person-to-person interview** is often regarded as the industry standard because of the high response rate. The interviewer, being at the scene, can make additional observations regarding subtle aspects of the interviewee's behavior; these may be used to help validate the interview. But this approach is costly; an alternative is the **telephone interview** (using random-digit dialing), which can be performed at approximately half the cost and produce essentially similar results. But telephoning introduces a new potential bias in that it excludes approximately 10% of households—those that do not have a telephone or that have an unlisted number. Still another approach is the **mailed questionnaire.** This costs less than person-to-person or telephone interviews and may be done anonymously. Mailed questionnaires rule out the problem of **interviewer bias;** respondents are less likely to be defensive about answering socially sensitive questions. But this approach does have a serious drawback: poor response rates. It usually requires at least two follow-up mailings to obtain a satisfactory number of responses. Other problems include uncertainty as to whether the intended targets actually completed the questionnaire, plus nagging doubts as to whether the respondents are truly representative of the target population.

Step 7: Establish the Time Frame

It is necessary to establish a time frame to realistically schedule survey events. The schedule should not be so tight as to jeopardize succeeding steps in case of a delay in preceding events. Plan backup procedures and personnel to avoid major delays. It is a good idea to have some trained interviewers on call.

Step 8: Design the Questionnaire

Questions need to be carefully worded so as not to confuse respondents or arouse extraneous attitudes. The questions should provide a clear understanding of the information sought. Be precise; avoid ambiguity and wording that might be perceived to elicit a specific response. Questions may be open-ended, multiple choice, completion, or a variation of these. You should studiously avoid overly complex questions. The key principles to keep in mind while constructing a questionnaire are that it should (1) be easy for respondents to read, understand, and answer; (2) motivate respondents to answer; (3) be designed for efficient data processing; (4) have a well-designed, professional appearance; and (5) be designed to minimize missing data.

Step 9: Pretest the Questionnaire

It is never possible to anticipate all the potential problems that may occur when you administer a questionnaire. So it is important to **pretest** it. A pretest will identify questions that respondents tend to misinterpret, omit, or answer inappropriately. It should be done on a handful of individuals similar to, but not included in, the target population and should utilize the same methodology that will be used in the actual survey.

Step 10: Obtain Informed Consent

Prior to conducting a research study, it is essential that you obtain institutional approval to do research using human subjects. Included in this approval process is the necessity of obtaining **informed consent.** Obtaining informed consent can sometimes be a difficult process, especially if minors are involved. Ross, Sundberg, and Flint (1999) identified 20 procedures that have proved effective in boosting response rates while providing a realistic level of informed consent for school-based studies.

1. Accommodate local prevailing practices in obtaining parental permission and student assent to participate.
2. Anticipate differences in how various cultural groups will interpret the consent process, and tailor processes accordingly.
3. Use multiple, culturally appropriate communication channels to broadcast advance publicity about the project and create a favorable climate of acceptance.
4. Identify as project spokesperson a popular staff member who can solidify support and cooperation from other staff members and students.
5. Develop background materials for use in explaining the importance of the project, anticipated uses of the data, local relevance, and project responsibilities for school personnel, especially those who will be responsible for distributing parental permission forms and encouraging student cooperation.

6. Prepare teachers and other school staff for their role in promoting the survey and in distributing and collecting parental permission forms.

7. Develop a parental permission form at a reading level appropriate to the intended readers.

8. Anticipate and provide answers to commonly asked questions on the reverse side of the parental permission form.

9. Provide participating schools with a sample parental permission form that they can adapt, as needed, to local circumstances and cultural requirements, and put on their local letterhead.

10. Identify major languages, other than English, spoken by the students' families.

11. Select a supportive classroom environment, such as homeroom, a health-related course, or classes taught by a sympathetic teacher, as the staging area for distribution of parental permission forms while maintaining the integrity of the sampling procedures.

12. Develop a brief script that teachers can use when they distribute parental permission forms.

13. Provide teachers with a system for maintaining accurate records of distribution, follow-up, and return of parental permission forms.

14. Provide ready access to the questionnaire and to members of the research team to respond to questions from parents.

15. Assess the effectiveness of established means for getting information home to parents.

16. Provide reminders to parents who do not return parental permission slips during a specified time period, including written reminder slips, telephone follow-up, the resending of forms by mail, and use of culturally appropriate networks.

17. Provide scripts for survey administration to ensure that the survey process is controlled and that survey administrators do not inadvertently make remarks that could affect participation in other classes.

18. While providing alternative activities for nonparticipants, ensure that they are not so attractive as to invite students to decline to participate or not bring home/back parental permission forms.

19. Provide makeup opportunities for students who originally did not have a signed parental permission form, were absent on the scheduled date of survey administration, or initially refused but subsequently decided to participate.

20. Provide a range of small but meaningful incentives for school, teacher, and student participation, including both intrinsic and extrinsic incentives.

For details about any of these steps, you may want to refer to the article by Ross, Sundberg, and Flint (1999).

Step 11: Select the Sample

You should select the sample in such a way that valid statistical inferences can be drawn regarding the target population. You wish to obtain a representative sample, one that minimizes **sampling bias** and is designed for economy in operation. A variety of sampling designs are available: simple random, systematic random, stratified random, and multistage. To determine the most appropriate design for a complex survey, consult a survey statistician.

Step 12: Collect the Data

With a completed and pretested questionnaire, you are ready for data collection. This step requires careful planning and supervision to ensure high-quality data. You want to attain the following objectives: (1) maximize the response rate by minimizing nonresponses, (2) keep track of the nonrespondents, (3) obtain some information on nonrespondents, (4) avoid duplication, (5) avoid failing to contact part of the sample, (6) protect confidentiality of the data, (7) provide anonymity, and (8) maintain a cooperative spirit in the target population. Interviewers should be well trained and coached with regard to how to approach respondents, how to conduct the interview, how to handle various answers, and how to inform respondents about what is expected of them during the interview.

Step 13: Edit and Code the Data

Editing of data is analogous to editing newspaper copy. The editor's job is to make sure that the text meets certain standards and that errors are corrected. The editor checks for missing data, for inconsistencies, and for problems that can be remedied. Editing of data should be done as soon as possible after data collection.

To permit computerized analysis of data, it is essential that the variables be reduced to a form in which a numerical value can be assigned to each possible choice. This process is referred to as **coding.** It is carried out simultaneously with editing. Coding may be done either by use of an ad hoc coding system specifically developed for your own database or by use of a standard coding system. A well-accepted technique for the coding of diseases or causes of death is the International Classification of Diseases (World Health Organization, 1977). This flexible system can provide either a broad categorization of disease groups or quite detailed coding of specific entities. For years, the standard procedure was to use punch cards for computer entry. The current method of choice is to enter data directly via an interactive terminal. In this way, a validation program is able to inform you immediately about possibly invalid data. To maintain accuracy, it is essential that, by program or otherwise, the data entry be verified.

Step 14: Analyze the Data

After data have been collected, edited, coded, and key-entered, they are almost ready for analysis. But a preliminary step is needed: some advance data analysis to ferret out possible outliers, look at the distribution of the various variables, provide an item analysis for the variables of special interest, and assess the amount of missing data. Once this analysis is completed, you are ready to perform the major analysis of data, a task dictated by the specific objectives of the survey.

Step 15: Report the Findings

The report should begin with background information that provides a rationale for the study. It should indicate the specific objectives that the survey seeks to accomplish. A "methods" section should describe the target population, the test instruments, and the sampling design. The "results" section should discuss the findings and possible future implications.

17.2   EVALUATING A RESEARCH REPORT

It is quite unlikely that all the users of this book will become regular producers of research literature. But, almost without exception, everyone will be a consumer of such literature. Research literature comes in many forms: books, journal articles, monographs, administrative documents, program evaluations, and the like.

A valuable skill to develop is the ability to critically read and evaluate research literature. Without this ability, you will not be able to differentiate between a pedestrian report and one of quality. A top-grade report stands unshaken under the critical process of **peer review.** In a sense, every user of literature, by doing a critical analysis, is carrying peer review to its ultimate end.

It is a well-known, if regrettable, fact that some research literature is of poor quality. After wading through a mire of jargon, inconsistencies, poor grammar, and qualifications, and some muddy logic, the user is expected to draw a brilliantly clear scientific conclusion. This problem is chronic in much scientific writing. A full discussion is well beyond the scope of this book. A parallel problem exists when dealing with the quantitative aspects of a report. We hope that by reading this section you will gain at least a glimmer of insight into how to be critical, analytical, and discriminating in your use of research literature.

Researchers, being human, must exercise constant vigilance to avoid bias while working toward a prized objective. As mentioned briefly in Chapter 1, bias may well creep in—usually inadvertently, perhaps subconsciously, and often as a consequence of some aspect of the research design. Although the best researchers are carefully trained in its avoidance, bias assumes so many forms that it is difficult to recognize and avoid them all. By examining a few of these, you should be more capable of effectively evaluating a research report. For a comprehensive catalog of research bias, see Sackett (1979).

Observer Bias

When the observer (or interviewer) is fully aware that the person being interviewed has a certain disease, the observer may subconsciously attribute certain characteristics to the subject. The result of this **observer bias** is that those characteristics are more likely to be recorded for cases than for controls. The solution of choice is to "blind" the observer as to whether the subject is a case or a control.

Sampling Bias

Bias may enter whenever samples are chosen in a nonrandom fashion. **Convenience sampling** (choosing only subjects who are easy to find) leads almost invariably to biased results. **Systematic sampling** (choosing every nth person from a list) carries the potential of subtle error, especially if the list has some cyclical pattern. Telephone and household sampling have their own potentials for bias. What if no one answers the phone or comes to the door? Should the interviewer skip that household? On the contrary. The interviewer should try again (and again), realizing that a household where no one is at home in the daytime is quite different from one where someone is nearly always present.

Selection Bias

Were the cases and the controls drawn from the same population? This question, which sounds simple, has profound implications. **Selection bias** may lead to a false association between a disease and some factor because of different probabilities of selecting persons with and without the disease and with and without the variable of interest. This problem was first quantified by Berkson (1946) and is sometimes called **Berksonian bias** or hospital selection bias.

Response Bias

When participation in a study is voluntary, **response bias** (sometimes called **nonrespondent bias** or **self-selection bias**) is important. Owing to their psychological makeup, internal motivation, concern for their own health, educational background, and many other reasons, persons who choose voluntarily to participate in research studies are known to differ from those who decline to do so. Nevertheless, many important research studies (e.g., the landmark Framingham Heart Study—the Massachusetts study that reported on the dangers to "yo-yo" dieters, who shorten their life expectancy by swinging through cycles of weight loss and gain) depend in part on volunteers. A way to control for response bias is to compare characteristics of volunteer subgroups with those of randomly chosen subgroups.

Dropout Bias

Dropout bias is the mirror image of response bias. In long-term studies, a certain proportion of participants, for reasons of their own, choose to drop out. These persons are likely to differ from those who continue.

Memory Bias

There are several well-known aspects of **memory bias** (also known as **subjective bias**). Memory for recent events is much more accurate than that for long-ago events. Hence, persons interviewed concerning past illnesses tend to report a greater prevalence in the recent past than in the distant past (Stocks, 1944). A perhaps more profound form of memory bias is the tendency of persons with a disease to overemphasize the importance of events they may consider to be predisposing causes (e.g., breast cancer patients who trace their disease to traumatic breast injury).

Participant Bias

Participant bias is an interesting form of bias that derives from the participant's knowledge of being a member of the experimental or control group and his or her perception of the research objectives. For example, a participant in a heart disease intervention study may report and exaggerate minor symptoms actually unrelated to the disease under study.

Lead-Time Bias

Does early detection of chronic disease actually result in improved survival rates, or does it merely provide a longer period between first detection and death? This fascinating question of **lead-time bias** is fully considered in Cole and Morrison (1980).

Keys to a Systematic Approach

Awareness of the potential for bias underlies a critical reading of any research report. But bias is not the only issue to keep in mind. A great deal may be learned by taking a systematic approach to a critique of any research literature. Here are some of the most important questions that should be considered:

1. *Research objectives.* Does the research report clearly state its objectives? Do the conclusions address the same objectives?
2. *Study design.* What type of study was it? Was sample selection random and appropriate to the study design? Were cases and controls comparable and drawn from the same reference group?
3. *Data collection.* Were criteria for diagnosis precisely defined? Were end points (or outcome criteria) clearly stated? Were research instruments (whether mechanical or electronic devices, or printed questionnaires) standardized? Can the study be independently replicated?
4. *Discussion of results.* Are results presented clearly and quantitatively? Do tables and figures agree with the text? Are various tables consistent with one another?

5. *Data analysis.* Does the report address the statistical significance of its results? If not, are you able to draw a reasonable inference of significance (or nonsignificance) from the data as presented? Were the statistical tests appropriate to the data? Does the report discuss alternative explanations for what might be spurious statistical significance?

6. *Conclusions.* Are the findings justified by the data? Do the findings relate appropriately to the research objectives originally set forth?

◆ CONCLUSION

Two fundamental research tools—the health survey and the research report—are inseparable parts of the same process: that of aiding scientists, managers, and public officials in their decision making. Health surveys need careful planning; a systematic, stepwise procedure is the best means of avoiding error in their use. Research reports are read by nearly everyone in the health sciences. It is important to develop a critical eye in order to distinguish between ordinary reports and those of quality. Especially when dealing with human populations, the research is susceptible to many sources of bias. An understanding of the origins of bias, and of the means to avoid bias in whatever form, helps you assess the quality of any research report.

◆ VOCABULARY LIST

coding	mailed questionnaire	response bias
consumer	memory bias	(nonrespondent bias;
convenience sampling	(subjective bias)	self-selection bias)
dropout bias	observer bias	sampling bias
editing	participant bias	selection bias
element	peer review	(Berksonian bias)
informed consent	person-to-person	systematic sampling
interviewer bias	interview	target population
lead-time bias	pretest	telephone interview

◆ EXERCISES

17.1   Prepare an outline for a health survey on a subject of special interest to you.

17.2   Locate a completed health survey. Is it constructed in keeping with the guidelines of this chapter? In what ways is it imperfectly planned? What would you do to improve it?

17.3   Choose a scientific article that reports on research in your field. Subject it to the evaluation process suggested in this chapter.

17.4   Using the survey of Exercise 17.2, the article for Exercise 17.3, or any health survey report, discuss how the authors handled potential bias. What steps did they take to minimize it? What types of bias may have crept in? How could these have been avoided?

◆ EPILOGUE

We hope that the techniques and methods presented in this book will provide you with some useful tools that you can use to separate fact from fiction, to determine the significance of experimental results, and, ultimately, to assist your search for truth. The road to truth is seldom an easy one, but a great deal of satisfaction can be attained while traveling it. This is particularly true when you are able to establish the significance of a new finding, to learn that a commonly accepted approach is not really valid, or to gain the kind of insight that begins to shed new light on the process of discovery. The journey may be rough, but it is surely worthwhile. Godspeed!

Appendix A Binomial Probability Table

| | | | | | | | | | p | | | | |
n	x	.01	.05	.10	.15	.20	.25	.30	1/3	.35	.40	.45	.50
1	0	.9900	.9500	.9000	.8500	.8000	.7500	.7000	.6667	.6500	.6000	.5500	.5000
	1	.0100	.0500	.1000	.1500	.2000	.2500	.3000	.3333	.3500	.4000	.4500	.5000
2	0	.9801	.9025	.8100	.7225	.6400	.5625	.4900	.4444	.4225	.3600	.3025	.2500
	1	.0198	.0950	.1800	.2550	.3200	.3750	.4200	.4444	.4550	.4800	.4950	.5000
	2	.0001	.0025	.0100	.0225	.0400	.0625	.0900	.1111	.1225	.1600	.2025	.2500
3	0	.9703	.8574	.7290	.6141	.5120	.4219	.3430	.2963	.2746	.2160	.1664	.1250
	1	.0294	.1354	.2430	.3251	.3840	.4219	.4410	.4444	.4436	.4320	.4084	.3750
	2	.0003	.0071	.0270	.0574	.0960	.1406	.1890	.2222	.2389	.2880	.3341	.3750
	3	.0000	.0001	.0010	.0034	.0080	.0156	.0270	.0370	.0429	.0640	.0911	.1250
4	0	.9606	.8145	.6561	.5220	.4096	.3164	.2401	.1975	.1785	.1296	.0915	.0625
	1	.0388	.1715	.2916	.3685	.4096	.4219	.4116	.3951	.3845	.3456	.2995	.2500
	2	.0006	.0135	.0486	.0975	.1536	.2109	.2646	.2963	.3105	.3456	.3675	.3750
	3	.0000	.0005	.0036	.0115	.0256	.0469	.0756	.0988	.1115	.1536	.2005	.2500
	4	.0000	.0000	.0001	.0005	.0016	.0039	.0081	.0123	.0150	.0256	.0410	.0625
5	0	.9510	.7738	.5905	.4437	.3277	.2373	.1681	.1317	.1160	.0778	.0503	.0312
	1	.0480	.2036	.3280	.3915	.4096	.3955	.3601	.3292	.3124	.2592	.2059	.1563
	2	.0010	.0214	.0729	.1382	.2048	.2637	.3087	.3292	.3364	.3456	.3369	.3125
	3	.0000	.0012	.0081	.0244	.0512	.0879	.1323	.1646	.1812	.2304	.2757	.3125
	4	.0000	.0000	.0005	.0021	.0064	.0146	.0284	.0412	.0487	.0768	.1127	.1563
	5	.0000	.0000	.0000	.0001	.0003	.0010	.0024	.0041	.0053	.0102	.0185	.0312
6	0	.9415	.7351	.5314	.3771	.2621	.1780	.1176	.0878	.0754	.0467	.0277	.0156
	1	.0570	.2321	.3543	.3994	.3932	.3559	.3026	.2634	.2437	.1866	.1359	.0938
	2	.0015	.0306	.0984	.1762	.2458	.2967	.3241	.3292	.3280	.3110	.2779	.2344
	3	.0000	.0021	.0146	.0414	.0819	.1318	.1852	.2195	.2355	.2765	.3032	.3125
	4	.0000	.0001	.0012	.0055	.0154	.0330	.0596	.0823	.0951	.1382	.1861	.2344
	5	.0000	.0000	.0001	.0004	.0015	.0044	.0102	.0165	.0205	.0369	.0609	.0938
	6	.0000	.0000	.0000	.0000	.0001	.0002	.0007	.0014	.0018	.0041	.0083	.0156

(Continued)

SOURCE: Reprinted with permission from *Handbook of Tables for Probability and Statistics*, ed. William H. Beyer (Boca Raton, Fla.: CRC Press, 1966). Copyright © 1966 by CRC Press, Inc., Boca Raton, Fla.

n	x	.01	.05	.10	.15	.20	.25	.30	1/3	.35	.40	.45	.50
7	0	.9321	.6983	.4783	.3206	.2097	.1335	.0824	.0585	.0490	.0280	.0152	.0078
	1	.0659	.2573	.3720	.3960	.3670	.3114	.2470	.2048	.1848	.1306	.0872	.0547
	2	.0020	.0406	.1240	.2096	.2753	.3115	.3177	.3073	.2985	.2613	.2140	.1641
	3	.0000	.0036	.0230	.0617	.1147	.1730	.2269	.2561	.2679	.2903	.2919	.2734
	4	.0000	.0002	.0025	.0109	.0286	.0577	.0972	.1280	.1442	.1935	.2388	.2734
	5	.0000	.0000	.0002	.0011	.0043	.0116	.0250	.0384	.0466	.0775	.1172	.1641
	6	.0000	.0000	.0000	.0001	.0004	.0012	.0036	.0064	.0084	.0172	.0320	.0547
	7	.0000	.0000	.0000	.0000	.0000	.0001	.0002	.0005	.0006	.0016	.0037	.0078
8	0	.9227	.6634	.4305	.2725	.1678	.1001	.0576	.0390	.0319	.0168	.0084	.0039
	1	.0746	.2794	.3826	.3847	.3355	.2670	.1977	.1561	.1372	.0896	.0548	.0313
	2	.0026	.0514	.1488	.2376	.2936	.3114	.2965	.2731	.2587	.2090	.1570	.1093
	3	.0001	.0054	.0331	.0838	.1468	.2077	.2541	.2731	.2786	.2787	.2569	.2188
	4	.0000	.0004	.0046	.0185	.0459	.0865	.1361	.1707	.1875	.2322	.2626	.2734
	5	.0000	.0000	.0004	.0027	.0092	.0231	.0467	.0683	.0808	.1239	.1718	.2188
	6	.0000	.0000	.0000	.0002	.0011	.0038	.0100	.0171	.0217	.0413	.0704	.1093
	7	.0000	.0000	.0000	.0000	.0001	.0004	.0012	.0024	.0034	.0078	.0164	.0313
	8	.0000	.0000	.0000	.0000	.0000	.0000	.0001	.0002	.0002	.0007	.0017	.0039
9	0	.9135	.6302	.3874	.2316	.1342	.0751	.0404	.0260	.0207	.0101	.0046	.0020
	1	.0831	.2986	.3874	.3678	.3020	.2252	.1556	.1171	.1004	.0604	.0339	.0175
	2	.0033	.0628	.1722	.2597	.3020	.3004	.2668	.2341	.2162	.1613	.1110	.0703
	3	.0001	.0078	.0447	.1070	.1762	.2336	.2669	.2731	.2716	.2508	.2119	.1641
	4	.0000	.0006	.0074	.0283	.0660	.1168	.1715	.2048	.2194	.2508	.2600	.2461
	5	.0000	.0000	.0008	.0050	.0165	.0389	.0735	.1024	.1181	.1672	.2128	.2461
	6	.0000	.0000	.0001	.0006	.0028	.0087	.0210	.0341	.0424	.0744	.1160	.1641
	7	.0000	.0000	.0000	.0000	.0003	.0012	.0039	.0073	.0098	.0212	.0407	.0703
	8	.0000	.0000	.0000	.0000	.0000	.0001	.0004	.0009	.0013	.0035	.0083	.0175
	9	.0000	.0000	.0000	.0000	.0000	.0000	.0000	.0001	.0001	.0003	.0008	.0020
10	0	.9044	.5987	.3487	.1969	.1074	.0563	.0282	.0173	.0135	.0060	.0025	.0010
	1	.0913	.3152	.3874	.3474	.2684	.1877	.1211	.0867	.0725	.0404	.0208	.0097
	2	.0042	.0746	.1937	.2759	.3020	.2816	.2335	.1951	.1756	.1209	.0763	.0440
	3	.0001	.0105	.0574	.1298	.2013	.2503	.2668	.2601	.2522	.2150	.1664	.1172
	4	.0000	.0009	.0112	.0401	.0881	.1460	.2001	.2276	.2377	.2508	.2384	.2051
	5	.0000	.0001	.0015	.0085	.0264	.0584	.1030	.1366	.1536	.2007	.2340	.2460
	6	.0000	.0000	.0001	.0013	.0055	.0162	.0367	.0569	.0689	.1114	.1596	.2051
	7			.0000	.0001	.0008	.0031	.0090	.0163	.0212	.0425	.0746	.1172
	8				.0000	.0001	.0004	.0015	.0030	.0043	.0106	.0229	.0440
	9				.0000	.0000	.0000	.0001	.0003	.0005	.0016	.0042	.0097
	10	.0000	.0000	.0000	.0000	.0000	.0000	.0000	.0000	.0000	.0001	.0003	.0010
11	0	.8953	.5688	.3138	.1673	.0859	.0422	.0198	.0116	.0088	.0036	.0014	.0005
	1	.0995	.3293	.3836	.3249	.2362	.1549	.0932	.0636	.0518	.0266	.0125	.0054
	2	.0050	.0867	.2130	.2866	.2953	.2581	.1998	.1590	.1395	.0887	.0513	.0268
	3	.0002	.0136	.0711	.1518	.2215	.2581	.2568	.2384	.2255	.1774	.1259	.0806
	4	.0000	.0015	.0157	.0535	.1107	.1721	.2201	.2384	.2427	.2365	.2060	.1611
	5		.0001	.0025	.0132	.0387	.0803	.1321	.1669	.1830	.2207	.2360	.2256
	6		.0000	.0003	.0024	.0097	.0267	.0566	.0835	.0986	.1471	.1931	.2256
	7			.0000	.0003	.0018	.0064	.0173	.0298	.0379	.0701	.1128	.1611
	8				.0000	.0002	.0011	.0037	.0075	.0102	.0234	.0462	.0806
	9					.0000	.0001	.0006	.0012	.0018	.0052	.0126	.0268
	10						.0000	.0000	.0001	.0002	.0007	.0020	.0054
	11	.0000	.0000	.0000	.0000	.0000	.0000	.0000	.0000	.0000	.0000	.0002	.0005

(Continued)

n	x	.01	.05	.10	.15	.20	.25	.30	1/3	.35	.40	.45	.50
12	0	.8864	.5404	.2824	.1422	.0687	.0317	.0138	.0077	.0057	.0022	.0008	.0002
	1	.1074	.3412	.3766	.3013	.2062	.1267	.0712	.0462	.0367	.0174	.0075	.0030
	2	.0060	.0988	.2301	.2923	.2834	.2323	.1678	.1272	.1089	.0638	.0338	.0161
	3	.0002	.0174	.0853	.1720	.2363	.2581	.2397	.2120	.1954	.1419	.0924	.0537
	4	.0000	.0020	.0213	.0683	.1328	.1936	.2312	.2384	.2366	.2129	.1700	.1208
	5		.0002	.0038	.0193	.0532	.1032	.1585	.1908	.2040	.2270	.2225	.1934
	6		.0000	.0004	.0039	.0155	.0401	.0792	.1113	.1281	.1766	.2124	.2256
	7			.0001	.0006	.0033	.0115	.0291	.0477	.0591	.1009	.1489	.1934
	8			.0000	.0001	.0005	.0024	.0078	.0149	.0199	.0420	.0761	.1208
	9				.0000	.0001	.0004	.0015	.0033	.0048	.0125	.0277	.0537
	10					.0000	.0000	.0002	.0005	.0007	.0025	.0068	.0161
	11						.0000	.0000	.0000	.0001	.0003	.0010	.0030
	12	.0000	.0000	.0000	.0000	.0000	.0000	.0000	.0000	.0000	.0000	.0001	.0002
15	0	.8601	.4633	.2059	.0874	.0352	.0134	.0047	.0023	.0016	.0005	.0001	.0000
	1	.1301	.3667	.3431	.2312	.1319	.0668	.0306	.0171	.0126	.0047	.0016	.0005
	2	.0092	.1348	.2669	.2856	.2309	.1559	.0915	.0599	.0475	.0219	.0090	.0032
	3	.0004	.0307	.1285	.2185	.2502	.2252	.1701	.1299	.1110	.0634	.0317	.0139
	4	.0000	.0049	.0429	.1156	.1876	.2252	.2186	.1948	.1792	.1268	.0780	.0416
	5		.0005	.0105	.0449	.1031	.1651	.2061	.2143	.2124	.1859	.1404	.0917
	6		.0001	.0019	.0132	.0430	.0918	.1473	.1786	.1905	.2066	.1914	.1527
	7		.0000	.0003	.0030	.0139	.0393	.0811	.1148	.1320	.1771	.2013	.1964
	8			.0000	.0005	.0034	.0131	.0348	.0574	.0710	.1181	.1657	.1964
	9				.0001	.0007	.0034	.0115	.0223	.0298	.0612	.1049	.1527
	10				.0000	.0001	.0007	.0030	.0067	.0096	.0245	.0514	.0917
	11					.0000	.0001	.0006	.0015	.0023	.0074	.0192	.0416
	12						.0000	.0001	.0003	.0004	.0016	.0052	.0139
	13							.0000	.0000	.0001	.0003	.0010	.0032
	14								.0000	.0000	.0000	.0001	.0005
	15	.0000	.0000	.0000	.0000	.0000	.0000	.0000	.0000	.0000	.0000	.0000	.0000
20	0	.8179	.3583	.1216	.0388	.0115	.0032	.0008	.0003	.0002	.0000	.0000	.0000
	1	.1652	.3773	.2701	.1368	.0577	.0211	.0068	.0030	.0019	.0005	.0001	.0000
	2	.0159	.1887	.2852	.2293	.1369	.0670	.0279	.0143	.0100	.0031	.0008	.0002
	3	.0010	.0596	.1901	.2428	.2053	.1339	.0716	.0429	.0323	.0124	.0040	.0011
	4	.0000	.0133	.0898	.1821	.2182	.1896	.1304	.0911	.0738	.0350	.0140	.0046
	5		.0023	.0319	.1029	.1746	.2024	.1789	.1457	.1272	.0746	.0364	.0148
	6		.0003	.0089	.0454	.1091	.1686	.1916	.1821	.1714	.1244	.0746	.0370
	7		.0000	.0020	.0160	.0546	.1124	.1643	.1821	.1844	.1659	.1221	.0739
	8			.0003	.0046	.0221	.0609	.1144	.1480	.1614	.1797	.1623	.1201
	9			.0001	.0011	.0074	.0270	.0653	.0987	.1158	.1597	.1771	.1602
	10			.0000	.0002	.0020	.0100	.0309	.0543	.0686	.1172	.1593	.1762
	11				.0000	.0005	.0030	.0120	.0247	.0336	.0710	.1185	.1602
	12					.0001	.0007	.0038	.0092	.0136	.0355	.0728	.1201
	13					.0000	.0002	.0010	.0028	.0045	.0145	.0366	.0739
	14						.0000	.0003	.0007	.0012	.0049	.0150	.0370
	15							.0000	.0001	.0003	.0013	.0049	.0148
	16								.0000	.0000	.0003	.0012	.0046
	17										.0000	.0003	.0011
	18											.0000	.0002
	19											.0000	.0000
	20	.0000	.0000	.0000	.0000	.0000	.0000	.0000	.0000	.0000	.0000	.0000	.0000

Appendix B Percentiles of the F Distribution

$F_{.95}$ (use with $\alpha = .05$)

N − k df_w	1	2	3	4	df_b 5	6	7	8	9
1	161.40	199.50	215.70	224.60	230.20	234.00	236.80	238.90	240.50
2	18.51	19.00	19.16	19.25	19.30	19.33	19.35	19.37	19.38
3	10.13	9.55	9.28	9.12	9.01	8.94	8.89	8.85	8.81
4	7.71	6.94	6.59	6.39	6.26	6.16	6.09	6.04	6.00
5	6.61	5.79	5.41	5.19	5.05	4.95	4.88	4.82	4.77
6	5.99	5.14	4.76	4.53	4.39	4.28	4.21	4.15	4.10
7	5.59	4.74	4.35	4.12	3.97	3.87	3.79	3.73	3.68
8	5.32	4.46	4.07	3.84	3.69	3.58	3.50	3.44	3.39
9	5.12	4.26	3.86	3.63	3.48	3.37	3.29	3.23	3.18
10	4.96	4.10	3.71	3.48	3.33	3.22	3.14	3.07	3.02
11	4.84	3.98	3.59	3.36	3.20	3.09	3.01	2.95	2.90
12	4.75	3.89	3.49	3.26	3.11	3.00	2.91	2.85	2.80
13	4.67	3.81	3.41	3.18	3.03	2.92	2.83	2.77	2.71
14	4.60	3.74	3.34	3.11	2.96	2.85	2.76	2.70	2.65
15	4.54	3.68	3.29	3.06	2.90	2.79	2.71	2.64	2.59
16	4.49	3.63	3.24	3.01	2.85	2.74	2.66	2.59	2.54
17	4.45	3.59	3.20	2.96	2.81	2.70	2.61	2.55	2.49
18	4.41	3.55	3.16	2.93	2.77	2.66	2.58	2.51	2.46
19	4.38	3.52	3.13	2.90	2.74	2.63	2.54	2.48	2.42
20	4.35	3.49	3.10	2.87	2.71	2.60	2.51	2.45	2.39
21	4.32	3.47	3.07	2.84	2.68	2.57	2.49	2.42	2.37
22	4.30	3.44	3.05	2.82	2.66	2.55	2.46	2.40	2.34
23	4.28	3.42	3.03	2.80	2.64	2.53	2.44	2.37	2.32
24	4.26	3.40	3.01	2.78	2.62	2.51	2.42	2.36	2.30
25	4.24	3.39	2.99	2.76	2.60	2.49	2.40	2.34	2.28
26	4.23	3.37	2.98	2.74	2.59	2.47	2.39	2.32	2.27
27	4.21	3.35	2.96	2.73	2.57	2.46	2.37	2.31	2.25
28	4.20	3.34	2.95	2.71	2.56	2.45	2.36	2.29	2.24
29	4.18	3.33	2.93	2.70	2.55	2.43	2.35	2.28	2.22
30	4.17	3.32	2.92	2.69	2.53	2.42	2.33	2.27	2.21
40	4.08	3.23	2.84	2.61	2.45	2.34	2.25	2.18	2.12
60	4.00	3.15	2.76	2.53	2.37	2.25	2.17	2.10	2.04
120	3.92	3.07	2.68	2.45	2.29	2.17	2.09	2.02	1.96
∞	3.84	3.00	2.60	2.37	2.21	2.10	2.01	1.94	1.88

(Continued)

SOURCE: Reprinted with permission from *Handbook of Tables for Probability and Statistics*, ed. William H. Beyer (Boca Raton, Fla.: CRC Press, 1966). Copyright © 1966 by CRC Press, Inc., Boca Raton, Fla.

$F_{.95}$ (use with $\alpha = .05$)

$N - k$ df_w	10	12	15	20	df_b 24	30	40	60	120	∞
1	241.90	243.90	245.90	248.00	249.10	250.10	251.10	252.20	255.30	254.30
2	19.40	19.41	19.43	19.45	19.45	19.46	19.47	19.48	19.49	19.50
3	8.79	8.74	8.70	8.66	8.64	8.62	8.59	8.57	8.55	8.53
4	5.96	5.91	5.86	5.80	5.77	5.75	5.72	5.69	5.66	5.63
5	4.74	4.68	4.62	4.56	4.53	4.50	4.46	4.43	4.40	4.36
6	4.06	4.00	3.94	3.87	3.84	3.81	3.77	3.74	3.70	3.67
7	3.64	3.57	3.51	3.44	3.41	3.38	3.34	3.30	3.27	3.23
8	3.35	3.28	3.22	3.15	3.12	3.08	3.04	3.01	2.97	2.93
9	3.14	3.07	3.01	2.94	2.90	2.86	2.83	2.79	2.75	2.71
10	2.98	2.91	2.85	2.77	2.74	2.70	2.66	2.62	2.58	2.54
11	2.85	2.79	2.72	2.65	2.61	2.57	2.53	2.49	2.45	2.40
12	2.75	2.69	2.62	2.54	2.51	2.47	2.43	2.38	2.34	2.30
13	2.67	2.60	2.53	2.46	2.42	2.38	2.34	2.30	2.25	2.21
14	2.60	2.53	2.46	2.39	2.35	2.31	2.27	2.22	2.19	2.13
15	2.54	2.48	2.40	2.33	2.29	2.25	2.20	2.16	2.11	2.07
16	2.49	2.42	2.35	2.28	2.24	2.19	2.15	2.11	2.06	2.01
17	2.45	2.38	2.31	2.23	2.19	2.15	2.10	2.06	2.01	1.96
18	2.41	2.34	2.27	2.19	2.15	2.11	2.06	2.02	1.97	1.92
19	2.38	2.31	2.23	2.16	2.11	2.07	2.03	1.98	1.93	1.88
20	2.35	2.28	2.20	2.12	2.08	2.04	1.99	1.95	1.90	1.84
21	2.32	2.25	2.18	2.10	2.05	2.01	1.96	1.92	1.87	1.81
22	2.30	2.23	2.15	2.07	2.03	1.98	1.94	1.89	1.84	1.78
23	2.27	2.20	2.13	2.05	2.01	1.96	1.91	1.86	1.81	1.76
24	2.25	2.18	2.11	2.03	1.98	1.94	1.89	1.84	1.79	1.73
25	2.24	2.16	2.09	2.01	1.96	1.92	1.87	1.82	1.77	1.71
26	2.22	2.15	2.07	1.99	1.95	1.90	1.85	1.80	1.75	1.69
27	2.20	2.13	2.06	1.97	1.93	1.88	1.84	1.79	1.73	1.67
28	2.19	2.12	2.04	1.96	1.91	1.87	1.82	1.77	1.71	1.65
29	2.18	2.10	2.03	1.94	1.90	1.85	1.81	1.75	1.70	1.64
30	2.16	2.09	2.01	1.93	1.89	1.84	1.79	1.74	1.68	1.62
40	2.08	2.00	1.92	1.84	1.79	1.74	1.69	1.64	1.58	1.51
60	1.99	1.92	1.84	1.75	1.70	1.65	1.59	1.53	1.47	1.39
120	1.91	1.83	1.75	1.66	1.61	1.55	1.50	1.43	1.35	1.25
∞	1.83	1.75	1.67	1.57	1.52	1.46	1.39	1.32	1.22	1.00

(Continued)

$F_{.99}$ (use with $\alpha = .01$)

$N-k$ df_w	1	2	3	4	df_b 5	6	7	8	9
1	4052.00	4999.50	5403.00	5625.00	5764.00	5859.00	5928.00	5981.00	6022.00
2	98.50	99.00	99.17	99.25	99.30	99.33	99.36	99.37	99.39
3	34.12	30.82	29.46	28.71	28.24	27.91	27.67	27.49	27.35
4	21.20	18.00	16.69	15.98	15.52	15.21	14.98	14.80	14.55
5	16.26	13.27	12.06	11.39	10.97	10.67	10.46	10.29	10.16
6	13.75	10.92	9.78	9.15	8.75	8.47	8.26	8.10	7.98
7	12.25	9.55	8.45	7.85	7.46	7.19	6.99	6.84	6.72
8	11.26	8.65	7.59	7.01	6.63	6.37	6.18	6.03	5.91
9	10.56	8.02	6.99	6.42	6.06	5.80	5.61	5.47	5.35
10	10.04	7.56	6.55	5.99	5.64	5.39	5.20	5.06	4.94
11	9.65	7.21	6.22	5.67	5.32	5.07	4.89	4.74	4.63
12	9.33	6.93	5.95	5.41	5.06	4.82	4.64	4.50	4.39
13	9.07	6.70	5.74	5.21	4.86	4.62	4.44	4.30	4.19
14	8.86	6.51	5.56	5.04	4.69	4.46	4.28	4.14	4.03
15	8.68	6.36	5.42	4.89	4.56	4.32	4.14	4.00	3.89
16	8.53	6.23	5.29	4.77	4.44	4.20	4.03	3.89	3.78
17	8.40	6.11	5.18	4.67	4.34	4.10	3.93	3.79	3.68
18	8.29	6.01	5.09	4.58	4.25	4.01	3.84	3.71	3.60
19	8.18	5.93	5.01	4.50	4.17	3.94	3.77	3.63	3.52
20	8.10	5.85	4.94	4.43	4.10	3.87	3.70	3.56	3.46
21	8.02	5.78	4.87	4.37	4.04	3.81	3.64	3.51	3.40
22	7.95	5.72	4.82	4.31	3.99	3.76	3.59	3.45	3.35
23	7.88	5.66	4.76	4.26	3.94	3.71	3.54	3.41	3.30
24	7.82	5.61	4.79	4.22	3.90	3.67	3.50	3.36	3.26
25	7.77	5.57	4.68	4.18	3.85	3.63	3.46	3.32	3.22
26	7.72	5.53	4.64	4.14	3.82	3.59	3.42	3.29	3.18
27	7.68	5.49	4.60	4.11	3.78	3.56	3.39	3.26	3.15
28	7.64	5.45	4.57	4.07	3.75	3.53	3.36	3.23	3.12
29	7.60	5.42	4.54	4.04	3.73	3.50	3.33	3.20	3.09
30	7.56	5.39	4.51	4.02	3.70	3.47	3.30	3.17	3.07
40	7.31	5.18	4.31	3.83	3.51	3.29	3.12	2.99	2.89
60	7.08	4.98	4.13	3.65	3.34	3.12	2.95	2.82	2.72
120	6.85	4.79	3.95	3.48	3.17	2.96	2.79	2.66	2.56
∞	6.63	4.61	3.78	3.32	3.02	2.80	2.64	2.51	2.41

(Continued)

					df_b					
$N-k$ df_w	10	12	15	20	24	30	40	60	120	∞
1	6056.00	6106.00	6157.00	6209.00	6235.00	6261.00	6287.00	6313.00	6339.00	6366.00
2	99.40	99.42	99.43	99.45	99.46	99.47	99.47	99.48	99.49	99.50
3	27.23	27.05	26.87	26.69	26.60	26.50	26.41	26.32	26.22	26.13
4	14.55	14.37	14.20	14.02	13.93	13.84	13.75	13.65	13.56	13.46
5	10.05	9.89	9.72	9.55	9.47	9.38	9.29	9.20	9.11	9.02
6	7.87	7.72	7.56	7.40	7.31	7.23	7.14	7.06	6.97	6.88
7	6.62	6.47	6.31	6.16	6.07	5.99	5.91	5.82	5.74	5.65
8	5.81	5.67	5.52	5.36	5.28	5.20	5.12	5.03	4.95	4.86
9	5.26	5.11	4.96	4.81	4.73	4.65	4.57	4.48	4.40	4.31
10	4.85	4.71	4.56	4.41	4.33	4.25	4.17	4.08	4.00	3.91
11	4.54	4.40	4.25	4.10	4.02	3.94	3.86	3.78	3.69	3.60
12	4.30	4.16	4.01	3.86	3.78	3.70	3.62	3.54	3.45	3.36
13	4.10	3.96	3.82	3.66	3.59	3.51	3.43	3.34	3.25	3.17
14	3.94	3.80	3.66	3.51	3.43	3.35	3.27	3.18	3.09	3.00
15	3.80	3.67	3.52	3.37	3.29	3.21	3.13	3.05	2.96	2.87
16	3.69	3.55	3.41	3.26	3.18	3.10	3.02	2.93	2.84	2.75
17	3.59	3.46	3.31	3.16	3.08	3.00	2.92	2.83	2.75	2.65
18	3.51	3.37	3.23	3.08	3.00	2.92	2.84	2.75	2.66	2.57
19	3.43	3.30	3.15	3.00	2.92	2.84	2.76	2.67	2.58	2.49
20	3.37	3.23	3.09	2.94	2.86	2.78	2.69	2.61	2.52	2.42
21	3.31	3.17	3.03	2.88	2.80	2.72	2.64	2.55	2.46	2.36
22	3.26	3.12	2.98	2.83	2.75	2.67	2.58	2.50	2.40	2.31
23	3.21	3.07	2.93	2.78	2.70	2.62	2.54	2.45	2.35	2.26
24	3.17	3.03	2.89	2.74	2.66	2.58	2.49	2.40	2.31	2.21
25	3.13	2.99	2.85	2.70	2.62	2.54	2.45	2.36	2.27	2.17
26	3.09	2.96	2.81	2.66	2.58	2.50	2.42	2.33	2.23	2.13
27	3.06	2.93	2.78	2.63	2.55	2.47	2.38	2.29	2.20	2.10
28	3.03	2.90	2.75	2.60	2.52	2.44	2.35	2.26	2.17	2.06
29	3.00	2.87	2.73	2.57	2.49	2.41	2.33	2.23	2.14	2.03
30	2.98	2.84	2.70	2.55	2.47	2.39	2.30	2.21	2.11	2.01
40	2.80	2.66	2.52	2.37	2.29	2.20	2.11	2.02	1.92	1.80
60	2.63	2.50	2.35	2.20	2.12	2.03	1.94	1.84	1.73	1.60
120	2.47	2.34	2.19	2.03	1.95	1.86	1.76	1.66	1.53	1.38
∞	2.32	2.18	2.04	1.88	1.79	1.70	1.59	1.47	1.32	1.00

$F_{.99}$ (use with $\alpha = .01$)

Appendix C Percentage Points of the Studentized Range for 2 Through 20 Treatments

					Upper 5% Points of q				
					k				
df_w	2	3	4	5	6	7	8	9	10
1	17.97	26.98	32.82	37.08	40.41	43.12	45.40	47.36	49.07
2	6.08	8.33	9.80	10.88	11.74	12.44	13.03	13.54	13.99
3	4.50	5.91	6.82	7.50	8.04	8.48	8.85	9.18	9.46
4	3.93	5.04	5.76	6.29	6.71	7.05	7.35	7.60	7.83
5	3.64	4.60	5.22	5.67	6.03	6.33	6.58	6.80	6.99
6	3.46	4.34	4.90	5.30	5.63	5.90	6.12	6.32	6.49
7	3.34	4.16	4.68	5.06	5.36	5.61	5.82	6.00	6.16
8	3.26	4.04	4.53	4.89	5.17	5.40	5.60	5.77	5.92
9	3.20	3.95	4.41	4.76	5.02	5.24	5.43	5.59	5.74
10	3.15	3.88	4.33	4.65	4.91	5.12	5.30	5.46	5.60
11	3.11	3.82	4.26	4.57	4.82	5.03	5.20	5.35	5.49
12	3.08	3.77	4.20	4.51	4.75	4.95	5.12	5.27	5.39
13	3.06	3.73	4.15	4.45	4.69	4.88	5.05	5.19	5.32
14	3.03	3.70	4.11	4.41	4.64	4.83	4.99	5.13	5.25
15	3.01	3.67	4.08	4.37	4.59	4.78	4.94	5.08	5.20
16	3.00	3.65	4.05	4.33	4.56	4.74	4.90	5.03	5.15
17	2.98	3.63	4.02	4.30	4.52	4.70	4.86	4.99	5.11
18	2.97	3.61	4.00	4.28	4.49	4.67	4.82	4.96	5.07
19	2.96	3.59	3.98	4.25	4.47	4.65	4.79	4.92	5.04
20	2.95	3.58	3.96	4.23	4.45	4.62	4.77	4.90	5.01
24	2.92	3.53	3.90	4.17	4.37	4.54	4.68	4.81	4.92
30	2.89	3.49	3.85	4.10	4.30	4.46	4.60	4.72	4.82
40	2.86	3.44	3.79	4.04	4.23	4.39	4.52	4.63	4.73
60	2.83	3.40	3.74	3.98	4.16	4.31	4.44	4.55	4.65
120	2.80	3.36	3.68	3.92	4.10	4.24	4.36	4.47	4.56
∞	2.77	3.31	3.63	3.86	4.03	4.17	4.29	4.39	4.47

(Continued)

Source: From Table 29 of Pearson, E. S., and Hartley, H. O. (1966), *Biometrika: Tables for Statisticians*, Volume I, Third Edition, published by Cambridge University Press.

					Upper 5% Points of q					
						k				
df_w	11	12	13	14	15	16	17	18	19	20
1	50.59	51.96	53.20	54.33	55.36	56.32	57.22	58.04	58.83	59.56
2	14.39	14.75	15.08	15.38	15.65	15.91	16.14	16.37	16.57	16.77
3	9.72	9.95	10.15	10.35	10.52	10.69	10.84	10.98	11.11	11.24
4	8.03	8.21	8.37	8.52	8.66	8.79	8.91	9.03	9.13	9.23
5	7.17	7.32	7.47	7.60	7.72	7.83	7.93	8.03	8.12	8.21
6	6.65	6.79	6.92	7.03	7.14	7.24	7.34	7.43	7.51	7.59
7	6.30	6.43	6.55	6.66	6.76	6.85	6.94	7.02	7.10	7.17
8	6.05	6.18	6.29	6.39	6.48	6.57	6.65	6.73	6.80	6.87
9	5.87	5.98	6.09	6.19	6.28	6.36	6.44	6.51	6.58	6.64
10	5.72	5.83	5.93	6.03	6.11	6.19	6.27	6.34	6.40	6.47
11	5.61	5.71	5.81	5.90	5.98	6.06	6.13	6.20	6.27	6.33
12	5.51	5.61	5.71	5.80	5.88	5.95	6.02	6.09	6.15	6.21
13	5.43	5.53	5.63	5.71	5.79	5.86	5.93	5.99	6.05	6.11
14	5.36	5.46	5.55	5.64	5.71	5.79	5.85	5.91	5.97	6.03
15	5.31	5.40	5.49	5.57	5.65	5.72	5.78	5.85	5.90	5.96
16	5.26	5.35	5.44	5.52	5.59	5.66	5.73	5.79	5.84	5.90
17	5.21	5.31	5.39	5.47	5.54	5.61	5.67	5.73	5.79	5.84
18	5.17	5.27	5.35	5.43	5.50	5.57	5.63	5.69	5.74	5.79
19	5.14	5.23	5.31	5.39	5.46	5.53	5.59	5.65	5.70	5.75
20	5.11	5.20	5.28	5.36	5.43	5.49	5.55	5.61	5.66	5.71
24	5.01	5.10	5.18	5.25	5.32	5.38	5.44	5.49	5.55	5.59
30	4.92	5.00	5.08	5.15	5.21	5.27	5.33	5.38	5.43	5.47
40	4.82	4.90	4.98	5.04	5.11	5.16	5.22	5.27	5.31	5.36
60	4.73	4.81	4.88	4.94	5.00	5.06	5.11	5.15	5.20	5.24
120	4.64	4.71	4.78	4.84	4.90	4.95	5.00	5.04	5.09	5.13
∞	4.55	4.62	4.68	4.74	4.80	4.85	4.89	4.93	4.97	5.01

(Continued)

Upper 1% Points of q

df_w	2	3	4	5	k 6	7	8	9	10
1	90.03	135.00	164.30	185.60	202.20	215.80	227.20	237.00	245.60
2	14.04	19.02	22.29	24.72	26.63	28.20	29.53	30.68	31.69
3	8.26	10.62	12.17	13.33	14.24	15.00	15.64	16.20	16.69
4	6.51	8.12	9.17	9.96	10.58	11.10	11.55	11.93	12.27
5	5.70	6.98	7.80	8.42	8.91	9.32	9.67	9.97	10.24
6	5.24	6.33	7.03	7.56	7.97	8.32	8.61	8.87	9.10
7	4.95	5.92	6.54	7.01	7.37	7.68	7.94	8.17	8.37
8	4.75	5.64	6.20	6.62	6.96	7.24	7.47	7.68	7.86
9	4.60	5.43	5.96	6.35	6.66	6.91	7.13	7.33	7.49
10	4.48	5.27	5.77	6.14	6.43	6.67	6.87	7.05	7.21
11	4.39	5.15	5.62	5.97	6.25	6.48	6.67	6.84	6.99
12	4.32	5.05	5.50	5.84	6.10	6.32	6.51	6.67	6.81
13	4.26	4.96	5.40	5.73	5.98	6.19	6.37	6.53	6.67
14	4.21	4.89	5.32	5.63	5.88	6.08	6.26	6.41	6.54
15	4.17	4.84	5.25	5.56	5.80	5.99	6.16	6.31	6.44
16	4.13	4.79	5.19	5.49	5.72	5.92	6.08	6.22	6.35
17	4.10	4.74	5.14	5.43	5.66	5.85	6.01	6.15	6.27
18	4.07	4.70	5.09	5.38	5.60	5.79	5.94	6.08	6.20
19	4.05	4.67	5.05	5.33	5.55	5.73	5.89	6.02	6.14
20	4.02	4.64	5.02	5.29	5.51	5.69	5.84	5.97	6.09
24	3.96	4.55	4.91	5.17	5.37	5.54	5.69	5.81	5.92
30	3.89	4.45	4.80	5.05	5.24	5.40	5.54	5.65	5.76
40	3.82	4.37	4.70	4.93	5.11	5.26	5.39	5.50	5.60
60	3.76	4.28	4.59	4.82	4.99	5.13	5.25	5.36	5.45
120	3.70	4.20	4.50	4.71	4.87	5.01	5.12	5.21	5.30
∞	3.64	4.12	4.40	4.60	4.76	4.88	4.99	5.08	5.16

(Continued)

					Upper 1% Points of q					
						k				
df_w	11	12	13	14	15	16	17	18	19	20
1	253.20	260.00	266.20	271.80	277.00	281.80	286.30	290.40	294.30	298.00
2	32.59	33.40	34.13	34.81	35.43	36.00	36.53	37.03	37.50	37.95
3	17.13	17.53	17.89	18.22	18.52	18.81	19.07	19.32	19.55	19.77
4	12.57	12.84	13.09	13.32	13.53	13.73	13.91	14.08	14.24	14.40
5	10.48	10.70	10.89	11.08	11.24	11.40	11.55	11.68	11.81	11.93
6	9.30	9.48	9.65	9.81	9.95	10.08	10.21	10.32	10.43	10.54
7	8.55	8.71	8.86	9.00	9.12	9.24	9.35	9.46	9.55	9.65
8	8.03	8.18	8.31	8.44	8.55	8.66	8.76	8.85	8.94	9.03
9	7.65	7.78	7.91	8.03	8.13	8.23	8.33	8.41	8.49	8.57
10	7.36	7.49	7.60	7.71	7.81	7.91	7.99	8.08	8.15	8.23
11	7.13	7.25	7.36	7.46	7.56	7.65	7.73	7.81	7.88	7.95
12	6.94	7.06	7.17	7.26	7.36	7.44	7.52	7.59	7.66	7.73
13	6.79	6.90	7.01	7.10	7.19	7.27	7.35	7.42	7.48	7.55
14	6.66	6.77	6.87	6.96	7.05	7.13	7.20	7.27	7.33	7.39
15	6.55	6.66	6.76	6.84	6.93	7.00	7.07	7.14	7.20	7.26
16	6.46	6.56	6.66	6.74	6.82	6.90	6.97	7.03	7.09	7.15
17	6.38	6.48	6.57	6.66	6.73	6.81	6.87	6.94	7.00	7.05
18	6.31	6.41	6.50	6.58	6.65	6.73	6.79	6.85	6.91	6.97
19	6.25	6.34	6.43	6.51	6.58	6.65	6.72	6.78	6.84	6.89
20	6.19	6.28	6.37	6.45	6.52	6.59	6.65	6.71	6.77	6.82
24	6.02	6.11	6.19	6.26	6.33	6.39	6.45	6.51	6.56	6.61
30	5.85	5.93	6.01	6.08	6.14	6.20	6.26	6.31	6.36	6.41
40	5.69	5.76	5.83	5.90	5.96	6.02	6.07	6.12	6.16	6.21
60	5.53	5.60	5.67	5.73	5.78	5.84	5.89	5.93	5.97	6.01
120	5.37	5.44	5.50	5.56	5.61	5.66	5.71	5.75	5.79	5.83
∞	5.23	5.29	5.35	5.40	5.45	5.49	5.54	5.57	5.61	5.65

Appendix **D** Critical Values of *n* for the Sign Test

In the body of the table, the first number of the pair usually refers to the positive values, and the second number to the negative values.

n	α(two-sided) 0.10 α(one-sided) 0.05	0.05 0.025	0.02 0.01	0.01 0.005
1				
2				
3				
4				
5	0, 5			
6	0, 6	0, 6		
7	0, 7	0, 7	0, 7	
8	1, 7	0, 8	0, 8	0, 8
9	1, 8	1, 8	0, 9	0, 9
10	1, 9	1, 9	0, 10	0, 10
11	2, 9	1, 10	1, 10	0, 11
12	2, 10	2, 10	1, 11	1, 11
13	3, 10	2, 11	1, 12	1, 12
14	3, 11	2, 12	2, 12	1, 13
15	3, 12	3, 12	2, 13	2, 13
16	4, 12	3, 13	2, 14	2, 14
17	4, 13	4, 13	3, 14	2, 15
18	5, 13	4, 14	3, 15	3, 15
19	5, 14	4, 15	4, 15	3, 16
20	5, 15	5, 15	4, 16	3, 17
21	6, 15	5, 16	4, 17	4, 17
22	6, 16	5, 17	5, 17	4, 18
23	7, 16	6, 17	5, 18	4, 19
24	7, 17	6, 18	5, 19	5, 19
25	7, 18	7, 18	6, 19	5, 20
26	8, 18	7, 19	6, 20	6, 20
27	8, 19	7, 20	7, 20	6, 21
28	9, 19	8, 20	7, 21	6, 22
29	9, 20	8, 21	7, 22	7, 22
30	10, 20	9, 21	8, 22	7, 23
31	10, 21	9, 22	8, 23	7, 24
32	10, 22	9, 23	8, 24	8, 24
33	11, 22	10, 23	9, 24	8, 25
34	11, 23	10, 24	9, 25	9, 25
35	12, 23	11, 24	10, 25	9, 26

(Continued)

_n_	α(two-sided) 0.10 α(one-sided) 0.05	0.05 0.025	0.02 0.01	0.01 0.005
36	12, 24	11, 25	10, 26	9, 27
37	13, 24	12, 25	10, 27	10, 27
38	13, 25	12, 26	11, 27	10, 28
39	13, 26	12, 27	11, 28	11, 28
40	14, 26	13, 27	12, 28	11, 29
41	14, 27	13, 28	12, 29	11, 30
42	15, 27	14, 28	13, 29	12, 30
43	15, 28	14, 29	13, 30	12, 31
44	16, 28	15, 29	13, 31	13, 31
45	16, 29	15, 30	14, 31	13, 32
46	16, 30	15, 31	14, 32	13, 33
47	17, 30	16, 31	15, 32	14, 33
48	17, 31	16, 32	15, 33	14, 34
49	18, 31	17, 32	15, 34	15, 34
50	18, 32	17, 33	16, 34	15, 35
51	19, 32	18, 33	16, 35	15, 36
52	19, 33	18, 34	17, 35	16, 36
53	20, 33	18, 35	17, 36	16, 37
54	20, 34	19, 35	18, 36	17, 37
55	20, 35	19, 36	18, 37	17, 38
56	21, 35	20, 36	18, 38	17, 39
57	21, 36	20, 37	19, 38	18, 39
58	22, 36	21, 37	19, 39	18, 40
59	22, 37	21, 38	20, 39	19, 40
60	23, 37	21, 39	20, 40	19, 41

Appendix E Random Numbers Table

Row Number										
00000	10097	32533	76520	13586	34673	54876	80959	09177	39292	74945
00001	37542	04805	64894	74296	24805	24037	20636	10402	00822	91665
00002	08422	68953	19645	09303	23209	02560	15953	34764	35080	33606
00003	99019	02529	09376	70715	38311	31165	88676	74397	04436	27659
00004	12807	99970	80157	36147	64032	36653	98951	16877	12171	76833
00005	66065	74717	34072	76850	36697	36170	65813	39885	11199	29170
00006	31060	10805	45571	82406	35303	42614	86799	07439	23403	09732
00007	85269	77602	02051	65692	68665	74818	73053	85247	18623	88579
00008	63573	32135	05325	47048	90553	57548	28468	28709	83491	25624
00009	73796	45753	03529	64778	35808	34282	60935	20344	35273	88435
00010	98520	17767	14905	68607	22109	40558	60970	93433	50500	73998
00011	11805	05431	39808	27732	50725	68248	29405	24201	52775	67851
00012	83452	99634	06288	98033	13746	70078	18475	40610	68711	77817
00013	88685	40200	86507	58401	36766	67951	90364	76493	29609	11062
00014	99594	67348	87517	64969	91826	08928	93785	61368	23478	34113
00015	65481	17674	17468	50950	58047	76974	73039	57186	40218	16544
00016	80124	35635	17727	08015	45318	22374	21115	78253	14385	53763
00017	74350	99817	77402	77214	43236	00210	45521	64237	96286	02655
00018	69916	26803	66252	29148	36936	87203	76621	13990	94400	56418
00019	09893	20505	14225	68514	46427	56788	96297	78822	54382	14598
00020	91499	14523	68479	27686	46162	83554	94750	89923	37089	20048
00021	80336	94598	26940	36858	70297	34135	53140	33340	42050	82341
00022	44104	81949	85157	47954	32979	26575	57600	40881	22222	06413
00023	12550	73742	11100	02040	12860	74697	96644	89439	28707	25815
00024	63606	49329	16505	34484	40219	52563	43651	77082	07207	31790
00025	61196	90446	26457	47774	51924	33729	65394	59593	42582	60527
00026	15474	45266	95270	79953	59367	83848	82396	10118	33211	59466
00027	94557	28573	67897	54387	54622	44431	91190	42592	92927	45973
00028	42481	16213	97344	08721	16868	48767	03071	12059	25701	46670
00029	23523	78317	73208	89837	68935	91416	26252	29663	05522	82562
00030	04493	52494	75246	33824	45862	51025	61962	79335	65337	12472
00031	00549	97654	64051	88159	96119	63896	54692	82391	23287	29529
00032	35963	15307	26898	09354	33351	35462	77974	50024	90103	39333
00033	59808	08391	45427	26842	83609	49700	13021	24892	78565	20106
00034	46058	85236	01390	92286	77281	44077	93910	83647	70617	42941
00035	32179	00597	87379	25241	05567	07007	86743	17157	85394	11838
00036	69234	61406	20117	45204	15956	60000	18743	92423	97118	96338
00037	19565	41430	01758	75379	40419	21585	66674	36806	84962	85207
00038	45155	14938	19476	07246	43667	94543	59047	90033	20826	69541
00039	94864	31994	36168	10851	34888	81553	01540	35456	05014	51176

(Continued)

Row Number										
00040	98086	24826	45240	28404	44999	08896	39094	73407	35441	31880
00041	33185	16232	41941	50949	89435	48581	88695	41994	37548	73043
00042	80951	00406	96382	70774	20151	23387	25016	25298	94624	61171
00043	79752	49140	71961	28296	69861	02591	74852	20539	00387	59579
00044	18633	32537	98145	06571	31010	24674	05455	61427	77938	91936
00045	74029	43902	77557	32270	97790	17119	52527	58021	80814	51748
00046	54178	45611	80993	37143	05335	12969	56127	19255	36040	90324
00047	11664	49883	52079	84827	59381	71539	09973	33440	88461	23356
00048	48324	77928	31249	64710	02295	36870	32307	57546	15020	09994
00049	69074	94138	87637	91976	35584	04401	10518	21615	01848	76938
00050	09188	20097	32825	39527	04220	86304	83389	87374	64278	58044
00051	90045	85497	51981	50654	94938	81997	91870	76150	68476	64659
00052	73189	50207	47677	26269	62290	64464	27124	67018	41361	82760
00053	75768	76490	20971	87749	90429	12272	95375	05871	93823	43178
00054	54016	44056	66281	31003	00682	27398	20714	53295	07706	17813
00055	08358	69910	78542	42785	13661	58873	04618	97553	31223	08420
00056	28306	03264	81333	10591	40510	07893	32604	60475	94119	01840
00057	53840	86233	81594	13628	51215	90290	28466	68795	77762	20791
00058	91757	53741	61613	62669	50263	90212	55781	76514	83483	47055
00059	89415	92694	00397	58391	12607	17646	48949	72306	94541	37408
00060	77513	03820	86864	29901	68414	82774	51908	13980	72893	55507
00061	19502	37174	69979	20288	55210	29773	74287	75251	65344	67415
00062	21818	59313	93278	81757	05686	73156	07082	85046	31853	38452
00063	51474	66499	68107	23621	94049	91345	42836	09191	08007	45449
00064	99559	68331	62535	24170	69777	12830	74819	78142	43860	72834
00065	33713	48007	93584	72869	51926	64721	58303	29822	93174	93972
00066	85274	86893	11303	22970	28834	34137	73515	90400	71148	43643
00067	84133	89640	44035	52166	73852	70091	61222	60561	62327	18423
00068	56732	16234	17395	96131	10123	91622	85496	57560	81604	18880
00069	65138	56806	87648	85261	34313	65861	45875	21069	85644	47277
00070	38001	02176	81719	11711	71602	92937	74219	64049	65584	49698
00071	37402	96397	01304	77586	56271	10086	47324	62605	40030	37438
00072	97125	40348	87083	31417	21815	39250	75237	62047	15501	29578
00073	21826	41134	47143	34072	64638	85902	49139	06441	03856	54552
00074	73135	42742	95719	09035	85794	74296	08789	88156	64691	19202
00075	07638	77929	03061	18072	96207	44156	23821	99538	04713	66994
00076	60528	83441	07954	19814	59175	20695	05533	52139	61212	06455
00077	83596	35655	06958	92983	05128	09719	77433	53783	92301	50498
00078	10850	62746	99599	10507	13499	06319	53075	71839	06410	19362
00079	39820	98952	43622	63147	64421	80814	43800	09351	31024	73167
00080	59580	06478	75569	78800	88835	54486	23768	06156	04111	08408
00081	38508	07341	23793	48763	90822	97022	17719	04207	95954	49953
00082	30692	70668	94688	16127	56196	80091	82067	63400	05462	69200
00083	65443	95659	18238	27437	49632	24041	08337	65676	96299	90836
00084	27267	50264	13192	72294	07477	44606	17985	48911	97341	30358
00085	91307	06991	19072	24210	36699	53728	28825	35793	28976	66252
00086	68434	94688	84473	13622	62126	98408	12843	82590	09815	93146
00087	48908	15877	54745	24591	35700	04754	83824	52692	54130	55160
00088	06913	45197	42672	78601	11883	09528	63011	98901	14974	40344
00089	10455	16019	14210	33712	91342	37821	88325	80851	43667	70883

(Continued)

Row Number										
00090	12883	97343	65027	61184	04285	01392	17974	15077	90712	26769
00091	21778	30976	38807	36961	31649	42096	63281	02023	08816	47449
00092	19523	59515	65122	59659	86283	68258	69572	13798	16435	91529
00093	67245	52670	35583	16563	79246	86686	76463	34222	26655	90802
00094	60584	47377	07500	37992	45134	26529	26760	83637	41326	44344
00095	53853	41377	36066	94850	58838	73859	49364	73331	96240	43642
00096	24637	38736	74384	89342	52623	07992	12369	18601	03742	83873
00097	83080	12451	38992	22815	07759	51777	97377	27585	51972	37867
00098	16444	24334	36151	99073	27493	70939	85130	32552	54846	54759
00099	60790	18157	57178	65762	11161	78576	45819	52979	65130	04860
00100	03991	10461	93716	16894	66083	24653	84609	58232	88618	19161
00101	38555	95554	32886	59780	08355	60860	29735	47762	71299	23853
00102	17546	73704	92052	46215	55121	29281	59076	07936	27954	58909
00103	32643	52861	95819	06831	00911	98936	76355	93779	80863	00514
00104	69572	68777	39510	35905	14060	40619	29549	69616	33564	60780
00105	24122	66591	27699	06494	14845	46672	61958	77100	90899	75754
00106	61196	30231	92962	61773	41839	55382	17267	70943	78038	70267
00107	30532	21704	10274	12202	39685	23309	10061	68829	55986	66485
00108	03788	97599	75867	20717	74416	53166	35208	33374	87539	08823
00109	48228	63379	85783	47619	53152	67433	35663	52972	16818	60311
00110	60365	94653	35075	33949	42614	29297	01918	28316	98953	73231
00111	83799	42402	56623	34442	34994	41374	70071	14736	09958	18065
00112	32960	07405	36409	83232	99385	41600	11133	07586	15917	06253
00113	19322	53845	57620	52606	66497	68646	78138	66559	19640	99413
00114	11220	94747	07399	37408	48509	23929	27482	45476	85244	35159
00115	31751	57260	68980	05339	15470	48355	88651	22596	03152	19121
00116	88492	99382	14454	04504	20094	98977	74843	93413	22109	78508
00117	30934	47744	07481	83828	73788	06533	28597	20405	94205	20380
00118	22888	48893	27499	98748	60530	45128	74022	84617	82037	10268
00119	78212	16993	35902	91386	44372	15486	65741	14014	87481	37220

Table of Probabilities for the Kruskal–Wallis One-Way ANOVA by Ranks*

Sample Sizes					Sample Sizes				
n_1	n_2	n_3	H	p	n_1	n_2	n_3	H	p
2	1	1	2.7000	.500	4	3	2	6.4444	.008
								6.3000	.011
2	2	1	3.6000	.200				5.4444	.046
								5.4000	.051
2	2	2	4.5714	.067				4.5111	.098
			3.7143	.200					
3	1	1	3.2000	.300					
					4	3	3	6.7455	.010
3	2	1	4.2857	.100				6.7091	.013
			3.8571	.133				5.7909	.046
								5.7273	.050
3	2	2	5.3572	.029				4.7091	.092
			4.7143	.048				4.7000	.101
			4.5000	.067					
			4.4643	.105	4	4	1	6.6667	.010
								6.1667	.022
3	3	1	5.1429	.043				4.9667	.048
			4.5714	.100				4.8667	.054
			4.0000	.129				4.1667	.082
								4.0667	.102
3	3	2	6.2500	.011					
			5.3611	.032					
			5.1389	.061	4	4	2	7.0364	.006
			4.5556	.100				6.8727	.011
			4.2500	.121				5.4545	.046
								5.2364	.052
3	3	3	7.2000	.004				4.5545	.098
			6.4889	.011				4.4455	.103
			5.6889	.029					
			5.6000	.050	4	4	3	7.1439	.010
			5.0667	.086				7.1364	.011
			4.6222	.100				5.5985	.049
								5.5758	.051
4	1	1	3.5714	.200				4.5455	.099
								4.4773	.102
4	2	1	4.8214	.057					
			4.5000	.076	4	4	4	7.6538	.008
			4.0179	.114				7.5385	.011
								5.6923	.049

(Continued)

*Adapted and abridged from W. H. Kruskal and W. A. Wallis (1952), Use of ranks in one-criterion variance analysis, *Journal of the American Statistical Association* 47, pp. 614–617. Reprinted with permission from the Journal of the American Statistical Association. Copyright 1952 by the American Statistical Association. All rights reserved. (The corrections to this table given by the authors in Errata, *Journal of the American Statistical Association* 48, p. 910, have been incorporated.)

Sample Sizes					Sample Sizes				
n_1	n_2	n_3	H	p	n_1	n_2	n_3	H	p
4	2	2	6.0000	.014				5.6538	.054
			5.3333	.033				4.6539	.097
			5.1250	.052				4.5001	.104
			4.4583	.100					
			4.1667	.105	5	1	1	3.8571	.143
4	3	1	5.8333	.021	5	2	1	5.2500	.036
			5.2083	.050				5.0000	.048
			5.0000	.057				4.4500	.071
			4.0556	.093				4.2000	.095
			3.8889	.129				4.0500	.119
5	2	2	6.5333	.008				5.6308	.050
			6.1333	.013				4.5487	.099
			5.1600	.034				4.5231	.103
			5.0400	.056					
			4.3733	.090	5	4	4	7.7604	.009
			4.2933	.122				7.7440	.011
								5.6571	.049
5	3	1	6.4000	.012				5.6176	.050
			4.9600	.048				4.6187	.100
			4.8711	.052				4.5527	.102
			4.0178	.095	5	5	1	7.3091	.009
			3.8400	.123				6.8364	.011
								5.1273	.046
5	3	2	6.9091	.009				4.9091	.053
			6.8218	.010				4.1091	.086
			5.2509	.049				4.0364	.105
			5.1055	.052					
			4.6509	.091	5	5	2	7.3385	.010
			4.4945	.101				7.2692	.010
								5.3385	.047
5	3	3	7.0788	.009				5.2462	.051
			6.9818	.011				4.6231	.097
			5.6485	.049				4.5077	.100
			5.5152	.051					
			4.5333	.097	5	5	3	7.5780	.010
			4.4121	.109				7.5429	.010
								5.7055	.046
5	4	1	6.9545	.008				5.6264	.051
			6.8400	.011				4.5451	.100
			4.9855	.044				4.5363	.102
			4.8600	.056					
			3.9873	.098	5	5	4	7.8229	.010
			3.9600	.102				7.7914	.010
								5.6657	.049
5	4	2	7.2045	.009				5.6429	.050
			7.1182	.010				4.5229	.099
			5.2727	.049				4.5200	.101
			5.2682	.050					
			4.5409	.098	5	5	5	8.0000	.009
			4.5182	.101				7.9800	.010
								5.7800	.049
5	4	3	7.4449	.010				5.6600	.051
			7.3949	.011				4.5600	.100
			5.6564	.049				4.5000	.102

Answers to Selected Exercises

Chapter 2

2.1 a. A parameter is a characteristic of a population, and a statistic is a characteristic of a sample.

  b. A sample is a subset of a population, and a census includes the entire population.

  c. A simple random sample is one in which each member of the population has an equal chance of being selected. A convenience sample is one in which each member has not been given an equal chance of being selected. The selected members are included because of some characteristic other than chance.

2.3 The sample should be representative of the population.

2.4 a. It avoids known and unknown biases on average.

  b. It helps convince others that the trial was conducted properly.

  c. It is the basis for statistical theory that underlies hypothesis tests and confidence intervals.

2.8 Stratified random sampling

2.10 a. The population is the entire list of 83 individuals with their blood pressure readings. The various samples are computer-generated random samples.

  b. The population is the entire list of 7683 subjects in the Honolulu Heart Study. Data from a sample of 100 subjects are shown in Table 3.1.

2.11 In the health sciences, subjects who drop out of a study often have different outcomes than subjects remaining in a study. This may lead to bias because the subjects remaining in the study may not be representative of the population.

Chapter 3

3.2 | Diastolic blood pressure | quantitative continuous |
| Sex | qualitative |
| Diet status | qualitative |

3.3 Extreme values are to the left in a negatively skewed distribution and to the right in a positively skewed one.

3.7 a. Bar graph

  b. Frequency polygon

c. Pie chart
d. Line graph

3.8   Stem-and-leaf display:

		Frequency
40–49	7 9	2
50–59	0 1 2 2 2 2 3 3 5 5 5 5 5 6 6 6 6 7 7 8 8 8 9 9 9 9 9 9 9 9	30
60–69	0 0 0 0 1 1 1 1 1 1 1 1 1 2 2 2 3 4 4 5 5 5 6 6 6 6 6 6 6 6 6 7 7 8 8 8 8 8 8	41
70–79	0 0 0 0 0 1 1 1 3 3 3 3 3 5 5 5 7 7 7 8	21
80–89	0 0 2 3 6	5
90–99	1	1
		Total 100

a. The smallest is 47, the largest is 91.
b. 61

3.10

		Frequency
150–154	0 2 2 2 2 2 2 4 4	9
155–159	5 5 5 5 5 5 5 5 7 7 7 7 7 7 7 7 9 9 9 9 9	22
160–164	0 0 0 0 0 0 0 0 0 0 0 0 0 0 1 1 1 1 2 2 2 2 2 2 2 2 2 4 4 4	31
165–169	5 5 5 5 5 5 5 5 5 5 5 5 5 5 5 5 6 6 6 7 7 9	24
170–174	0 0 0 0 0 0 0 0 1 1 2 2 3	13
175–179	5	1
		Total 100

a. The smallest height is 150, and the largest is 175.
b. The most frequent is 165.

3.12   a. Smokers ($n = 37$)   b. Nonsmokers ($n = 63$)

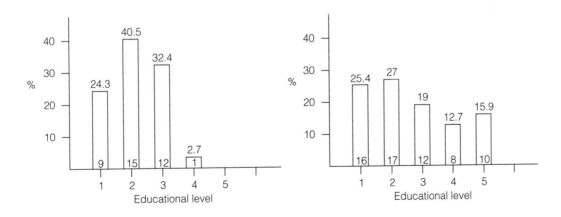

There is a higher proportion of nonsmokers with a high school (#4) and technical school (#5) education level.

3.14   Pie chart

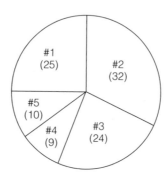

3.16   a. Frequency Table of Weight Loss (in pounds) of 25 Individuals Enrolled in a Weight-Control Program.

Weight Loss (lb)	f	%
2–3	3	12
4–5	5	20
6–7	3	12
8–9	7	28
10–11	6	24
12–13	1	4
	25	100

b. and c.

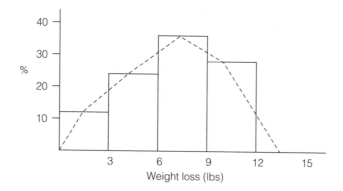

d. The distribution appears to be negatively skewed. A possible interpretation is that there are more individuals with small losses than large losses.

e. The most common weight loss was 9 lb.

Chapter 4

4.1 Mean $= \dfrac{\Sigma x}{n} = \dfrac{24}{6} = 4$

Median $= 4$
Mode $= 5$
Range $= 8 - 1 = 7$

Variance $= \dfrac{\Sigma(x - \bar{x})^2}{n - 1} = \dfrac{32}{5} = 6.40$

Standard deviation $= \sqrt{\text{variance}} = 2.53$

4.3 Range $= 102 - 40 = 62;$ median $= 72;$ mode $= 70$

4.7 a. $CV_H = \dfrac{100s}{\bar{x}} = \dfrac{100(5.60)}{161.75} = 3.46$

$CV_W = \dfrac{100s}{\bar{x}} = \dfrac{100(8.61)}{64.22} = 13.41$

b. The CV for weight is approximately four times larger.

4.8 a. $\bar{x} = \dfrac{13{,}010}{100} = 130.10$

$s^2 = \dfrac{1{,}737{,}124 - 1{,}692{,}601}{99} = 449.73 \qquad s = 21.21$

b. 108.89, 151.31
c. 87.68, 172.52
d. 66.47, 193.73
e. 68.3%, 95.4%, 99.7%

4.10 Variance $= s^2 = (38.82)^2 = 1506.99$

4.14 a. i. 138, 190, 128, 152, 134, 108, 118, 138, 108, 126, 176, 112, 92, 152, 98, 112, 120, 140, 94, 150, 144, 156, 140, 150, 162

ii. 116, 130, 136, 134, 162, 162, 118, 142, 104, 140, 142, 112, 116, 134, 108, 114, 154, 128, 116, 140, 122, 122, 172, 128

$\bar{x}_1 = \dfrac{\Sigma x}{n} = \dfrac{3338}{25} = 133.52$

$s_1 = \sqrt{\dfrac{\Sigma x^2 - (\Sigma x)^2/n}{n - 1}} = \sqrt{\dfrac{460{,}748 - 445{,}689.76}{24}} = \sqrt{627.43} = 25.05$

$\bar{x}_2 = \dfrac{\Sigma x}{n} = \dfrac{3152}{24} = 131.33$

$s_2 = \sqrt{\dfrac{\Sigma x^2 - (\Sigma x)^2/n}{n - 1}} = \sqrt{\dfrac{421{,}472 - 413{,}962.67}{23}} = \sqrt{326.49} = 18.07$

b. The first set has the larger standard deviation: $25.05 - 18.07 = 6.98$.
c. The first set of observations is more dispersed than the second.

4.16 The median becomes 3.5, and the mean and standard deviation both become smaller.

4.18   a. $CV = \dfrac{21.21}{130.1} \times 100 = 16.3\%$

b. $CV = \dfrac{38.82}{216.96} \times 100 = 17.9\%$

c. The CV for blood pressure is somewhat less than the CV for cholesterol. The CV is a unit-free measure.

4.20   a. Negatively skewed
b. Positively skewed
c. Symmetric

4.23 $\sigma = \sqrt{\sigma^2} = \sqrt{144} = 12$

4.25   a. If mean = median = mode, then the frequency distribution is symmetrical.
b. If mean = 15, median = 10, and mode = 5, then the frequency distribution is positively skewed.

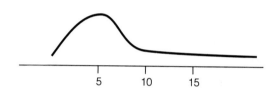

4.26   The sample mean $\bar{x} = \dfrac{\Sigma x}{n}$ is based on the sample size n, and the population mean

$\mu = \dfrac{\Sigma x}{N}$ is based on the entire population N.

Chapter 5

5.1   {TT, TH, HT, HH}

$P(0H) = (\tfrac{1}{2})(\tfrac{1}{2}) = \tfrac{1}{4}$

$P(1H) = (\tfrac{1}{2})(\tfrac{1}{2}) + (\tfrac{1}{2})(\tfrac{1}{2}) = \tfrac{1}{2}$

$P(2H) = (\tfrac{1}{2})(\tfrac{1}{2}) = \tfrac{1}{4}$

5.3   {TTT, TTH, THT, THH, HTT, HTH, HHT, HHH}
a. $P(2H) = \tfrac{3}{8}$
c. $P(\text{at most } 2H) = \tfrac{7}{8}$

5.4   {GGG, GGB, GBG, GBB, BGG, BGB, BBG, BBB}
a. $P(2B + 1G) = \tfrac{3}{8}$
c. $P(0G) = \tfrac{1}{8}$
e. $P(2B \text{ followed by } 1G) = \tfrac{1}{8}$. Note that (a) does not consider order.

5.7   a. $P(\text{sum } 8) = \dfrac{5}{36}$

d. $P(\text{sum 7 and both dice} < 4) = 0$

5.8   a. $P(\text{O or R}) = \dfrac{10 + 15}{10 + 30 + 20 + 15} = \dfrac{25}{75} = \dfrac{1}{3}$

c. $P(\text{not B}) = \dfrac{55}{75} = \dfrac{11}{15}$

e. $P(\text{R, W, or B}) = \dfrac{60}{75} = \dfrac{4}{5}$

5.9 $P(\text{white mouse in 10 hours}) = \dfrac{7}{10}; P(\text{black mouse in 10 hours}) = \dfrac{9}{10}$

a. $P(\text{both alive}) = \left(\dfrac{7}{10}\right)\left(\dfrac{9}{10}\right) = \dfrac{63}{100}$

b. $P(\text{black alive and white dead}) = \left(\dfrac{9}{10}\right)\left(\dfrac{3}{10}\right) = \dfrac{27}{100}$

d. $P(\text{at least one alive}) = \dfrac{7}{10} + \dfrac{9}{10} - \dfrac{63}{100} = \dfrac{97}{100}$

5.10 a. $P(\text{vegetarian}) = \dfrac{18 + 22}{18 + 22 + 20 + 23} = \dfrac{40}{83}$

c. $P(\text{male vegetarian}) = \dfrac{18}{83}$

5.11 a. $P(\text{completed high school or technical school}) = \dfrac{19}{100}$

c. $P(\text{physically inactive}) = \dfrac{49}{100}$

e. $P(\text{serum cholesterol} > 250 \text{ and systolic blood pressure} > 130) = \dfrac{9}{100}$

5.12 $5! = 120$

5.13 $P(10,4) = \dfrac{10!}{(10 - 4)!} = \dfrac{3,628,800}{720} = 5040$

5.15 $C(9,5) = \dfrac{9!}{5!(9 - 5)!} = \dfrac{362,880}{(120)(24)} = 126$

5.16 b. $C(6,4) = \dfrac{6!}{4!(6 - 4)!} = \dfrac{720}{24(2)} = 15$

$P(n,r) > C(n,r)$ because order is considered.

5.17 $C(10,4) = \dfrac{10!}{4!(10 - 4)!} = \dfrac{3,628,800}{(24)(720)} = 210 = C(10,6)$

5.18 a. $P(\text{3 out of 5}) = \dfrac{5!}{3!(5 - 3)!}(.5)^3(1 - .5)^2 = \dfrac{120}{6(2)}(.5)^3(.5)^2$

$= .3125$

c. $P(\text{at most 1}) = P(0) + P(1) = .03125 + \dfrac{5!}{1!(5 - 1)!}(.5)^1(.5)^4$

$= .03125 + .15625 = .1875$

5.19 $n = 20, p = .25$

a. $P(3) = .1339$

c. $P(< 3) = 1 - P(\geq 3) = 1 - .9087 = .0913$

5.20 $n = 10, p = .1$
a. $P(10) = 0$
c. $P(\geq 3) = 1 - (.3487 + .3874 + .1937) = .0702$

5.21 $n = 12, p = .25$
a. $P(4) = .1936$
c. $P(\geq 4) = 1 - .6488 = .3512$

5.22 10 males, 15 females; $P(\text{M smoke}) = \frac{1}{2}$, $P(\text{F smoke}) = \frac{1}{3}$
a. $[P(4 \text{ of } 10 \text{ M smoke}) = .2051 \text{ and } P(6 \text{ of } 15 \text{ F smoke}) = .1786]$
$P(4\text{M and }6\text{F}) = (.2051)(.1786) = .0366$
c. $[P(0 \text{ of } 10 \text{ M smoke}) = .0010 \text{ and } P(0 \text{ of } 15 \text{ F smoke}) = .0023]$
$P(0\text{M and }0\text{F}) = (.0010)(.0023) = .0000$

5.25 a. $P(A) = \dfrac{432}{4075} = .1060$

b. $P(B) = \dfrac{768}{4075} = .1885$

c. $P(B|A) = \dfrac{P(A \text{ and } B)}{P(A)} = \dfrac{42/4075}{.1060} = \dfrac{.0103}{.1060} = .0972$

d. Because $P(B) \neq P(B \mid A)$ (that is, $.1885 \neq .0972$), events A and B are *not* independent.

5.27

Class Interval	Nonsmokers f_i	Smokers f_i	Total
90–109	10	5	15
110–129	24	15	39
130–149	18	10	28
150–169	9	3	12
170–189	2	2	4 ⎫
190–209	0	2	2 ⎬ 6
Total	63	37	100

a. $P(A) = \dfrac{63}{100} = .63$

b. $P(B) = \dfrac{37}{100} = .37$

c. $P(C) = \dfrac{6}{100} = .06$

d. $P(C|A) = \dfrac{P(C \text{ and } A)}{P(A)} = \dfrac{2/100}{.63} = .0317$

e. $P(C|B) = \dfrac{P(C \text{ and } B)}{P(B)} = \dfrac{4/100}{.37} = .1081$

The conditional probability of selecting someone with a blood pressure $\geq$ 170 from smokers is three times that of selecting someone from nonsmokers. Because $P(C \mid B) \neq P(C)$ (that is, $.1081 \neq .06$), smoking status and blood pressure are *not* independent.

Chapter 6

6.1   a. .4911   c. 2(.4678) = .9356   e. .4990

6.2   a. .5 − .4582 = .0418   c. 5 − .4946 = .0054   e. 0

6.3   a. 1.645   c. ±1.96   e. ±1.645

6.4   a. 1.645   c. 0   e. −.84

6.5

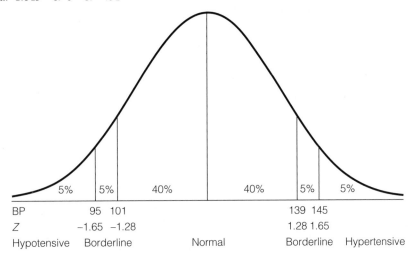

6.6   a. $Z_1 = (x − \mu)/\sigma = (45 − 60)/10 = −1.5$
       $Z_2 = (75 − 60)/10 = 1.5$; area = 2(.4332) = .8664 = 86.6%
   c. <50 Z = (50 − 60)/10 = −1; area = .5 − .3413 = .1587 = 15.9%
   e. ≥75 Z = (75 − 60)/10 = 1.5; area = .5 − .4332 = .0668 = 6.68%

6.7   Mean = 75, σ = 8; 90th percentile; Z = 1.28
   1.28 = (x − 75)/8; x = (1.28)8 + 75 = 85.24 = 85%

6.8   Mean = 50, σ = 12
   P(x < 35) = (35 − 50)/12 = −1.25; area = .5 − .3944 = .1056

6.9   a. The standard normal distribution has mean = 0 and SD = 1.0. Other distributions have a variety of means and standard deviations.
   b. Because the area is easily obtained for the standard normal distribution

6.11   a. $\bar{x}$ = 55; SD = 6

$$Z = \frac{65 − 55}{6} = \frac{10}{6} = 1.67$$

       P(Z) > 1.67 = .5 − .4525 = .0475

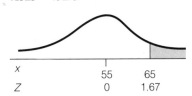

     A little less than 5% will live another 65 years.
   b. That life expectancy is normally distributed

6.12   a.

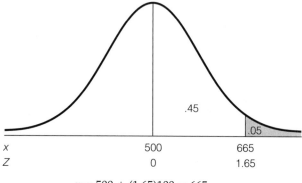

$$x = 500 + (1.65)100 = 665$$

b. 5% of 1,000,000 = 50,000

c.

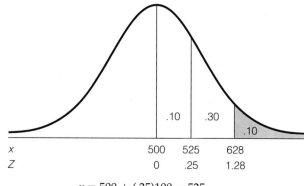

$$x = 500 + (.25)100 = 525$$
$$x = 500 + (1.28)100 = 628$$

d. 30% of 1,000,000 = 300,000

e.

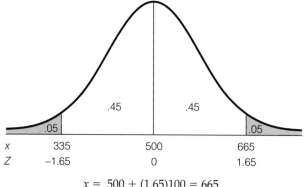

$$x = 500 + (1.65)100 = 665$$
$$x = 500 + (-1.65)100 = 335$$

The middle 90% have scores between 335 and 665.

f.

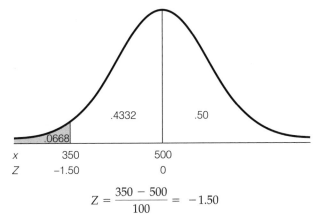

.4332		.50

.0668

x	350	500
Z	−1.50	0

$$Z = \frac{350 - 500}{100} = -1.50$$

.0668 or about 7% would score less than 350.

6.15 $\bar{x} = 4.7G$; SD = .8G

P(pilot with < 3.5G) =

$$P\left(Z = \frac{3.5 - 4.7}{.8} = \frac{-1.2}{.8} = -1.5\right)$$

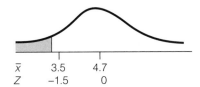

$\bar{x}$	3.5	4.7
Z	−1.5	0

Area = .5 − .4332
      = .0668

6.20   a. $x = \mu + Z\sigma$; $x = 195 + 1.645(10) = 211.45$ and higher

   c. $Z = \dfrac{x - \mu}{\sigma}$; $Z = \dfrac{180 - 195}{10} = \dfrac{-15}{10} = -1.50$; area = .0668 or 7%

   e.

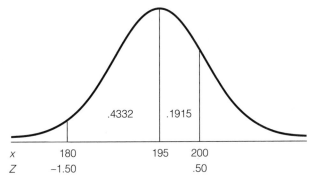

.4332		.1915

x	180	195	200
Z	−1.50		.50

.4332 + .1915 = .6247 or 62%

Chapter 7

7.1 $n = 36, \mu = 120, \sigma = 15$

Follows an approximately normal distribution with a mean equal to the population mean and a standard deviation of $\sigma/\sqrt{n}$

7.2 $n = 25, \mu = 60, \sigma = 10$

a. $P(57 < \bar{x} < 63); Z_1 = (57 - 60)/(10/5) = -1.5;$
$Z_2 = (63 - 60)/2 = 1.5; A = 2(.4332) = .8664 = 86.6\%$

c. $P(\bar{x} > 61); Z = (61 - 60)/2 = 0.5; A = .5 - .1915 = .3085 = 30.9\%$

7.5 $\mu = 50, \sigma = 12$

a. $\text{SE}(\bar{x}) = \dfrac{12}{\sqrt{16}} = 3$

c. $\text{SE}(\bar{x})$ decreases when n increases.

7.6 $\mu = 71, \sigma = 5, n = 15$

a. $P(\bar{x} \geq 77); Z = (77 - 71)/(5/\sqrt{15}) = 4.65; A = .999; P(\bar{x} > 77) < .001$

b. $P(65 < \bar{x} < 75)$

$$Z_1 = \frac{65 - 71}{5/\sqrt{15}} = -4.65$$

$$Z_2 = \frac{75 - 71}{5/\sqrt{15}} = 3.099; \text{ total } A = .999; P(65 < \bar{x} \; 75) = .999$$

7.7 $\mu = 52.5; \sigma = 4.5; P(\bar{x} > 56)$

a. $n = 10; Z = (56 - 52.5)/(4.5/\sqrt{10}) = 2.460; A = .0069$

7.8 $\mu = 3360, \sigma = 490$

a. $Z_1 = (2300 - 3360)/490 = -2.1633; A = .4846$
$Z_2 = (4300 - 3360)/490 = 1.9184; A = .4726; \text{ total } A = .9572;$
$P(2300 < x < 4300) = .96$

c. $Z = (5000 - 3360)/490 = 3.3469; A = <.001$

7.9 b. $Z_1 = (3100 - 3360)/(490/\sqrt{49}) = -3.7143; \text{ total } A = .999;$
$P(3100 < \bar{x} < 3600) = .999$
$Z_2 = (3600 - 3360)/(490/\sqrt{49}) = 3.4286$

c. $Z = (2500 - 3360)/(490/\sqrt{49}) = -12.2857; A < .001; P(\bar{x} < 2500) < .001$

7.12 a. The distribution of observations is more variable than the distribution of sample means. The distribution of sample means has the same mean as the parent distribution, but it has a smaller variance.

b. The standard deviation is a measure of variation of the individual x's. The standard error is a measure of variation of a sample of x's expressed as $\bar{x}$. Consequently, it is smaller.

c. In discussing the location of the individual x's, we would want to use the standard deviation. In trying to make inferences about the group (sample) mean, $\bar{x}$, we would want to use $\text{SE}(\bar{x})$.

7.14 $\mu = 200, \sigma = 25, n = 49$

$$\sigma_x = \frac{\sigma}{\sqrt{n}} = \frac{25}{\sqrt{49}} = \frac{25}{7} = 3.57$$

$$Z_1 = \frac{190 - 200}{3.57} = \frac{-10}{3.57} = -2.80; \; Z_2 = \frac{205 - 200}{3.57} = \frac{5}{3.57} = 1.40$$

$$-2.80 \leq P(Z) \leq 1.40 = .4974 + .4192 = .9166$$

7.16 $\mu = 2400, \sigma = 400, n = 64$

$$\sigma_x = \frac{400}{\sqrt{64}} = 50$$

a. $P(\bar{x}) > 2500$

$$P(Z) = \frac{2500 - 2400}{50} = 2$$

$P(Z) > 2 = .5 - .4772 = .0228$

b. $2300 \le P(\bar{x}) \le 2500$

$-2 \le P(Z) \le 2$

$2(.4772) = .9544$

c. $P(\bar{x}) < 2350$

$$P(Z) < \frac{2350 - 2400}{50} = \frac{-50}{50} = -1.0$$

$P(Z) < -1 = .5000 - .3413 = .1587$

7.18 $\mu = 118, \sigma = 12$

a. $112 < P(x) < 124$

$$\frac{112 - 118}{12} < P(Z) < \frac{124 - 118}{12}$$

$$\frac{-6}{12} < P(Z) < \frac{6}{12}$$

$-.5 < P(Z) < .5 = 2(.1915) = .3830$

b. $112 < P(\bar{x}) < 124$

$$\frac{112 - 118}{12/\sqrt{16}} < P(Z) < \frac{124 - 118}{12/\sqrt{16}}$$

$$\frac{-6}{3} < P(Z) < \frac{6}{3}$$

$-2 < P(Z) < 2 = 2(.4772) = .9544$

c. The reason for the threefold difference in the probabilities of the events is that in (a) we are dealing with x—the individual blood pressure of a girl—and in (b) we are dealing with a much less variable entity: the $\bar{x}$ blood pressure based on a group of $n = 16$ girls.

7.20 $\bar{x} = 73, s^2 = 121$

a. $P(80 < x < 100)$; $Z_1 = (80 - 73)/11 = .64$; $Z_2 = (100 - 73)/11 = 2.45$;

$A = .4929 - .2389 = .254$

c. $P(x > 90)$; $Z = (90 - 73)/11 = 1.55$; $A = .5 - .4394 = .0606$

7.23 $n = 100, \bar{x} = 15, s = 40, \text{SE}(\bar{x}) = 4$

$$P(\bar{x} < 160) \quad \text{or} \quad P\left(Z < \frac{160 - 150}{\text{SE}(\bar{x})} = \frac{10}{4} = 2.50\right)$$

$P(Z < 2.50) < .9938$

7.25 We could use the central limit theorem to justify performing a test of hypothesis.

Chapter 8

8.1 a. $H_0: \mu \le 30, \ H_1: \mu > 30$

d. $H_0: \mu \ge 31.5, \ H_1: \mu < 31.5$

e. $H_0: \mu = 16, \ H_1: \mu \ne 16$

8.5 a. -1.645 or 1.645
c. -3.012 and 3.012
e. -2.03 and 2.03

8.6 a. Z test in (a) and (d)
b. t test in (b), (c), and (e)

8.7 a. -1.96 and 1.96
c. -2.576 and 2.576
e. -2.602
f. -1.6759

8.8 a. Fail to reject H_0.
c. Reject H_0.
e. Fail to reject H_0.
f. Reject H_0.

8.12 a. 95% CI $= 122 \pm 2.0003(11/\sqrt{61}) = 119.18 < \mu < 124.82$
c. 95% CI $= 177 \pm 1.96(21/\sqrt{51}) = 171.24 < \mu < 182.76$
f. 95% CI $= 48 \pm 1.96(12.8/\sqrt{91}) = 45.37 < \mu < 50.63$
g. 99% CI $= 48 \pm 2.5758(12.8/\sqrt{91}) = 44.54 < \mu < 51.46$

8.14 95% CI $= 64 \pm 1.9840\ (8.61/\sqrt{100}) = 62.29 < \mu\ 65.71$
99% CI $= 64 \pm 2.6260(8.61/\sqrt{100}) = 61.74 < \mu < 66.26$

8.19 a. $H_0: \mu \leq 170, H_1: \mu > 170$
b. Z
c. $\alpha = .05,\ Z$ critical value $= 1.645$
d. $Z = \dfrac{177 - 170}{16/\sqrt{25}} = 2.19$
e. Reject H_0. Results are significant.
f. Based on this sample, there is evidence that Minnesota males are heavier than the population mean of U.S. males.
g. 95% CI $= 177 \pm 1.96(16/25) = 170.73 - 183.27$. There is a 95% probability that μ (population mean weight) lies between 170.73 and 183.27.
h. One-tailed $P = .0143$
i. $P < .05$
j. Because the exact P value is less than $\alpha = .05$, the results are significant.
k. Type I. In order to minimize the possibility of either a type I or a type II error, a study can be replicated with a larger sample size.

8.20 a. $H_0: \mu \leq 170,\ H_1: \mu > 170$
b. t
c. $\alpha = . 05,\ df = 25 - 1 = 24,\ t$ critical value $= 1.71$
d. $t = \dfrac{177 - 170}{16/\sqrt{25}} = 2.19$
e,f,k. Same as Exercise 8.19
g. 95% CI $= 177 \pm 2.0639\ (16/\sqrt{25}) = 170.40 < \mu < 183.60$
h. An exact P value cannot be calculated because we do not have raw data.
i. $P < .05$
j. Because the exact P value is less than $\alpha = .05$, the results are significant.

8.23 a. H_0: $\mu \le 950$, H_1: $\mu > 950$
b. t
c. $\alpha = .05$, df $= 30 - 1 = 29$, t critical value $= 1.70$
   $\alpha =. 01$, df $= 30 - 1 = 29$, t critical value $= 2.46$
d. $t = \dfrac{975 - 950}{60/\sqrt{30}} = 2.28$
e. Reject H_0 at $\alpha = .05$; fail to reject H_0 at $\alpha = .01$. Results are significant at .05 but not at .01.
f. Based on this sample, there is evidence that the soup has more sodium than listed at $\alpha = .05$; however, at $\alpha = .01$, we would conclude that there is not sufficient evidence to believe that the soup contains more sodium than listed.
g. 95% CI $= 975 \pm 2.0452(60/\sqrt{30}) = 952.60 < \mu < 997.40$
   99% CI $= 975 \pm 2.7564(60/\sqrt{30}) = 944.81 < \mu < 1005.19$
   There is a 95% probability that μ (population mean sodium level) lies between 952.60 and 997.40. There is a 99% probability that μ (population mean sodium level) lies between 944.81 and 1005.19.
i. $P < .05$, $P > .01$
j. Results are significant at .05 but not at .01.
k. Depending on the α used, there is either a type I or a type II error. We won't know which until further studies are conducted with a larger sample.

8.26 a. H_0: $\mu \le 200$, H_1: $\mu > 200$
b. t
c. $\alpha = .05$, df $= 49 - 1 = 48$, t critical value $= 1.68$
d. $t = \dfrac{211 - 200}{16.67/\sqrt{49}} = 4.62$
e. Reject H_0. Results are significant.
f. Based on this sample, there is evidence that overweight men have significantly elevated serum cholesterol levels.
g. 95% CI $= 211 \pm 2.0086(16.67/\sqrt{49}) = 206.22 < \mu < 215.78$. There is a 95% probability that μ (population mean serum cholesterol) lies between 206.22 and 215.78.
i. $P < .05$
j. Results are significant at .05.
k. Type I. In order to minimize the possibility of either a type I or a type II error, the study can be replicated with a larger sample size.

8.29 a. H_0: $\mu \ge 750$, H_1: $\mu < 750$
b. t
c. $\alpha = .01$, df $= 15 - 1 = 14$, t critical value $= -2.62$
d. $t = \dfrac{730 - 750}{24.2/\sqrt{15}} = -3.20$
e. Reject H_0. Results are significant.
f. Based on this sample, there is evidence that the vitamin C pills contain less than 750 mg of vitamin C.
g. 99% CI $= 730 \pm 2.9768(24.202/\sqrt{15}) = 711.40 < \mu < 748.60$. There is a 99% probability that μ (population mean vitamin C level) lies between 711.40 and 748.60.

h. One-tailed $P = .0032$, computer-generated
i. $P < .01$
j. Because the exact P value is less than $\alpha = .01$, the results are significant.
k. Type I

Chapter 9

9.3

	Mean	s	n	
Males	74.9	12.0	38	$s_p^2 = 131.51$
Females	71.8	11.0	45	

$$3.10 \pm 2.64(11.47)\sqrt{\frac{1}{38} + \frac{1}{45}}$$

$$-3.57 < \mu_1 - \mu_2 < 9.77$$

9.7   a. 95% CI for $\mu_1 - \mu_2$ $= 255 - 231 \pm 2.01(49.5)\sqrt{1/25 + 1/25}$
$= 24 \pm 2.01(49.5)(.2828) = 24 \pm 28.1$
$-4.1 < \mu < 52.1$

b. 99% CI for $\mu_1 - \mu_2$ $= 255 - 231 \pm 2.68(49.5)\sqrt{1/25 + 1/25}$
$= 24 \pm 2.68(49.5)(.2828) = 24 \pm 37.5$
$-13.5 < \mu < 61.5$

9.9   a. $n = \left(\dfrac{Z\sigma}{d}\right)^2 = \left(\dfrac{257(1.6)}{0.5}\right)^2 = (8.22)^2 = 67.6$ or 68

b. $n = \left(\dfrac{Z\sigma}{d}\right)^2 = \left(\dfrac{1.96(1.6)}{0.5}\right)^2 = (6.27)^2 = 39.34$

9.13   a. $H_0: \mu_1 = \mu_2, H_1: \mu_1 \neq \mu_2$
b. Independent t test. These are two different, unrelated groups.
c. $\alpha = .05$, df $= 54 + 85 - 2 = 137$, critical value $= \pm 1.98$
d. $t = 2.59$
f. $P < .05$
g. 95% CI $= 0.61 < \mu < 4.59$. We are 95% certain that college males will consume anywhere from .61 to 4.59 more drinks per drinking occasion than college females.
h. Reject H_0. The results are significant.
i. There is evidence that the maximum daily alcohol consumption of college males is greater than that of college females.
j. Because H_0 was rejected, there is a possibility of a type I error.

9.15   a $H_0: \mu_1 = \mu_2, H_1: \mu_1 \neq \mu_2$
b. Independent t test. These are two different, unrelated groups.
c. $\alpha = .01$, df $= 27 + 30 - 2 = 55$, critical value $= \pm 2.68$ (50 df used)
d. $s_p = .17$

$$t = \frac{.64 - .51}{.17\sqrt{(1/27 + 1/30)}} = \frac{.13}{.045} = 2.88$$

f. $P < .01$

g. 99% CI = 0.13 ± 2.68(.045) = .01 < μ < .25. We are 99% certain that the tumors in treatment B are between .01 cc and .25 cc larger than those in treatment A.

h. Reject H_0. The results are significant.

i. There is evidence to indicate that the tumors in treatment A are smaller than those in treatment B.

j. Because H_0 was rejected, there is a possibility of a type I error.

9.17 a. $H_0: \mu_1 = \mu_2, H_1: \mu_1 \neq \mu_2$

b. Independent t test

c. $\alpha = .05$, df = 40 + 43 − 2 = 81, critical value = ±1.99

d. $s_p = 11.55$

$$t = \frac{73.5 - 72.9}{11.55\sqrt{(1/40 + 1/43)}} = .236$$

f. $P > .05$

g. 95% CI = 0.6 ± 1.99(2.53) = −4.43 < μ < 5.63. We are 95% certain that nonvegetarians' diastolic blood pressure may be from 5.63 points higher to 4.43 points lower than that of vegetarians.

h. Accept (fail to reject) H_0. The results are not significant.

i. The evidence is insufficient to indicate a difference in mean blood pressure between the two groups.

j. Because H_0 was accepted, there is a possibility of a type II error.

9.20 a. $H_0: \mu_1 = \mu_2, H_1: \mu_1 \neq \mu_2$

b. Paired t test. Each lab is analyzing blood from the same persons.

c. $\alpha = .01$, df = 10 − 1 = 9, critical value = ±3.25

d. $s_d = \sqrt{\dfrac{2486 - (144)^2/10}{9}} = 6.77$

$$t = \frac{14.4 - 0}{6.77/\sqrt{10}} = 6.73$$

e. Exact P value is < .0001.

g. 99% CI = −21.36 < μ < −7.44. We would expect the readings from lab 1 to be between 7.44 and 21.36 points *lower* than the readings from lab 2 99% of the time.

h. Reject H_0. The results are significant.

i. There is a significant difference in cholesterol readings between the two labs.

j. Because H_0 was rejected, there is a possibility of a type I error.

9.22 a. $H_0: \mu_1 = \mu_2, H_1: \mu_1 \neq \mu_2$

b. Independent t test. These are two different, unrelated groups.

c. $\alpha = .05$, df = 14 + 18 − 2 = 30, critical value = ±2.04

d. $t = 2.982$

e. Exact P value is .0056.

g. 95% CI = 3.47 < μ < 18.53. We would expect the heart rate of smokers to be anywhere from 3.47 to 18.53 beats per minute higher than that of nonsmokers 95% of the time.

h. Reject H_0. The results are significant.

i. The heart rate for smokers is significantly higher than for nonsmokers.

j. Because H_0 was rejected, there is a possibility of a type I error.

Chapter 10

10.1 A $-F$ ratio is not possible. There is an error in the calculations.

10.2
a. In a one-way ANOVA, you can partition the variation into two sources and test one of them. In a two-way ANOVA, you can partition the variation into three sources and test two of them.

b. That the observations are independent. Furthermore, that the observations of each group are normally distributed and that the variances of the various groups are homogeneous.

c. $H_0: \mu_1 = \mu_2 = \cdots = \mu_k$ for a one-way ANOVA

$\left.\begin{array}{l} H_0: \mu_{1\cdot} = \mu_{2\cdot} = \cdots = \mu_{k\cdot} \\ H_0: \mu_{\cdot 1} = \mu_{\cdot 2} = \cdots = \mu_{\cdot n} \end{array}\right\}$ for a two-way ANOVA

10.3
a. For $\alpha = .05$: $F_{1,16} = 4.49$; $F_{3,16} = 3.24$; $F_{3,36} = 2.88$

b. For $\alpha = .01$: $F_{1,16} = 8.53$; $F_{3,16} = 5.29$; $F_{3,36} = 4.41$

10.8
a. $H_0: \mu_1 = \mu_2 = \mu_3$ (mean number of children is same for all groups)

b.

Source of Variation	SS	df	MS	F Ratio
Between	381.67	2	190.84	26.84
Within	191.90	27	7.11	$F_{.95}(2,27) = 3.35$
Total	573.57	29		

c. $\text{HSD} = q(\alpha, k, N - k)\sqrt{\dfrac{\text{MSW}}{n}} = 3.53\sqrt{7.10/10} = 3.53(.843) = 2.97$

	1.7	7.7	10.2
1.7	—	6.0	8.5
7.7		—	2.5
10.2			—

Because only 6.0 and 8.5 exceed 2.97, they are the only significant pairs at $\alpha = .05$.

e. Reject H_0, and conclude that the need for family planning counsel differs by the number of children per family.

10.10
b.

Source of Variation	SS	df	MS	F Ratio
Between	8,290.62	2	4,145.38	23.92
Within	3,118.33	18	173.24	$F_{.95}(2,18) = 3.55$
Total	11,408.95	20		

c. $\text{HSD} = 3.61\sqrt{173.24/7} = 3.61(4.975) = 17.96$

	23.0	71.3	41.9
23.0	—	48.3	18.9
71.3		—	29.4
41.9			—

Because all differences exceed the critical difference of 17.96, all pairs are significantly different from each other at the $\alpha = .05$ level.

e. Reject H_0: $\mu_1 = \mu_2 = \mu_3$, and conclude that the mean ages of the three communities are different.

10.12 b. $SS_t = 8299 - 7980 = 319$ $SS_r = 319 - 116 - 143 = 60$
$SS_{tr} = 6(1352.01) - 7980 = 132$
$SS_b = 8123 - 7980 = 143$

Source	SS	df	MS	F
Treatment	132	2	66.0	13.75
Blocks	139	5	27.8	5.79
Residual	48	10	4.8	
Total	319	17		

c. Because $13.75 > F_{2,10} = 4.1$ at the $\alpha = .05$ level, there is a significant difference in the recidivism of the three programs.

d. Tukey's HSD is $q(\alpha, 3, 15)\sqrt{10/6} = 3.67(1.29) = 4.74$.

	24.9	19.8	18.5
24.9	—	5.0	6.3
19.8		—	1.3
18.5			—

All differences are significant except B and C at the $\alpha = .05$ level.

e. Because $4.8 > F_{5,10} = 3.33$ at the $\alpha = .05$ level, it appears that weight also is influential in recidivism.

10.13 b. ANOVA Table

Source	SS	df	(MS) or s^2	F
Between	131.6	4	32.9	10.6
Within	94	30	3.1	
Total	225.6	34		

c. The calculated F is 10.6.
The critical $F_{.05}$ at df (4, 30) is 2.69.
The critical $F_{.01}$ at df (4, 30) is 4.02.
The F ratio is significant at .05 and .01.

d. The q value from Appendix C is 4.10 for a .05 level of significance and 5.05 for a .01 level of significance.
The critical HSD for a .05 level of significance is 2.69, and for a .01 level of significance it is 3.36.
There is a significantly greater weight gain in the following pairs at a .05 level of significance: A–B, A–C, A–E, B–C, C–D, C–E.
There is a significantly greater weight gain in the following pairs at a .01 level of significance: A–C, C–D.

10.14 b.

Source of Variation	Sum of Squares	df	Mean Squares (s^2)	F Ratio	Critical F	P value
Between	3,127,499	2	1,563,750	9.18	3.29	.0007
Within	5,619,875	33	170,299			
Total	8,747,374	35				

c. The calculated F is 9.18.
The critical $F_{.05}$ at df (2, 33) is 3.29.
The critical $F_{.01}$ at df (2, 33) is 5.33.
The F ratio is significant at .05 and .01.
d. The q value from Appendix C is 3.48 for a .05 level of significance and 4.42 for a .01 level of significance.
The critical HSD for a .05 level of significance is 415, and for a .01 level of significance it is 527.
There is a significant difference between the birth weight of infants born to mothers who do not smoke and that of infants born to mothers who smoke 1+ pack/day, and between the birth weight of infants born to mothers who smoke 1 pack/day versus 1+ pack/day at $\alpha = .05$. At $\alpha = .01$, the only significant difference is between the birth weight of infants born to mothers who do not smoke versus those who smoke 1+ pack/day.

10.15 Notice that when you complete the Tukey post hoc analysis you find that zone C had significantly more calls than any other zone and that zone A had significantly fewer calls than any other zone. This might lead you to conclude that fewer resources are needed in zone A and more resources are needed in zone C.

Chapter 11

11.1 a. p_1 (none) = 25/100 = .25
p_2 (primary) = 32/100 = .32
p_3 (intermediate) = 24/100 = .24
$p_4 + p_5$ (high school and technical school) = 19/100 = .19
c. p_1 (mostly sitting) = .49; p_2 (moderate) = .51; p_3 (much) = 0

11.2 $\mu = np = 7683(.37) = 2842.71$
$\sigma = \sqrt{npq} = \sqrt{7683(.37)(.63)} = 42.32$

11.3 $H_0: p_H = .31, H_1: p_H \neq .31$
$\alpha = .05$
Critical region: $Z > 1.96, Z < -1.96$
$Z = \dfrac{p_H - p}{\sqrt{pq/n}} = \dfrac{.37 - .31}{\sqrt{(.31)(.69)/100}} = 1.30$
Fail to reject H_0, and conclude that the evidence is insufficient to indicate that the proportion of smokers in Honolulu is significantly different from that in the United States in general.

11.5 $p_1 = 4/7 = .57; p_2 = 7/21 = .33$
$p' = \dfrac{4 + 7}{7 + 21} = .39$

$$SE(p_1 - p_2) = \sqrt{\frac{(.39)(.61)}{7} + \frac{(.39)(.61)}{21}}$$

$$= .213$$

$H_0: p_1 - p_2 = 0, H_1: p_1 - p_2 \neq 0$

$\alpha = .05$

$$Z = \frac{.57 - .33}{.213} = 1.127$$

$Z(.025) = \pm 1.96$

Fail to reject H_0. There is no difference in the proportion of smokers between the two groups.

11.6 90% CI for $p_1 - p_2 = p_1 - p_2 \pm 1.645 \sqrt{\frac{(.57)(.43)}{7} + \frac{(.33)(.67)}{21}}$

$$= .24 \pm .35$$

$$= -.11 < p_1 - p_2 < .59$$

11.8 $p = 29/99 = .293$

99% CI for $p = .293 \pm 2.576 \sqrt{\frac{(.293)(.707)}{99}}$

$$= .293 \pm .118$$

$$= .175 < p < .411$$

11.10 $p_1 = \frac{55}{219} = .251; p_2 = \frac{117}{822} = .142$

$\alpha = .01$

$$p' = \frac{55 + 117}{219 + 822} = .165; q' = .835$$

$$SE(p_1 - p_2) = \sqrt{\frac{(.165)(.835)}{219} + \frac{(.165)(.835)}{822}} = .028$$

$H_0: p_1 - p_2 = 0$

$$Z = \frac{.251 - .142}{.028} = 3.893 \qquad \text{Critical region is } \pm 2.576 \text{ (for } \alpha = .01\text{)}.$$

Reject H_0, and conclude that there was a significantly higher proportion of those who started smoking at an earlier age among "abusers" than among "nonusers."

11.12 a. For Exercise 11.10:

99% CI for $p_1 - p_2 = p_1 - p_2 \pm 2.576 \sqrt{\frac{(.251)(.749)}{219} + \frac{(.142)(.858)}{822}}$

$$= .109 \pm .082$$

$$= .027 < p_1 - p_2 < .191$$

11.13 a. $\mu = n\pi, \sigma = \sqrt{n\pi(1 - \pi)}$

b. p is the estimate of the parameter π.

c. The mean is $\frac{x}{n}$ and $\sigma_p = \sqrt{\frac{\pi(1 - \pi)}{n}}$.

d. When $n\pi \geq 5$ and $n(1 - \pi) \geq 5$ are satisfied

11.15 a. $p_1 = \frac{60}{100} = 0.6$ of males; $p_2 = \frac{70}{100} = 0.7$ of females

b. 99% CI for $\pi_1 - \pi_2 = p_1 - p_2 \pm Z \sqrt{\dfrac{p_1(1-p_1)}{n_1} + \dfrac{p_2(1-p_2)}{n_2}}$

$$= 0.6 - 0.7 \pm 2.58 \sqrt{\dfrac{.6(.4)}{100} + \dfrac{.7(.3)}{100}}$$

$$= -.1 \pm 2.58(.0671) = -.1 \pm .17$$

$$= -.27 \text{ to } .07$$

c. Because the CI for $\pi_1 - \pi_2$ includes zero in its interval, the difference is not a significant difference.

11.17 $p_1 = \dfrac{43}{100} = 0.43; p_2 = \dfrac{22}{100} = 0.22$

$p' = \dfrac{43 + 22}{100 + 100} = \dfrac{65}{200} = 0.33$

$SE(p_1 - p_2) = \sqrt{\dfrac{.33(.65)}{100} + \dfrac{.33(.65)}{100}} = \sqrt{.00429} = 0.0655$

1. $H_0: \pi_1 - \pi_2 = 0, H_1: \pi_1 - \pi_2 \neq 0$
2. $\alpha = .01$
3. $Z = \dfrac{p_1 - p_2 - 0}{SE(p_1 - p_2)} = \dfrac{.21}{.0655} = 3.21$
4. Critical region is area beyond 2.58.
5. Because $3.16 > 2.58$, we reject the H_0 of equality and declare that geographics appears to play a significant role in allergies.

11.19 $P = \dfrac{13}{100} = .13$ and 95% CI for $\pi = .13 \pm 1.96 \sqrt{\dfrac{P(1-P)}{n}}$

$$= .13 \pm 1.96 \sqrt{\dfrac{.13(.87)}{100}}$$

$$= .13 \pm 1.96(.0336)$$

$$= .13 \pm .066$$

$$= .06 \text{ to } .20$$

Include a 95% CI for π and indicate that workers have a significant toxic exposure.

11.20 a. Proportions for Oregon: before 0.29, after 0.24
Proportions for Washington: before 0.28, after 0.29

b. Oregon: $p' = 1275 + 1023$ divided by $4475 + 4168 = .266$; SE $= .01$
$H_0: p_1 - p_2 = 0, H_1: p_1 - p_2 > 0$
$\alpha = .05$
$Z = \dfrac{.29 - .24}{.01} = 5.00$
$Z(.05) = 1.64$
Reject H_0. The proportion of fatally injured drivers, in Oregon, is lower after the enactment of the 0.08% law.
Washington: $p' = \dfrac{1735 + 1582}{6184 + 5390} = .287$; SE $= .008$
$H_0: p_1 - p_2 = 0, H_1: p_1 - p_2 > 0$

$\alpha = .05$

$$Z = \frac{.28 - .29}{.008} = -1.25$$

$Z(.05) = 1.64$

Fail to reject H_0. The proportion of fatally injured drivers, in Washington, is not lower after the enactment of the 0.08% law.

Chapter 12

12.1 a.

	Smoker		Nonsmoker	
	Observed	Expected	Observed	Expected
None	4	6.73	16	13.26
Primary	15	10.78	17	21.22
Intermediate	12	8.08	12	15.92
Senior high	1	3.03	8	5.97
Technical school	0	3.37	10	6.63

H_0: There is no association between smoking and educational level.

$\alpha = .05$

$\chi^2 = 14.17$ and $\chi^2_{.05}(df = 4) = 9.49$

Reject H_0.

b.

	Smoker		Nonsmoker	
	Observed	Expected	Observed	Expected
None	4	6.73	16	13.26
Primary	15	10.78	17	21.22
Intermediate	12	8.08	12	15.92
Senior high and technical school	1	6.40	18	12.60

$\alpha = .05$

$\chi^2 = 13.91$ and $\chi^2_{.05}(df = 3) = 7.81$

Reject H_0, and conclude that smoking is dependent on educational level—namely, smoking is less frequent among the more highly educated.

12.3 a.

	Egg Consumption							
	0		1		2–4		Daily	
	O	E	O	E	O	E	O	E
Low	5	5.36	13	13.66	8	9.91	4	1.07
Medium	4	6.79	20	17.30	14	12.55	0	1.36
High	11	7.86	18	20.04	15	14.54	0	1.57

H_0: There is no association between egg consumption and age at menarche.

$\alpha = .05$

$\chi^2 = 14.59$ and $\chi^2_{.05}(df = 6) = 12.59$

Reject H_0, and conclude that age at menarche is dependent on level of egg consumption.

b.

| | Egg Consumption | | | | | |
	0		1		2–7	
	O	E	O	E	O	E
Low	5	5.36	13	13.66	12	10.98
Medium	4	6.79	20	17.30	14	13.91
High	11	7.86	18	20.04	15	16.11

H_0: There is no association between egg consumption and age at menarche.

$\alpha = .05$

$\chi^2 = 3.26$ and $\chi^2_{.05}(df = 4) = 9.49$

Fail to reject H_0: The data do not refute the H_0 of *no* association between age at menarche and egg consumption.

12.4 a.

| | Smoking | | No Smoking | | |
	O	E	O	E	Total
Hypertension group	4	2.75	3	4.25	7
Control group	7	8.25	14	12.75	21
Total	11		17		28

H_0: $p_1 = p_2$ (there is no difference in the proportion of smokers in the two groups)

$\alpha = .05$

$\chi^2 = 1.25$ and $\chi^2_{.05}(df = 1) = 3.84$

Fail to reject H_0: The data do not refute the H_0 of no association between smoking and hypertension.

12.5

| | Heartbeat | | | | |
Age Interval	O	E	$O - E$	$\dfrac{(O - E)^2}{E}$	
25–34	18	43.13	−25.12	14.63	
35–44	33	38.56	−5.56	0.80	$E_1 = \dfrac{140{,}195(188)}{611{,}152} = 43.13$
45–54	54	37.17	16.83	7.62	
55–64	48	30.42	17.58	10.16	
≥65	35	38.72	−3.72	0.36	
	188			33.57	

H_0: The age distribution of the Heartbeat group is the same as that of the MSA.

$\alpha = .05$

$\chi^2 = 33.58$ and $\chi^2_{.05}(df = 4) = 9.49$

Reject H_0: The Heartbeat age distribution is significantly different from the MSA age distribution.

12.7 a. The basis is the probability multiplication rule.

b. They are computed by multiplying the two marginal totals of the frequency and then dividing the product by the total frequency.

12.9 The odds ratio is $\dfrac{a/b}{c/d} = \dfrac{25/10}{14/51} = \dfrac{2.5}{.2745} = 9.1$.

The risk of developing heart disease among smokers is 9.1 times that of nonsmokers.

12.11 $RR = \dfrac{a/(a+b)}{c/(c+d)} = \dfrac{20/3299}{1/6701} = 40.6$

According to these data, the RR of developing lung cancer among smokers is 40.6 times that of nonsmokers.

12.13

	M	F	Total
Overweight	15	36	51
Not overweight	85	64	149
Total	100	100	200

$\alpha = .05$
H_0: Both groups are homogeneous.

$$\chi^2 = \frac{200(15(64) - 36(85))^2}{100 \times 100 \times 51 \times 149} = 11.61$$

Conclusion: The two groups are not homogeneous at the .05 level because $\chi^2 = 11.61 > 3.84$.

12.15 a.

	M	F	Total
Belt	60	70	130
No belt	40	30	70
Total	100	100	200

$\alpha = .01$
H_0: Sexes are homogeneous.

$$\chi^2 = \frac{200(60(30) - 70(40))^2}{100 \times 100 \times 130 \times 70} = 2.20$$

b. Because $\chi^2 = 2.20 < 3.84$, there is no significant difference in seat belt use between the sexes.

c. $\chi^2 = \dfrac{(60 - 65)^2}{65} + \dfrac{(70 - 65)^2}{65} + \dfrac{(40 - 35)^2}{35} + \dfrac{(30 - 35)^2}{35} = 2.20$

They are the same.

12.17

Substance Abuse	High	Low	Total
Alcoholic family	28	12	40
Nonalcoholic family	13	15	28
Total	41	27	68

$\alpha = .05$

$$\chi^2 = \frac{68((28)(15) - (13)(12))^2}{41 \times 27 \times 40 \times 28} = 3.82$$

Because $\chi^2 = 3.82 < 3.84$, there is no significant difference in juvenile substance abuse between alcoholic and nonalcoholic families.

Family Violence	Police Called to Home One or More Times	No Police Calls	Total
Alcoholic family	25	15	40
Nonalcoholic family	6	22	28
Total	31	37	68

$\alpha = .05$

$$\chi^2 = \frac{68((25)(22) - (15)(6))^2}{31 \times 37 \times 40 \times 28} = 11.2$$

Because $\chi^2 = 11.2 > 3.84$, there is a significant difference in the incidence of family violence between alcoholic and nonalcoholic families.

Neglect	Left Alone for Long Periods	Not Left Alone for Long Periods	Total
Alcoholic family	5	35	40
Nonalcoholic family	8	20	28
Total	13	55	68

$\alpha = .05$

$$\chi^2 = \frac{68((5)(20) - (35)(8))^2}{13 \times 55 \times 40 \times 28} = 2.75$$

Because $\chi^2 = 2.75 < 3.84$, there is no significant difference in the incidence of juveniles left alone between alcoholic and nonalcoholic families.

12.18

Race	Mutagen-Containing Meats						
	0–1 Servings		2–3 Servings		4 or More Servings		
	O	E	O	E	O	E	Total
African American	68	77.2	36	29.6	11	8.2	115
White	73	63.8	18	24.4	4	6.8	95
Total	141		54		15		210

H_0: There is no relationship between race and the consumption of mutagen-containing meats.

$\alpha = .05$

$\chi^2 = 7.60$ and $\chi^2_{.05}(df = 2) = 5.99$

Reject H_0: There appears to be a relationship between race and the consumption of mutagen-containing meats.

12.19   a. The odds ratio is 3.8.

Chapter 13

13.1   a. Range −1 to 1

     b. The sign tells the direction of the slope.

     c. It tells the strength of the linear relationship.

d. It tells how good the prediction is likely to be.
e. Yes, they would have the same sign. No, they would not have the same magnitude.

13.4 The limitations are
  i. it measures only straight-line relationships
  ii. it does not prove a cause-and-effect relationship

13.5 a. To test $H_0: \rho = 0$ we need to make the following assumptions:
    i. The pairs were obtained randomly.
    ii. x and y must be normally distributed.
  b. To test $H_0: \beta = 0$, we need to make the following assumptions:
    i. The means of each distribution of y's for a given x fall on a straight line.
    ii. The variances are homogeneous for each distribution of y's for each value of x.
    iii. The distribution of y's is normal for a given x.

13.8 The strongest correlation is $-.71$. The closer you are to either -1.00 or 1.00, the stronger the correlation. Conversely, the closer you are to 0.00, the weaker the correlation. The weakest correlation is $.08$.

13.9 a. $n = 25, .25-.80$ $n = 50, .39-.75$ $n = 100, .45-.71$

13.10 If you had 105 correlations, you would expect that by chance alone 5% or approximately 5 of the correlations would be significant at the .05 level of significance.

13.14 Plot of systolic blood pressure in row 3 (R3) versus cadmium level in row 1 (R1):

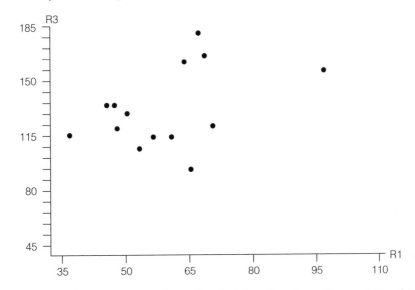

f. The plot does not support the notion that there is a strong linear relationship between the two variables.

g. Plot of zinc level in row 2 (R2) versus cadmium level in row 1 (R1):

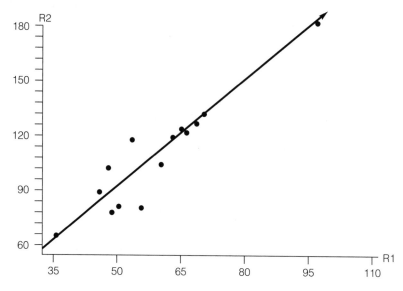

Correlation of R1 and R2 = .931

h. Yes, since it appears to follow a straight line.

i. $b = \dfrac{94{,}517 - (823)(1516)/14}{51{,}169 - [(823)^2]/14} = 1.936$

$a = 108.286 - (1.936)(58.786)$
$= -5.523$
$\hat{y} = 1.936x - 5.523$

j. $\hat{y} = 1.936(80) - 5.523 = 149.36$

k. $H_0: \beta = 0;\ \alpha = .05;\ b = 1.936$

$SE(b) = \sqrt{\dfrac{232.363}{46{,}364.357}} = .071;\ t = \dfrac{1.936 - 0}{.071} = 27.3$

Reject H_0, and conclude that the population regression coefficient is significantly different from zero.

l. No, because this is not possible to assess with this method.

13.15 a. $r = \dfrac{14{,}269.8 - \dfrac{(84)(2030)}{12}}{\sqrt{\left(589.2 - \dfrac{84^2}{12}\right)\left(346{,}940 - \dfrac{2030^2}{12}\right)}} = \dfrac{59.8}{\sqrt{(1.2)(3531.7)}} = \dfrac{59.8}{65.10} = 0.919$

d. 95% CI for ρ = .70 to .96

13.16 a. $r = \dfrac{169{,}140 - \dfrac{(6640)(226)}{11}}{\sqrt{\left(5{,}440{,}400 - \dfrac{6640^2}{11}\right)\left(6018 - \dfrac{226^2}{11}\right)}}$

$= \dfrac{32{,}718}{\sqrt{(1{,}432{,}255)(1375)}} = \dfrac{32{,}718}{44{,}377} = 0.7373$

b. At $\alpha = .05$, $t = \dfrac{0.7373}{\sqrt{(1 - .54)/9}} = \dfrac{0.7373}{0.2261} = 3.26$

Because $t = 3.26 > 2.26$, the critical t value at the .05 level, there is a significant correlation between current death rates and previous cigarette consumption. The correlation coefficient of 0.73 is quite high, indicating a strong association of current death rates with cigarette consumption 20 years earlier.

c. $r^2 = .54$ provides an estimate of the total variation in y that is explained by the variation in x.

13.17 With $n = 28$: $r = .23$, 95% CI $= -.16$ to .56

With $n = 15$ (initial): $r = .44$, 95% CI $= -.10$ to .78

With $n = 13$ (follow-up): $r = .17$, 95% CI $= -.42$ to .66

None of the correlations are significant; $P > .05$.

13.19 e. $b = \dfrac{3,371,580 - \dfrac{(15,214)(21,696)}{100}}{2,611,160 - \dfrac{(15,214)^2}{100}} = \dfrac{70,750.6}{296,502.1} = 0.2386$

$a = \bar{y} - b\bar{x} = \dfrac{21,696}{100} - .2386\left(\dfrac{15,214}{100}\right) = 217 - 36.3 = 180.7$

$\hat{y} = 180.7 + .2386x$

$H_0: \beta_1 = 0, \alpha = .01$

$t = \dfrac{b - 0}{SE(b)} = \dfrac{.2386}{.0656} = 3.64$

$s_{y \cdot x}^2 = \dfrac{\Sigma y^2 - a\Sigma y - b\Sigma xy}{n - 2}$

$= \dfrac{4,856,320 - 181(21,696) - .2386(3,371,580)}{98}$

$= 1274.3$

$SE(b) = \sqrt{\dfrac{1274.3}{296,502.1}} = \sqrt{.004298}$

$= .0656$

Because $t = 3.64 >$ the critical $t = 2.58$, we reject H_0 in favor of $H_1: \beta_1 \ne 0$.

Chapter 14

14.1

	Breast-Fed			Not Breast-Fed	
No.	Age	Rank	No.	Age	Rank
1	14	10	1	9	4
2	15	11	2	10	5.5
3	12	7.5	3	8	3
4	13	9	4	6	1.5
5	19	12	5	10	5.5
			6	12	7.5
			7	6	1.5
			8	20	13

$W_1 = 49.5$, $W_2 = 41.5$

$\bar{R}_1 = 9.90$, $\bar{R}_2 = 5.2$

a. H_0: There is no difference in age of first cavity comparing breast-fed and non-breast-fed babies.

b. H_1: Breast-fed babies have older age of first cavities than non-breast-fed babies.

c. $W_e = 35$ $\sigma_W^2 = 46.67$; $\sigma_W = 6.83$ $Z = \dfrac{W_1 - W_e}{\sigma_W} = \dfrac{49.5 - 35}{6.83} = 2.12$

One-tailed test: $Z(.05) = 1.64$

Reject H_0 in favor of H_1 and conclude that breast-fed babies have older age of first cavities than non-breast-fed babies.

14.2   a. Vegetarians: $W_1 = 295$; $\overline{R}_1 = 16.4$; $n_1 = 18$

Nonvegetarians: $W_2 = 408$; $\overline{R}_2 = 21.5$; $n_2 = 19$

$W_e = \dfrac{18(18 + 19 + 1)}{2} = 342$; $\sigma_W = 32.9$

$Z = (295 - 342)/32.9 = -1.43$

Because $Z = -1.43$ is less than $Z(\alpha = .05) = -1.96$, we conclude that there is no significant difference in diastolic blood pressure between the two groups.

14.3   a. H_0: The number of cavities for town A is the same as for town B.

b. H_1: The number of cavities for the two towns is different.

c.

	Town A			Town B	
Person	# Cavities	Rank	Person	# Cavities	Rank
1	0	1	1	3	15
2	1	4	2	2	9
3	3	15	3	2	9
4	1	4	4	3	15
5	1	4	5	4	19.5
6	2	9	6	3	15
7	1	4	7	2	9
8	2	9	8	3	15
9	3	15	9	4	19.5
10	1	4	10	3	15
		$W_1 = 69$			$W_2 = 141$
		$R_1 = 6.9$			$R_2 = 14.1$

$W_e = 105$, $\sigma_W = 13.2$

Because $Z = -2.73$, which is less than -1.96, reject H_0.

$\Sigma r_d = 55$ $\Sigma r_{d(+)} = W_1 = 51.5$

$W_e = 27.5$ $\Sigma r_{d(-)} = W_2 = 3.5$

$Z = \dfrac{51.5 - 27.5}{\sqrt{(20 + 1)27.5/6}} = 2.45$

Because $Z = 2.45$ is greater than 1.96, we reject H_0 in favor of H_1 and conclude that the two towns have different cavity levels; that is, the level is higher in the town with unfluoridated water.

14.5   a. H_0: There is no association between the cleanliness rankings of the two inspectors.

b. H_1: There is an association between the cleanliness rankings of the two inspectors.

c.

Row	Inspector 1 Column: C1 Count: 11	Inspector 2 C2 11	Inspector 1 Rank C11 11	Inspector 2 Rank C22 11
1	2	1	3.5	1.5
2	3	3	6.5	7.0
3	2	3	3.5	7.0
4	3	2	6.5	4.0
5	1	2	1.5	4.0
6	4	5	9.5	11.0
7	5	4	11.0	9.5
8	3	2	6.5	4.0
9	1	1	1.5	1.5
10	3	4	6.5	9.5
11	4	3	9.5	7.0

Correlation of C11 and C22 = .736

$$t = \frac{736\sqrt{9}}{\sqrt{1 - (736)^2}}$$
$$= 3.262$$

Two-tailed test: $t(.975, 9) = 2.26$

$\alpha = .05$

Because $t = 3.262$ is greater than $t(.975, 9) = 2.26$, we reject H_0 and conclude that there is a high correlation between the cleanliness rankings of the two inspectors.

14.7 a. For the Wilcoxon rank-sum test, we need to be able to rank the combined distribution of two separate samples. We must be able to assign ranks to each of the observations and list and sum separately the ranks for the two samples.

b. For the Wilcoxon signed-rank test, we need a situation where we can obtain differences on each observation, as in a before-and-after situation. We then rank these differences according to the size of their absolute value and restore the original sign to each rank. There should be an equal number of positive and negative ranks if H_0 is true.

c. For the Spearman rank-order correlation coefficient, we need to have two observations on each item observed. We then obtain these ranks separately for the x's and the y's. Next we obtain the differences between the ranks and square, and sum them. The smaller the sum, the larger the coefficient.

14.9 a. $r_s = 1 - \dfrac{6(13.5)}{11(121 - 1)} = 1 - \dfrac{81}{1320} = 0.94$

b. H_0: There is no association between exercise and blood pressure.
H_1: There is an association between exercise and blood pressure.

$$t = \frac{.94\sqrt{9}}{\sqrt{1 - .94^2}} = \frac{2.82}{0.34} = 8.3$$

Because $t = 8.3 > t_{(.99)} = 3.25$ with 9 df, we reject H_0 in favor of H_1 and conclude that the correlation coefficient is significantly different from zero.

14.11 a. For

A	B	Total
4	2	6
1	4	5
5	6	11

$$P_1 = \frac{5!\,5!\,6!\,6!}{11!\,4!\,4!\,2!\,1!} = \frac{5 \cdot 5 \cdot 2 \cdot 3 \cdot 4 \cdot 5 \cdot 6}{7 \cdot 8 \cdot 9 \cdot 10 \cdot 11 \cdot 2} = \frac{25}{154}$$

$$P_1 = 0.162$$

and for

A	B	Total
5	1	6
0	5	5
5	6	11

$$P_2 = \frac{5!\,5!\,6!\,6!}{11!\,5!\,5!\,0!\,1!} = \frac{1 \cdot 2 \cdot 3 \cdot 4 \cdot 5 \cdot 6}{7 \cdot 8 \cdot 9 \cdot 10 \cdot 11} = \frac{1}{77}$$

$$P_2 = 0.013$$

so $P_1 + P_2 = 0.162 + 0.013 = 0.175$ and $2(.175) = .350$

a and b. H_0: The responses to A and B are the same.

α .05

Because $P = 0.35 > .05$, we do not consider the response to be significant.

14.13 $W_1 = 125.5$; $W_e = 143$; $Z = -1.36$

At a .05 level of significance, we fail to reject the null hypothesis. There is no difference between low-income African-American women and low-income white women with respect to their consumption of meat.

14.16 $Z = 2.37$. Exact P value $= .0178$. Reject H_0. There is evidence that Coloplast Corporation's new product leads to greater improvement among sufferers from xerosis than current moisturizers.

Chapter 15

15.1 1970: 205.1 million
1980: 227.7 million
1990: 250.4 million

15.3 a. 196,000
b. 421,000

15.5

	Alaska	Kansas
Birthrate	21.8/1000	15.0/1000
Death rate	3.9/1000	8.9/1000

15.6 (1) Diseases of the heart; (2) malignant neoplasms; (3) cerebrovascular diseases; (4) accidents; and (5) chronic obstructive pulmonary diseases

15.7 1950: whites, 61.1 per 1000; nonwhites, 221.6 per 1000 (excludes Alaska and Hawaii)

15.9

	Deaths		
	Total	Infant	Neonatal
Riverside	8438	170	101
San Bernardino	8931	281	163

15.10 a. Alaska, 21.8 per 1000 population; Arizona, 18.7 per 1000 population
b. The birthrate in Alaska is higher because of the higher proportion of the population in the childbearing age group.

15.11 The state with the highest birthrate in 1993 can be found in Table 93 of the *Statistical Abstract of the United States* for 1996.
The state with the highest birthrate is Utah, with 20.00/1000; and the highest fertility rate is for Utah, at 85.9.

15.12 The age-adjusted sex-specific death rate for cirrhosis of the liver can be found in Table 132. It is 18/1000 for men and 9.3/1000 for women.

15.13 The cause-specific death rates for 1993 for the three states and the United States can be found in Table 133 of the same reference as in 15.11.

	Cancer	Heart Disease	Diabetes	Accidents
Michigan	203.5	302.6	22.3	30.3
Utah	110.9	158.3	18.2	34.8
Tennessee	217	314.3	21.7	48.1
United States	205.6	288.4	20.9	18.8/1000

15.15 The three states in 1993 with the highest HIV death rates were (see Table 133): New York with 37.4, New Jersey with 28.0, and California with 20.3.

Chapter 16

16.1

Age Interval	l_x	$_nd_x$	$_nL_x$	T_x	$\hat{e}_x$
70–74	67,638	11,282	310,551	895,649	13.24
75–79	56,356	14,923	245,220	585,098	10.38
80–84	41,433	15,036	168,072	339,878	8.20

16.4 a. $_1q_0 = \dfrac{_1d_0}{l_0} = \dfrac{1260}{100,000} = .0126$

c. $_5q_0 = \dfrac{_5d_0}{l_0} = \dfrac{1260 + 257}{100,000} = .01517$

16.5 b. $_{10}q_{35} = \dfrac{_{10}d_{35}}{l_{35}} = \dfrac{851 + 1327}{95,641} = .02277$

16.6 $_{45}p_{20} = \dfrac{l_{65}}{l_{20}} = \dfrac{76,540}{97,668} = .7837$

16.7 At birth, $\hat{e} = 73.62$
At 35 years, $\hat{e} = 41.25$

Bibliography

Abramson, J. H. 1974. *Survey Methods in Community Medicine.* Edinburgh: Churchill Livingstone.

Backstrom, C. H., and G. D. Hursh. 1963. *Survey Research.* Evanston, Ill.: Northwestern University Press.

Berkson, J. 1946. Limitations of the application of fourfold table analysis to hospital data. *Biometrics Bulletin* 2:47–53.

Brown, B. W., and M. Hollander. 1977. *Statistics: A Biomedical Introduction.* New York: Wiley.

Cappelleri, J., and Trochim, M. 2000. Cutoff designs. In S. C. Chow (ed.), *Encyclopedia of Biopharmaceutical Statistics* (pp. 103–109). New York: Marcel Dekker.

Carey, K. B., and C. V. Correia. 1997. Drinking motives predict alcohol-related problems in college students. *Journal of Studies on Alcohol* 58:100–105.

Chew, R. 2000. Protocol development. In S. C. Chow (ed.), *Encyclopedia of Biopharmaceutical Statistics* (pp. 103–109). New York: Marcel Dekker.

Chiang, Chin Long. 1984. *The Life Table and Its Applications.* Malabar, Fla.: Robert E. Krieger.

Chow, S. 2000. Good statistics practice. In S. C. Chow (ed.), *Encyclopedia of Biopharmaceutical Statistics* (pp. 244–248). New York: Marcel Dekker.

Cole, L., and C. Nesbitt. (In press). A three-year multiphase pressure ulcer prevalence/incidence study in a regional referral hospital. *Ostomy/Wound Management.*

Cole, P., and A. S. Morrison. 1980. Basic issues in population screening for cancer. *Journal of the National Cancer Institute* 64:1263–1272.

Cox, R. H. 1994. Dietary cancer risks of low-income African-American and white women. *Community Health* 17:49–59.

Cutler, S. J., and F. Ederer. 1958. Maximum utilization of the life table method in analyzing survival. *Journal of Chronic Diseases* 8:699–713.

Digest page: Study of tamoxifen and raloxifene (STAR) trial. Retrieved July 22, 2003, from http://www.nci.nih.gov/clinicaltrials/digestpage/STAR

Doll, R. 1955. *Etiology of Lung Cancer. Advances in Cancer Research* (Vol. 3). Cambridge: Oxford University Press.

Elveback, L. R., C. L. Guillier, and F. R. Keating. 1970. Health, normality, and the ghost of Gauss. *Journal of the American Medical Association* 211:69–75.

Emerging risk factors. Retrieved August 23, 2003, from http://www.framingham.com/heart/4stor_02.htm

Framingham heart study: 50 years of research success. Retrieved July 22, 2003, from http://www.nhlbi.nih.gov/about/framingham/

Gourevitch, M. N., D. Hartel, E. E. Sehrenbaum, et al. 1996. A prospective study of syphilis and HIV infection among injection drug users receiving methadone in the Bronx, N.Y. *American Journal of Public Health* 86:1112–1115.

Grizzle, J. E. 1967. Continuity correction in the χ^2 test for 2×2 tables. *The American Statistician* 21:28–32.

Guinn, B., L. Jorgensen, T. Semper, and V. Vincent. 2002. Weight preoccupation in female Mexican American adolescents. *American Journal of Health Education* 33:173–177.

Hammond, E. C. 1966. Smoking in relation to the death rates of one million men and women. *National Cancer Institute Monograph* 19:217–224.

Hingson, R., T. Hereen, and W. Winter. 1996. Lowering state legal blood alcohol limits to 0.08%: The effect on fatal motor vehicle crashes. *American Journal of Public Health* 86:1297–1299.

International Conference on Harmonization. May 1997. Good clinical practice: Consolidated guidelines. www.fda.gov/cder/guidance (as cited in Chew, 2000).

Kirkpatrick, L. A., and B. C. Feeney. 2003. *A Simple Guide to SPSS for Windows.* Belmont, Calif.: Wadsworth/Thomson Learning.

Kuzma, J. W. 1967. A comparison of two life table methods. *Biometrics* 23:51–64.

Kuzma, J. W., and W. J. Dixon. 1966. Evaluation of recurrence in gastric adenocarcinoma patients. *Cancer* 19:677–688.

Kuzma, J. W., and D. G. Kissinger. 1981. Patterns of alcohol and cigarette use in pregnancy. *Neurobehavioral Toxicology and Teratology* 3:211–221.

Kuzma, J. W., and R. J. Sokol. 1982. Maternal drinking behavior and decreased intrauterine growth. *Alcoholism: Clinical and Experimental Research* 6:396–401.

Lang, T. 2003. Common statistical errors even you can find. Part 1: Errors in descriptive statistics and in interpreting probability values. *American Medical Writers Association Journal* 18:67–71.

Lee, N., J. Greely, and T. Oei. 1999. The relationship of positive and negative alcohol expectancies to patterns of consumption of alcohol in social drinkers. *Addictive Behaviors* 24:359–369.

MacMahon, B., and F. Pugh. 1970. *Epidemiology: Principles and Methods.* Boston: Little, Brown.

MacMahon, B., S. Yen, D. Trichopoulos, J. Varren, and G. Nardi. 1981. Coffee and cancer of the pancreas. *New England Journal of Medicine* 304:630–633.

McGaha, J. E., and E. L. Leoni. 1995. Family violence, abuse, and related family issues of incarcerated delinquents with alcoholic parents compared to those with nonalcoholic parents. *Adolescence* 30:473–482.

McMillen, M. M. 1979. Differential mortality by sex in fetal and neonatal deaths. *Science* 204:89–91.

Mainland, D. 1963. *Elementary Medical Statistics,* 2d ed. Philadelphia: Saunders.

Mehta, C. R. 1994. The exact analysis of contingency tables in medical research. *Statistical Methods in Medical Research* 3:135–156.

Muir, C. S., and J. Nectoux. 1977. Role of the cancer registry. *National Cancer Institute Monograph* 47:3–6.

National Center for Health Statistics. *Monthly Vital Statistics Report.*

———. *Vital and Health Statistics Series.* Washington, D.C.: Government Printing Office.

———. *Vital Statistics of the United States.* Vol. 1, *Natality;* vol. 2, *Mortality;* vol. 3, *Marriage and Divorce.* Washington, D.C.: Government Printing Office.

———. 1976. *Vital Statistics of the United States, 1972.* HRA Publication no. 75-1101. Rockville, Md.

———. 1981. *User's Manual—The National Death Index.* Public Health Service Publication no. 81-1148. Hyattsville, Md.: U.S. Department of Health and Human Services, Public Health Service.

———. 1982. Advance report: Final mortality statistics, 1979. *Monthly Vital Statistics Report* 31(6), suppl. 4.

Norusis, M. 2002. *SPSS 11.0 Guide to Data Analysis.* Upper Saddle River, N.J.: Prentice-Hall.

Paul, O. 1976. The multiple risk factor intervention trial (MRFIT). *Journal of the American Medical Association* 235:825–827.

Pavkov, T. W., and K. A. Pierce. 2000. *Ready, Set, Go! A Student Guide to SPSS 9.0 for Windows.* Mountain View, Calif.: Mayfield.

Phillips, Roland L. 1972. *Familial aggregation of coronary heart disease and cerebrovascular disease.* Johns Hopkins University. Ph.D. dissertation.

Publication Manual of the American Psychological Association, 5th ed. 2001. Washington, D.C.: American Psychological Association.

Rimm, A. A., A. J. Hartz, J. H. Kalbfleisch, A. J. Anderson, and R. G. Hoffmann. 1980. *Basic Biostatistics in Medicine and Epidemiology.* New York: Appleton-Century-Crofts.

Rosa, L., E. Rosa, L. Sarner, and S. Barrett. 1998. A close look at therapeutic touch. *Journal of the American Medical Association* 279:1005–1010.

Ross, J. G., E. C. Sundberg, and K. H. Flint. 1999. Informed consent in school health research: Why, how, and making it easy. *Journal of School Health* 69:171–176.

Sackett, D. L. 1979. Bias in analytic research. *Journal of Chronic Diseases* 32:51–63.

Schechtman, K. 2000. Clinical trials. In S. C. Chow (ed.), *Encyclopedia of Biopharmaceutical Statistics* (pp. 117–124). New York: Marcel Dekker.

Shyrock, H. S., and J. S. Siegel. 1973. *The Methods and Materials of Demography.* Washington, D.C.: U.S. Bureau of the Census.

Siegal, S. 1956. *Non-Parametric Statistics.* New York: McGraw-Hill.

Simpson, W. S. 1957. A preliminary report on cigarette smoking and the incidence of prematurity. *American Journal of Obstetrics and Gynecology* 73:808–815.

Stocks, P. 1944. The measurement of morbidity. *Proceedings of the Royal Society of Medicine* 37:593–608.

Tessaro, I., et al. 1997. Readiness to change smoking behavior in a community health center population. *Journal of Community Health* 22:15–31.

Ting, N. 2000. Carry-forward analysis. In S. C. Chow (ed.), *Encyclopedia of Biopharmaceutical Statistics* (pp. 103–109). New York: Marcel Dekker.

Tukey, J. W. 1953. "The Problem of Multiple Comparisons." Princeton University, Princeton, N.J. Mimeo. Cited in Roger E. Kirk, *Experimental Design: Procedures for the Behavioral Sciences.* Belmont, Calif.: Brooks/Cole, 1968.

————. 1977. *Exploratory Data Analysis.* Reading, Mass.: Addison-Wesley.

United Nations, Secretariat, Department of Economic and Social Affairs, Statistical Office. 1990. *Demographic Yearbook.* New York: United Nations Publishing Service.

U.S. Bureau of the Census. *Decennial Census of Population.* Washington, D.C.: U.S. Government Printing Office.

————. *Statistical Abstract of the United States.* Washington, D.C.: U.S. Government Printing Office.

U.S. Department of Health, Education and Welfare. 1965, 1971. *Health Consequences of Smoking: A Report to the Surgeon General.* Washington, D.C.: Public Health Service, Health Services and Mental Health Administration.

————. 1979. *Smoking and Health: A Report to the Surgeon General.* Washington, D.C.: Public Health Service, Office of Smoking and Health.

Veterans Administration Cooperative Study Group on Antihypertensive Agents. 1970. Effects of treatment on morbidity in hypertension: II, Results in patients with diastolic blood pressure averaging 90–114 mmHg. *Journal of the American Medical Association* 213:1143.

————. 1972. Effects of treatment on morbidity in hypertension: III, Influence of age, diastolic pressure, and prior cardiovascular disease; further analysis of side effects. *Circulation* 45:991.

Windle, M., and R. C. Windle. 1996. Coping strategies, drinking motives, and stressful life events among middle adolescents: Associations with emotional and behavioral problems and with academic functioning. *Journal of Abnormal Psychology* 105:551–560.

Winslow, C. E. A., W. G. Smillie, J. A. Doull, and J. E. Gordon. 1952. *The History of American Epidemiology.* St. Louis: Mosby.

World Health Organization. 1977. *Manual of the International Statistical Classification of Diseases, Injuries, and Causes of Death.* Geneva: WHO.

Index

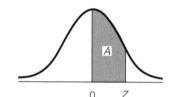

Table A Areas Under the Normal Curve

Z	.00	.01	.02	.03	.04	.05	.06	.07	.08	.09
0.0	.0000	.0040	.0080	.0120	.0160	.0199	.0239	.0279	.0319	.0359
0.1	.0398	.0438	.0478	.0517	.0557	.0596	.0636	.0675	.0714	.0753
0.2	.0793	.0832	.0871	.0910	.0948	.0987	.1026	.1064	.1103	.1141
0.3	.1179	.1217	.1255	.1293	.1331	.1368	.1406	.1443	.1480	.1517
0.4	.1554	.1591	.1628	.1664	.1700	.1736	.1772	.1808	.1844	.1879
0.5	.1915	.1950	.1985	.2019	.2054	.2088	.2123	.2157	.2190	.2224
0.6	.2257	.2291	.2324	.2357	.2389	.2422	.2454	.2486	.2517	.2549
0.7	.2580	.2611	.2642	.2673	.2704	.2734	.2764	.2794	.2823	.2852
0.8	.2881	.2910	.2939	.2967	.2995	.3023	.3051	.3078	.3106	.3133
0.9	.3159	.3186	.3212	.3238	.3264	.3289	.3315	.3340	.3365	.3389
1.0	.3413	.3438	.3461	.3485	.3508	.3531	.3554	.3577	.3599	.3621
1.1	.3643	.3665	.3686	.3708	.3729	.3749	.3770	.3790	.3810	.3830
1.2	.3849	.3869	.3888	.3907	.3925	.3944	.3962	.3980	.3997	.4015
1.3	.4032	.4049	.4066	.4082	.4099	.4115	.4131	.4147	.4162	.4177
1.4	.4192	.4207	.4222	.4236	.4251	.4265	.4279	.4292	.4306	.4319
1.5	.4332	.4345	.4350	.4370	.4382	.4394	.4406	.4418	.4429	.4441
1.6	.4452	.4463	.4474	.4484	.4495	.4505	.4515	.4525	.4535	.4545
1.7	.4554	.4564	.4573	.4582	.4591	.4599	.4608	.4616	.4625	.4633
1.8	.4641	.4649	.4656	.4664	.4671	.4678	.4686	.4693	.4699	.4706
1.9	.4713	.4719	.4726	.4732	.4738	.4744	.4750	.4756	.4761	.4767
2.0	.4772	.4778	.4783	.4788	.4793	.4798	.4803	.4808	.4812	.4817
2.1	.4821	.4826	.4830	.4834	.4838	.4842	.4846	.4850	.4854	.4857
2.2	.4861	.4864	.4868	.4871	.4875	.4878	.4881	.4884	.4887	.4890
2.3	.4893	.4896	.4898	.4901	.4904	.4906	.4909	.4911	.4913	.4916
2.4	.4918	.4920	.4922	.4925	.4927	.4929	.4931	.4932	.4934	.4936
2.5	.4938	.4940	.4941	.4943	.4945	.4946	.4948	.4949	.4951	.4952
2.6	.4953	.4955	.4956	.4957	.4959	.4960	.4961	.4962	.4963	.4964
2.7	.4965	.4966	.4967	.4968	.4969	.4970	.4971	.4972	.4973	.4974
2.8	.4974	.4975	.4976	.4977	.4977	.4978	.4979	.4979	.4980	.4981
2.9	.4981	.4982	.4982	.4983	.4984	.4984	.4985	.4985	.4986	.4986
3.0	.4987	.4987	.4987	.4988	.4988	.4989	.4989	.4989	.4990	.4990